MONEY
PLAYERS

Other Books by the Authors

ROD CAREW'S ART AND SCIENCE OF HITTING
  by Rod Carew with Frank Pace and Armen Keteyian

CALLING THE SHOTS
  by Mike Singletary with Armen Keteyian

BIG RED CONFIDENTIAL—INSIDE NEBRASKA FOOTBALL
  by Armen Keteyian

CATFISH—MY LIFE IN BASEBALL
  by Jim "Catfish" Hunter and Armen Keteyian

RAW RECRUITS—THE HIGH STAKES GAMES COLLEGES PLAY TO GET
THEIR BASKETBALL STARS*
  by Alexander Wolff and Armen Keteyian

DITKA—MONSTER OF THE MIDWAY*
  by Armen Keteyian

THE SELLING OF THE GREEN—THE FINANCIAL RISE AND MORAL
DECLINE OF THE BOSTON CELTICS
  by Harvey Araton and Filip Bondy

*Published by POCKET BOOKS

MONEY PLAYERS

Days and Nights Inside the New NBA

Armen Keteyian
Harvey Araton
Martin F. Dardis

POCKET BOOKS

New York   London   Toronto   Sydney   Tokyo   Singapore

POCKET BOOKS, a division of Simon & Schuster Inc.
1230 Avenue of the Americas, New York, NY 10020

ISBN: 0-671-56809-4

First Pocket Books hardcover printing May 1997

10 9 8 7 6 5 4 3 2 1

POCKET and colophon are registered trademarks of
Simon & Schuster Inc.

NBA is a registered trademark of NBA Properties, Inc.

Printed in the U.S.A.

Contents

UNIFORM PLAYER CONTRACT

Exhibit 1 -- Compensation

Player: Shaquille O'Neal

Team: The Los Angeles Lakers, Inc.

Date: July 17, 1996

Season	Current Compensation	Deferred Compensation
1996-1997	$10,714,286.00	None
1997-1998	$12,857,143.20	None
1998-1999	$15,000,000.40	None
1999-2000	$17,142,857.60	None
2000-2001	$19,285,714.80	None
2001-2002	$21,428,572.00	None
2002-2003	$23,571,429.20	None

Payment Schedule (if different from paragraph 3):

   (a) On October 1, 1996, Team shall pay to Player an amount equal to the entire amount of the Current Compensation due for the 1996-1997 season.

   (b) On October 1, 1997, Team shall pay to Player an amount equal to 50% of the Current Compensation due for the 1997-1998 season.

   (c) On February 2, 1998, Team shall pay to Player an amount equal to 50% of the Current Compensation due for the 1997-1998 season.

   (d) On October 1, 1998, Team shall pay to Player an amount equal to the entire amount of the Current Compensation due for the 1998-1999 season.

   (e) All Current Compensation due for the remaining seasons under this Contract shall be paid in accordance with the provisions of paragraph 3 of this Contract.

   (f) In the event that Player dies or becomes totally and permanently disabled so that he is unable to play professional basketball, then in such event the total remaining unpaid sum of Current Compensation due to Player under this Contract for all of the remaining years of the term shall be paid in equal monthly installments over the following number of years:

Initialled:

Player _____ Team _____

ONEALEX1.LAL (S)
L7312-

ACCEPTED & RECORDED

JUL 3 2 1996

1

Introduction

ONE SUNDAY AFTERNOON IN MID-AUGUST OF 1994, DAVID STERN stood under the makeshift bleachers of the mammoth SkyDome in Toronto, Canada, and made a bold pledge that revealed two most un–Stern-like public qualities: anger and ego.

"We are going to take back our game," Stern vowed, as the so-called Dream Team II warmed up for its gold medal game against Russia at the World Championship of Basketball.

This was no strain of xenophobia Stern had suddenly caught. The man deified as the most successful pro sports commissioner of his time, maybe all time, was certainly willing to share his game with Russians, Italians, Spaniards, or anyone willing to sign a lucrative deal to pull NBA games down from the almighty satellite. No, in this case, the "we" was Stern's league administration. "They" were the players. The star maker was fed up with his stars.

For two excruciating weeks, Stern had watched the collection of players the league had assembled for its second "national team" competition exhibit the same antisocial behavior that was turning people off back home in the States. Marvelously gifted players such as Derrick Coleman, Larry Johnson, Alonzo Mourning, and Shawn Kemp were no global ambassadors or gadfly salesmen.

They were not like Magic Johnson at the Barcelona Olympics in 1992. These new pro basketball stars, commonly referred to as Generation X, were flaunting themselves, and embarrassing Stern.

In 1992, original Dream Teamers such as Johnson, Michael Jordan, and Larry Bird were happy to have pictures snapped with starstruck opponents from around the world. Coleman, Johnson, Mourning, and Kemp were more interested in staring them down. Any hard foul was taken as a challenge. Any chance to slam-dunk was perceived as a gleeful show of superiority. In one unforgettable and deeply symbolic spectacle, Johnson stuffed the ball in a game against Puerto Rico. While play resumed without him, he caressed himself in front of the television camera behind the baseline.

Johnson was no lovable Grandmama. Ugly American was the more prevalent notion. And if Johnson and company represented the NBA's best, then what was to be said about the NBA? These players had not chosen themselves to represent the league. More deserving but less sexy players had stayed home.

Dream Team II symbolized the delicate and unhappy position Stern suddenly found himself in. Despite his stated desire to create a more homogeneous product, the reality was the NBA could go only where a handful of leading men could take it. He knew it. They knew it. And if they didn't know it, agents, family, friends, and assorted sycophants told them about it. The New NBA was even more than a "players' league," as it had long been referred to. It was a superstars' league, riding the backs of the transcendent, telegenic few. The league's objectives had long since been established: create marketable superstars, then hawk them the way Hollywood sells its Academy Award winners.

"The single biggest reason pro basketball became popular is March Madness, three weeks of the most intense television in sports," said David Falk, the leveraged superagent for Jordan and other NBA stars. "You think back through the years: Bird and Magic; Michael hitting the last shot for North Carolina against Georgetown; Olajuwon against Ewing. I remember once they were talking about the shape of Grant Hill's ears! By the time he got to the NBA, people felt like they knew Hill for years. Alonzo Mourning. Bobby Hurley. What other sport do you see that in?"

Not baseball. Not hockey. Much less in football, the sport of costumed warriors. In a 1996 list of the one hundred most powerful men in sports, the *Sporting News* included four men from the NBA: Stern (9); deputy commissioner Russ Granik (29); executive vice president and chief marketing officer Rick Welts (39); senior vice president and director of operations Rod Thorn (91). By comparison, the NFL had two (Paul Tagliabue and Neil Austrian), as did the NHL (Gary Bettman and Brian Burke). Major league baseball had nobody.

No team-sport athletes were as visible as NBA stars. In no other sport did they seem to embody the spirit of their teams and markets. Speaking at an International Radio & Television Society luncheon at the Waldorf in New York on January 18, 1996, Stern effectively captured the virility of his league and one of baseball's obvious weaknesses when he played a wickedly delicious game of word association.

"Magic Johnson—Lakers," Stern said. "Larry Bird—Celtics. Michael Jordan—Bulls."

He paused.

"Dave Winfield . . . ," he said, letting the name of the future Hall of Fame outfielder dangle, those in the audience free to choose from among the half dozen uniforms this gifted ballplayer had modeled. To Stern, this was hard-core evidence of baseball's instability—and inability to maximize its earning potential.

The worth of the average franchise in the so-called national pastime ($115 million) was now less than that of the average NBA team ($127 million), according to the May 1996 edition of *Financial World*. Five NBA teams were worth more than every baseball team except the New York Yankees, whose value was in part due to a local-television contract George Steinbrenner had, ironically, with the corporation that owned the Knicks. Stern's league had come a long way since the storied Boston Celtics, with Larry Bird already on their team for three seasons of sold-out games at Boston Garden, exchanged hands in 1983 for the sum of $17 million, liabilities included.

The NBA's incessant deal-making had been especially good for its players, too. Stern always argued that although the salary-cap system restricted movement, there were commercial benefits to staying put. It was difficult to argue with him. When *Forbes* magazine ranked the top forty earners for 1995, twenty-three team-sport athletes made the list. Seven were NBA players, but of the $100 million Forbes reported those twenty-three athletes to have earned from endorsements, the NBA players commanded roughly 70 percent.

Jordan, of course, took the lion's share, $40 million. But even without Jordan, the remaining six NBA stars earned slightly more than the other sixteen combined. Baseball's two most glamorous players, Barry Bonds and Ken Griffey Jr., combined for $2.4 million, about half the take of Grant Hill, in his second year with the Detroit Pistons. Of course, as Falk correctly analyzed, Hill hadn't exactly damaged his Q score during his four years at Duke.

Thanks primarily to Jordan's corporate pioneering—perhaps his most significant legacy—these younger players had mind-numbing endorsement contracts that went way beyond the conventional sneaker deal. They hawked burgers and tacos, soft drinks and cars. Shaquille O'Neal cut best-selling rap albums. He opened Shaq's Place at Universal Studio's Orlando theme park and, with other superstars such as Griffey Jr., Joe Montana, Andre Agassi, and Monica Seles, partnered the All-Star Cafe in Times Square in New York and another in Orlando. O'Neal and even Hill launched home pages on the Internet (shaq.com and granthill.com).

O'Neal and Anfernee Hardaway were cast in starring Hollywood roles before they'd ever won a playoff game. In the late spring of 1996, a slew of NBA players appeared with Whoopi Goldberg in *Eddie*. O'Neal showed up again on the big screen in *Kazaam*, as a three-hundred-pound rappin' genie. Jordan had a court built by Warner Brothers for his full-court workouts while he was filming *Space Jam*, starring him and Bugs Bunny.

Then there was Dennis Rodman, who ascended from rogue rebounder to cult rebel without a cause when he attached himself in the fall of 1995 to Michael Jordan and the record-breaking 72-win Chicago Bulls. Rodman wrote a book, called *Bad As I Wanna Be*, in which he claimed that "fifty percent of life in the NBA is sex. The other fifty is money." These days, many of the players showing up to play are all too ready to believe that and get their cut.

Along the way to the Bulls' fourth championship, Rodman arrived for a downtown-Chicago book-signing by rounding the corner of Michigan and Pearson on his Harley chopper, done up as a silver-haired, heavily made-up and tattooed drag queen. He parked his bike, flipped his fuchsia boa over his shoulder, and proceeded to sign 1,400 copies. Howard Stern of the hardwood, a real nineties celebrity.

The book, naturally, soared to No. 1 on the *New York Times'* best-seller list, where it remained for weeks.

As colorful as David Stern wished his players to be, this was not exactly Disney-on-parade, a family values night out. Yes, corporate America was buying, more than ever, but what could it possibly be thinking? Celebrity did not always guarantee long-term likability. And there was something increasingly troubling about the NBA's mind-altering orgy of earnings. You could see it on the court almost every night.

Until Jordan and Magic Johnson reversed retirements and plugged themselves back into the league a year apart, the perception had been growing that the NBA was more about fantastically wealthy and self-absorbed young men than it was about professionalism, even about basketball.

While attendance records were set and television ratings soared during the 1995–96 season, at times it seemed it was all Stern could do just to maintain some semblance of order, to hold rein on the young, the reckless, and the rebellious. During one very long two-week stretch in March, Stern's office suspended Denver's Mahmoud Abdul-Rauf for refusing to stand for the national anthem, Philadelphia's Jerry Stackhouse and Vancouver's Greg Anthony for punching opponents, Seattle's Gary Payton for head-butting an opponent, and Chicago's Rodman for head-butting a ref, Ted Bernhardt.

In addition, the Los Angeles Lakers' co-captain Cedric Ceballos left his team in the middle of the race for a crucial playoff seeding and went waterskiing in Arizona, his excuse being "personal problems," which many had speculated more or less amounted to a feud with his coach over playing time. Ceballos was upset after he'd lost minutes and control of the ball following the comeback of Magic, one of the greatest players of all time.

Not long after that, the team's other cocaptain, Nick Van Exel, vented his frustration over being ejected by forearming another official, Ron Garretson, over the scorer's table. Van Exel was suspended seven games, one more than Rodman. At a damage-control press conference, Van Exel apologized to his sneaker company, Reebok, and not Garretson.

Rodman's outburst was one thing, Van Exel's another. But when

Magic Johnson, of all people, one week later bumped still another official, Scott Foster, while protesting a technical foul in a nationally televised game against Phoenix, it was a mind-altering experience for the league. In other words, never mind the notion that unbridled youth was all that ailed it.

But perhaps the most symbolic act of malfeasance during this unsightly period was committed by an Orlando Magic bench player named Anthony Bowie, who was having himself a career night against the Detroit Pistons, a team in search of a championship identity lost to erosion, age, and the degradations of the new-age NBA.

Being fed his statistics by the Magic's public relations people near the bench, Bowie learned that he was one assist short of a coveted "triple double"—double figures each in points, rebounds, and assists. With four seconds left in a 20-point Orlando rout, word reached the court and the Magic fouled Detroit's Theo Ratliff.

Ratliff missed a free throw and the ball was tipped to Bowie, who called time-out with 2.7 seconds left. Here, Pistons coach Doug Collins knew that his Orlando counterpart, Brian Hill, had a choice: he could do the right thing, which was to tell his players to forget it, or simply remove Bowie from the game. But by doing so, he risked the wrath of his two youthful stars, O'Neal and Penny Hardaway, who were enjoying Bowie's fifteen minutes of fame.

Hill chose to let the Magic do as they wished, but to distance himself from the huddle, which was a lack of clear thinking or loss of control of his team. Collins decided it was up to him to stage the protest. Fuming, he pulled his players off the floor, allowing Bowie free access to his precious assist.

Bowie approached Collins after the horn, grabbing at his arm behind the scorer's table. "Get the fuck away from me," Collins told him. Collins also blew off Hill when the Magic coach asked if they could talk. Hill did address his team for five minutes after the game and publicly apologized. But those words meant little to Collins and hundreds of others around the country, who flooded the Pistons' office with faxes in support of what Collins had done, who bristled at the league's fining of Collins for taking his team off the court.

Collins wanted no part of what he considered a desecration of a sport he'd played, coached, or broadcasted almost his entire life.

This was antithetical to what he, as a first-year coach in Detroit, had been preaching to his young players as he tried to acquaint them with their championship ancestry—the part of it that wasn't too scandalous to talk about, anyway. The mere fact that Bowie knew what his stats were before the game was over was, to Collins and others, a sad commentary on what the league had become.

Stern, for his part, reflexively recognized the dangers in this type of behavior in a league once shunned by Madison Avenue, with all of the predictable racial typecasting. In the early 1980s, though obviously more talented than in the past, NBA players by reputation played "unstructured," or unintelligent, ball. They were paid too much to work too little. Nothing ever happened until the last two minutes of the game.

By the nineties, though, there was a new world order. Jordan had the same appeal and panache as any black comedian, actor, or singer. The increasingly black NBA was a more-than-billion-dollar-a-year enterprise, though events such as the Finals did not stand alone as a name brand, such as the Super Bowl or World Series. It was more a vehicle for Magic to go against Bird, for Charles Barkley to challenge Jordan, for Hakeem Olajuwon to post up O'Neal. The bigger the stars, the higher the ratings. Stern refused to admit it, but the NBA lived year to year, crossing its fingers for the right ratings matchups. It seemed the whole world had grown accustomed to the NBA's being able to deliver new episodes of Star Wars every season.

Like a hungry shark, the league had invaded Europe, and even Asia. It had forged a powerful alliance—or, it could be argued, a friendly corporate takeover—with FIBA, the raucous international basketball coalition. It had elbowed its way past outdated and hypocritical Olympic amateur ideals. It had crossed the border into Canada, placing teams in Toronto and Vancouver for the start of the 1995–96 season. It was turning its attention south, toward Mexico City.

When it came to the art of the deal, mining promising new markets, the NBA moved with exceptional flair but with a crafty politician's image-grooming spin. When Toronto was granted its franchise, for instance, it was with the condition that the province of Ontario remove basketball betting from its Pro-Line sports lottery. The province, which helped fund cash-strapped health care with the estimated $15 million annual take from basketball betting, began to balk. Sorry, the league said, we'll have to go someplace else. We have a reputation to uphold. Ontario backed down.

The fan-friendly league that stood firm with powerful governments has been far less assertive with its own foot soldiers, however. The NBA could afford to fight for its stated ideals as long as its adversaries were faceless bureaucrats, or even its own naughty owners who would dare challenge the one-for-all edicts of Stern. Confronting its rebellious poster children was much, much trickier. Bring them down, and where was the league?

"We spend most of our time promoting these guys," Stern said one day in his spacious Fifth Avenue office in midtown Manhattan. "We're not going to try to bury them."

And right there, in two candid declarative sentences, was the great NBA dilemma. It was the paradox that had helped Stern build what from the outside looked to the world like a wondrous, shiny castle on the hill, but from the inside, more often resembled a rickety house of cards.

In this painstakingly researched and reported book, the many levels of that enormously profitable but highly flammable infrastructure are explored in depth, often with disturbing results. The book goes deep inside the frantic system that simultaneously creates and corrupts Stern's would-be heroes, the parallel basketball and merchandising markets that try to sink their tentacles into impressionable teenagers such as Kevin Garnett, that peddles them to corporate America while distorting basic values vital to team sport and personal growth. A system so tantalizingly seductive that it can exaggerate one's sense of worth and warp one's priorities to the point of disarray, of scandal, or worse.

In the money-mad world of the NBA, even what should be the best-case scenarios are not. For most of his rookie season, for instance, young Joe Smith seemed to have his world in perfect working order. But beneath the surface were the system's insidious by-products eroding good intentions, dragging the player and the one man who could have made a difference into a dangerous and ultimately destructive drama.

The compelling stories of Smith and his would-be career guide, former pro Len Elmore, convey the random and unstable nature of the NBA millionaire's club, even in its most embryonic stages. But it wasn't much different at the other end of the spectrum, as veteran Buck Williams grew weary of teams—such as his Portland outfit—hopelessly infected with the Me First virus. As president of the Players' Association, Williams also presided over a union as dysfunctional as the most fractious NBA team, even as it battled its canniest and most dangerous opponent, David Stern.

Not even the chosen few, the most celebrated superstars of all, have operated on a foundation of bedrock. Much more frightening and much more threatening to the league is the information presented here baring dangerous and volatile conditions at the very top of the player heap.

In recent years, the stench of scandal has been detected in major NBA outposts such as Phoenix, Detroit, Boston, and Chicago, involving some of its greatest stars and most powerful teams. All of it was swiftly and skillfully "investigated," then virtually ignored by the powerful NBA public relations machine. This book reopens these complex cases, bores deep inside them, and presents its leading men—powerful figures such as Jordan and former Detroit Pistons Bad Boy leader Isiah Thomas—in entirely different lights than the NBA mythmakers have.

In Jordan's case, it meant wild betting sprees that reportedly left him more than a million dollars in debt to the likes of a convicted cocaine dealer and shady characters, as well as habitual high-stakes gamblers, and entangled the NBA's foremost meal ticket in a web of deceit and secret payoffs. In Thomas' case, it looked like the NBA's worst imaginable nightmare come true: the superstar point guard who held an NBA season in the palm of his hand said to be in staggering debt to members of a gambling ring involved with organized crime. In these and other cases, the pattern was the same: NBA stars, living fast and loose, open to serious questions about how deep their criminal involvement might be.

In many ways a most progressive team-sports industry, the NBA is not meant to be cast here as an evil empire, but more one that, it often seems, selectively sees no evil and hears none either. The issue is the NBA's near-desperate dependency on its stars, and what the league would do—or wouldn't do—to protect its image. What it closed its eyes to or, as in the tragic case of Reggie Lewis, inadvertently caused with its self-righteous mandate set by Stern, the brilliant architect.

The NBA's version of history is rewritten here, while a rich cast of characters is visited and revisited, set in an event-filled season highly charged by Jordan's Bulls and Magic Johnson's dramatic return. From the 1995 college draft in Toronto to the 1996 draft in New Jersey, with many stops along the glamorous NBA trail, the book defines a New NBA in all its expansive brilliance and all the encroaching shadows that threaten to send it back to its dark ages.

Stern privately understood the forces that could undermine his work. He had long since realized that he had to at least make an attempt to achieve a better balance of power before it was too late. He'd dedicated his professional life and too much of his personal life as well to the growth and prosperity of his league. It infuriated him to be squeezed by these increasingly leveraged players and by more audacious owners who didn't share his vision of how the NBA should operate. In Stern's mind, they were creating alternative paths, a double vision, that could only court chaos. He became determined to demonstrate that he, as NBA head coach, had his boardroom and his locker rooms under control. On that August afternoon in Toronto, he was chatting with a longtime league reporter when he shook his head and made his vow about taking back the game.

The reporter asked how.

Stern, his thoughts racing ahead, already laying out the plan, just said, "You'll see."

As it turned out, he would start by getting his house of cards in order the old-fashioned way. By disciplining the kids.

1

Lottery Tickets

THERE IS NO MORE COMPELLING OUTSIDE-THE-LINES PAGEANTRY IN professional sports than the NBA draft. Part coronation, part lottery drawing. The opportunity of a lifetime, broadcast in prime time.

In 1950, the draft rights to the first great NBA entertainer, Bob Cousy, were selected at the league's cramped office from Syracuse Nationals owner Danny Biasone's hat. Now, the draft was a marquee event, NBA cities submitting bids as if it were the Super Bowl.

Stars aren't quite born on NBA draft night. They are made, in the mercurial manner of the mob. To be a top draft pick has meant becoming instantly untouchable, to demand staggering amounts in player and endorsement contracts. It has been the cue to take the ceremonial and symbolic walk from the roots of poverty to unimagined wealth, a one-way ticket from the working-class struggle of urban America.

Joe Smith's turn to take that walk came on June 28, 1995, at Toronto's SkyDome, shortly after 7:30 P.M., in a scene with all the atmospherics and elegant trappings of a political convention.

The Golden State Warriors, with the leadoff pick of the 1995 college draft, used all but twelve seconds of their allotted five

11

minutes before announcing the player they hoped would revital-
ize their moribund and dissension-racked team. Why wait to
announce a selection the Warriors had weeks to make? Live
television, of course. Dramatic effect. Documentary in the making. "Hoop Dreams '95," as the inscription read inside the
projected basketball on one of the huge walls behind the
fabricated stage.

The predraft show had moved along like some three-ring circus
under the SkyDome, one well-orchestrated act after another. A
troop of tight-butted women busting out of black tops and hot
pants as they raged through a hip-hop routine; a slam-dunk
contest; a fireworks show; the mascot for the new Toronto
Raptors—one of two Canadian expansion franchises—sliding
down a wire from the rafters and crashing through a banner.

Then it was time to bring out the leading man.

Upon a backdrop of ocean and electric blue, with huge placards
of major sponsors looming high above an empty draft board, with
a dozen clean-cut security and public relations people whispering
into walkie-talkies, NBA Commissioner David Stern strode stiffly
across the stage. He was, as always, immaculately coiffed, wearing
a dark suit, blue shirt, and red tie. His roundish face revealed a
fresh coat of Pan-Cake makeup, and his wire-framed glasses
glistened from the camera lights below.

There would be no game-show banter with so much money at
stake. Stern always knew whom the fans had come to see. Smiling
benevolently, he lowered his head slightly and cut right to the
chase. "With the first pick of the 1995 NBA draft, the Golden State
Warriors select Joe Smith."

The crowd of 21,268, paying as much as $15 a head, erupted in
cheers. The spotlight shifted to the left of the stage, to the front
entrance of a large tent, the so-called green room, where the
players, their family members, and friends awaited this stomach-
churning roll call. Within seconds, a tall, slender figure emerged, a
white cap tipped back on his head. The cap had the Warriors' logo
on its front and the official draft logo on its side. From here began
the procession of patronage: a step to the platform for a handshake and photo with Stern; a quick hello to NBA radio; a sit-
down in the Turner Network Television booth with no less than
the coaching and industry know-it-alls Rick Pitino and Hubie
Brown.

"Joe, this way," the photographers called out as they scrambled to snap a close-up shot.

"Joe, over here," others cried.

Back in the green room, more than a dozen members of Joe Smith's family had had their prayers answered. His mother, Letha Smith, had uttered a prayer for all of her youngest child's games since high school. In a quiet moment that very morning, she had whispered it to herself: "Lord, put wings on his feet and strength in his arms and let him do what he has to do."

All nineteen-year-old Joe Smith had to do, at least on this indelible night, was look into the television cameras and smile the winning smile. He was a long way from Maury High School in downtown Norfolk now. He was where his boyhood hero, Magic Johnson, had once been. A sophomore picked No. 1 in the draft, on top of his class, which understandably was his world.

His decision to leave school had been made during an NCAA playoff game back in March, his Maryland team against the University of Connecticut. He couldn't recall which UConn player had raced ahead for a first-half layup on the fast break, only that he'd gone all out to block the shot.

"Someone cut my legs out from under me," said Smith. He landed on his back. His hip ached for the rest of that game. He thought afterward, "If I come back next year, I could mess up my career."

That game had been played at the Oakland Coliseum, which happened to be the Golden State Warriors' home court. The Warriors' general manager, Dave Twardzik, was a former college backcourt mate of Smith's high school coach, Jack Baker, at Old Dominion in Norfolk. When Baker took Smith to his first pro game, an exhibition in Norfolk between Atlanta and Charlotte, he took his fourteen-year-old freshman down to the court and introduced him to Twardzik, who at the time was the Hornets' director of player personnel. Twardzik removed the championship ring he'd won as a starting guard for Bill Walton's Portland Trail Blazers in 1977. He handed it to Smith, who inspected the diamond-studded jewel. When Twardzik momentarily looked away, Smith put the ring in his pocket. They all shared a laugh. Smith went home with a dream.

Now it had all come true, almost as if it were mysteriously ordained. The Warriors were seeking a big young forward after losing their previous lottery prize, Chris Webber, following an acrimonious battle with former coach Don Nelson. The Webber-Nelson debacle had wrecked a season and tarnished the coach's reputation and left the franchise adrift. Twardzik this time wanted to be certain he was getting "a good kid," one he could sell to the Bay Area community without fear. He trusted the judgment of his old friend Baker, among other Norfolk friends who knew Joe Smith. He even passed on North Carolina's Jerry Stackhouse, in whom some saw traces of Michael Jordan.

The decision by Smith to turn pro early seemed certain to pay off handsomely now. When he was in high school, Smith had the habit of scribbling his name in script, on the blank pages of his notebook, twenty or thirty times a page. Such a common name it was, but Smith imagined that someday, somehow, it would be a signature that was well worth perfecting. Suddenly it was. He was the No. 1 pick in the NBA draft. All he would have to do was wait for his agent to strike a deal, then sign that name on the dotted line.

While Smith was taking a hero's chauffeured ride in a golf cart through the bowels of the stadium to meet the national media, another career-launching triumph was quietly being celebrated near the back entrance to the green room, out of public view. There, forty-three-year-old, six-foot-ten-inch Len Elmore was holding a cellular telephone to his ear, smiling broadly as he chatted with an associate of his three-year-old player representative agency. As Stern continued to announce the first-round selections, as the fans responded with cheers and jeers, other agents scurried past, pausing to nod.

"How does it feel?" Elmore would say, repeating a question after getting off the phone. "We're ecstatic. I'd be lying if I didn't say certain elements of prestige are attached to the number one pick. As a somewhat new player and an African-American, it underscores the fact that we are *here!*"

There was a moment when Elmore paused but obviously wanted to say more. "Regardless of what my counterparts might say," he added, not trying too hard to hold back his smile.

What were they saying? What he kept hearing was that others resented him because he hadn't "paid his dues." That he was trying to undercut the market by charging clients 3 percent fees on negotiating contracts instead of the industry standard 4. And there were whispers far worse than that. Elmore hadn't realized the extent of them until he called up Norman Blass, a New York–based attorney who had once upon a time been Elmore's agent. The word on the basketball-agent grapevine, Blass told him, was that Elmore had taken a $2-million loan in order to pay off Joe Smith.

Elmore shook his head. He said the notion was too demeaning to even deny. "It only tells me they know we're out here now," he said.

In his own calm, self-contained way, Elmore was commenting on the nature of his new vocation. It was, he had discovered during the last couple of years, as fiercely competitive as the most vicious NBA game. And when it came to landing the jewels of this or any other draft, downright cutthroat.

Providing up-front cash and other gifts to draftbound players and their families had, for years, been widespread, part of the territory. And while not all agents felt the need to back up their sales pitches with graft, and while many of the top agents decried the practice, it was virtually impossible to control and even know who was being sincere. In most cases, the players being so young, it was the parents, guardians, and coaches who delivered the player to his agent. Deals were often made based on what was in it for them.

Newcomers were not exactly welcomed into this fraternity of backroom operators. It was simply a case of so much pie to go around. The more successful agents there were, the fewer bonanzas there were going to be for the industry superstars, such as David Falk, a George Washington University Law School graduate who knocked on the door of ProServ's Donald Dell in 1975 and talked his way into a law clerk's job.

The son of a New York butcher and language scholar, Falk rose to prominence as ProServ's basketball guru. He signed Michael Jordan in 1984 and Patrick Ewing one year later. He sought leverage for his clients like a barracuda. With Jordan as his nuclear weapon, he challenged and defeated standard NBA licensing practices regarding the use of Jordan's likeness. He bragged how he understood the league's arcane salary cap better than most general managers, and he probably did. With his large stable of players, he took it upon himself to arrange trades when his clients were in the final season of contracts and their teams were afraid they would lose them without any form of compensation. Falk would shop his player as if he were a general manager, as he did when he successfully moved Alonzo Mourning to Miami on the opening day of the 1995–96 season, and Kenny Anderson from New Jersey to Charlotte months later.

"Oh, we do that all the time," he said without any apparent regard for how suspect it made the NBA look. If Falk was allowed to negotiate with Miami and could establish a market figure without Mourning's having to actually play out his contract, then what chance did Charlotte have of re-signing its franchise player before he became a free agent? None. It made David Falk—or any other agent in that position—look to be in charge of the league's competitive balance. Which made Falk's day.

If you asked Elmore, Falk may have been too consumed with power mongering and less passionate about the individual needs of his clients. He never stopped brokering, networking, pushing for more leverage.

The night before the draft, as the families of the future pros congregated in the lobby of Toronto's Westin Hotel, Smith was standing around with members of his family when they spotted Denver center Dikembe Mutombo, chatting with Falk, his agent. Willie Brown, Smith's uncle on his mother's side, innocently walked over, intending to ask Mutombo if he would mind having his picture snapped with Smith.

As he began to speak, Falk snapped, "Can't you see we're talking here?"

Brown retreated in silence. Elmore, witnessing this episode, remembering the full-court press Falk had put on Smith and his family just months before, believed there was a moral in there somewhere.

As a sports agent, he was a long way from David Falk's league, though he claimed he didn't necessarily intend to join. He didn't see himself as a shark, nor did he much look like one. His light-brown glasses made him look bookish. His long, thin legs moved stiffly from years of grinding his surgically repaired knees to a pulp on the basketball court. His most passionate sermons were usually issue-oriented, not self-promoting.

Elmore's stated agenda was as different from Falk's as his

background. Elmore, out of Harvard Law, had more to offer than Ivy League credentials. He had played the game. And as rare as an African-American agent was, a former player making a serious move into the agent game was downright revolutionary. In Elmore's mind, it was also a statement. The onetime meek, their humble roots notwithstanding, could inherit the sport.

Elmore was born in the same Brooklyn neighborhood that would later produce Mike Tyson. He was raised in Queens and played high school basketball at Power Memorial, following Lew Alcindor (later Kareem Abdul-Jabbar). Despite what was then crippling knee surgery early in his pro career, his sound pivot skills carried him through ten seasons, in the old American Basketball Association and then as a classic NBA journeyman. He retired in 1984 and decided to go to law school. After graduation, he worked in the Brooklyn district attorney's office for Elizabeth Holtzman, a liberal Democrat. Holtzman's programs, Elmore said, were attractive to him because they had no overriding sense of loyalty to the law enforcement establishment. But in 1990 Holtzman left to run for city comptroller. Elmore, who had begun to moonlight as a television analyst, was drawn back to the game.

He founded Precept Sports in 1992, opening shop in Columbia, Maryland. Elmore played his college ball in nearby College Park, at the University of Maryland, for Lefty Driesell. He was a campus sports legend, his No. 41 jersey retired at Cole Fieldhouse, a 1974 All-America who helped put Maryland on the college basketball map. Now Maryland was helping establish Elmore in the agent business. Walt Williams, a Terrapin forward, was his first name client in 1992.

The following year, he got lucky with Sam Cassell, a Baltimore kid who was drafted by Houston late in the first round. Cassell had unexpectedly become one of the most flamboyantly appealing young players. With a handful of NBA clients, with Hall of Fame tight end Kellen Winslow working the football side, Precept's future looked bright indeed. But the defining moment, make no mistake, was when Smith was announced as No. 1.

In the weeks before Toronto, Elmore surmised it was a close race between Smith and Stackhouse, North Carolina's explosive guard. Both were sophomores out of the Atlantic Coast Conference, arguably the country's best college league. Both were

17

regarded as coachable kids. Smith did have the Twardzik connection in his favor, but Stackhouse, like Jordan, had played for a coaching legend, Dean Smith.

Elmore believed that the decision would ultimately be made from the individual workouts the top players would be asked to participate in. He summoned Smith to the gym and kept him there.

"I think the greatest impact I made was helping him get prepared, helping him understand what teams were expecting of him," Elmore said outside the green room. "Every drill I put him through, I'll be damned that, in those two days, they put him through all of them. Spot shooting, ball handling, even the Mikan drill, which hardly anyone does. Layup left hand, layup right. Whatever they asked him to do, he'd been there, seen that.

"People tend to forget that, how important experience is, in every situation you put these kids in. That's why this lack of respect for elders that you see in some of these players just baffles me. Joe is different. There's a certain level of humility. When I say humble, I don't mean retiring. It's just not braggadocio. It's the way I tried to be when I was playing. Joe, I think, is a throwback. He was raised to be respectful."

The person who raised Smith soon joined Elmore outside the tent. Letha Smith, a roundish woman with large glasses dominating her face and soft buttermilk skin, wore a white dress and white Warriors cap.

So often it seemed as if it was the mothers vouching for their sons at the NBA draft. Five years earlier at the Jacob K. Javits Convention Center on the West Side of Manhattan, Derrick Coleman's mother, Dassie, wiped away tears and lectured a reporter who questioned her son's integrity after he was picked first in the draft by New Jersey. "He's nobody's problem, no matter what anyone says or writes," she said. It didn't work out that way, but what was a mother to do? The fathers were often out of the picture, or trying to sneak back in.

Letha Smith dropped out of high school in 1953, had six kids in nine years, and was divorced three years later. Joe was born almost a decade later, when Letha was thirty-eight, the son of a man named Joe McFarland, who Letha never married. McFarland was 6-5, which explains why, at 6-10, Joe is eight inches taller than any of his siblings. McFarland played basketball at Booker T.

Washington in Norfolk but no longer lived there. He was married, with teenaged twin daughters, living in Clinton, Maryland. He worked as a police officer. When Joe was growing up, McFarland occasionally dropped by the house to talk to Letha and see Joe. Once, he attended Joe's game at Maryland, but their relationship had been almost nonexistent before Joe became a college star. Now, on the verge of his becoming a millionaire, there was almost no chance it could grow.

"I'd feel it might be because of the money or the celebrity," Joe said. He thought about it for a moment, then added, "Actually, I kind of look at my mother as my father."

So this night belonged to Letha, as much as it did to Joe. This was her last baby, the one she would go looking for in the neighborhood the minute after he was due home. "I was his taxi, his bus driver, his everything," she said as Elmore, nearby, turned his attention to his other major client, Wake Forest guard Randolph Childress. "Saturday was always Joe's day."

She worked as a maid and, after earning her high school equivalency diploma, as a naval medical clerk. She was never frivolous with money. She said the only things she ever bought on credit in all her years of raising kids were their shoes. Her children were raised with the fastidious work ethic her own father, Jasper Smith, preached to her and her six siblings, all boys. All of Letha's children graduated high school. Their diplomas, she said, were displayed in her living room, on what she called her Proud Table.

Just days before the draft, her father had called her and said, "You know what? This is the only day I can remember in my life that I woke up and I didn't have anywhere to go to make money at."

Jasper Smith was a handyman who sold whatever he could get his hands on. He became a landscaper when Letha was in high school and remained one until his retirement, days before his grandson became the first pick in the draft. He was eighty-one years old. Letha Smith figured it was just as well. With Joe going out West, there would be some late nights staying up to watch his games on TV.

Tears welled in her eyes as she spoke of the joy this unexpected, late-in-life child had brought her. There were fewer tears, however, than when Joe had announced he was leaving Maryland in the spring, several months before. Only that day, it had been his turn to cry. He made the announcement, then bent over and sobbed in his mother's lap. Prospective millions notwithstanding, she knew he was still her baby. She knew it was too soon to let him go.

Soon the word came that Joe's press conference was about to begin. Letha hurried over, but the conference was delayed while technicians completed a video hookup to Oakland, where the Warriors' brass was assembled to welcome him to their lineup. While she waited, Letha Smith signed autographs, dozens of them, writing "Joe's Mom."

Finally, the West Coast connection was made. There, on the small monitor, were Twardzik and Rick Adelman, the new Warriors coach.

Twardzik: "Were you nervous, Joe?"

Smith: "Oh, yeah. Very nervous. Beyond nervous. It was the longest four and a half minutes of my life."

Twardzik: "We're really excited about having you with us, Joe. It's a good start for us and a good start for you."

Smith: "Oh, yes. It's a great accomplishment and I'd like to thank both you guys for having me."

Twardzik: "How about a number, Joe? What number do you want?"

Smith: "Thirty-two."

Twardzik: "I think we can arrange it. And, hey, Joe, tell your mother you'll be in good hands out here."

Smith: (laughing) "That's not going to change her mind."

And it didn't. Letha Smith, who had already been promised by her son her dream house on the Virginia shore, said that night she would be his California roommate for his rookie season. "He's still growing. Still a boy. He needs that guiding just a little while longer," she said. "I don't want him out there alone."

She always watched over him this way. When he was just a boy and was five minutes late coming home, she was out in the neighborhood, combing playgrounds, knocking on doors. When he became a high school basketball star, she set the rules—no earrings, no offbeat haircuts, none of what she called that "in-your-face thing." In college, Smith did get a tattoo, a snarling bulldog on his chest that represented his nickname, Beast. Letha still bristled over that.

For the most part, though, he respected her wishes and would do so now. She would be his rookie roommate.

"I guess," Joe said, "I'm just a momma's boy."
It was all music to Dave Twardzik's and Rick Adelman's ears.

After months of grievances by owners, coaches, veteran players, media, and fans about how irresponsible, overpaid young players were dragging the NBA down, not one player in his junior or senior year could crack the top five of the 1995 college draft. To magnify the contradiction of the argument to the point of embarrassment, the fifth pick was a skinny nineteen-year-old only weeks removed from his high school prom.

The Warriors, Clippers (Alabama forward Antonio McDyess), 76ers (Stackhouse), and Bullets (North Carolina forward Rasheed Wallace) were all content to hitch themselves to sophomores. The next prize catch was Kevin Garnett, a 6-11 prodigy who was raised poor in South Carolina but spent his senior high school season honing his skills against inner-city kids at Farragut Academy on Chicago's West Side.

Garnett had declared himself eligible for the draft on May 15, conducting a press conference at the Home Run Inn, one of Chicago's renowned neighborhood pizza joints. It was like a scene from the school of performing arts, a kid imitating what he watches on TV. Garnett announced his dream was to go to the NBA and have a Nike shoe named after him. When asked about the prospect of millionaire bachelorhood, he assumed a cocky posture and said, "Come on, ladies, come on." While his homeroom homeys cheered him on, a former Farragut Academy assistant principal, a middle-aged black woman named Arleen Daag, stood off to the side and wondered what the NBA's responsibility should be.

"The problem as I see it is that the NBA doesn't have anything in place, a support system to help these kids once they get there," she said. "Maybe they should use Kevin as a test case. There's a lot of talent at the high school level, and a lot of these kids are going to be looking to see how Kevin does."

Or, more to the point, what he earned.

Garnett said he wanted to play at Michigan but he didn't achieve the required test scores. The prospect of higher education became academic when pro scouts began flocking to his games. One of the Farragut coaches, Cesar Calimee, counted twenty-three teams during the season.

The Garnett story did not have the maternal poignance of Joe and Letha Smith's. To begin with, Garnett's mother, Shirley Irby, had been unsuccessful in protecting her son from the flesh peddlers and power brokers, from the colleges and the pros. She had long since been displaced as the controlling influence in his life.

The person who seemed to have Garnett's ear most of the time was a young black man named Billy Taylor, fresh off the streets of Chicago, with no apparent athletic skills but becoming a Money Player in his own right. His mysterious rise to power as the gateway to this potential gold mine was the source of serious concern to many NBA teams. How did he get so close to the player who had become, in some ways, the focal point of the draft? What did it say about Garnett, whom some scouts were already calling a bigger version of Scottie Pippen, the most versatile player in the game? He had too much raw talent to ignore, to risk being second-guessed on years later.

With the four sophomores taken, Minnesota was next up with the fifth pick. The Timberwolves were one of the worst teams of all sports, with a six-year record of 126–366. Their best players were Isaiah Rider and Christian Laettner, two of the most despised Generation X players in the league. Now, however, Kevin McHale was on board as vice president of basketball operations. McHale brought some old-fashioned Celtics credibility with him. The way McHale looked at it, the Timberwolves were still the equivalent of an expansion team, such as Toronto and Vancouver. They could afford to wait for Garnett to mature. McHale, convinced that he would, had the same intuitive explanation that Red Auerbach had given again and again about Bill Russell, John Havlicek, Dave Cowens, Larry Bird. He had sensed a certain pride, a Celtic pride. "I looked him right in the eye and I saw something that erased all my fears," said McHale. "A look like, 'I want to be special.'"

The clock ticked away . . . 3:14 . . . 2:12 . . . finally down to fifty-five seconds. Here came Stern once more. "With the fifth pick, the Minnesota Timberwolves select . . ."

Cut to the green room, where Garnett stood and began, like a piston, to furiously pump his fist. He hugged his mother, but turned immediately to a chunky, light-skinned black man. They hugged, then Garnett took the walk across the stage, toward

Stern. He made the rounds, then hopped on the golf cart. Soon, he bumped right into Rasheed Wallace.

"Hi, Kevin," Wallace said, sounding like an excited kid about to go see his first game with his dad.

"Hi, Rasheed," Garnett said in kind. They giggled and went to their respective podiums.

Garnett made a point of saying that he didn't think of himself as a star: "I'm not trying to be no Michael Jordan, or nothing like that."

What did he want to do now that he was in the NBA?

"Just stay Kevin," he said. "Stay Kevin."

His said that his mother and his grandmother had given him that advice. But then he began to talk about how much friends meant to him, how they would remain important to him, even in this new world of bright lights, of high rollers. He mentioned his old buddy and teammate from South Carolina, Jamie "Bug" Peters. And he went out of his way to mention one more name. It was the man he'd hugged in the green room. The man, it turned out, who had helped him get where he was today. Billy Taylor.

The name would be one to remember for next year's draft as well. Taylor, a budding general manager of the streets, was out looking for more players like Garnett to "draft."

The following morning, in every NBA city whose team had drafted a player in the first round, there would be a requisite photo on the lead sports page of the newspaper, that city's pick dwarfing the gray-haired commissioner as they shook hands and made small talk. Sociologists might have a field day with these awkward poses—a liberal, Jewish New York lawyer as the patron saint to the young, flamboyant African-Americans. Only this year, the handshake was decidedly less welcoming.

As the college stars fell into the NBA's seductive embrace that night in Toronto, none could realize the extent of the smoldering feuds and peculiar alliances that were about to create the most bizarre off-season in NBA history, as well as rewrite the tickets they thought they were holding.

Hours before the draft, in fact, Michael Jordan and Patrick Ewing, along with five other players, had filed a class action lawsuit in a U.S. District Court in Minneapolis against the NBA, challenging the legality of not only the draft but the league's salary cap and free agent system. As usual, David Falk was right behind the insurgents.

Falk, along with other distinguished agents, had successfully moved to block the NBA Players' Association's hastily negotiated collective bargaining agreement, a deal reached after Stern threatened a summer lockout and league-wide shutdown. Beyond fixed rookie pay slotting, the purported deal closed loopholes teams were using to stimulate free agent movement. But the real battleground was over the gutting of what was known as the Larry Bird exception, or a team's ability to go well above its salary cap to pay its own players. The deal called for a 100 percent tax on every dollar over the cap.

Baseball's owners and its union had waged so calamitous a war over such a tax system that there was widespread belief the sport might not survive. Hockey players swallowed all kinds of contractual restrictions rather than agree to a tax. Now Jordan and Ewing, having submarined union director Simon Gourdine's agreement with Stern, were espousing union decertification and a shift of NBA labor troubles to federal court.

"We're trying to eliminate the owners from locking us out," Jordan said that afternoon. "We're trying to ensure that the game goes on and the public doesn't have the same ill feelings toward us that they had toward baseball."

That was the public relations spin, anyway. The players had other, more selfish reasons, as did their agents. Stern was mad as hell that his deal was dead, for the time being. But he was also cheered by the awareness that Simon Gourdine, a former NBA deputy commissioner, and union president Buck Williams were closer to his camp than they were to the agents and dissident players. They did not want to court chaos. They wanted to deal.

"We're used to this," Stern said with a shrug when he climbed down off the stage after the first round was done. "Just another fight over a billion dollars a year."

It was more money than Stern himself could have imagined when he took over the league not much more than a decade before.

2

Stern Leadership

DAVID STERN BEHOLDS NEW YORK CITY FROM FIFTEEN FLOORS ABOVE Fifth Avenue, from a grand corner-office window presenting the glory of St. Patrick's Cathedral, and a midtown backdrop of dazzling shadow and light that is right out of Woody Allen's *Manhattan*. The high-rise is called Olympic Tower, an appropriate perch for a driven man who keeps wanting the bar to be raised, the leap for the gold to get higher and higher.

What Stern most loathes is the idea of rattling around the office he inherited from an old Kennedy-family confidant named Larry O'Brien, admiring the view, living off the medals he earned four years ago and four years before that. Stern habitually seeks the high of cognitive challenge, the thrill of heated debate, the way Michael Jordan hungers for the ball in the final minute of a one-point game.

In fact, the parallels are there to be drawn: Stern as the Jordan of sports commissioners.

The truth is that when Stern, in 1978 at age thirty-six, left what he grew up believing to be his professional dream, a New York law partnership, he wasn't sure he'd find his calling in a troubled professional basketball league. But he soon came to realize that running the sport had the potential to be the next-best thing to playing it. That, from the fifteenth floor of Olympic Tower, this onetime fraternity athletic chairman at Rutgers University, himself a roundish 5-9, could work his own pick-and-rolls, back-door passes, and that when subtlety just wouldn't do, he could throw a few mean elbows, too.

"He was always trying to coach the house football and basketball teams, and they just abused him, but in a way where you abuse people you know can take it," said Roger Cohen, a Stern fraternity brother at Rutgers. "When I found out that David had gone to work for the NBA, I just said, 'Perfect.'"

Had he peered west on an early winter morning, in the direction across the Hudson River to East Rutherford, New Jersey, Stern might have noticed the latest brush fire in his ever-expanding kingdom. The New Jersey Nets were suing their entrepreneurial landlord, the New Jersey Sports and Exposition Authority, a clear and ominous outbreak of domestic franchise turbulence.

During Stern's largely triumphant reign as NBA Commissioner, the Nets had been a microcosm of the league before Stern took over: consistently chaotic, their obscure and fractious group of investor owners comically trying to tie loose ends together like the cast of *Seinfeld*. And always, embarrassingly, right in Stern's backyard.

He couldn't be blamed for advising them to pack up their pouty guards and power forwards to find a place where they'd be out of the shadow of Madison Square Garden's Knicks, if not his hair. But upon hearing such a suggestion, Stern pursed his lips and shook his finger, like a parent warning a child not to point a finger near a heated stove.

"You spend so much time encouraging teams to make investments in their communities," he said. "If you say, 'Okay, that's it, we're going on to the next market,' then your pleas don't ring true. I'd rather hold the owner responsible in the market than blame the fans."

This was classic, conciliatory Stern. Would he have picked up the telephone and advised an owner to move a franchise if he believed it made sense for the team and the league? In a heartbeat. There was no opinion that Stern kept to himself, and there was no escaping Stern when he was determined to express it. Publicly, though, what Stern long ago realized was that the most delicate and significant aspect of being a contemporary sports commissioner was making the heartfelt impression that he was no mere owners' front man. He had to be much more than that. He had to be the ever-composed leader of the basketball revolution.

Stern succeeded somehow in convincing far more people than he had a right to—especially in the media—that he was advocate for all, from the Microsoft-rich Portland owner, Paul Allen, to the highest-paid player, right on down to the teenaged ball boys. This wasn't always easy, as when he was challenged by Jordan and the other rebel players during the 1995 summer decertification movement, or when he locked his officials out for the start of the following season to force them to drop what he said were exaggerated contractual demands.

"David Stern screwed us, treated us like dogshit," one veteran official said long after his union voted 27–26 to accept the deal that ended the lockout and the short, chaotic run of the scab referees. But the ref wouldn't make this call for attribution. He conceded that wouldn't be fair to Stern, who had never publicly said anything so inflammatory about anyone who worked for the NBA, and never would.

According to Stern, Jordan was naturally only doing what he had the right to do, pick a side in a family fight. Even before the union eventually voted to accept the contract, Papa Stern telephoned his meal-ticket megastar to make sure there were no lingering hard feelings. But as for David Falk and those other agents Stern accused of fanning the labor flames, they were not part of his brood at all and thus could publicly be treated with unbridled disdain. To Stern, they were "parasites," enemies of the NBA.

Under Stern's protective umbrella, he insisted there were none of those, only adversaries, those who required that figurative elbow to the ribs. And there had been many over the years, including upstart owners who wouldn't play ball the way Stern wanted them to. When he became commissioner in February 1984, it in fact took just months before one was determining how much he could get away with. Right from the start, Stern showed that he didn't back down.

It was right about this time that the Oakland Raiders had busted the NFL in federal court, winning some $50 million in damages and legal fees plus the right to move to Los Angeles. On May 15,

1984, Donald Sterling decided similarly to take on the NBA. He announced he was moving his woeful Clippers from San Diego to the Sports Arena in L.A. The league filed suit to block the move.

So Stern and his team of lawyers went to work, preparing the legal defense. The result: in startling contrast to the NFL, Sterling eventually paid the NBA $3.2 million for its permission to move. Stern's line in the sand was drawn.

The league's ever-widening profit margin stabilized the franchise-hopping threat, but owners found other ways, equally maddening, to challenge Stern. Many—including supposed Stern ally Jerry Colangelo—tried to circumvent his beloved salary cap to gain a competitive edge. Chicago sports magnate Jerry Reinsdorf defied the league by putting Bulls games on superstation WGN, which to Stern was an obvious subversion of national television deals, the league's lifeblood. He went right to court, as he almost always did, and kept his legal staff up night after night until 2 and 3 A.M. preparing for the case. "Stern was a maniac about the WGN suit," said one attorney from the NBA's firm, Proskauer Rose Goetz & Mendelsohn. (The case was eventually settled out of court.)

Stern claimed it was nothing personal with Reinsdorf. Businessmen had differences of opinion all the time. That's why they invented courts. "There is a difference between an enemy and an adversary," he said. Making this clear distinction, he believed, helped prevent the NBA from sinking to baseball's level, to where the owners were regarded as—his words—"stupid" and the players as "greedy."

Stern was forever working this angle, and this particular year more than ever, as the labor fight led to the abolition of the right of first refusal on all free agents, and a wild escalation on superstar salaries loomed for the summer of 1996.

He hated talking about salaries, especially his own expired five-year, $27.5-million deal that was being reworked. Stern knew the figures for players like Jordan and Shaquille O'Neal would be staggering, exceeding $20 million a year. He began to lay the PR groundwork. "New figures startle people, but it's our job to educate them," Stern said. "I accept that. I've been hearing this since Jerry Buss signed Magic Johnson for one million dollars a year. It was the end of the world. But I don't think the great players are begrudged money by our fans. I think they accept them as the cream of the entertainment business, like Eddie Murphy or Tom Hanks. When Joe Dumars or Alonzo Mourning makes a lot of money, I don't think the fans mind. They tend to make harsher judgments on players who don't deserve it, the .220-hitting shortstop."

Even in making this seemingly innocent point, Stern's remarkable spin-doctoring skills were obvious. The deserving players were basketball stars. The undeserving were banjo hitters from the former pastime. Unmentioned were 38 percent shooting guards or muscular centers who couldn't make a free throw.

It was the world as David Stern simply wished it to be.

Union attorney James Quinn said Stern doesn't mind playing with the facts when it suits him "I remember it happening on a number of occasions. We almost came to blows over it one time during the mid to late eighties. It related to a particular provision in some prior agreement that obligated the league to make payments of several million to the Players' Association. He just flatly denied that's what the provision meant, even though all the evidence was to the contrary, including people on his own side.

"His response to our side was, 'You're just too stupid to understand.' He uses his brilliance as a weapon, pulls his intelligence out as a sword."

And, when necessary and always behind closed boardroom doors, Stern could posture and bully like George Steinbrenner in heat.

"David under the polish and veneer has a terrible temper," said Marc Fleisher, whose perspective was shaped from his father's own private tirades and the occasional collective bargaining session Larry let him sit in on. "He can be very rough, where *fuck* is every other word out of his mouth. All the things Gary Bettman is known for. Only David was able to clean up his act, let Bettman be the bad guy."

Others, like James Quinn, argued that Stern's tirades were never hysterical, always calculated. "Like all people with great egos, he knows how and when to use it," Quinn said. "He could play his temper like a fiddle."

In day-to-day operational matters, Stern was careful to avoid being drawn into muddy waters. If the issue was sanguine, Magic Johnson's returning to the NBA, Stern would dash off a quick statement welcoming the legend back with open arms. A more difficult issue might be left to Russ Granik, or vice president of operations Rod Thorn.

Case in point: When Mahmoud Abdul-Rauf refused to stand for the national anthem in March 1996, citing religious reasons as a Muslim, Stern decided to suspend him indefinitely, but Granik's name was on the press release. This was a difficult and emotional issue, one in which the predominantly black player constituency figured to support Rauf. Stern had to be careful. And there was a less calculating side to this, Stern's own deep-rooted liberalism, his ever-growing ties to the Democratic Party. Here was a man who worried about his ability to be an appropriately deferential host when Bob Dole's people called to say the candidate would attend a May 1996 Bulls-Magic playoff game in Orlando.

Stern was, in his own words, the CEO of a successful corporation now. Compromises had to be made for expediency, or his sense of it anyway. In his early days, the NBA was still more of a grassroots operation. Stern knew everyone remotely connected to it, his life story. He greeted everyone at the door, by name, at the league's annual postseason party. When Nat "Feets" Broudy, the longtime league mailroom employee and famed Madison Square Garden timekeeper, died in 1991, Stern delivered a compassionate eulogy at a chapel on Manhattan's Upper West Side.

Thousands more people were connected with his league now, people whose language he didn't even speak. Expansion breeds anonymity, and anonymity breeds social disengagement. Even at home, with twenty-nine teams and players dropping in and out as if the league were a department store, Stern was fighting harder to walk the line between benefactor and boss. He was forced to play aggressive defense, for example, when the agents said, sure, he doesn't mind Jordan making $20 million, as long as he can screw everyone else.

He was asked about the charges made by agents like Fleisher and David Falk that within three years of the new labor deal, half the players would be making minimum salary to accommodate the stars' monster deals.

These were exactly the moments that Stern waited for, when the dogged litigator in him lit up the room.

He said he'd read those same charges printed in a *Boston Herald* article—most NBA clippings passed by his desk—and they drove him crazy. "There are some statements that are just so inherently bizarre that it is journalistically irresponsible to even print them," he said.

Stern loosened his tie, stood up, reached for the handle on a cabinet attached to the back wall. It opened to a chalkboard and he proceeded to draw lines for categories of players who will earn different-level salaries under the new system. When he finished, he pointed to the figures with a ruler and began his lecture.

"How does David Falk say that half the players will play for the minimum?" he said, voice rising. "It can't be. You have a draft pick every year. And you can pay him anything you want after two years. Now you have a whole roster that's there, and then every other year you have a million-dollar exception. Are there loopholes that say you can't hold a guy for a year? No. That was never meant to be. Now everyone knows these are the rules. We know them. Let's go. If the Bulls want to pay Michael, fine. Shaquille, fine.

"Listen, if you think I think taking advantage of players is good for us, you're crazy. It's bad business. How does anyone look at this and say half of these guys are going to be earning the minimum? Now I understand. Falk says it is going to happen. I say it's not. I can't wait for the next two years to come. It's not going to happen. It's just not!"

The level of certitude in all this was indeed unsettling. It made you wonder how so much unrestrained passion could possibly be an act. And if it wasn't, then wasn't the next assumption that Stern was on the level? And that perhaps this charming, conversant man really was basketball's advocate for everyman?

Well, at the very least, he was the smartest, slickest, and clearly the most vigorously ambitious person you could come across who was running a professional sport. And those who were close to him on his way up, those he'd left behind, said they were not surprised. Not surprised at all.

David Joel Stern was born September 22, 1942, in New York City, the son of William and Anna (Bronstein) Stern. Although Stern has commonly been described as a child of Manhattan's Chelsea section, where his second-generation Russian-immigrant father operated a delicatessen several blocks from where today's

Madison Square Garden stands, most of his development occurred west of the Hudson River, in the leafy New Jersey suburb of Teaneck.

Even upon his graduation from Teaneck High, the personal bio accompanying the youthful Stern pose (trademark half-smile with a Brylcreem, pre-Beatles cut) could do justice to the Stern image of the 1990s: clever, focused, and deliberately ambiguous. Under his name and address (446 Churchill Road) and his activity résumé (debating club, French club, student service, tennis), Stern was thusly described:

"That fellow behind the 'pat' hand is 'Dave' . . . possesses a good sense of humor and good sense for cards . . . he looks for honesty and sincerity in others . . . sports favorites are basketball and tennis . . . will remember his 'dealings' with Miss Devany . . . plans to attend college in pursuit of a law career."

At Rutgers, Stern majored in history, becoming a Henry Rutgers scholar. He was no campus luminary, losing a race for a seat on the interfraternity council, but was well liked within his fraternity, Alpha Sigma Mu.

Besides being athletic chairman, he was pledge master and managed to leave at least one freshman with memories of a pleasant hazing, of Stern in the familiar role of benevolent dictator. "There was a trip to Roosevelt Raceway to scour the grounds for empty Marlboro boxes, and afterward we were taken to Coney Island, treated to hot dogs at Nathan's," said Roger Cohen. "We got back to the campus at five or six A.M. It was wonderful. It was also clear that we were pledges and the others were brothers, but rather than his being one of them, Stern was a link, with a witty remark, a laugh, a way to calm everyone down.

"He always had a way with people. Dave was a frustrated athlete, but, oh, was he smart. The brains, the patience, the ability to get people to do things they might not want to, but do them because David asked you to. It was the kind of thing that you didn't want to disappoint him."

He could apparently incite people, too, to the point of throwing a punch. But usually not at him.

"One particular day, we were going to catch the races at Garden State Park, but Dave [Stern] said he couldn't go to the track because he had to study, so another friend, Dave Kaufman, was going to drive," said another former Rutgers classmate, Bob Fish.

"On the way out to the turnpike, we stopped off at the apartment. Well, I get out of the car and Kaufman gets out and throws some candy wrapper on the ground.

"Now, we were very conscious of our neighborhood because, here we were, four college kids living in a residential area. So I said, 'Dave, please pick it up.' He said he wouldn't. One thing led to another and I started to lose my temper. I said, 'You don't pick it up, I'm going to deck you.'"

At this point, upon hearing the commotion, here came Stern to the second-floor window, wearing only his boxer shorts.

"Go ahead, deck him," Stern yelled down.

"But he's driving me to the races," Fish said.

"If you deck him, I'll take you," said Stern.

"So I decked him. And Stern drove me." It was a classic Stern story his old friends never forgot. The main point was this: Stern, while no party boy, knew how to have a good time, usually managing to keep himself out of trouble.

By his sophomore year, Stern had settled into Rutgers life with a core of close friends—Fish, Herb Towell, Cliff Goldman—who decided to move off campus, to a two-bedroom apartment in a two-family home on Lawrence Street in New Brunswick.

Once, after a roommate left unexpectedly, they were short rent money, so they went down to the New Brunswick barbershop where a local bookmaking operation was run, put $20 on a horse that paid $12, and wound up with three months' reserve fund. They played all-night card games, bowled for hours at Edison Lanes. They held their own "Davis Cup" tennis tournaments. They drove up to the Bronx to see the Yankees play in the World Series. They rooted for the inept Knicks and did their own Knick imitations in the C and D fraternity divisions.

Stern was better at tennis but best with words. By then a loyal Kennedy Democrat, he entertained his friends with JFK impersonations that sometimes took on serious tones. The fraternity was almost entirely Jewish, and Stern, said Fish, pressed for change. "We were in what was called the liberal wing of our fraternity," said Fish. "The liberals would push for gentiles and blacks to be in the fraternity."

Stern's old friends have watched him from afar, amazed when they read of the millions Stern has reeled in for the NBA and for himself. Fish, who was an usher at Stern's wedding (to Dianne

Bock) at the Hotel Delmonico in New York on Thanksgiving Day, 1963, went on to teach high school and coach track in California. Cohen went back to Rutgers in the journalism department. Several years ago, he visited Stern for a piece he was doing for a cable television program called *Rutgers Sports Review*. He remembers Stern's secretary telling him, "David will be with you in a moment," and being relieved that it wasn't "the commissioner" or "Mr. Stern."

He said it was nice to know that Stern was still one of the guys. Or acting like one, at least.

After Rutgers, Stern headed for Columbia Law, where during his sophomore year he became friends with another student, Michael Cardozo. They both were newlyweds. They worked together at *Columbia Law Review*. They would sit in Morningside Park, munching sandwiches and talking politics in these early days of 1960s campus unrest.

Stern may have been a Kennedy liberal, but he was no flag burner, no radical. He studied. He played cards. Not necessarily in that order.

"We would play cards more than we should have—until the deadlines," Cardozo said. "He would always claim he wasn't very good."

Stern was usually bluffing, feeling out his opponent, his poker face revealing little. "Easy Dave," a nickname he would give himself years later during one Oscar-worthy media briefing on NBA labor, was in the formative stage.

In 1966, while Cardozo went off to spend a year clerking for a judge, Stern landed his first job, with a starting attorney's salary of $7,800 a year. But money was not the point, not yet, for Stern was about to get an education Columbia or any other law firm could not provide. He didn't yet know it but he was soon going to study the business of NBA basketball, under an all-time great named George Gallantz.

At eighty-three years of age, slowed by the onset of Parkinson's, George Gallantz's mind remained sharp and facile one afternoon in the midtown-Manhattan offices of Proskauer Rose Goetz & Mendelsohn. Off the tip of his tongue rolled names of judges thirty years past, cases, venues, details, the essence of complicated legal arguments long since won or lost. He was retired from the seventh-largest firm in New York City, employing 425 lawyers and leasing eleven floors in a gleaming granite monstrosity on Broadway between Forty-seventh and Forty-eighth Streets. But as was his habit, he was checking in, keeping up as best he could with firm business.

Not a tall man, Gallantz bore a vague resemblance to the late character actor Ralph Bellamy. The wisps of gray hair trimming the sides of his head accented a gray, bushy mustache, and his shallow gray eyes shone behind brown tortoiseshell glasses. On the desk in front of him, just like old times, was a legal pad with the firm's moniker printed on top and a pile of sharpened pencils.

His small office was more of a storage bin now. It was stark, not a stitch on the walls, cluttered with boxes of legal documents and dusty Rolodex files. Gallantz was mostly interested in touching base with the younger attorneys who were now the stars of the firm. They were "students," as he said many of them had been.

"How about next week?" he said, trying to arrange lunch with a partner just back from a trial in Europe and some round-the-clock partying at the Cannes Film Festival in the south of France.

"I haven't even had a chance, you know, to check my calendar," the partner demurred.

"I'll call you next week," Gallantz said. It was apparent that the old lion's memory and sense of loyalty may have been better than that of some of the now-affluent and jet-setting men he'd trained.

He came up a different way, from the old school. He grew up in New York City so poor that "as a kid [I] used to go to the toilet in the hall." Then he went to City College and Brooklyn Law School, then to the firm Simpson Thacher & Bartlett. He was, by many accounts, a courtroom giant, a fearless litigator hailed for his oratory, tactical skills, and demonic belief in preparation.

In other words, his was a style strikingly similar to one that would eventually be ascribed to the young man whose law school record Gallantz reviewed in the mid-1960s, the young man he took on to assist him with a litigation caseload that had grown too heavy.

Thus did David Stern go to work at the knee of Gallantz, who by this time had long since held a marginal yet intriguing account of a scuffling professional basketball league.

Gallantz's basketball involvement traced to a man named Maurice Podoloff, the son of a New Haven real estate man who happened to own an arena in that Connecticut city. After the younger Podoloff got a law degree from Yale, he took over management of his father's arena, where he booked hockey games and eventually fielded an offer to become president of the National Hockey League.

In 1946, when owners of several pro basketball franchises formed their own shaky alliance, they approached Podoloff and wondered, in the spirit of frugality, if he could handle both jobs. Podoloff presided for a time over the NHL and the Basketball Association of America (BAA), which would soon become the NBA. Eventually, the basketball people decided they needed their own man and convinced Podoloff to drop hockey. He moved into an office in the Empire State Building with the idea that he would run the league and be its attorney. Then up came a complicated case involving a player for the Fort Wayne Pistons who was ensnared in a police wiretap talking to bookmakers.

The player's name was Jack Molinas. Molinas was a Money Player before the phrase became a buzzword in professional sport. After an All-American career at Columbia, the six-foot-six forward with the brilliant mind and movie-star looks was drafted No. 1 by the Fort Wayne Pistons in 1953, and quickly became not only the highest paid rookie but an all-star as well. Molinas eventually admitted placing bets up to $500—all to win, he said—on at least 10 Pistons games.

"Podoloff gets a telephone call one day and he's told about this," said Gallantz. "He hops on a plane and goes to Fort Wayne, goes to the police station where Molinas was being held. He asks some questions. Molinas admits talking to them but says, 'I didn't make any bets.' The police get him to sign a statement, and Podoloff takes this statement and says, 'You're finished.' That was it. He assumed the power to tell a player that was that."

Embittered about being banned from the league, Molinas became a lawyer. In 1959, after joining a Manhattan law firm, he filed a $3 million lawsuit against Podoloff and the NBA in the New York State Supreme Court in the Bronx, seeking reinstatement and damages. Podoloff, realizing he couldn't handle such a case, called Ned Irish, who owned the New York Knicks.

"Who is your lawyer in New York?" he asked.

"Simpson Thacher & Bartlett," Irish said.

And so the seed that would one day give rise to David Stern was planted as the league's first de facto commissioner attempted to sort out the sordid, league-threatening specter of gambling and point shaving.

"Podoloff comes right down with this piece of paper in his hand," said Gallantz. "At this stage, I have been with the firm a dozen years, and I will tell you that I was recognized as a mature litigator fazed by no kind of litigation. I had dubbed myself vice president of oddball litigation. If it was off the beaten path, send it to George Gallantz."

Gallantz won the Molinas case for Maurice Podoloff, as well as an appeal, in which he said the judge was half-persuaded to rule for Molinas on the basis that he said he didn't actually bet.

"And I said, 'Judge, he kept bookmakers *informed* about whether he agreed or disagreed with the point spread.'

"The judge said, 'Where'd you get that?'

"'He told us, from the stand. He called up the bookmaker. He'd ask the bookmaker what the point spread was. When the bookmaker told him, he'd either bet or didn't bet—but not on his own teams. What do you suppose the bookmaker was doing with that information?'"

Later, the true colors of this high-rolling, life-of-the-party boy who claimed no dishonesty in life emerged in a burst of shocking news: Molinas was named as the so-called master fixer of a mob-backed game-fixing operation whose tentacles stretched into at least 47 players at 27 colleges in 17 states from 1957 to 1961 Players were "contracted" to dump 43 games, and press reports from that period suggest at least 20 others may have been on the list. Molinas was directly tied to 14 players at six colleges and three bribe payments. In 1963 he was convicted of bribery and sentenced to 10 to 15 years in Attica.

Five years later, after cooperating with federal authorities probing mob activities, Molinas earned early parole. But he never stayed out of trouble. He was indicted for transporting pornography across state lines; his lover-boy lifestyle resumed, fueled by fast cars, fine women, and compulsive betting.

So it was on the night of August 2, 1975, with a $55,000 blue Rolls-Royce convertible in the garage and a beautiful brunette looking at the sparkling lights of Los Angeles below his Hollywood Hills home, that an assassin shot and killed Molinas with a bullet fired from a silencer-equipped automatic. Later it turned out he had been murdered in a complicated plot involving a $50,000 gambling debt to a L.A. bookie. He was 43.

With the deft handling of Molinas, Gallantz's association with pro basketball was cemented. The client would follow him after he left Simpson Thacher to start his own small firm and then on to Proskauer in 1963. He would work with Podoloff's successor, Walter Kennedy, and Kennedy's successor, Larry O'Brien. He would work on every major piece of NBA legislation through its most convulsive years. He would even play a role in the future of the players' union, locating and hiring for the NBA a bright young lawyer after Kennedy told him he needed a black attorney. That attorney's name was Simon Gourdine.

And one day, as fate would have it, that young litigator Gallantz had hired from Columbia knocked on his door.

Stern had heard that a young Proskauer associate working with Gallantz on the NBA matters was taking another job in Philadelphia. In the words of Michael Cardozo, who had by now joined his friend Stern at Proskauer, "When David heard the young lawyer was leaving, before the ink was dry—and I say that metaphorically—he walked into Gallantz's office. He said, 'You must need an assistant, and I'd like to be that assistant.'"

Added Gallantz, "I think he caught wind of the possibility, and that he would not be my first choice. But as an office politician . . ."

Stern got the job and the chance to specialize and absorb the encyclopedic knowledge of NBA history that George Gallantz was all too willing to impart.

"I taught him how to do things," Gallantz said.

The old man chuckled, then went on:

"We would sit and have a brainstorming session. Try this case with Judge X. What sort of guy is X? What's he likely to ask? How do you handle him? Do you handle him man-to-man or like lawyer and judge? If you're summing up before a jury, don't tell a jury you're going to be brief. *Be brief!* I wrote a little five-page pamphlet how to prepare for a deposition. . . . I did the talking. It's a hands-on, extremely practical method of teaching, but if you don't have the ability to absorb, you're not going to make it."

Stern, Gallantz said, "had what the doctor ordered." And his timing wasn't bad either, since the NBA was entering a period of fractious litigation. There was Connie Hawkins, launching his ultimately successful challenge to a Molinas-like ban. There was the Oscar Robertson suit, representing the players' push for long-denied freedoms. There was Spencer Haywood's legal fight to play as an underclassman. There was all-out war and eventual peace to negotiate with the American Basketball Association.

Michael Cardozo was soon brought on to help handle the burgeoning NBA caseload. In 1975, Walter Kennedy retired and was replaced by Larry O'Brien, who was no basketball maven and, according to insiders, was intimidated by Gallantz. Stern, young and amiable, made his move, quickly becoming O'Brien's right-hand man.

"When O'Brien wanted to call his lawyer, he called David Stern," said Gallantz. "David would keep me informed."

And one day, a couple of years later, Stern walked into Gallantz's office and said that O'Brien had offered him a job as legal counsel. He wanted Gallantz's opinion. He asked for it and got it.

"Well, you schmuck, he's not that nice of a guy to work for," Gallantz said. "How can you put your life in the hands of *one* client?"

As it turned out, Stern was merely being polite. His mind was made up. "I'll give it a try," he said.

As Stern rose through the NBA ranks, his people began to fall into place behind him. Gary Bettman had landed at Proskauer and he wound up working on the NBA. Cardozo became Proskauer's partner in charge of NBA litigation, where he remains. Howard Ganz would be the firm's point man for NBA labor issues. The axis of lawyers who would dominate and protect the league for years to come was formed.

And Simon Gourdine, the bright black attorney Gallantz had discovered for Walter Kennedy, got out of Dodge.

"As fast as he could, when David ultimately became commissioner, before David could shaft him," said Gallantz. "Gourdine had worked with O'Brien, and when O'Brien indicated he wanted to quit, Simon thought he was the next commissioner."

Gourdine was not part of Stern's team and he knew it. Years later, Gourdine would engage Stern from the other side, the players' side. Again, Stern would use him as a springboard to greater heights.

In the twilight years of his career, Gallantz saw it all unfold, the

NBA's dramatic rise with Stern at the helm. It would occur to him that Stern had known exactly where he was going from the day he knocked on the door and invited himself to be Gallantz's assistant on that "oddball" account.

"What I didn't realize was that this young man was very well-informed," he said. "He had a vision."

Stern argued that there was "never any master plan," that he was less visionary and more opportunistic. And perhaps that was what Gallantz was getting at when he said that while "[I] admire Stern's skills and enjoy his prosperity," he sadly no longer feels that he has a place in his former student's life. He said he feared that Stern had come to view himself too much as a product of his own genius, a victim of the same syndrome afflicting too many basketball stars.

Or so he has heard.

"It's true, since he became a millionaire," Gallantz said, agreeing with James Quinn's assessment that Stern can be an intellectual bully. "If you think you can talk to your lawyers as if they are vassals, you are a lesser human being. I think, in David's case, he has no insight in that department. I think he's more self-important than I'd like him to be. I'd like to sit down and say, 'What the hell is going on, David?'"

He has tried, but Stern, like the Proskauer partner just back from the French Riviera, never seems to have checked his calendar.

"I make jokes when I'm going to have lunch with him . . . ," Gallantz said. "You can *beg* for a lunch date just so much."

He was asked how many times he had tried.

David Stern's mentor laughed and said rather mournfully, "I'm an old man. How many times should I try?"

About the time Stern was making his way toward law partnership in New York City, learning the pro basketball ropes from George Gallantz, he also was preparing for what would one day become the NBA's greatest challenge: how to get control of divisive socioeconomic conditions and how to integrate itself into the curious and volatile mix of prejudicial mainstream culture.

Stern, it turned out, got all the practice he needed right in his own backyard.

Four distinguished women who knew firsthand of how hard

Stern practiced for this walk on a tightrope decided their much-talked-of reunion was long overdue and met early in 1996, at the Hackensack, New Jersey, high-rise apartment of Gilda Yolles Mintz.

Mintz was the president of her own public relations and marketing firm. Phoebe J. Slade was a professor in sociology and anthropology at Jersey City State College. Barbara Lotz Griffin was in creative advertising. Lee Porter was executive director of the Fair Housing Council of Northern New Jersey.

The group was racially mixed, Mintz and Griffin both white, Slade and Porter black. It seemed the way it was supposed to be, for their story, this very reunion, represented a history of working together for peaceful coexistence, for racial tolerance.

They were bound by issues and principles, by a decades-old battle against bigotry that shook wealthy Bergen County in northern New Jersey and, in the end, all of America right to its core. And when it came to the subject of legal acumen, of coolheaded guidance, they shared the belief that one man, more than any other, had helped steer them right.

That man was David Stern, and Lee Porter, sipping coffee with her old friends, told the story of how the now internationally famous NBA commissioner had impacted their community-driven lives.

Ensconced at Proskauer, the young attorney and his wife had settled back in his hometown to begin raising a family. Just a few miles from the George Washington Bridge, Teaneck offered an easy commute to midtown Manhattan, and a stable, diverse community described in 1976 by the *New York Times* as a "national model for successful suburban integration. It was once adjudged an All-American community, and it was the first Northern suburb to vote in favor of busing to achieve integrated schools in the early 1960s."

It was natural for a town striving for that rare place in racially and economically polarized America to have its own watchdog group to maintain the qualitative but fragile balance. In 1973, a group of citizens became concerned about perceived racial steering practices by the town's real estate brokers. Blacks were being encouraged to buy in Teaneck; whites were not. That is when a group called Teaneck Together was formed. Stern joined, offering pro bono legal work, but never dreaming he was about to take on what amounted to a full-time job moonlighting as a civil rights litigator and spiritual adviser.

At the time, three towns in Bergen—Teaneck, Englewood, and Hackensack—housed 82 percent of the county's blacks. Most of the neighboring towns were almost entirely white. At a time when housing discrimination suits were catching on as a means to integrate white-dominated neighborhoods, Teaneck Together began to send out test couples, black and white, who pretended to look for homes in the same price range.

"They would never be shown the same houses," Porter said.

The group decided it had to do something, but what? And to whom?

"Our problem at first was that we were entirely focused on just our town," Porter said. "But it was David who was able to look beyond Teaneck and Englewood. I remember him saying, 'You've got to stop looking at it this way.' He made us see that whatever was going on outside our towns was affecting us. So we began studying other towns. We'd send a black couple to Ridgewood, and they would be sent right to Teaneck."

Teaneck Together reached out, merged its campaign with the Fair Housing Council, of which Stern would eventually become president. On March 8, 1976, this coalition of open-housing advocates, acting in concert with the municipality of Englewood, filed a class action civil complaint in Newark's federal district court, charging most of the county's real estate brokers with perpetuating a racially segregated housing market.

The suit was described by the *New York Times* as groundbreaking. The *Times* reported that, unlike previous housing claims, "the suit attacks what fair housing advocates regard as one of the most sinister and pervasive forces in the suburban housing market: the practice of racial steering."

Lee Porter described the lawsuit as "massive" and, predictably, one that dragged on for four years. Block-to-block battlelines were drawn, especially in Teaneck, whose town government refused to join Englewood in filing the suit. Commitments were tested. Tempers flared, but not in public, if master spin doctor Stern could help it.

"We'd go on television shows with people from the other side, and David would be in the studio telling me, 'Lee, you can't say that. You can't!' " Porter said. "One time, I remember the interviewer was a guy named Bill Boggs. I was younger then, emotional. There was a guy from Glen Rock, one of 'those' towns. The minute David saw him, he said, 'Don't call the guy from Glen Rock an SOB.' David was only in his early thirties, but he seemed older, much more composed, than a man his age. The other lawyers were all older, but he commanded respect."

Porter said that Fair Housing naturally hired its own attorney, but that Stern was the real legal authority and mastermind. Every press release, every document, had to pass by his desk. She would rush into Manhattan to get a form signed, or show up at his home at the crack of dawn, so often that all these years later she still remembered the address: "Thirteen thirty-one Hudson Street," she said.

Stern would conduct meetings Sundays at 7 A.M., and one time Porter blurted out to his wife, "Dianne, how can you stand it?"

"Oh, it goes with the territory," Dianne Stern replied.

Whatever drove Stern, it wasn't publicity. "So much of what he did usually went unnoticed," Porter said. "He had to stay in the background, to make sure there wasn't the appearance of him using his affiliation with Proskauer to help us." And, in all probability, because a crusading liberal might not endear himself to the corporate mentality. It might negatively affect his climb toward partnership.

The suit was settled, with Fair Housing gaining the right to examine the records of Bergen County's real estate brokers and to monitor the towns and homes that whites and blacks were being shown. Fair Housing dropped a demand to have each broker pay $100 a year to better finance the group.

"It's a long time ago now," Porter said. "Things did improve, but of course there have been setbacks. We're still fighting."

For Stern, this particular war ended soon after the suit was settled. He said that while his young sons, Eric and Andrew, had derived "tremendous benefits" from attending Teaneck's integrated grammar schools, and that they had thanked him years later, he also believed it was time to move on. He was moving up the establishment ladder now, making more money, defining comfort in new, upscale ways. Stern and his family relocated to Scarsdale, an extremely wealthy enclave known for being predominantly Jewish, in suburban Westchester County north of New York City.

There, his wife began to write book reviews for the Westchester Gannett newspaper chain. His sons, who, according to Stern family friends, suffered due to the long hours their father habitually worked, attended schools that were overwhelmingly white. Stern discourages them from giving interviews, in keeping with his desire to keep the family's home life private. But success clearly changed the way Stern made choices.

Once again, Stern moved on, and up, and didn't look back.

At Gilda Mintz's apartment, the women said they had not seen Stern in many years. But they, too, with fascination and awe, had watched him drive icons of the black community to the heights of white, mainstream America. Lee Porter said the man in Olympic Tower across the river doesn't strike her as much different from the one she knew. He still sees the big picture better than most and still somehow gets enough people to see it his way. "I never met his parents, but somewhere along the way, he acquired a lot of sensitivity, and I mean a lot!" she said. "I see what he's done in basketball and I'm not surprised that he's able to work with owners and players. He's been able to make the owners see that they're not going anyplace without the players."

Or, for that matter, David Stern.

"The game is really bigger than the individual, no matter how spectacular that individual has been," Stern said. "When that individual retires, on time or early, the sun is going to rise."

In Stern-speak, it was obvious what he was saying: Michael Jordan, great as he is, is not The Game as much as what has been created, in essence, by Stern.

Jordan, supported in part by soaring financials and the chest-beating David Falk, would be inclined to disagree. He was indeed big enough to carry the league, to dramatically affect its fortunes and fate.

But lesser lights could, in this star-crossed setting, do devastating damage as well. Even though the league often did everything it could to squelch the damage before it could surface.

3

Puff Policy

THIRTEEN MEN GATHERED IN A CONFERENCE ROOM IN JULY 1994 AT
Boston's Deaconess Hospital. Twelve were some of the top cardiac
specialists in the country. The thirteenth knew little of heart
disease, and less about basketball.

Soon, however, Ron Suskind would know more about both
subjects than he would ever have bargained for. And he would
become David Stern's worst nightmare, a dogged reporter who
had somehow slipped inside the heart of the powerful NBA spin-
doctoring machine to uncover the story behind a tragic death that
might have been prevented—had it not been, in part, for the
NBA's compulsive need to keep its public believing that its house
of cards was steel and brick.

The results of Suskind's work would more than taint one of
Stern's most embellished achievements and put someone who
was more used to the calculated offensive thrust into an unsteady
and warranted defensive crouch. It would expose the NBA's
celebrated drug plan as mostly public relations fluff, and not the
progressive policy it was hailed and promoted as. It would
summarize it in humiliating headline fashion: "NBA: Don't Ask,
Don't Tell."

The conference had been called to discuss athletes' hearts and sudden death, a disturbing trend, particularly among young basketball players. As slides of the damaged hearts of several fallen athletes appeared on the screen in the darkened room, Ron Suskind was equally unenlightened as to who they were. The name of Len Bias, for example, meant nothing to him.

Suskind was no NBA beat writer fishing for trade rumors for his Sunday notes column, though. He was a Pulitzer Prize–winning reporter for the *Wall Street Journal,* working on his first sports story: the controversial death of Boston Celtics star Reggie Lewis on July 27, 1993.

Like any good reporter, Suskind scribbled notes and figured he'd catch up, while the eminent physicians pinpointed a small tissue scar possibly caused by cocaine and potentially life-threatening, especially to large, muscular athletes.

When the lights came on, the discussion continued and several of the doctors turned to a short, heavyset man with a shock of gray hair and a tweed sport coat. His name was Stanton Kessler, deputy medical examiner for the state of Massachusetts, and the man who had prepared Reggie Lewis' final autopsy report, which listed the official cause of death as heart damage caused by a common cold virus.

The doctors were actually laughing as Kessler was peppered with questions like "What about the Lewis autopsy? What about that virus, Stan?"

Kessler, squirming, looking down, stammered that legal threats had been made by the Lewis family and that he was bound by Massachusetts law not to discuss the case. He quickly left the room and clearly hoped the case would be left closed.

That was not going to happen now, not with Suskind picking up the scent of something foul.

Following Lewis' ominous fainting spell during an April 1993 playoff game at the Boston Garden, Dr. Gilbert Mudge of Brigham and Women's Hospital publicly said initial tests indicated that the player was suffering from a corrective fainting condition and could likely continue his career. But that promising diagnosis had come shortly after a so-called Dream Team of specialists concluded that Lewis was in much worse shape and would have to retire, only to have Lewis and his wife, Donna Harris Lewis, flee New England Baptist Hospital for Brigham and Women's in the middle of the night. A second team of consultants called in several months later by Dr. Mudge reached the same conclusion as the Dream Team.

Suskind didn't know Lewis' scoring average, but he could see as he worked backward on the story that more questions had been raised than answered in the days and weeks following Lewis' death. Something was wrong with the loose ends being tied together by "this one doctor screwing everything up with one misdiagnosis." No doctor in his right mind, having seen the X rays and heard the previous diagnosis, would put himself out on a limb like that. It just didn't fit with Suskind's notion of "how the world works."

Months later, Ron Suskind would go to another conference and would tell a group of fellow investigative reporters that, as it turned out, Mudge had been the perfect fall guy in a story that was really about what happened, or didn't happen, as Lewis lay in his bed at New England Baptist, refusing doctors' requests to test him for cocaine after X rays of his heart revealed damage consistent with that drug's use. How the Lewis family fortune and the NBA's public relations concerns seemed to be a greater priority than the damaged heart of the stricken star.

As long as people believed that Lewis was misdiagnosed, that his death was not drug related, the player's widow and the team would receive more than $15 million in insurance on his contract.

The Celtics, in the midst of several business deals involving their own Boston media outlets in the outset of the post–Larry Bird era, would have no scandal on their hands, no Len Bias sequel. Ditto the ever-protective NBA.

"It was too easy," Suskind said. "Everyone hates doctors." And no one in the Boston sports community wanted to believe that Lewis, a local star at Northeastern University who'd succeeded Bird as captain of the revered Celtics, could be anything less than a tragic victim.

Lewis handed out turkeys every Thanksgiving in poor Boston neighborhoods. He was spokesman for the local YMCA, the proverbial sports role model. It was too complicated to even consider the possibility that Lewis might have been another Bias, too conspiratorial to imagine that he might have been saved had fear and self-interest not been involved.

Suskind had gone to college in Boston and lived there for a time, as well. But now his home was in Washington, D.C. In Boston, he was an outsider, with no emotional ties to Lewis or the Celtics. That day at Deaconess Hospital, Suskind intuitively knew that he was on to something big from the moment Stanton Kessler could not look his peers in the eye.

So, long before Suskind would rock Boston and the NBA with his devastating March 9, 1995, *Journal* account of the cloak of silence that surrounded the Lewis case, seemingly in order to protect reputations and financial interests, he began calling NBA people to ask a simple question:

How does your drug program work?

There would be no resistance by America's most media-savvy sport. At the time, the NBA was bigger than ever, coming off the ratings bonanza of a championship series between Michael Jordan's Bulls and Charles Barkley's Suns. NBA people loved to talk about any piece of the league's blueprint for success. And the drug program, by reputation, was one of the crown jewels of the 1983 collective bargaining agreement often cited as the single event that reversed the fortunes of a sagging sport.

"The NBA was so happy to tell me about the drug policy, delighted," Suskind said. "It was, 'Oh, yes, another reporter. It's the best anywhere, are you kidding? We had a drug problem in '83 and back then'—and this is [union president] Charlie Grantham talking—'the *L.A. Times* wrote that seventy-five percent were using drugs.'"

Suskind—recalling this conversation in an animated, cynical manner—said, "'Really, Charlie?'

"'Yeah, yeah, but then David came up with this policy, amazing policy.'

"I said, 'What happened?'

"'Then it worked.'

"So I said, 'All of a sudden, drugs were eradicated?' I said, 'How come you people haven't been contacted by Oslo?'

"'Oslo?'

"'Yeah, Oslo, Nobel Prize.'

"'Is that supposed to be sarcastic?'

"I said, 'How many players have been tested since the policy started?'"

Suskind said Grantham guessed maybe a half dozen, then said he'd get back to him. Grantham, he said, didn't return his calls after that. He'd apparently figured out this was one reporter who wasn't interested in the fluff.

The "Anti-Drug Program of the National Basketball Association and the National Basketball Players' Association" was heralded in the September 29, 1983, sports section of the *New York Times*. The headline above the story: "NBA Will Ban Drug Users." A secondary headline over the second of three columns read: "Stern Plan Adopted."

The reference, ironically, was not to David Stern, who, as the league's general counsel and rising star, helped craft the policy. It was a summation of its perceived severity.

In declaring the immediate cancellation of any contract and a minimum two-year suspension for players testing positive after the league established "reasonable cause," the NBA was creating the most punitive penalty in professional sports. At the same time, it believed it was sending a message with its third-strike ban that drug use was unacceptable, the policy also had its intended benevolent side. It enabled a player to be suspended with pay if he came forward for treatment on strike one, and without pay on strike two.

Strike three and the player was out, for at least two years, as if he'd tested positive after reasonable cause.

The logic of the plan was that once players understood that their careers would be in jeopardy if they were caught, they would be more inclined to ask for help. Seeing through this impressive rhetoric right from the start was the league's most notorious abuser at the time, Micheal Ray Richardson.

"The NBA doesn't understand that drugs are a disease that changes your entire life," Richardson said in the same *Times* article. "The big problem is that people who are on drugs are ashamed to admit it. They have this terrible fear of getting up in the morning and seeing a newspaper headline that so and so is on drugs."

Years later, medical experts would take a hard look at the results the drug policy was producing and determine that Richardson knew what he was talking about. The addict knew bullshit when he read it. Dr. Robert Millman, an adviser to Major League Baseball's drug policy, said, "We encourage players to come forward because we assure that their privacy will be protected."

That was likely to happen only during the off-season for an NBA player. If he sought help during the season, he might as well have snorted a gram right in the middle of Times Square.

"Labeling somebody a drug user, taking a famous athlete and telling the world publicly that they have a drug problem, has got to be realized as something inhibiting somebody's willingness to come forward," said Dr. Arnold Washton, who, while treating Richardson at his New York institute in the early 1980s, dealt with the NBA at its most frantic point.

He argued that players who stepped forward for help should be evaluated to determine a "malignancy of use pattern," not subjected to immediate punitive measures such as being sent away from their teams to a treatment facility.

He added that the league approached the plague of drugs as a "business decision, an image problem." In a clinical sense, he said, the NBA drug program was really no drug program at all.

"Only if you see athletes as racehorses," he said. "If one horse gets injured, you put in another horse."

Richard Dumas, in the impersonal vernacular of comparing athletes with animals, was more thoroughbred than workhorse, a well-proportioned and long-limbed, 6-7, 210-pound small forward out of Oklahoma State. But he had had problems with substance abuse in college and had been drafted in the second round of the 1991 draft by the Phoenix Suns with trepidation regarding his past.

For good reason, as it turned out. Before he ever played a minute of NBA ball, Dumas took a urine test during training camp, as all rookies did, and failed.

He was suspended and disappeared from the Suns' camp, into John Lucas' Houston rehab residence for wayward athletes, to be known for the next year and a half as that kid with the scarlet D on his chest.

"I think you're branded," Dumas said one day, relaxing in a Phoenix hotel room. "I mean, you go through something like that, you don't want the whole world to know."

Dumas and anyone else entangled with the NBA drug program

didn't have much choice. The suspension guaranteed, as Richardson forecast way back in 1983, immediate headlines, and public scorn.

"People start to look at you," Dumas said. "If something goes wrong, you wonder what they're thinking. They're probably thinking, 'You're doing this, you're doing that.'"

That day at the Biltmore Hotel, Dumas was dressed in a gray T-shirt with a sky blue Nike logo, head shaved, hoop earring dangling from his left lobe, diamond stud in his right. A gold chain hung around his neck.

For all this flash, for all his painful struggles with nightlife stimulants, Dumas tended to whisper his way through interviews, though without the impishness of the soft-spoken Shaquille O'Neal. Dumas was shy, not terribly articulate. He almost never made eye contact. For the taping of a television interview that same day, he wanted to wear dark sunglasses until he was reminded that, considering his image, he was better off without them.

One could understand why Dumas, at least in Phoenix, felt he was better off incognito. In this ultraconservative environment, playing for a team whose most famous fan and franchise friend was Rush Limbaugh, Dumas was treated more like a man who was destroying his team than one who was killing his career, if not himself.

His boss, Suns president and CEO Jerry Colangelo, one of the NBA's longtime power brokers, was on record that he didn't even believe drug addiction to be a disease.

"That may get me in trouble with advocacy groups, but that's how I feel," he said.

Dumas would nonetheless get his chance to prove he could score in the NBA, as easily as he did in the street. Not long after he was finally cleared to play for the Suns in December 1992, he became a starting forward on a team that went all the way to that six-game championship series against the Bulls. Dumas played well, averaging 15 points during the regular season, 11 in the playoffs.

He played the game above the rim, swooping in from the baseline for a variety of highlight-reel dunks. "Dr. J with a jump shot," Lucas, who'd scrimmaged with Dumas during his Houston rehab, called him. When the season was over, he signed a multiyear contract worth millions. He appeared on the verge of stardom.

During the championship series, however, there had been ominous spottings of Dumas in Chicago pubs. He appeared nervous and distant to teammates, league officials, and reporters. By the end of the summer, the sad word was out: he was back in Houston, in Lucas' care.

"The guy had gone from rehab to starting in the NBA Finals," said Lucas. "He was out there. He was under pressure and had a difficult time dealing with it. People want to say he had a drug problem. I like to say he has a living problem."

In his counseling of athletes, including notorious NBA cases such as Lloyd Daniels, Chris Washburn, and Roy Tarpley, Lucas said, he had encountered all the appalling calamities, every imaginable emotional and physical violation. "Violence, incest, substance abuse, you name it," he said.

Colangelo, a proud, self-made man with roots on Chicago's working-class South Side, didn't want to hear what he called "liberal excuses." To him this was simply a case of betrayal, of waste. Dumas wasn't Dr. J with a jump shot anymore. He was Richard Dumas with a drug habit.

Though this was technically his first strike—a positive rookie test did not count as one, according to the drug agreement— Colangelo said he would challenge that rule. He didn't think he should have to pay Dumas' salary. He announced that Dumas had blown his future in Phoenix.

John Lucas didn't blame Colangelo for feeling as he did. "It's hard for the layman to see this as more than irrational behavior," he said. "People tend to look at the drug, not the life—until it's someone you love."

To Lucas, Dumas was more than an investment turned sour. He knew him as the scared and lonely twenty-three-year-old, out on the road with the Suns, calling his counselors back in Houston in the middle of the night, wanting very much to be talked out of cracking open the mini-bar in his room. One February day in 1993, he was the excited new father of a baby boy on the telephone to Lucas' business adviser and mentor, Joyce Bossett, thanking her again and again for all her support.

Dumas missed the entire 1993–94 season. Perhaps motivated by a crippling knee injury to star forward Danny Manning,

Colangelo eventually accepted Dumas back in March of 1995, but not before forcing his agent, James Sears Bryant, to agree to contract modifications allowing for Dumas' suspension and release should he so much as test positive for alcohol. He demanded that Dumas make a humiliating apology to the city of Phoenix.

Clinical drug specialists everywhere had to shake their heads in dismay.

Dumas was one of two NBA players in the first half of the 1990s suspended for drugs. None were suspended after testing positive by reasonable cause. Only six had been since the implementation of the policy in 1984.

This, according to Peter Bensinger, former director of the Drug Enforcement Administration, was nearly a statistical impossibility.

"That tells me the policy isn't working," Bensinger said.

According to the National Institute on Drug Abuse, in 1995, drug use nationwide for males nineteen to thirty-two—the relative age range for NBA players—was running about 17 percent. The NBA number for positive drug tests was about 1 percent. While the league regularly used these figures as evidence that it had cleaned up its act, Bensinger said they were more likely representative of a farce.

"I think the NBA is putting its head in the sand, saying, 'Well, we don't want to hear the bad news,'" he said. "They have a reasonable-suspicion provision, but it's not being used."

Reasonable-cause testing was not exactly what the NBA had in mind to combat its 1980s drug woes. It was a compromise after the Players' Association rejected the league's effort to have mandatory testing. It eventually agreed in 1988 to rookie testing four times a year, but held firm that veterans' privacy would be violated by mandatory testing.

"If someone is going to go into his house and use cocaine recreationally, it's our job through education, through reinforcement, to counsel about the evils and dangers," said David Stern. "Not to accompany them into their bathroom."

If testing veterans was such a bad idea, then why test rookies? This concept seemed backward to Arnold Washton, Richardson's drug rehabilitation counselor.

"As players get on in experience, become more famous, become wealthier, and get inducted in a lifestyle, you could argue their chances of getting involved with drugs goes up, not down," he said.

The reasonable-cause plan allowed for an independent arbitrator to determine, based on evidence submitted by the NBA, that a player be tested as many as four times over six weeks. What evidence might constitute reasonable cause? According to former NBA drug arbitrators, a police officer seeing a player buying drugs would qualify as reasonable cause. A player's association with a known dealer or presence in a drug den would not.

Hundreds of other scenarios were possible, all open to interpretation and manipulation. These incredibly ambiguous guidelines become further obscured because NBA teams, unlike baseball's, are under no obligation to report information they receive regarding a specific player to the league.

So let's say Team X hears from local police sources on the eve of the playoffs that its star forward has been involved in drug transactions. The choices are for the team to create a scandal and lose its leading scorer, to risk early playoff elimination and the revenue created by sellout crowds, or to do nothing—under no threat of league penalty—and hope the situation somehow remedies itself.

According to Wes Matthews, a former Atlanta Hawk, Philadelphia 76er, San Antonio Spur, Los Angeles Laker, and Chicago Bull, the obvious result of such a policy was that a journeyman player such as himself was at far greater risk than the stars who carry the league.

"If you're a megastar, they ain't gonna fuck with you," Matthews said, persevering, at thirty-six, in the spring/summer United States Basketball League in 1995. "If you're the megaman, or next to the man, they're not gonna mess with you. If you're Joe Blow, it was, 'We're gonna get you.' "

Maybe it wasn't that simple. But logic dictated that no team would pursue its star unless the situation was completely out of control, as in the case of Richardson. And the statistics overwhelmingly supported the assertion that the policy didn't work or was not designed to.

Peter Bensinger said the fact that the NBA had two players suspended in the first half of the 1990s—none for reasonable cause—out of an estimated sixteen hundred man-years indicated that the league was letting anywhere between two to three hundred players slip by. And the numbers might be higher when drugs the league was *not* testing for were factored in.

"From talking to my players and what I've observed, alcohol is clearly widespread and marijuana is, too," said Dumas' agent, Bryant, an Oklahoma district judge from 1981 through 1986, now working for ProServ. "There is widespread soft-drug use."

Dumas, offering some insight as to what the NBA players' current drug of choice might be, suggested the league has good reason to limit its testing to heroin and cocaine: "If they tested for marijuana, there probably wouldn't be no NBA."

And if they suddenly had the right to substitute random testing for veterans in place of reasonable cause, what might they find?

"I know no stars ever got caught, so that's all the comment I have," Dumas said.

What did that say?

"It says I need to become a star."

That wasn't going to happen in Phoenix. Obviously a troubled man, Dumas was never going to outrun his self-destructive habits in such a hostile, demeaning workplace. He was mired in a drug program that didn't properly treat the few it identified and sounded much worse than it really was for those who were hiding.

Dumas was waived in May 1995 by the Suns after violating the drinking clauses in his contract. John Lucas, coaching a bad Philadelphia team and making a noble and sometimes knee-jerk, self-cleansing habit out of throwing lifelines to drowning players, signed him for the 1995–96 season.

Dumas was better off away from Phoenix. Colangelo, building what would become a magnificent sports empire in the desert, was relieved to amputate this annoying appendage. It reminded him too much of a far more disheartening brush with the scourge of drugs, and the NBA's improvisational means of wishing them away.

Back in the spring of 1987, there were no professional football or hockey teams in Arizona, and the notion of major league baseball in an area littered with spring training bases was barely a gleam in Jerry Colangelo's eye. His NBA franchise had for nineteen years been the only game in town. Its players were popular mainstays and community heroes.

Then came one of the darkest days the Valley of the Sun had known, the largest bust in the history of professional sports tearing like a stake right through the heart of Phoenix, of Maricopa County, piercing its way all the way to Olympic Tower in New York.

"I think any of us who went through it at the time would look at it as a bad memory for the community, the franchise, the league, and as a prosecutor, for me because there was so much of a public backlash," said James Keppel, a local attorney turned crime fighter who learned much more about his favorite NBA team than he ever wanted to know.

Keppel grew up in Mesa, went to law school at the University of Arizona, and joined the county attorney's office in 1979. By 1987, he was head of the organized-crime unit, working bookmaking, drugs, theft rings, money laundering, and the like. Tall and rangy, with a gray mustache and bearing more than a slight resemblance to television gunslinger Dennis Weaver, Keppel sipped a Diet Pepsi in a Phoenix hotel suite during Super Bowl week in late January of 1996, remembering how a lawman's natural curiosity led him and others into the dark, inner sanctum of a troubled NBA team.

It started with Walter Davis, the Suns' five-time All-Star and leading career scorer, coming forward under the NBA drug agreement, asking for help with his cocaine addiction. That was shocking enough for Phoenix's sports community. But one day, as Keppel and a fifteen-year veteran detective named Gary Ball lounged in the office, the subject got around to connecting small dots to bigger ones. If Davis was using cocaine, it was unlikely that he was getting it from some low-level dealer in the back of a college frat house.

"We knew there was a big drug problem with kids in the community," Keppel said. "Here's this guy, the best player the Suns had, a role model. A big basketball star with all this money, he's out there buying cocaine, why doesn't somebody find out who's dealing?"

That was a question Keppel said he eventually raised with a

local contact for NBA security, a supposed watchdog for drug-related issues.

"I remember asking this guy when we found out that Davis had this drug problem, 'Did the league ever ask you to investigate who was selling him the drugs?'

"He goes, 'Nope, they told me just to put it aside. . . . They don't seem to be interested in that.'"

It was law enforcement's job, not the NBA's, to monitor the flow of drugs in Phoenix's streets and bars, if not its locker rooms. But in Keppel's and Ball's opinions, Davis' drug use should have set off alarms, in the Suns' and league office. If there was a legitimate system to work with police and seek evidence that would allow the league to exercise its "reasonable cause" option, the NBA should have been responding with the attitude that fire was in the vicinity of the smoke.

"Our expression to the district attorney's office was if there's independent things, go for it," Stern said at the time. "But if it's because of the publicity surrounding it [Davis' drug use], it would not be a good thing because we're trying very hard in a program that has been praised by the DEA, FBI, the presidential drug counselor as at least a start, an attempt to do something right."

The right thing to do, in the opinion of Phoenix police chief Ruben Ortega and Keppel's boss, Tom Collins, was to proceed with the investigation, starting with Davis' being subpoenaed before a grand jury for information on his suppliers. Ortega and Collins paid a visit to Colangelo at the Suns' old offices on N. Central Avenue.

"Tom and Ruben basically laid it out, advised him we were conducting this investigation," Keppel said. "Jerry was very disturbed, offended, that we would start an investigation without coming to him. Ruben mentioned to him, 'Here I am, chief of police investigating criminal activity, and are you saying you'd rather have me come to you and have you handle it in-house?'

"And Jerry's response was: 'Yes, I would have preferred that.'"

While Ball said Colangelo was the only NBA person who seemed genuinely concerned for the players, Keppel added that Colangelo was also in denial. "I don't think he wanted to accept the fact there could be the extensive drug use on this team it turned out to be," he said.

There wasn't supposed to be. The NBA drug program was almost four years old by this time and universally hailed as the best in the business. The rules were in place. The lessons, absorbed in hard and tragic ways by the likes of Micheal Ray Richardson and Len Bias, should already have been learned. But that wasn't the case, no more than the NBA's feel-good umbrella program could have reduced drug use in the league to a few scattered, insignificant drops in the bucket.

According to Ball, now retired and living in Pocatello, Idaho, then deputy commissioner Gary Bettman lived up to his reputation as Stern's bad cop. In a meeting at the county courthouse, NBA Director of Security Horace Balmer hardly said a word. Bettman, meanwhile, fit a desert lawman's image of a blustery New York lawyer to a T.

"Arrogance, absolute arrogance" is how Ball described Bettman. "It was: 'Why are you doing this? Nobody else does.' They just wanted, as far as I was concerned, to protect their image, sweep it under the rug."

Keppel said that Bettman, who declined comment, kept trying to talk them off their investigation, claiming it was going to ruin their drug program, which Keppel said he "didn't think was that effective in the beginning."

Not in Phoenix it wasn't. It turned out, based on the investigation and on the admissions of the players involved, that members of the Suns had been using cocaine for years.

And so it was on a Friday afternoon in April 1987—a Good Friday turned very, very bad—that a shopping cart brimming with copies of the indictments by the Maricopa County grand jury charging nine men with twenty-one felony counts of possessing or trafficking in cocaine or marijuana, or conspiring to do so, was rolled into a jam-packed press conference.

Three of those indicted were current members of the Suns— thirty-one-year-old center James Edwards, starting guard Jay Humphries, and a rookie, Grant Gondrezick. Two others were retired Suns, Mike Bratz and Garfield Heard, who at the time was a member of the mayor's task force on drug abuse.

Several other present or former Suns were linked to the case, described by police as "being present or having knowledge of illegal drug transactions." The current team members were Davis and that season's No. 1 draft pick, William Bedford. The former players were Don Buse, Johnny High, and Alvin Scott.

If the dishonor of a drug scandal wasn't bad enough for the NBA, the scent of a sordid little sports-gambling investigation was making hairs stand on end back at the NBA office in New York.

Three days before the drug indictments came down, Keppel, the assistant DA and the lead prosecutor in the case, was talking just as tough about what he called a "gambling point-shaving" probe. "Given the nature of this area, the beautiful climate, rapidly growing—a lot of money is flowing into Phoenix," Keppel said. "Gambling seems to just follow."

The NBA's worst nightmare, of course, was precisely the fast nightlife scene, the mix of high rollers and wealthy athletes and the potential of a drug trail leading to inside information being passed in return for a few sniffs of powder.

Indeed, it was the arrest of two Phoenix men, John "Red" Chase and Orest J. "Babe" Alex, for running a million-dollar bookmaking operation that same spring that convinced police that much more was going on with the Phoenix Suns beyond Walter Davis. In an interview, Alex, a former member of the ASU Sun Devil Advisory Board, bragged of his close ties to football coaches and other members of the team. Alex later died in a mysterious early-morning one-car accident. The link between Alex and the Suns was a gambler named Charles Keenan, named in the indictments for "conspiring to accept wagers" for Chase at several local bars frequented by Suns and other NBA players, including a club named Malarkey's.

After his arrest, Keenan became a wired-up informer for the district attorney's office. Phones were tapped. With Keenan in place, the gambling part of the investigation began to focus on one game, a February 21, 1987, encounter between the Suns and Milwaukee Bucks, concerning the over-under betting line of 226 points. The word in the betting community was that something was up, and to take the "under."

Charles Keenan had reportedly told the grand jury that James Jordan, who tended bar at Malarkey's, gave cocaine to Bucks reserve center Paul Mokeski before the Suns game and had met with Mokeski and his teammate Jack Sikma in an upstairs VIP lounge frequented by athletes. (Mokeski and Sikma publicly denied any involvement in gambling or drug use.) Ball also testified that Keenan told him Jordan was nervous about police learning the players had been in to see him.

The Suns lost the game at home, 115–107, a victory for the "under."

With almost nine years between him and the Suns investigation, some of the details have blurred for Keppel, now a Maricopa County Superior Court Judge.

Asked if point-shaving was involved in that February 21 game, Keppel replied bluntly, "We received information to that effect."

He talked of unsubstantiated details prosecutors had linking Mokeski or Sikma with passing along information to bartender Jordan about the return of Terry Cummings to the Bucks and how this would impact the team's performance against Phoenix.

But this also was the part of the case that brought back haunting memories, he said.

"Whether it was grand jury leaks, all this stuff gets put in the media," he said. "Some of the allegations of the drug use could be substantiated. This other stuff about the gambling, with Mokeski and Sikma, as I recall, could not be substantiated to the extent that any criminal prosecution could be brought. We never really contemplated that. Still, it was out there in the media and we're getting blamed for bringing this all up and ruining people's reputations. That was the point where this case started coming undone."

By the following November, he said, there were questions about Charles Keenan's credibility, about changed or recanted testimony, about the political agendas of District Attorney Collins and Police Chief Ortega. The notion of Davis as star witness unraveled, as he, naturally fearing for his future in the league, was reluctant to give any concrete evidence. Only nonplayers were ever convicted of drug charges. None of the Suns ever went to trial, and the charges against James Jordan were dismissed.

"A witch-hunt," Colangelo called the whole affair nine years later. "Rumors, innuendo, absolutely nothing."

Yet out of that debacle came what Colangelo called an "opportunity," his opening to organize a group, with him as controlling partner, to purchase the tainted Suns for $44.5 million from

Donald Pitt and Richard Bloch. By 1996, housed in sparkling America West Arena, Colangelo's investment had quadrupled.

The continued growth of the league and the blossoming of Phoenix as a shining jewel of a franchise may have obfuscated those dark days of 1987. At its roots, though, the Suns story showed how vulnerable the league was—and still is—to a gambling scandal, how drugs and inside betting information easily mix in upscale restaurants and bars or late-night parties, carrying overtones of organized crime. How uncomplicated it would be to suck NBA players in, set them up. The typical NBA player has more downtime than baseball players, more overnight road stays than football players. They are out there, wealthy and sometimes willing targets.

"The marketing of heroes" is what Stern once called the NBA's mission. His mission. But how far does one go to protect those who don't have the same understanding of how fragile that marketing can be? Those who would put the entire league's image at risk?

"There is a difference between having a league and a police state," Stern said. He was right about that. But James Keppel and Gary Ball were left with the impression that this seemingly progressive conviction was more the work of patronizing capitalists, that the NBA was much too willing to separate itself from drug scandals and law enforcement in the interests of keeping those cash registers ringing.

The consequences, even those leading to tragedy, be damned.

In the final analysis, Ron Suskind's story in the *Wall Street Journal* was essentially about how a hollow NBA drug policy disrupted the normal chain of medical events, how doctors could not do for twenty-seven-year-old Reggie Lewis what they could have done for another twenty-seven-year-old who walked in off the street with the same condition Lewis had.

It was not about tarnishing Reggie Lewis. It was whether his life might have been saved. It was to determine who was most culpable.

The doctors, even Gilbert Mudge, eventually talked to Suskind because they apparently didn't want to play the NBA image game anymore. They knew the score on this one, and it seemed to have taken a toll on them. They told Suskind they had wanted to test for cocaine and were told the Lewis case did not meet the reasonable-cause standard.

"The guy is falling down on the court, no one knows why, his X rays were medically consistent with cocaine, and it doesn't *meet the standard?*" Suskind said.

In his opinion, it was precisely at this time that Lewis needed a guiding angel to step forward, help him make the right decision. Someone smart and caring from the Celtics—who for decades had bragged how they took care of their own. Someone from the NBA family, which was in close contact with the Celtics through the ordeal. Someone who should have walked into Lewis' hospital suite, whispered in his ear that if he was worried about his contract, his pregnant wife, and his little boy's future, then he didn't have to worry. He could step forward, accept a drug strike, still get paid under the league's drug plan.

The treatment Mudge would ultimately nudge Lewis toward, the insertion of a device that would have controlled his heartbeat, could have been done long months before it was too late. Lewis might have been saved.

"It would have been a terrible day for the Celtics, the NBA, another drug scandal," Suskind said. "But Lewis would be here today doing public service announcements. He would have been alive. That's what I feel. That's what a lot of people in the case felt, and that's why they ended up talking."

Several weeks after Suskind's story appeared, the Celtics retired Lewis' number, 35, raising it on a green-and-white banner that also contained Kevin McHale's 32, Dennis Johnson's 3, and Larry Bird's 33. By that time, a former high school and college teammate of Lewis' named Derrick Lewis (no relation) had told the *Journal* that Lewis was a drug user. He later recanted, but the dam blew and unattributed sources surfaced in the Boston newspapers to allege that Lewis did everything from buy crack on ghetto streets to play high at Boston Garden.

It was ugly and unwarranted, a smear campaign that had no relation to Suskind's dogged and comprehensive report. In its counterattack, the NBA managed to lump everything together.

On Reggie Lewis Night, Stern climbed a small stage in the cramped, beer-stained corridor outside the Celtics' locker room to denounce the "feeding frenzy." He again effectively defended the drug program as one "praised by the FBI, DEA," etc, etc. Much of the mainstream media, including NBA partner NBC, would play down the Suskind story, claim it went way too far. Lewis' death continued to be blamed on circumstance, on bad luck.

By the following year, familiar NBA drug rhetoric was again being heard.

"It was a problem and a perception the league had, which [Stern] saw, attacked, and basically solved," the Detroit Pistons' managing partner and strong Stern ally Bill Davidson said in a rare interview more than halfway through the 1995–96 season. The underlying message being, if the perception was that the problem was resolved, then the problem had been resolved.

Stern held out the possibility that the drug program could be toughened in future collective bargaining negotiations. But when labor war came, the drug issue was long since buried as a memory and a priority. As in the Lewis case, the battles would be about money, money, money. And they would tear at the league, balkanize it, as never before. Inside the camps, it wasn't hard to see why Reggie Lewis had no chance to get the break he desperately needed to save his life.

4

Labor Pains

THE AUGUST AFTERNOON WAS HOT AND STICKY, PROFESSIONAL basketball a dim yesterday and a distant tomorrow. From owners to agents, midsummer has always been the long lunch season for NBA people. But this day, August 8, 1995, Marc Fleisher sat at the head of a rectangular conference table in a sterile office complex in downtown Stamford, Connecticut. A turkey sandwich, a bag of chips, and a diet soda were scattered in front of him. There was no going out with so many calls coming in, with the NBA's financial future on the line.

One by one, Fleisher's new best friends were dialing him up. A big union meeting was set for later that evening in New York City. The agents' grapevine was abuzz with anxiety. Were Simon Gourdine and Buck Williams finally going to jump into their union decertification camp? What did David Stern, who had shut down his league in an unprecedented summer lockout, have up his sleeve?

From the reception area, Fleisher's secretary called out the names, a staggered roll call of agent all-stars. Steve Kauffman. Arn Tellem. Jimmy Sexton. Bill Strickland. And, of course, David Falk. Fleisher would lean over, press down the button of the speaker phone, sit back, confide in men he would normally not turn his back on.

This was, he said, one industry benefit to the summer-long NBA labor strife. "Guys who hate each other have actually gotten to know each other," he said.

What they considered to be dire circumstances for the players, and obviously for themselves, had drawn them together, like rival revolutionary warlords battling an autocratic central government. Only this burgeoning conflict was against what seemed to be another uneasy partnership, in Stern and Gourdine. The union leadership was struggling to stay afloat. It was in Stern's and the NBA's interests for it to succeed. If the agents won, if the union decertified and dissolved, anarchy loomed.

Marc Fleisher, for his part, had incited the mutiny weeks earlier, on the Friday afternoon of Father's Day weekend, days after the NBA had finished the season without a collective bargaining agreement.

Just before Houston completed its sweep of Orlando for the 1994–95 title, Stern went on television to announce "substantial progress" in contract talks with the union. It was an abrupt turnaround after a year in which no contract progress was made. It looked as if Stern would not have to go through with his threat to impose an off-season lockout.

It was Stern's second lockout threat within nine months. In October 1994, with baseball players on strike, with hockey players locked out, the NBA seemed certain to follow the winds of sports labor war. An eleventh-hour no-strike, no-lockout moratorium, which included a freeze on all existing player contracts, averted the league's first shutdown.

Stern and Charles Grantham, the union director at the time, were hailed as pragmatic sportsmen. Actually, the deal was more about union acquiescence. Grantham knew his players were not about to strike or tolerate being locked out. Now Stern knew it, too.

The average NBA salary was $1.7 million. Most contracts were multiyear and almost all were guaranteed. The typical NBA star was no union activist. He never formed a lasting bond to his sport in a minor league clubhouse or rode fume-fouled buses or plugged his way through the frozen tundra of junior hockey. He was pampered at every turn, the king of his high school and college court. He was guaranteed millions before his first professional dribble.

Stern, who by spring was dealing with Gourdine after Grantham's mysterious April exit from the union, preyed on Gourdine's obvious weakness. He insisted that a deal be struck before the summer, long before regular-season games could actually be threatened. He claimed player contracts were rising 20 percent against 8 percent annual revenue growth. In other words, the NBA, for all its growth, was crying poverty.

Following Stern's televised show of optimism from the NBA Finals, Fleisher became suspicious. On that Friday before Father's Day, he began calling management contacts such as Phoenix's Jerry Colangelo, who gleefully reported union concessions such as a drastic rookie wage scale and the severe modification of the Bird exception via a 100 percent luxury tax (for any veteran's raise over 10 percent). In return, the salary cap was to increase over six years, from the $23 million in 1995–96 to $32.5 million by the turn of the century. Meetings were being set for Monday and Tuesday, for union leadership and the owners to vote on the deal. Without losing one game, Stern was on the verge of accomplishing what baseball and hockey had failed to do despite damaging and lengthy shutdowns.

With Gourdine and Stern unavailable under the terms of a news blackout, Fleisher guessed this Stern-Gourdine express was about to make a high-speed run through union station. He picked up the telephone and dialed David Falk.

"Something had to be done," Fleisher said.

Only Falk, he knew, had the clients to do it. Falk had Michael Jordan, Patrick Ewing, Alonzo Mourning, and others. And Falk was always ready for a fight. By the beginning of the following week, those names were on a petition to the National Labor Relations Board with nearly two hundred others to decertify the union and shift the labor fight to federal court. Soon, Gourdine and Williams were forced to summon Stern back to the table. The deal was not going to fly.

Once thinking he was home free for a deal-sealing slam dunk, Stern suddenly found himself stripped of the ball.

* * *

"My father was always a firm believer and always told me that a union is only as strong as its stars," Marc Fleisher said on August 8 between incoming calls. "Stars are the ones who have the power to deal with the owner, but, unfortunately, in Charlie's regime, and even more so in Simon's, there seems to be a shift away from that and more towards the old football sensibility, to go for the everyday player and not worry about the stars.

"Maybe it's because the stars are making so much money now. But they've lost track of the whole concept that works in pro basketball. The stars are the ones who are going to make David Stern give them more. Stern doesn't care about the players at the lower end because they can be replaced in two seconds. He damn well cares about the Michael Jordans, Patrick Ewings, and Alonzo Mournings of the world."

As if to have his father forever remind him of this, the only personal touch in Fleisher's office was a wall-mounted copy of a *New York Times* sports column by Ira Berkow, dated May 11, 1989. The headline on the column read: "When 15 7-Footers Trailed Him." The column told of how a fiery Harvard Law School graduate named Larry Fleisher had organized a threatened boycott of the 1964 All-Star Game in snowy Boston, unless the owners agreed to give the players a pension plan.

The struggling NBA was having its All-Star Game televised nationally that year for the first time. In the Berkow column, Oscar Robertson recalled how Fleisher defiantly marched under the stands to confer with the owners, with the muscular giants of the day, Wilt Chamberlain and Bill Russell among them, treading carefully behind. The game was delayed fifteen minutes. The owners caved. The lesson was clear. Basketball stars had clout. If Larry Fleisher didn't found the NBA Players' Association, he certainly empowered it, after becoming its executive director in 1961. He believed passionately in fighting for players' rights, though he was more pragmatic dealmaker than fanatic crusader, like his baseball counterpart, Marvin Miller.

Miller liked Fleisher but always believed he had sold his players out and forever compromised sports labor leverage by not striking a militant posture, by agreeing to a so-called soft, or flexible, salary cap in 1983. Fleisher argued that NBA teams would have folded without it. Jobs would have been lost.

Negotiating for basketball players, collectively and individually, consumed Larry Fleisher. He relished his personal relationships with 1970s greats such as John Havlicek, Paul Silas, and Willis Reed. Bill Bradley once called him "the big brother I never had."

In the Fleisher home, to the teenaged Marc and Eric, basketball owners were portrayed quite differently from the players. They were shallow, arrogant, elitist, racist. "My father was very vocal, even to us, to anyone who would listen, about how badly the owners had treated the players," Marc Fleisher said.

It was a New York teenager's dream, the likes of Bradley and Earl Monroe sleeping in the guest bedroom at their home in the northern New York suburbs. The town, Chappaqua, New York, was as white as any bedroom community in America. Forgetting for the moment the family's choice to live there in the first place, Marc said that, in his opinion, his father derived great pleasure from parading the players through the small Westchester County village.

He once bought from Monroe a silver Rolls-Royce with a black-power-fist symbol on the side. It became the family shopping car, drawing a cautiously curious crowd wherever it was parked. "My father's attitude was, fuck 'em. He was not going to be shy in who he socialized with," Marc said.

In the off-seasons, long before Stern began his global march, there were union-organized barnstorming swings through Europe, South America, and Asia. The young Marc Fleisher's passport was stamped in China, Brazil, and the Ivory Coast. If these trips helped the sport progress, that was fine. According to his son, Larry Fleisher believed that many players, especially those from the inner cities, would never have traveled abroad on their own. When stars from different teams mingled, they became friends. Fleisher's union became stronger.

By 1988, after negotiating his final collective bargaining agreement with Stern, Fleisher was less emotionally connected to the players for whom he had fought. He was fifty-seven years old. His old allies were now on the sidelines as coaches or in the front office or the United States Senate.

The average NBA salary was $600,000 and climbing. For Fleisher, the battles were now more about principle than passion. Few players, if any, were being abused. Once, Larry told Marc, half-joking, that maybe the union had done too good a job. "He was concerned how difficult it would be to get them to strike, if necessary," Marc said.

But there was also mounting pressure for him to quit. Though he forsook agent fees that typically were as high as 10 percent and charged clients by the hour, his dual role was perceived by anti-agent players such as Isiah Thomas, Magic Johnson, and Buck Williams as a severe conflict of interest.

Larry Fleisher stepped aside in 1988. He formed the International Services Group with his two sons. Sensing a new frontier in the European market, the Fleishers landed as clients the first European invaders into the NBA. But in early May 1989, Fleisher finished a workout at his health club, walked into the shower, suffered a heart attack, and died.

The business was left to Marc, the lawyer son, and Eric, the business school graduate.

Marc Fleisher bears a fair resemblance to Larry. Stocky build. Dark hair. Glasses. During the summer of 1995, at the age of forty, he declared himself at war in the name of his dead father.

"I don't want to see everything he fought for for twenty-five years handed right back to the owners," he said. "I don't want to see NBA players no longer get guaranteed contracts. Absolutely, I'm sure this is what my father would have done."

Funny how he wound up in battle against David Stern. In Larry's shadow was the last place Marc Fleisher wished to be when he finished law school in 1979. He wanted to make his own name. The irony was that while Larry was teaming with Stern to battle the NBA's drug culture during the mid-1980s, Marc was experiencing far worse than either could imagine.

He moved to San Francisco, and into the music business. His clients, among others, were Aerosmith, Santana, and Blue Öyster Cult.

"Not to say that athletes are angels, but at least they use their bodies as a tool, and most realize if they abuse it, it will affect their career," Fleisher said. "In rock, it's the complete opposite. They think if they don't abuse their body, they're not fulfilling their fantasy. I can't tell you the trouble we had to get our clients out of.

"One group we represented played their last tour on the West Coast. We were able to clean up the lead singer for the tour, but the last night we find him in the bathroom of the hotel room with a heroin needle in his arm and a hooker doing unspeakable things to him. I saw things like that all the time."

There was one irrefutable benefit to being a rock-star attorney, though. "Lawyers of rock groups weren't paying rock groups to be their clients," he said. "The whole thing in pro sports is ridiculous, very dirty."

By the time the Fleisher brothers began to go at it alone, the NBA Players' Association was trying to clean it up.

Months before Larry Fleisher officially announced in a letter dated August 23, 1988, that he was quitting, a committee of past union presidents was formed to consider replacement candidates. That committee included Junior Bridgeman, Paul Silas, and Bob Lanier. Fleisher believed that the director should be a lawyer, given the countless suits that would inevitably be filed when opposing bargaining positions became entrenched.

One of the candidates, ironically, was a former NBA attorney named Simon Gourdine. But less than one month later, the union president, Alex English, wrote in a letter to the league's players:

"In February, 1988, a committee was formed to seek a replacement for Larry. After much debate, and research on my part, it was decided that the chief operation officer of our Union need not be a lawyer.

"Therefore, as per the NBPA Constitution and by-laws, the officers and player representatives took the following steps to secure a replacement for Larry:

"1. Naming Charles Grantham as Executive Director of the NBPA.

"2. Request of the Executive Director to present 3 Legal Candidates for the position of General Counsel."

With this announcement, it was clear that a purge was under way. Committee members Bridgeman, Silas, and Lanier were all onetime Fleisher clients and loyalists. Grantham, a smartly dressed former director of admissions at the Wharton School of Business and longtime assistant to Fleisher, was the candidate pushed by Isiah Thomas, who was about to succeed English as president.

When Grantham was announced by English—as essentially the anti-lawyer/agent director—the committee dashed off a bitter statement that was read at a union meeting on September 26:

"Even though we were on the committee to search for these

people, the choice was made without our being able to actually have a search take place. We believe this was neither done democratically or in the best interests of the players in the league."

The statement was initialed "J.B., B.L., P.S." Bridgeman resigned as a union official. It was clear that this union was not a happy one. But now that the Fleisher faction was excised, player agents who always had a window to the Players' Association through Fleisher would be shut out. And with Thomas assuming the presidency, life for agents was going to get worse.

Beneath the surface of these union politics, a more significant conflict was smoldering, as the increasingly leveraged black men who drove the sport struggled for a greater say in how it ran. Until Grantham succeeded Fleisher, white attorneys ran the league and its union. White attorneys represented almost all the players.

Thomas, for one, perceived himself as an agent for change. He was that rare star whose ambition exceeded the next sneaker contract placed in front of his face. "I wasn't interested in endorsing products," he said. "My paradigm was different. I wanted to hire the people who would endorse my product."

Little Thomas ever did as an NBA superstar was publicly endearing. Instead of being viewed as a cuddly 6-1 guard, he was cast as a cunning, backroom operator. Most players, especially teammates, were in awe of Thomas' intellect, wary of his motives, and afraid of his wrath.

Thomas spoke out, sometimes clumsily, on racial stereotypes. He and his teammates were perceived as dirty players. He feuded with Michael Jordan. He went after Jordan's agent, David Falk, and his kind.

Thomas believed the agents were an inherent bane on the sport. He no longer employed one and regularly warned player representatives at union meetings to watch out for them. One of those player reps, Buck Williams, was paying close attention. Williams disassociated himself from David Falk.

Not long after Grantham and Thomas took control of the union, agent fees for contracts were capped at 4 percent. By 1990 they initiated a plan that would allow former players to draw retirement benefits early. Led by Falk, agents protested because the plan took 8 percent off the top of the revenue pot for current players. That meant less money for contemporary stars, and less for agents.

That year, Falk and some of his most leveraged clients—Jordan, Ewing, and James Worthy—stormed out of a union meeting during All-Star weekend in protest of the pre-pension plan. Battle positions that were to be taken up in the summer of 1995 were clearly drawn.

As Marc Fleisher and David Falk hastily spearheaded the rush toward union decertification, Simon Gourdine, who had returned to pro basketball on the labor side as general counsel in 1990, saw it as the agents' long-awaited revenge.

"I remember David Falk saying to me after the pre-pension thing, 'You beat us,' but with the implication, 'We'll see you again.' I'm not so sure this isn't the 'again.'"

Actually, decertification was no novel concept. In 1988, Gene Upshaw—with the help of New York attorneys James Quinn and Jeffrey Kessler—decertified the National Football League players' union to begin a successful six-year fight for a far better deal.

In a memo to NBA players dated July 12, Gourdine had tried to assert that Quinn and Kessler—whose firm, Weil Gotshal & Manges, had represented the NBA players for Larry Fleisher—had saddled the NFL players with a bad deal via decertification. That prompted Gene Upshaw, the NFLPA's executive director, to dash off an angry letter to Gourdine on July 25, which said:

"The ultimate result was a settlement which gave NFL Players both the most liberal free agency in professional sports and also the highest percentage of gross revenues (63) of any group of pro athletes. . . . The NBA players are in the same position we were then, and they deserve a true account of what happened in the NFL as opposed to the inaccurate one you gave them in your July 12 memo."

Even before the NFL union decertified, Len Elmore claimed that Larry Fleisher had threatened to do likewise in the 1988 collective bargaining talks. "He had four hundred names on a decertification petition to Stern, and suddenly Stern was saying he intended to strike a deal with the players," said Elmore. "Guess what? It worked."

Even the man whom Gourdine had replaced four months earlier, no great friend of the agents, believed they were right. As the dispute dragged on through the summer, Charles Grantham said that decertification had been a viable and carefully outlined option since the courts had, in recent years, more or less ruled that a sports union could not win an antitrust suit against a league unless it decertified for collective bargaining purposes.

Doc Rivers, one of the league's most respected veterans, supported Grantham's claim. "Charlie was saying all winter that we might have to go that route if it became obvious the NBA wasn't going to give us a good deal," Rivers said. "Anyway, if you can get around negotiating with David Stern, why wouldn't you? That's like going one-on-one with Jordan."

This contract was to have been Grantham's baptism under collective bargaining fire. His credibility as a tough negotiator was on the line. He was mindful of Larry Fleisher's shadow, and of his responsibility as the first black man leading the union.

Grantham would gladly have traded a rookie cap on length of contracts and other minor concessions for more total revenue. In the 1988 deal, even Marc Fleisher admitted that his father failed to anticipate the explosion in NBA licensing revenue. In 1995, the players were netting a ridiculous $500,000 a year from a gross revenue pot of more than $3 billion. Stern was ready to share more of it but was demanding what Grantham viewed as outrageous concessions in return. More than capping rookie contracts, he wanted to limit what they earned. He wanted to gut the Bird exception. He wanted, in effect, to turn a soft cap into a hard cap.

At a time when the NBA was perceived to be doing better than ever, Grantham was infuriated at the thought of anything that would be seen as less than the status quo. Domestic television revenues alone had escalated 28 percent, to $1.1 billion, since the previous collective bargaining agreement.

Grantham didn't trust the league when it came to accurate reporting of the defined revenue, of which players were guaranteed 53 percent. He had recruited former FBI agent turned Albuquerque accountant Charles Bennett to uncover numerous underreportings of income by NBA teams in 1991. The Detroit Pistons, for instance, reported none of the $11 million they earned each year in luxury-suite revenue. Teams routinely didn't report income from playoff tickets and various advertising. In February 1992, Bennett's sleuthing earned the players a settlement of $100 million.

"If you buy their argument that they're not making money, then you go in and make the deal," Grantham said. "I said, 'I'm not buying your bullshit here.' I want the information on skybox revenue and everything else."

Thus negotiations were dormant as the 1994–95 season dragged on. And then, on the afternoon of April 14, Grantham was suddenly gone.

No explanation beyond "philosophical differences" was given. Player reps around the league claimed they had no idea why a man with nearly two decades in the union would close a book in midchapter.

Soon there were unsubstantiated claims in newspaper columns that Grantham had been fired for padding his expense accounts. Grantham later denied this, saying, "The allegations were not substantial. I'm not going to tell you if you looked at my expense accounts, I didn't have a dinner here, a car there. I didn't steal money. I go to the U.S. Open and use the union car service— you're telling me I've got to pay for that bullshit? My whole job is about engaging people, getting information. I wasn't going to give those people up."

Months later, however, in the Players' Association's annual report (Form LM-2) filed by Gourdine on October 4, 1995, with the U.S. Department of Labor, the following paragraph was written on page 2 in the box requesting additional information for receipts and disbursements, referred to as Item #15:

"In early 1995, an internal review was conducted concerning expenses incurred by the Association staff. That review disclosed that the executive director had been reimbursed over the course of several years in the amount of approximately $165,000 for expenses that were not, the Association determined, incurred in the performance of Association duties. The Association obtained reimbursement."

According to the LM-2's disbursements-to-officers report, Grantham was paid off the remainder of his contract, which ran through the end of 1995. The $165,000 was deducted from his gross income of $578,654. (Gourdine's salary as combined executive director and general counsel was $275,000.)

"Charlie had a great gig," said Marc Fleisher. "His salary would have gone up to $900,000 had he stayed."

Fleisher, who'd known Grantham all his adult life, believed he would have fought the charges had they been untrue. On the other hand, Fleisher said that the timing of Grantham's exit clearly suggested a motive beyond crime and punishment. Why the sudden "internal review" when the union was facing a crucial collective bargaining challenge? Grantham's extravagant habits had hardly been a state secret.

"Simon was put in by Buck, and it was sort of confirmed by the executive committee after the fact," Marc Fleisher said. "We had a bunch of conferences with players who said, 'Who is Simon Gourdine?' Charlie got the job in a coup and he lost it in a coup. The union the last few years has been run like a banana republic."

Months later, this last charge would bring acrimony to Buck Williams' eyes and passion to his voice:

"How much communication do you think there was when Larry Fleisher ran this union? The agents say, 'Simon and Buck didn't keep us informed.' When Larry Fleisher made a deal with the NBA, that was it. There was no communication. Everyone just went along with what he did. Now we go and negotiate and we're under attack. Why is that?"

Williams hesitated to say but decided to answer his own question. It sounded like a subject Len Elmore might have lectured a young forward on years ago in the back of the New Jersey Nets' bus.

"You see it all the time: blacks don't believe that another black man can do for them what a white man can," Williams said. "I'm not a racist person, but here you have all these white, Jewish attorneys on both sides, and in the middle you have black players questioning the intelligence of their black union leaders."

Williams argued that his union, unlike baseball's and football's, did not have the resources or support to battle for years in court, or to help its members through a strike or lockout. In its LM-2 report, it listed $1,408,687 in assets and $2,256,418 in liabilities for 1995.

"I would've loved to have told David Stern to go shove his offer," Williams said. "But I know what this union has and I know its membership."

It was easy, he said, for the agents to support the more militant strategy. "They don't have their entire families dependent on them, the way many players did," Williams said. While admitting that decertification had always been an option, Williams said the agents would never admit that it was a risky, expensive one. If a decertified union couldn't get an injunction declaring Stern's lockout illegal, then where would it be?

"Players would go pouring back in," he said. "But the agents would never deal with that possibility."

Even Elmore disappointed Williams with a bylined *New York Times* article in which he discussed the notion of the players' secession from the NBA to form their own league. "Lenny admitted that players would have to accept less money from a new league," Williams said. "That means sacrificing for the future. And that's naive."

The union members Williams knew would not even suffer an increase in dues. At one point during the '94–'95 season, he said he made what he thought was a simple request. To help cover the costs of the potential contract impasse, he asked to increase dues $3,000. Players who earned the minimum salary paid $4,000. Everyone else paid $5,000. He was told to forget it.

"These guys are paying four percent of their money to their agents and they wouldn't kick in an extra three thousand dollars," Williams said. "You tell me what a union president is supposed to make of that."

With the decertification movement under way in July, with negotiations between the union and the league in limbo, Williams met with Jordan and Ewing in Los Angeles at the Beverly Hills Hotel. He admitted to them that the original deal wasn't very good. But it had been negotiated when the superstars were admittedly asleep on labor issues.

"I said to Michael and Patrick, 'Tell me what you want. We'll go back and see if we can get a deal we can live with. If we can't, then we'll all decertify. We'll get people back together.'"

He said Jordan and Ewing expressed no interest in a deal. Only in decertification, which meant the fall of the union leadership and the rise of the agents.

There were times, Williams said, when he felt like washing his hands of the whole union deal. He worked some nights until 2 A.M. Other nights he would lie awake and ask himself, "What do I need this for?" He certainly wasn't getting paid. But Williams didn't get thousands of offensive rebounds without being a proud, persistent man. Too proud, said one of his more amicable critics.

"Buck's a good man, but he dug himself in early in the summer," Elmore said.

Williams left his meeting with Jordan and Ewing even more determined to fight. Stern was by now frantically pressing buttons, trying to scare people out of the decertification camp. He made personal appeals to influential players such as David Robinson and Reggie Miller. Fringe players were contacted and told they could lose their jobs. On August 3, Stern announced with great solemnity that, with tip-off three months away, he was "resigned to the fact that there won't be a season."

Williams and Gourdine decided to pressure Stern by announcing their intention to step aside as the players' bargaining agent if no improved deal was reached by midnight, August 9. The union called a meeting for the evening of August 8 in midtown Manhattan. There was an eerie silence over the following few days.

On the afternoon of August 8, when David Falk called Marc Fleisher, he asked, "What do you hear?"

Fleisher said he'd heard that other, less-vocal agents had received calls from Williams or Gourdine wanting to know what might be enough for the dissidents' approval on a deal.

"They must know it's not going to be easy, if the response they got was what I think," Fleisher told Falk. They hung up, promising a late-night telephone rendezvous.

Outside the Sheraton Hotel on Seventh Avenue in the early evening of August 8, a satellite truck was already parked. Down on the ballroom level, a press room was equipped with telephone lines to allow reporters to file their stories. A beverage table was in the corner. A television set had been wheeled in, set to the Yankees game, in anticipation of a long night's wait.

This sort of press-ready operation was most unlike the Players' Association, which did not even employ a public relations person. The NBA, of course, had a virtual platoon of almost forty, led by Brian McIntyre, the league's bearded and affable communications vice president and general manager. McIntyre, with assistants Jan Hubbard and Teri Washington, just happened to be in attendance.

"Anyone up for pizza?" McIntyre asked the assorted reporters and technicians. Many hands went up, and soon an unofficial milestone was being established: the first known union meeting catered by management.

McIntyre said that Stern, deputy commissioner Russ Granik,

and the NBA legal staff were behind closed doors, with Gourdine, Williams, and several surprise guests. When they emerged, just before the union-imposed twelve-o'clock deadline, it was obvious that something more surreptitious was up.

While McIntyre and staff orchestrated the show as if it were the NBA draft, Gourdine, Williams, Granik, and Stern strolled in and sat themselves at a table equipped with microphones. Anonymous attorneys from both sides stepped to the side. Then, marching in in eerie silence, came twenty-five players, none of them named Jordan or Ewing.

Clyde Drexler. Joe Dumars. Mark Price. Danny Manning. Charles Smith. John Stockton. Doc Rivers. There was one common denominator here: these players, for the most part, were either union board members or highly respected, certified NBA good guys.

Now this was all beginning to make sense. The satellite truck. The pressroom setup. It turned out that Stern, like another famous point man named Magic, did have something up his sleeve. It was the ball he'd been stripped of weeks before.

Several of the players later admitted that there were no actual negotiations going on that night at the Sheraton Hotel. A modified NBA offer had already been made by Stern earlier that day. The union leadership was ready to make a final push to pin the dissidents to the mat.

The players formed a human chain, behind Stern and Gourdine. A list of their names under the heading "NBA News" was handed out. There was a New York, August 8, dateline, and the ensuing statement: "The following players were in attendance at the negotiating session last night that resulted in a new collective bargaining agreement between the National Basketball Association and the Players' Association."

While Stern stared pensively into the lights, Granik announced that the league had removed the luxury tax from the deal. The Larry Bird exception would continue. Those who were seeking decertification had what they wanted.

Actually, they didn't. There were still crucial owner achievements. The rookie wage scale. The tightening of the system that agents claimed would create, in effect, an inflexible cap. And they were still guaranteed "merely" no less than $25 million a year from merchandising, the fastest-growing source of league revenue. Falk and Jeffrey Kessler had been telling their players they could legally challenge the league's right to any merchandising monies. The agents denounced the deal as slightly improved but still a disaster for the players. They would press ahead for the National Labor Relations Board's decertification vote.

They didn't know it yet, but that vote was already a foregone conclusion, with Stern having convinced the majority that a vote for decertification meant a vote for killing the season. That became obvious on August 30, the first of two voting dates at NLRB offices nationwide. Outside Room 3614 at 26 Federal Plaza in downtown Manhattan, Knicks forward Anthony Mason received last-minute counsel from his New York–based agent, Donald Cronson. Nearby stood Marc Fleisher, who said he'd come to observe.

A rough-edged Queens kid who had bounced around the basketball bush leagues and even played in Turkey before finding his place in 1991 with Pat Riley's brutish Knicks, Mason was now an established player, the 1994–95 winner of the Sixth Man award. He was about to cash in as a free agent for $4 million a year. He couldn't risk a shutdown.

Mason listened patiently as Cronson animatedly made the case for decertification. Twenty minutes went by before he stepped into Room 3614. He emerged to say that while details of the contract troubled him, he had voted against his agent's advice.

"Basically, if you decertify, there'll be a lot of time consumed while this is going on," Mason said. He agreed that the players were giving too much, but not enough to make them push back hard enough to potentially provoke a salary loss.

In other words, Buck Williams was certainly right about the union having negotiated without any real clout behind it.

The final margin accepting the deal was bigger than the worst NBA blowout, 226–134. The count turned into a packed media event, with reporters conducting their own buck-a-head pool. Where baseball presented the gloomy personas of Bud Selig and Donald Fehr, the NBA concluded its summer-long lockout with a live labor lottery. A typical David Stern telemarketing production.

Stern had come just far enough to sway a membership whose majority had no stomach or attention span for a long-term fight. In the vernacular of the sport, he said, "We decided that we were going to step up and do what's necessary here. We had owners demanding the end of the Bird exception. I forced this down their throats."

This was nonsense, argued Kessler's partner, James Quinn, who considers himself one of Stern's admirers and friends.

"This contract will cost the players one billion dollars over the life of the deal," said Quinn. "There was essentially no need, because the NBA is so successful, for David to put the Players' Association, with its weakened leadership, in the position he put them in. The fact is, David could have avoided a lot of the fighting.

"He has no respect for Gourdine. He had him basically doing his bidding, fighting the rest of the membership. David may think in the short term he's made a few bucks. In the long run, he's created enormous unhappiness among the players."

The worst thing, said veteran forward John Salley, was the underlying racial tensions and the specter of failed black leadership. Gourdine's intelligence and intentions were publicly challenged time and again. Buck Williams's dedicated service was forgotten. Charles Grantham's reputation was smeared. Even black agents such as Elmore and Fred Slaughter resented how Fleisher and Falk were held up as the brains behind the rebellion.

As for the players, Salley said they had let the NBA and the agents divide them into warring factions the public perceived as the haves against the have-nots. They came off looking, he said, like "house Negroes and field Negroes."

Salley knew enough American history to understand this wasn't the first time something like this had occurred.

"Blacks in this country have always been divided and it never did us any good," he said. "The NBA is a very black league, so we must be careful of the message we send."

In effect, Salley's message was that no matter how successful it became, how big it got, 1970s racial perceptions would never go away for a predominantly black league selling to a white corporate crowd.

Sadly, he may have been right, judging by the media's general response to the summer of labor strife. After at least acknowledging baseball and hockey players had the right to fight for their best deal, many sports journalists more or less rolled their eyes and advised the basketball players to be happy with whatever they got. Stern was held up as the sport's shining knight. Jordan, as if he needed the money, was cast as a greedy infidel. One national sports commentator referred on television to Jordan's involvement as the "equivalent of a drive-by shooting."

That even brought out the less polished, 1960s liberal in Stern.

"Fuck the people who say that Michael was being greedy, that he should just shut up and play," Stern said. "That's a code."

With the labor war over, Stern was quickly reverting to his more preferred paternal self. He didn't have to talk trash anymore, like Derrick Coleman and Shawn Kemp. He didn't have to play public hardball or accuse Marc Fleisher of being obsessed with his family's regaining control of the union as revenge for his dead father.

In defeat, Fleisher wasn't blaming Stern, though. "He was just doing his job," he said. The real enemy, he said, was Simon Gourdine, the next target to go after. Fleisher and Co. would not be licking their wounds for long.

For Fleisher, though, another blaze was breaking out, right in his office in downtown Stamford.

By the winter, brother Eric, one and a half years younger, was breaking up their company, now called Entersport, and suing him to boot. In court papers, Eric Fleisher claimed Marc had neglected their business and diverted money in a callous attempt to seize control of the players' union. It seemed that Marc Fleisher's own brother was telling him, like Stern, that he'd stuck his nose where it didn't belong.

Marc claimed that Eric, after landing a hot young client like Kevin Garnett, was feeling more and more like a Money Player, an industry rival more than a sibling rival, who didn't want to share in the score he'd made. Eric argued, "Sometimes people want to go in different directions, with different styles."

Marc accused Eric of pilfering the records and files from the company they had started with their father. Eric said his brother was on a power trip. Family friends said their father was probably turning over in his grave. It was all enough to convince you that no relationship was worth more than the need to cash in. Who needed brotherly love when one could have Kevin Garnett?

The bottom line was this: If Marc and Eric Fleisher couldn't coexist, what chance did others have to look beyond the money in front of them, to see the big picture? To create for the players a clear, united front? There were no easy answers, even for a man named Buck.

5

Maryland Connection

FUTURE MARYLAND STAR JOE SMITH WAS SIX YEARS OLD, BARELY bouncing a basketball with one hand at the Hunton YMCA on Charlotte Street in Norfolk, when another All-America Terrapin, Charles Linwood Williams, was drafted third overall into a very different NBA by the New Jersey Nets in June of 1981. If Smith's destiny was to be an NBA star for the nineties, to reap all that was sown in the bridge-building eighties, then Williams, in many ways, was the Joe Smith of the previous generation: sturdy, strong, and sincere.

Williams was 6-8 and 225 pounds of sculpted muscle. He was movie-star handsome, with a genial, leisurely manner about him until he walked out onto the court and the ball was bouncing off the rim, up for grabs. That's when it became clear why Williams was known as Buck.

In his three seasons at the University of Maryland under garrulous Lefty Driesell, Williams was no great scorer, no NCAA poster boy. He was every coach's dream, though. A power rebounder, a tireless worker, a modest small-town kid from Rocky Mount, North Carolina.

Larry Brown, a restless but splendid tactician who that year stepped out of John Wooden's unfillable shoes at UCLA to become the Nets' head coach, used a second first-round pick to take Albert King, Williams' Maryland frontcourt mate. The younger brother of Bernard King, out of Brooklyn's Fort Hamilton High School, Albert was one of the first scholastic players to create a recruiting spectacle that seemed more like a nationwide manhunt.

Albert King was so famous by the age of seventeen that Buck Williams chose Maryland in large part for the opportunity to play with him. At Maryland, they became close friends. Williams was ecstatic when they wound up on the same NBA team, albeit one that had ignominiously pawned off Julius Erving, the Michael Jordan of his time, in 1976. The Nets had since been one of the worst eyesores in a league that had plenty.

The NBA to which Williams arrived was beginning its third year of the Magic Johnson/Larry Bird era. Both players had already won a championship with their respective teams, the Lakers and the Celtics. Despite these revolutionary talents, who came pre-packaged from their 1979 NCAA championship showdown between Johnson's champion Michigan State team and Bird's upstart Indiana State runners-up, the NBA was still very much on the launching pad. It was strapped by red ink, by Madison Avenue's notion that America would not buy a sport that was predominantly black.

By today's standards, the NBA of the early 1980s was giving off unimaginably endangered signals. There was financial chaos, the result of fractious ownership, an unfocused league office, and player salaries that had escalated from a superstar's salary of roughly $75,000 in the late 1960s to $500,000 and $600,000 by the late 1970s. Reckless expansion had diluted the talent, created too many unattractive matchups, increased travel costs. At the time, the league had a four-year, $74-million contract with CBS, which ignored most of the teams and televised, week after week, the same contenders in the few appealing markets.

While ratings had improved from the 1960s—when they were routinely labeled by Nielsen as IFR (insufficient for reporting)—they were falling from the early 1970s, when Kareem Abdul-Jabbar and Red Holzman's Knicks in New York gave the sport a promising boost. By the late 1970s, interest was seriously waning. The league was sliding out of prime time. One of its greatest individual performances, Johnson's lighting up Philadelphia for 42 points and 15 rebounds in the 1980 finals while subbing at center for injured legend Kareem Abdul-Jabbar, was televised in many big markets on delayed tape. The title-clinching sixth game was not deemed worthy by CBS of preempting its Friday-night rerun of *Dallas.*

At least six teams were in grave danger of folding, a potential loss of at least seventy-two player jobs. In the 1980–81 season, sixteen of the twenty-three teams lost money. Forty-two percent of all seats were empty. And in August 1982, the *L.A. Times* estimated that "40 to 75 percent" of the players in the league were using drugs.

Later that year, John Lucas, a Washington Bullets guard, admitted to The *Washington Post* that he was addicted to cocaine.

"There was little or no self-awareness of how we were perceived, that it could be destructive to the league," said Len Elmore, a onetime teammate of Lucas' at Maryland during the early 1970s, a less tumultuous time than when Williams entered the league, but primitive in relation to Joe Smith's era. "Even though people would look at the league and say, 'Oh, it's drug infested'—and it was—we knew where the drugs were coming from.

"It was the guys on Wall Street, the high rollers, the people who wanted to rub shoulders with the athletes. That was the irony. In an indirect way, or sometimes in a direct way, the people making decisions—'Oh, we can't get involved with the NBA'—were the ones facilitating it. Any guy who played in that era will tell you the parties, the women—all these things had their roots in people of means.

"By the same token, there was a balance. You had guys who had little or no control of their lives but another group who played the game, took care of themselves, interacted with the community. If we had the NBA of today, with its public relations machine, I dare say the perception would've been different. We didn't have that. We only had what was in print."

However astonishing the *Times'* 40-to-75 percent figure was, that paper was hardly alone with its gloomy forecast. The year before, the *Boston Globe* was preparing to publish a series on pro basketball's woes when the league's thirty-eight-year-old general counsel, David Stern, paid a sudden visit to the *Globe's* sports editor, Vince Doria.

"The predictions were dire," Doria said. "Stern was doing

everything to talk us out of it. He was arguing about how great the league would be."

Doria smiled. Newspapermen, unlike soon-to-be visionary commissioners, live in the moment. The *Globe* ran its series. And if Los Angeles and Boston had a negative perception of the NBA, what was the rest of Bird-less and Johnson-less America supposed to think?

Such negativism, a fear of apocalypse, brought the negotiating sides to the table in 1983. The drug agreement within the 1983 collective bargaining agreement, also known for the implementation of a salary cap, was born.

James Quinn, the longtime Players' Association attorney, admitted that the *Times* report and others had moved activist players such as Paul Silas and Bob Lanier to act, to rouse the union to work with the league. "There was a desire to get tough, to clean up the problem," said Quinn. "They did not want people to think there were a bunch of drug addicts in the league."

The league's celebrated drug policy was set. But order was far from being restored.

The New Jersey team that Buck Williams joined was a mixture of promising young players—Williams and King, plus second-year center Mike Gminski from Duke—and retread veterans. By lucky chance for Williams, Len Elmore was one of the vets. The Nets were his fourth team in four seasons. But the new coach knew him from the ABA. He viewed Elmore as the perfect pivot tutor for Gminski, as a role model for others.

Williams already knew Elmore from summer scrimmages at Cole Field House. "There was sort of a generation gap between Lenny and myself, so we didn't hang out," he said. But in the back of the team bus, normally a venue for players to insult each other or put their minds at ease between headphones, Elmore offered sermons on politics, religion, and race.

"I was twenty-one years old," Williams said. "I didn't have a lot to say back."

This, for the most part, was the way of the NBA world back then. Veterans spoke. Rookies listened. Elmore tried to be a role model for Williams, the way he would offer his counsel for Joe Smith almost fifteen years later, when a young player couldn't count on joining a team that had any wise old heads. Or when many young players, instant millionaires and far more obedient with their marketing representatives, had had enough philosophy during their short college careers. They believed their contracts and endorsement deals gave them all the status they were going to need.

"There were always some young players who came into the league with an attitude," Elmore said. "But generally, young guys would listen to you. They respected experience, accomplishment. The apparatus in place today didn't exist—all these people who want a piece telling them how great they are, convincing them they don't have to respect the process, instead of telling them how hard it's going to be. When a guy like Buck came in, you could see it in his eyes, how much he wanted to learn, to make sure he didn't lose what he had."

What Williams had from day one was the ability to go get the ball. In his rookie season he retrieved 1,005 rebounds, an average of 12.3 per game, third best in the league. Coaches, who pray for such selfless, durable players, voted him onto the Eastern Conference All-Star team. Against the best frontline players in the league, he grabbed another 10 rebounds in twenty-two minutes. Brown, whose biggest complaint with the pros was that the players weren't coachable enough, naturally fell in love with the prize rookie he called Bucko.

"Buck Williams came into the league as a ten-year veteran," he raved.

By today's standards, Williams earned peanuts, but no veteran in his right mind could say he wasn't worth every cent. And the $300,000 he made as a rookie happened to be a staggering amount for someone who, as a young boy, prayed his family could escape its tattered house and enjoy the luxury of indoor plumbing. Williams' family was poor, yet proud, mostly of a hard day's work. With no child-care option, his mother, Betty, carried her baby son Charles in the bag into which she dropped the cotton she picked for $4 per hundred pounds. Later, when her children were older, she worked as a maid.

Her husband, Moses, quit school in the third grade and once worked on a construction gang for ten cents a day. As his family grew to five children, three boys and two girls, Moses Williams seldom made it home from work as a cement finisher before his children were asleep.

"But I woke up every morning and saw him getting ready to go to work," Buck said. "There were no sick days or 'I don't feel like going in.' I might have taken it for granted at that time, but it's amazing how that shaped my personality, this work ethic I've had. It made me understand the value of a dollar."

The joke among the Nets was that Williams squeezed his cash tighter than he did a rebound. These were the days when pro basketball salaries were beginning to set the industry standard. The Lakers' owner, Jerry Buss, shocked the sports world by signing Magic Johnson to a twenty five-year deal worth $25 million.

Such sudden wealth to young men from impoverished backgrounds meant status. Even rookies felt pressured into making a statement by driving a Mercedes. Not Williams. He tooled around north Jersey in his 1979 Buick, with no regrets.

He remembers telling his teammates, "If I get a Mercedes now, what will I get later?"

This was how young Buck Williams viewed the world. Work hard. Get better. Be rewarded. It was a formula that prevailed for him, and his team. The 1981–82 Nets unexpectedly made the playoffs with a late-season rush. Playing alongside Williams energized Elmore, who more than doubled his minutes and rebounds from the previous season and averaged a career-high 9.1 points per game.

Everything seemed to be pointing in the right direction. The following season, Brown smartly sensed that his team needed more talent to advance beyond the first round of the playoffs. All-Stars weren't just out there for the taking, and desirable free agents didn't quite pound on New Jersey's door. Brown decided to take a chance by trading for Micheal Ray Richardson, the electric but troubled player, banished the previous year by the New York Knicks to Golden State.

The pieces were now in place for a tragedy to unfold, for the worst of the NBA to be played out spectacularly on the back pages of the New York tabloids. Richardson was inarticulate, unpredictable, irresponsible and self-destructive. Yet he was an All-Star caliber player, a 6-5 point guard who could dominate a game with raw power, speed, and a flowing energy tap. He had a strong upper body, long arms, thin but muscular legs, and steel grips for hands. Willis Reed, then coach of the Knicks, plucked him third in the 1978 draft, ahead of Larry Bird. Reed was convinced he'd found a sleeper in this hyperactive kid from Denver out at the University of Montana. He compared him to a legendary Knick, Walt Frazier.

This was well intentioned, but a public relations disaster, another example of how the NBA did not understand the social forces it was setting loose as a means of attracting a larger clientele. On the day Reed introduced Richardson, visions of the next Frazier, urbane and poised, flashed through the minds of the cynical New York media. The first question to Richardson was why he was nicknamed Sugar. Painful moments passed before Richardson blurted out, "B-because I'm s-sweet on the court." Richardson had a terrible stuttering problem, and more emotional baggage to carry around town.

Richardson's father had disappeared from his life when he was a toddler. In basketball, some would-be surrogate always promised to be there for him but didn't keep his word. When Jud Heathcote, who recruited Richardson to Montana, left for Michigan State after his freshman year, Richardson cried, begged to go with him, then raged that he never wanted to see him again. When Reed was fired by the Knicks fourteen games into Richardson's rookie season, he demanded that the Knicks jettison him, too, preferably to his hometown Denver Nuggets. Richardson befriended an older man named Sam Cohen who owned an electronics store near Madison Square Garden. He called Cohen "Daddy."

Now Larry Brown, who saw the potential greatness in Micheal Ray Richardson, said he wanted to be his father figure. Brown couldn't deliver either. Near the end of the 1982–83 season, Brown was offered the head coaching position at the University of Kansas, one of the country's more historic programs. When this became public knowledge, the Nets organization told Brown to make an immediate decision. The Nets were about to begin the playoffs as the favorite in a cross-river series against the Knicks. Brown could no more resist Kansas than could Dorothy. He left. His players, in particular Williams and Richardson, were crushed. They were swept by the Knicks.

Buck Williams, a pillar of strength, was getting the idea that the NBA was a house of cards. "Everything kept changing," he said. "You never knew what was coming next."

After Brown, there would certainly be no more coach worshiping. This was a business. Williams went back to Maryland to finish his degree in business administration. He was going to look out for himself.

He was more inclined to bond now with teammates, especially Richardson, whose boyish vulnerability was maddening yet charming. Many NBA people already suspected or knew that he was more than dabbling with cocaine. He suffered wild performance and mood swings. Butch Beard, an assistant coach when Richardson was a Knick, did the unthinkable, going public with Richardson's cocaine use. "I thought he was basically a good kid," Beard said. "I wanted to help."

Even those he would eventually let down, even betray, felt sympathy for Richardson. How could they not? Here was a young man with such a rickety psyche that, for years, he allowed people to misspell his first name. It wasn't M-i-c-h-a-e-l, he sheepishly revealed one day as a Net. It was M-i-c-h-E-A-l.

Williams embraced Richardson as sort of a long-lost and troubled brother, tried to be what Elmore had been for him. But there would be no harnessing the raging emotions and hormones. "I loved him," Williams said. "We spent a great deal of time together. I know he wanted to do the right thing, but he had a lot going against him. But I'll tell you what. Nobody I ever met in this league had a bigger heart than Micheal."

Williams may have realized this one day riding in a shuttle van between Cleveland's Hopkins Airport and a Marriott Hotel. In the van with him were Richardson and Otis Birdsong, a veteran shooting guard. Williams was engaged to be married, and the subject was whether to seek a prenuptial agreement. Birdsong had one with his wife and was encouraging Williams to do likewise. He told Williams he would be making millions of dollars over his career. He had to protect himself.

Williams nodded. It seemed like the prudent thing to do, especially for a financially conservative man such as himself. That is, until Richardson butted in.

"Buck," he blurted out. "Y-you can't do t-that. I-it'd break her h-heart."

It was pure Micheal Ray, innocent, illogical, and irresistible. Williams dropped the idea.

Richardson was Williams' teammate for parts of three tortured seasons under three different coaches. The Nets were a team on the brink of contention and proved it by upsetting the defending champion Philadelphia 76ers of Erving and Moses Malone in the 1984 playoffs. But the ultimate fate of every NBA team is irrevocably tied to the character of its leading man. Williams may have been the Nets' blue-collar soul, but Richardson, without question, was their pulse.

More and more, they assumed his unpredictable nature. They added players who were closer to Richardson in spirit than Williams. Darryl Dawkins, who had jumped to the pros from high school in 1976, the year Kevin Garnett was born; Mickey Johnson, a talented but volatile forward; Stan Albeck, who replaced Brown as coach, bolted his contract two years later to coach the young Michael Jordan in Chicago; Dawkins, famous for the wacky names he gave the dunks that brought down rims and backboards, slipped in a hot tub and hurt his back.

Through all of this, the team somehow continued to show promise. In December of 1985, the Nets won nine of ten games and took the third-best record in the league, trailing only Bird's Celtics and Johnson's Lakers going into Christmas. They began to entertain hopes of making the NBA Finals. As long as Richardson had command of the ball and control of himself.

"We tried to stay close to him," Williams said. "I would say, 'Micheal, you okay?' He told me he wasn't doing drugs. I believed him, which shows you how naive I was."

At the team's Christmas party that season at a restaurant in Moonachie, New Jersey, in the shadow of the Meadowlands, Richardson and Dawkins set off together for a hotel bar close by. Richardson left Dawkins at the bar, headed out into the cold suburban night. He was AWOL for three days and soon checked into drug rehab for cocaine abuse. It was his third rehab visit, second under the NBA's new policy. One more strike and he would be out.

Richardson missed a month and rejoined the Nets. But the ball of yarn was unraveling fast. At a game in Landover, Maryland, against the Washington Bullets, he looked distant and played erratically. The players, trying to deal with this hardship, buckled under the stress. The coach, Dave Wohl, got into a screaming match with Mickey Johnson. Gminski and Johnson argued in the locker room. Johnson punched a hole through a blackboard.

The Nets, their season evaporating, skulked home the next morning, only to be met at the airport by Horace Balmer, director of league security, and Charles Grantham of the players' union. The players stood around watching. They didn't have to guess what was up.

Richardson had failed his mandated urinalysis. He was automatically banned from the league.

"We always knew it was possible, but it was still devastating," Williams said. "First, because of how bad we felt for the guy. Second, because it cut the legs out from under us, physically and psychologically."

Micheal Ray Richardson left the NBA after a dizzying eight-year run and never returned. He ventured into the European leagues where he remained, at forty years of age during the 1995–96 season, a formidable player.

During his NBA career he managed to become the player who put a face on the league's drug subculture, who may even have been most responsible for the adoption of the 1983 policy. Dr. Arnold Washton, who treated Richardson for his addiction, said it was clear to the NBA that to "prevent all the insanity surrounding Micheal Ray's case," it was time to "bang out" something that would demonstrate to the public a more proactive attitude.

For Buck Williams, the Richardson debacle was a haunting, demoralizing, and career-shaping experience. While he couldn't hold personal grudges against a troubled man whose sad childhood contrasted with his comparatively stable environment, it forever cast him as an enemy of the unprofessional. Before he was mercifully traded to Portland in 1989, three years of bad basketball followed in New Jersey. So depressing were those post-Richardson years that the normally chatty Williams would brush past his wife, Kim, after another awful loss and hole up in the loft of their home, fiddling until the wee hours with remote-control model planes.

"I didn't think anything could be worse than what happened with Sugar," he said.

He was wrong about that. One year later, Len Bias died. A powerful link on the Maryland connection was lost forever.

Just before the 1984–85 season, the Boston Celtics traded Gerald Henderson, a starting guard, to Seattle for a first-round draft pick. Henderson had been a hero of the previous season's championship series. His steal of James Worthy's pass in the backcourt saved the Celtics from losing two games at home to the Lakers. They eventually won the series in seven.

Henderson, however, was a free agent the following summer. He held out into training camp, then signed a contract. Upon reporting to the team, he got a shocking call from the coach, K. C. Jones. He'd been traded to Seattle for the SuperSonics' first-round draft pick in 1986.

The Celtics had wanted to give to Henderson's starting spot to Danny Ainge for a long time. Red Auerbach used the contract dispute to make his move. When Seattle finished the 1985–86 season with a 31-51 record, Auerbach was hailed, once more, as the NBA's once and forever genius. One of the league's strongest teams had the second pick in the college draft.

At the recommendation of his good friend, former Celtic and Georgetown coach John Thompson, Auerbach had his eye on Maryland's Len Bias. With the first pick, Philadelphia would take North Carolina center Brad Daugherty. Auerbach had his man, a flashy power forward who could run and score and prolong the career of Larry Bird. The Celtics were buoyant. They flew Bias to Boston the next day for an introductory press conference. That night, they had Ainge show him around town.

Bias, about to join the NBA's most famous team, signed a $1.62 million contract to endorse Reebok products. He returned triumphantly to College Park to celebrate with friends. In the wee hours of June 19, he snorted cocaine with some of his teammates in his Washington Hall dormitory suite. At about 6:30 A.M., he suffered a cardiac arrest. By the time he was rushed to the hospital, he had no pulse, no heartbeat. He was gone that morning before the Maryland campus had stirred to life.

The timing of this tragedy gave it a sense of impossibility. For Bias, there would be no first and second NBA strikes.

"I had just seen him the past summer, played with him down at Coach Driesell's camp," said Buck Williams. "It was . . . unbelievable." It was much more than that. Here, finally, was the proof that there was far more to lose than games and money. The drug of choice did not bow to stardom.

At the time of Bias' death, Williams did not know him well enough to ask himself how this could be; nor did Maryland's other famous frontcourt alumnus, Len Elmore. But while Elmore was naturally stunned, he could not feel actual astonishment that a famous athlete had lost everything in return for an artificial high.

Elmore was gone from the NBA by then, into his second year at Harvard Law. On the morning of June 19, he was driving into the parking lot, on his way to his summer job working for the Massachusetts public defender. The news bulletin came over the radio. Elmore sat in his car for several minutes, unable to move. He thought about this incredible waste of talent, of life, and about a grief-stricken family trying to make some sense of it all. His mind drifted from Bias, whom he hardly knew, to other young men who had suffered similar fates. To those whom he knew all too well.

He thought of his brothers, then began to weep.

As a young boy in Brownsville, Brooklyn, in the city's outer envelope, Len Elmore knew the joys of New York street life. Punch ball and stickball games in the schoolyard, a life of Spaldeens and twelve-ounce Cokes purchased from the corner candy store. A neighborhood that ultimately became one of the city's most notorious. Elmore remembers Brownsville as a carefree playland, shared with his younger brothers Cliff and Rob, who were two and a half years and one year and seven months younger than him.

His family, which lived in a city housing project, was decidedly working class. His father, like Buck Williams', was named Moses. He worked for the New York City sanitation department. His mother, Gladys, worked various jobs, as a clerk for the city, as a maid. For several years, she worked night shifts, her four children awakening to the smell of a fresh Entenmann's cake she would cart home as their favorite treat.

"Probably the thing that ate at my mother more than anything was that, as a high school senior, she had a choice—go to Southern University on a scholarship or come to New York, work, and send money home to her family," said Elmore. "She used to lament how the person who ultimately took that scholarship eventually wound up at Columbia University. She could've been a professional. She always talked about that."

Her oldest of four children paid close attention. Already, Len had been included in the public schools' "S.P." program for children evaluated as advanced. "I guess I was considered to be somewhat bright," he said.

Within his family, that wasn't uncommon. "If Cliff had applied himself, he probably was brighter than I was," Elmore said. "He had an awful lot of electronic, scientific acumen. Dissecting frogs, making transistor radios, math problems. Cliff could figure out anything."

When Len was twelve, his grandparents combined savings with his parents for a down payment on a house in a working-class residential neighborhood in Queens. The American dream. Move up. Help your children do better. His father, who never graduated from high school, built a small study, its walls packed with bookshelves. There was only enough room for a table, four chairs—one for each child.

By the time he was fourteen, Len was already 6-5. He wasn't much of a basketball player, though. A junior high school teacher helped steer him to Power Memorial High School, the school made famous in the 1960s by Kareem Abdul-Jabbar. Elmore's picture appeared next to a *New York Times* story that suggested he might be the next Abdul-Jabbar.

"The day after I played my first game, nobody ever made that comparison again," he said.

He improved, though, and was soon on track to becoming a prized recruit of Lefty Driesell, who was building Maryland into the so-called UCLA of the East. To get to school in Manhattan on time, Elmore had to awaken at 6 A.M., take a bus, then the subway. He joined the student council, eventually becoming president, which required early-morning meetings twice a week. During the basketball season, he didn't return home until 7:30 P.M. When the season was over, he stayed late and cleaned the school to help defray tuition costs.

"What happened, I think, was that my brothers and I started to grow apart," he said. Even more than his brothers, he became detached from his neighborhood, from a place where many teenagers were beginning to drift toward more perilous paths.

In the late 1960s, with the drug culture expanding, family stability in New York City was not necessarily the exemption from trouble that it may have been for Buck Williams several years later in Rocky Mount, North Carolina.

Cliff, Len said, had already begun using drugs in high school. At 6-5, he was the shortest of the three brothers. He played linebacker on the high school football team, then briefly at Wichita State. But according to a longtime family friend, Steve Shalin, "Cliff didn't care about sports. Of the three, Lenny was the star athlete and opinionated scholar; Robert was the quiet, sensitive one, a big teddy bear; and Cliff, he was the handsome flower child, the one who lit up the room."

Steve Shalin played and coached basketball in various leagues with the Elmores in New York, then helped steer Rob and Cliff to Wichita State, where he had been a graduate assistant coach. Cliff briefly played football, then immersed himself in campus life. Rob, a center, helped the school's basketball team make the NCAA tournament as a senior. He was drafted by the New Jersey Nets. In the fall of 1977, right after Erving had been dealt to Philadelphia, he tried out for the demoralized Nets, but was cut on October 10. He was immediately signed by Rome's Lazio-Eldorado of the Italian league, considered the best pro ball in Europe.

A little more than one month later, Rob Elmore, at twenty-three, was dead.

On November 26, he was found in his hotel room, a syringe and packet of heroin beside him, needle marks in his arm. Friends such as Steve Shalin back in the States said they had no knowledge of prior hard drug use. "There were no signs then," he said, "though now, in hindsight, I guess there are. The thing is, as independent as Lenny always was, Robert was very vulnerable to peer pressure. He was as good as the people around him."

Even for those few short weeks, Len could imagine what life was like for his shy, uncharismatic brother in a strange, freewheeling city where he couldn't speak the language. "From what I got, he took up with expatriate Americans," Len said. "Artists, musicians, people who were into heroin. And he was unlucky."

Playing at that time for the Indiana Pacers, Len was devastated. Having shockingly and suddenly lost one brother, he reached out to Cliff, who was at the time dealing with his own hard-drug habit. Len asked him to come to Indianapolis. They became roommates. Cliff eventually got a job, his own apartment. He married a local woman. They had two children. He was clean, happy. Then came tragedy, too much for Cliff Elmore to bear.

Shortly after his second child's birth, his wife hemorrhaged and bled to death. Left with two children and his grief, he turned to drugs again. Late in Len's playing career, still struggling in Indianapolis, Cliff Elmore became gravely ill. Doctors offered various diagnoses but it soon became apparent to Len that his brother had contracted the new plague called AIDS. Cliff Elmore ultimately returned home to New York, where he died in April 1985.

Len did not see his brother in the final weeks of his life. "I just couldn't bear to see him like that," he said, admitting that he was trying too hard to cover his grief, to numb his pain.

About a year after being left brotherless, Len sat in the parking lot and heard the news of Len Bias' senseless death. And it was all starting to catch up with him now, young men he loved or simply knew who were dying too young.

A Maryland college teammate, Owen Brown, died of cardiac arrest in February 1976. Another teammate, Chris Patton, died of Marfan's syndrome two months later. Then Rob. Then Cliff. He watched his parents suffer these losses, the emotional wounds taking a physical toll on his mother, who died—prematurely, and partially from grief, in his mind—in 1993. He saw his brother's two young children become orphaned.

No matter how composed Elmore came across as a player, a broadcaster, a Harvard-educated lawyer, Steve Shalin said the devastation of losing two brothers was never buried too deep. Once, Shalin held a reunion luncheon for the guys from the old neighborhood and asked Elmore to come. It was at a restaurant in Flushing. Elmore at one point looked up at Shalin through glassy eyes. "Steve, I've got to go see my brothers," he said. They were buried across the street.

For years, Elmore said he blamed himself. Maybe he'd been too self-absorbed and hadn't done enough. Why had he survived, even thrived? What right did he have? And sometimes he felt as if he were sinking, too, and maybe ought to be. He drowned himself in self-pity, in too many bars. He stayed out late. He put stress on his marriage, on his work, on himself. If his brothers couldn't be like him, maybe he would have to be like them.

"I didn't learn how to grieve and let it manifest in behavior I'm not proud of," he said.

The irony was that people, if only from a distance, still looked at him with admiration, even awe. He had credentials. And so, in the aftermath of the Bias tragedy, he was asked to participate in a special task force assembled by the University of Maryland Chancellor John B. Slaughter. The results, revealing a marginal relationship between Maryland academics and athletics, ultimately forced Driesell out.

"I think he would have admitted that he'd stopped recruiting a certain type of young man and was looking to win a national championship," Elmore said. He couldn't bring himself to say that Driesell and those like him were bad for the game. Elmore believed Driesell to be a good man, even something of a scapegoat in the Bias case. There had to be some personal accountability in all this. Nonetheless, involvement in the undoing of the man who had given him his college scholarship was just another disillusioning jolt.

In 1990, Len's wife, Gail Segal, became pregnant with the first of their two sons. Elmore was at his crossroads. He was tired of running around. He wanted to go home, in more ways than one. He sought professional help for his drinking. He embraced the memories of his brothers' lives and deaths, instead of running away. He finally buried them in peace.

The years from the mid-1980s until the end of the decade had not been happy ones. For all of Elmore's academic achievement at Harvard, for all his work at the Brooklyn district attorney's office, for all the respect he was earning as someone who had transcended jockdom, he knew in his heart that, in many ways, he was like any other washed-up athlete. He missed the spotlight. He missed the game.

And it crossed his mind that if it was difficult for him, how must it be for those who had nothing to make the transition to? He looked around the NBA, growing exponentially, but still churning out players who were flushing away money, their health, and their careers.

For all of the league's new spit-shined image and slick drug-policy PR, these were still young, suddenly affluent men under incalculable pressures in a world of constant temptation.

Len Bias' class of 1986 alone was a study in neglect and waste, a sign that it wasn't as simple as three strikes and you're out. Potential stars such as Chris Washburn, Roy Tarpley, and William Bedford became classic drug flameouts. At least two first-rounders from that class, Buck Johnson and Billy Thompson, succumbed to cocaine use. Another talented big man, John Williams, let his weight balloon to corpulent heights. He was ridiculed far more than he was helped.

Elmore, now going after drug dealers and dirty cops in the Brooklyn district attorney's office, never took his eye off the NBA. He stayed close to the action by broadcasting college games for CBS. But every year that went by, he missed the league and the life more and more.

"I'd given a greater part of my life to sports and received most of what I had from it," he said. "And while I'd had designs on any number of things, including politics, from a business standpoint, I was looking for some purpose, something to make sense of everything that had happened."

He founded his agency, Precept Sports, in 1992, setting up shop in the University of Maryland's backyard. Of course he wanted to make the best living he could. He was a family man now. Why shouldn't he be a capitalist? But if it was just about money, his degree, his intellect, and his name would certainly have opened any number of doors in the business world.

He wanted something more than that. He wanted to help shape the young lives in which he saw potential, in which he saw hope. In the likes of Joe Smith, Elmore saw a chance to ease his own pain.

His parents by this time had taken in his brother Cliff's two orphaned children. The Elmores were not young anymore. But they could mold young lives again, hope for a better parental shake this time around.

"Maybe I wanted a second chance to be a kind of big brother, too," Len Elmore said. "Maybe I did."

He got that chance, only to end up in pain again.

6

Education of a Rookie

THE FIRST PLAYER CHOSEN IN THE 1994 DRAFT, GLENN ROBINSON, was guaranteed $68 million over ten years by the Milwaukee Bucks before he played his first professional game. Joe Smith, taken in the same position as Robinson one year later, was "offered" $8.5 million over three years by the Golden State Warriors. Take it or leave it.

Smith became the biggest loser in the new collective bargaining agreement, which had eliminated his right to bargain.

"We thought that since they didn't have the rookie cap in by the draft or the summer, they would hold it off until the next year," Smith said. "That's why most of us came out as underclassmen in the first place."

At nineteen, Smith had come out one year too late. David Stern had reached into the pockets of the rookies and pulled out whatever leverage they once had. It was, at least in part, his way of keeping his vow to "take back" his game, starting with those who many believed were demanding too much of it in the first place.

Antonio McDyess was also feeling Stern's sting. A soft-spoken and muscular power forward from Quitman, Mississippi, McDyess was shipped off to Denver minutes after being picked by the Los Angeles Clippers on draft night. It was a rude welcoming into the professional ranks, but as the second pick in the draft, he at least figured to command long-term financial security.

By summer's end, he realized he would need to grab a couple of thousand rebounds before that could happen. The rookie scale allocated not a penny more than $7.634 million over three years for the No. 2 pick. "Before, you had a long-term deal, so it took the pressure off you," said McDyess. "Now, you may never get one."

Now, it was still possible for a team to make a big mistake on draft night, but not have to pay for it beyond a comparatively modest scale. The Warriors would not get stuck with the likes of a Donyell Marshall anymore.

Marshall, taken fourth in 1994 by Minnesota, signed for nine years and $42.6 million. During his rookie season, the Timberwolves traded him to a Golden State team reeling over its loss of Chris Webber. After two years, Marshall was perceived as no better than an average player and as bad as a total bust. He was still set for life, with absolutely no financial pressure to succeed or improve, unlike his far more talented teammate Joe Smith.

Under the new system, if a player such as Smith didn't come close to fulfilling his promise by the end of his third season, he would become another in the army of those seeking summer-league auditions. If he became a star, his contract could be reworked by the end of his second year for as much as his team was willing to pay him.

The achievers would undoubtedly still make out, but the potential saving just for the first three years was enormous. By David Falk's arithmetic, the entire 1995 first round's total pay for all three seasons was less than the combined guaranteed deals of the previous year's top three picks—Robinson, Jason Kidd, and Grant Hill.

It should never have come to that, Falk said. He, like Charles Grantham, was not staunchly opposed to limiting the number of years a rookie could sign for, allowing that forcing teams to pay $50 million over seven years to a player who might flop was punitive to the teams and to more deserving players. "But all you would have needed for a meritocracy was a three-year cap," he said.

The National Football League's rookie cap, by comparison, was much more liberal, allowing for incentive bonus possibilities. The NBA scale called for only a 20 percent increase on the figures, though they were set so low that, as Falk surmised, "the 20 percent had to be automatic, especially at the top end." Thus Smith's scale—$7.1 million ($2.06, $2.37 and $2.68)—became $8.53. In the first year of a much longer deal, Robinson earned $3.9. This was money that Smith would never earn back.

Not every top rookie, of course, fit the popular stereotype of being overindulged and overpaid. When Shaquille O'Neal was selected first by Orlando in 1992, he transformed the Magic from a 21-win team into a 41-win team. But, far more significantly, he gave the Magic a powerful drawing card.

As an expansion team of the late 1980s in sports-starved central Florida, the Magic had sold out every home game but were a hopeless dud on the road. "Just when we were struggling for something, Shaq provided us immediate credibility in almost everything," said John Gabriel, the team's vice president of basketball operations.

From nine road sellouts in 1991–92, the Magic packed thirty-seven of forty-one visiting arenas during O'Neal's rookie season. Though road teams didn't share in gate receipts, this was still the most accurate way to gauge a star's commercial appeal. And there were, naturally, many ways for the Magic to cash in. Home ticket prices were raised. Sales of merchandise soared. On the verge of Pepsi's signing O'Neal to a lucrative endorsement contract, a deal to stock the Orlando Arena with the soft drink followed.

"Do we do that deal without Shaq?" Gabriel said. He didn't have to answer that question.

Before his forced resignation by the Players' Association, Grantham tried to reason with the outspoken critics of rookie salaries, Charles Barkley among the loudest. Grantham appealed to the previous season's beneficiaries, Hill and Kidd, to stand up for future classes. But it was too late. The antics of the Larry Johnsons and Derrick Colemans had taken their toll. And there was little sympathy for rookies around the league, especially when Stern was attacking the veterans' free agent rights at the same time.

"There is no company in corporate America where someone walks in and makes more than the CEO," Buck Williams said. "With this rookie slotting, maybe these kids will come into the league and develop a respect for what the veterans have already done, for the years that people like Magic and Michael and Kareem put in. That's a real meritocracy."

There was, Williams insisted, one other substantial benefit.

"Now these agents who negotiate these $68 million contracts right off the bat and then won't return phone calls and are just concerned about the next $68 million contract are going to have to be accountable," he said. "They'll have to work for these guys, otherwise the player will just go find someone else."

Which, in effect, put the agents in the same position as the rookies. They had to prove themselves before they could make the big score.

So the gravy train left the station in 1994, with Robinson, Kidd, and Hill all aboard. The pendulum of power had now swung the other way, much the way the old-timers remembered it when they were young and eager, when they had as much negotiating leverage as did Joe Smith.

Five pro basketball apprentices lounged on sofas on the ballroom level of Orlando's Marriott World Center one early September afternoon in 1995, their long legs outstretched, alternately talking tough and then innocently probing one another for inside information they might use down the road. Maryland's Joe Smith was there. Duke's Cherokee Parks. Alabama's Antonio McDyess. Kansas' Greg Ostertag. And Farragut Academy's Kevin Garnett.

They rambled from subject to subject, from Dennis Rodman's alleged relationship with Madonna to his rebounding training techniques to the seven-foot Ostertag's shooting a cameo role in the Whoopi Goldberg film *Eddie* ("I'm the dumb, white rookie," he said) to all of them facing the long, winding, and sometimes hopelessly depressing NBA season.

"I asked Laettner, 'Chris, what's it like after forty games and you're, like, six and thirty-four?'" Parks said, referring to his former Duke teammate who had spent three disastrous seasons with the Minnesota Timberwolves after winning two NCAA championships.

Parks pointed to Garnett, whose slender, 6-11 frame was slouched under a baseball cap pulled down so low that you couldn't see his eyes.

"That's where Garnett's going," Parks said, he and the others giggling away.

The high school refugee had a quick and effective rejoinder for the preppyish Duke grad.

"I seen Dallas right there in the lottery with Minnesota," he said.

Parks dropped the subject and the needling, realizing Garnett was not going to just sit there and take it.

While they chattered on, the doors to an elevator just down the hall opened, and out stepped a distinguished figure who might have offered them all a few pearls of wisdom on what was to come. But that would have required knowing who Earl Monroe was.

"I heard the name, I think," said Ostertag, a draft pick of the Utah Jazz.

The others acted as if they hadn't.

By then, Monroe, who has had both hips replaced, had walked stiffly past the rookies, without one of them so much as turning his head.

Within a few hours, on the first night of the NBA's weeklong Rookie Transition Program, Monroe formally introduced himself. He took the microphone from the league's vice president of player programs (and the Rookie Transition Program's administrator), Tom "Satch" Sanders, and shared with fifty-six wanna-bes one personal tale that effectively kicked off a crash course, Perspective 101.

After hearing Monroe's story, they would have a hard time complaining about their contract slotting, which set their salary for three years, at least not until they got home and listened to their friends and relatives all over again.

As the second overall pick by the Baltimore Bullets of the 1967 draft, Monroe told of being taken by limousine from his home in Philadelphia to New York, where he was given a two-year contract and an ultimatum: Sign this first-and-last offer, or not play. Monroe, with no agent present, signed, for $20,000 a year. "I found out later that I was the lowest paid of the top rookies in the league," he said.

Heads shook all around, though it was debatable whether the disbelief was over the Baltimore Bullets' duplicity or the $20,000 salary, which sounded like chump change to the class of '95.

In any event, the rookies soon understood that Monroe had gone on to a fabulous career, creating spin moves that had never been seen, teaming with Walt Frazier in the backcourt as the New York Knicks won the championship in 1973. But Monroe didn't want their sympathy, and they certainly weren't getting his, or anyone else's, at what was billed as the Legends Talk.

Monroe was there to tell them that there was more to this game than stuffing their pockets. They certainly had a responsibility to their families, to themselves. But, speaking directly to the black players for a moment, he reminded them that there had been a league before Magic, before Jordan. And it wasn't exactly the windfall of opportunity they saw it as today.

"When I first got into the NBA, I heard about the quota system," Monroe said. "That there could only be five or six blacks on a team. That changed because guys worked hard, because they took pride in what they had, because they were involved in the civil rights movement of the times."

If Monroe's time seemed ancient to these rookies, Bailey Howell was downright prehistoric. Having played in the NBA from 1959 through 1971, Howell was old enough to speak of five-hour rides on DC-3s from Minnesota to Detroit. He didn't know what the current pay system was and didn't care.

"You've got to be really dumb, even if you play a few short years, if you don't leave the league with a lot of money," he said, leaving no room for tact. Which, in effect, would be the week's most profound message.

The Rookie Transition Program—attendance: mandatory—was created by the league in conjunction with the Players' Association in 1986. It was certainly no vacation week for the players, who roamed the hotel corridors with informational packets and notebooks under their arms, like the rest of the corporate warriors from Philip Morris, Bayer USA Inc., Ford Motor Company, and the Japan Travel Bureau. There were no excursions to Disney World, little time to lounge by the pool.

The rookies filled out forms called the NBA Rookie Player Game Card. It asked questions such as "How do you see your NBA career five years from now? After five years in the NBA, what do you want people to say about you?"

Players used to expressing themselves as flamboyant individuals were split into groups identified by different-color T-shirts. One day found them attending seminars and workshops on public relations (*USA Today* basketball beat writer David DuPree as guest moderator), finance, personal care, HIV/AIDS, gambling (guest speaker: a made New York City mob guy), and drugs (lecture by a Drug Enforcement Administration official).

"We work hard on this," said Horace Balmer, the league's vice president of security. "Everyone knows it's the best rookie educational program in team sports."

Once a New York City detective, the gray-haired Balmer was raised, ironically, like Joe Smith, in Norfolk, Virginia. He was a ubiquitous presence at league events, often cheering for NBA players during international games from whatever press-row seat he could squeeze into. He and his director, another ex–New York detective named Larry Richardson, were international players now, working with Interpol during the Olympics, and with the German, French, and Italian authorities for various McDonald's Opens.

Balmer said the league had spent about $250,000 on a sports gambling video that took eighteen months to produce, with access to FBI files. The video, he said, was targeted to inform players, not scare them, a departure from the league's past tactics. "When I first started with the NBA, we used to bring in law enforcement agencies and more or less talk about what would happen if you get caught," he said. "I think the trend of education has to change."

He was most pleased this particular week that he could arrange, from his New York detective days, for an appearance by a made Mafia guy. The players, apparently having seen their share of Martin Scorsese films, were looking forward to this session more than any other.

Fine, thought Balmer. The more they focused on gambling, the bigger success the week would be.

It turned out that the Mafia man—appearing anonymously, of course—was short and unimposing. "He walked in the room and we all said, 'This guy?'" said Smith. "But that was the whole point. He told us how people will try to trick you into dealing with them, like, 'How could a little guy like me hurt a big guy like yourself?' He told us how easy they'll make it sound. 'Oh, you don't have to lose the game, just miss a shot here and there.'"

But it was not just the gamblers and the drug dealers that the players would have to be careful of, the players were warned. One evening, Smith and Atlanta rookie guard Travis Best were asked to participate in a skit with an acting troupe from New York University called the Creative Arts Team.

An actress played a woman—NBA players called aggressive women Body Snatchers—who had gone out to the West Coast with Best as he reported to his new team. The couple was supposed to marry, but over dinner at a restaurant, Best made an attempt to break the engagement. When he ran into trouble, he summoned the waiter, Smith, for some advice.

The two of them were no match for the actress.

By the end of the session, Smith was cracking up and Best was practically saying "I do."

"People are going to ask you for things," Alex English, the former Denver Nuggets star who was now the $125,000-a-year director of player services for the Players' Association, told the rookies. "If you say no, your homeboys will say, 'Oh, man, you changed.' Well, you have changed. You've moved to another level."

The highest level of the sport was represented that night by Julius Erving, the high-wire sensation who preceded Magic, Bird, and Jordan as basketball's predominant star. The rookies were bewildered when he joked about wearing his hair during the 1970s like Jimi Hendrix. The rock guitarist was dead by the time most of them were born. But they sure knew Dr. J. He was a legend. He was NBA royalty. It helped that he was also on television every week during the season, trying to get a word in as the polished Bob Costas and the acerbic Peter Vecsey chirped away during NBC's pregame and halftime shows.

Erving, a serious man and an eloquent speaker, was unsuited for mere sound bites. He looked around the room that night and seemed to make eye contact with everyone. Kevin Garnett straightened up in his seat. Rasheed Wallace, who had nodded off as the others spoke, looked up and folded his hands in his lap. Even league officials, who had been whispering to one another in the back, snapped to attention.

"I remember after making moves and scoring forty, fifty points, people would say, 'Are you going to the party?'" Erving said. "They'd say, 'You should be the life of the party because you were the life of the game.' I thought about that. I decided I wasn't Dr. J at the party. I was Julius Erving.

"Who are you going to be associated with socially and professionally? What kind of domestic situation are you going to create for yourself? You are going to have to make some choices, even involving the people you love, because there is charity and there is dependency. You're going to have to learn to say no, no, no."

The following night, Marvin Davis found himself in that very position. He wasn't a rookie, or even a player. He was an actor named Zack Minor from the Creative Arts Team, portraying a young NBA point guard whose brother was begging him for cash.

"They'll kill me," the brother pleaded, on his knees, referring to drug dealers. "Do you want them to kill me? You know what that would do to Momma."

The actors froze. A moderator appeared. He asked the rookies to tell him what they thought of the brother in need.

There were no takers until Kevin Garnett, sitting a couple of rows from the front, finally spoke out.

"He's a junkie," Garnett said softly.

"But he's Marvin's brother," the moderator responded. "Marvin loves him. And you heard his brother—what about his mother?"

"He's still a junkie," Garnett said, louder this time.

The moderator nodded approvingly at Garnett. The kid without a college credit had aced his first Rookie Transition exam. But then, he had already learned from firsthand experience about the game of basketball, how the whole exploitative system really worked.

How tall and gangly Kevin Garnett from Mauldin, South Carolina, went from small-town prodigy to the NBA lottery in less than one year is something of a tangled, land-of-opportunity tale that began in a quiet bedroom community near Greenville and continued amid the urban blight of Chicago's West Side.

However backward that was, Garnett's story began to look like an unsavory and prototypical study of basketball flesh-peddling, a textbook case of the system cranking into gear the moment a diamond is discovered in the rough.

This was no new process, just one that was more out of control than ever. With more players leaving school earlier and earlier, it stood to reason that those who wanted a piece of the dream identify and inveigle potential stars that much sooner. Often by the time they were just in the sixth and seventh grades.

After years of buckling under the weight of corruption and greed, the system seemed close to collapsing into chaos, with the NCAA's Enforcement Division essentially unable to police the lucrative and ever-expanding shoe company–financed summer league circuit, where so many of the shady relationships have formed between brokers and athletes. Where the hordes descended on players in an effort to "control the product."

These so-called uncles or street agents are often camouflaged as summer league coaches, family friends, and in a more recent and frightening twist, cash-rich drug dealers who court young prospects with sneakers, tickets, and rides around town. Detroit and Chicago are two prime examples, coaches claim, of cities where the drug-dealer phenomenon is growing. And it was in the latter, at Farragut Academy, where the battle for Kevin Garnett raged.

Flash back to December 1994. The location: a Chicago television production house. The scene: an interview with a proud, pretty woman decked out in a snazzy black pants suit and matching gaucho hat.

Her name was Shirley Irby, the mother of Kevin Garnett, the most talked-about high school basketball player in the country. She was new in town, claiming she had picked up and left South Carolina after a hallway brawl that resulted in the hairline ankle fracture of a Mauldin High School student and the arrest of five classmates, including her son. She said she would never forget the sight of "K," as she called him, being led away in handcuffs. And even though the charges were eventually dropped in return for her son attending a pretrial diversion program for first-time offenders, Irby's anger over what she considered a lack of support from the Mauldin High administration and coaching staff did not subside.

"A coach is supposed to take his player and shelter him, nuture him, like a mother hen brings her chicks in," she said. "No, you didn't have that at Mauldin High, no way."

She insisted the move was not what the persistent rumors suggested it was, a Nike-financed production to move her son along the assembly line, place him right where the shoe company and the minions working the dark corners of the streets wanted him to be.

"I tell you what, you can do all the snooping you want," Irby told a reporter from ESPN's *Outside The Lines*. "I worked very hard when I was in South Carolina and I didn't spend my money. I guess what intrigues everyone is that it's not often you find a young black woman who can just uproot somewhere, but I'm just fortunate that I'm in a position to do that. That's why I'm here, trying to save my son."

The irony, however, was that Irby was soon desperately trying to save her rightful place in her son's life. She was destined to fail.

When her boy was just a baby, Irby drove a forklift on the night shift, eleven to seven, at a South Carolina manufacturing plant. She never married his father, giving Kevin her maiden name. When he was five, she married Ernest Irby, who was no great surrogate dad. "My mom worked real hard and she was always tired and cranky," Kevin has said. "My stepfather treated me like dirt. I've never had a father."

In time, Shirley went into cosmetology, opening a beauty salon. Much of her spare time went to studying with Jehovah's Witnesses; by religious dictum, Kevin was forbidden to decorate the house for holidays, give gifts, or celebrate birthdays. Ernest Irby wouldn't let him put up a basketball hoop. Kevin eventually took to sneaking out of the house before dawn, shooting hoops with his best friend, Bug Peters. Bug and ball. Hoops and hope. That's what kept Garnett going, despite his mother's indifference or, at times, abhorrence to his spending so much time bouncing a ball.

She wanted him to get an education. Even after the arrest, by which time she understood just how good a player he was and that there was no turning back from the basketball court, she considered sending him to a prep school in Maine. Another possibility was Oak Hill Academy, the Nike-funded basketball factory. But Irby was turned off by Oak Hill's travel schedule and its reputation for avoidance of serious academic issues.

That summer, the first week of July 1994, Garnett attended an elite Nike camp in Deerfield, Illinois, at the Chicago Bulls' practice facility. Here, he was reunited with an explosive guard named Ronnie Fields, the reigning star at Farragut. (The two had hit it off the previous fall at Nike's "Fab 40" weekend at its world headquarters in Oregon.)

The Chicago event was supervised by Forrest Harris, Nike's longtime local youth league representative. Assisting him was his former Nike partner Ron Eskridge, a smooth-talking, sharp-dressing elementary-school teacher who was a volunteer assistant coach at Farragut. Garnett soon found himself on a camp team coached by William "Wolf" Nelson, who, in only his second season as Farragut head coach, was trying to turn a longtime also-ran into a public-school power.

That was no easy chore in talent-laden Chicago, but it would be a lot easier with a standout like Garnett. "Everyone's talking around the room and I'm thinking, 'They're gonna get him,'" Nelson said, referring to the state's high school coaching kingpins, who were all at the camp, drooling over Garnett. They had all heard the whispers that Garnett might be leaving the South. They were all green with envy when it became apparent that Garnett had struck up a friendship with Ronnie Fields.

"But, you know, he landed in my lap," Wolf Nelson would eventually say. "Everybody says, 'Sure, sure,' and I hadn't done anything."

Several hundred miles away, James "Duke" Fisher stood at the counter of the Garden Spot variety store, where he often worked weekends, and worried. With his close-cropped hair and military mien, the Mauldin coach seemed more suited to the 1950s. Truth was, Fisher had been looking forward to the 1994–95 season like no other. How many kids like Kevin Garnett, the state's Mr. Basketball as a junior, come along in a fifteen-year coaching career?

For the coach of a team in Mauldin, the answer was: one. Garnett was one in a lifetime.

With any luck, the state title was well within reach. Still, Fisher was insecure. Like thousands of other high school coaches, he knew the booming summer-league circuit was corrupting a sport that was already full of dubious repute. The unrelenting flow of free shoes, bags, jewelry, and travel being offered the blue-chip junior high and high school kids was eroding the integrity of the game. Fisher knew top stars were more likely to listen to the AAU or summer-league coaches, the shoe company guys, than they were to the coach back home.

He knew what was in it for the hustlers at every level of the game if they could move a kid like Kevin Garnett.

"They're just making money off someone else's talent, and that's not right," Fisher said. "I didn't get paid any more for coaching him or any less. Every coach wants to get a player like this, wants him to get some exposure. But how much, and where does it go from there?"

These questions would echo back in Chicago, where a steady procession of college assistants eased their way to Shirley Irby's side during the Nike camp. The smarter ones knew her last name was not Garnett, but every last one of them was awed as her son tore the camp apart. He could do it all, including pass, typically the missing piece to the best player's game.

By the time the camp ended, the word that Garnett was Farragut-bound was whipping through Chicago like the lakeshore wind. "The first time I heard it, I didn't believe it," said the *Chicago Tribune*'s longtime scholastic beat reporter Barry Temkin. "I mean, a kid's not going to come from a fairly decent area in South Carolina to the West Side of Chicago, to a school that's got its share of gang problems. It doesn't make any sense."

It did, if the kid had decided that's what he wanted. And Garnett decided he wanted to play with Ronnie Fields. He wanted to play with and against the best.

In the end, Duke Fisher didn't have a prayer. His championship dreams turned to dust. And Shirley Irby, behind the bravado, could only try to stay close to her son, try to steer from the rear.

She and her daughter moved with Garnett to Chicago, a place for which nothing she had experienced could have prepared her. "I cried the minute I got there," she said.

Then things began to go wrong. An anticipated job with a beauty salon fell through. A semisafe apartment barely big enough for four—Bug Peters initially accompanied his best friend north—made Mauldin rents seem nonexistent.

Even Garnett wondered what he was doing there. He had not come as some anonymous transfer student. He said some gang member threw a hot dog at him on his first day of school and nearly triggered a brawl. Police were stationed at all four corners after the final bell. For the longest time, Garnett feared walking to school in a neighborhood controlled by Hispanic crime lords such as Seven-Gun Marcello. "It was a jungle," he said. "I never want to live like that."

Shirley Irby eventually found work in a HUD office. The family found a cleaner two-bedroom apartment on South Ashland not far from school. It was in the very same building where Coach Wolf Nelson lived.

Early on, Irby wanted very much to believe she had some control of her son. She disputed rumors that he might jump right from high school to the pros. "If the NBA comes down the road, that's fine," she said. "Education is the key for my young man."

Garnett, for his part, said his college contenders were Michigan, North Carolina, South Carolina, Illinois, and Duke. But beyond the issue of his grades and test scores came the question of people trying to make a choice for him. The only mail Irby said she was receiving at home was coming from Illinois and Wabash Valley (Ill.) Junior College. She began to suspect that Ron Eskridge was censoring her son's mail in an effort to steer him in-state.

Irby's suspicions grew stronger when she called an assistant coach at one of the schools she preferred. She asked if the school was still interested in her son. Certainly, the assistant said. He added that he had sent Kevin some forty letters since August, in care of the coach, but had not heard back.

Eskridge denied controlling Garnett's mail. "The mother saw all the mail with Wolf or my address on it," he said.

Adidas basketball czar Sonny Vaccaro, no virgin in this game by any means, had a similar experience. About the same time, he recalled sending two invitations for Garnett to play in the annual Magic Johnson Roundball Classic in suburban Detroit, only to be told Garnett never received either one.

"A lot of people were trying to sell that kid," claimed the coach of a major Midwestern school, who, refusing to be more specific, said that someone offered to "deliver" Garnett in exchange for a coaching job. "To be honest," he said, "it was really sad."

By late winter, 1995, much of that sadness had rubbed off on Shirley Irby. She was losing Kevin, day by day, deal by deal. One night, Vaccaro picked up his telephone in California. It was 2 A.M. in Chicago. Irby was on the line, in tears.

"She said she had lost control," Vaccaro said. " 'These people.' She always referred to 'these people.' She alluded to promises that had been made. She said, 'I don't have anything here. I have to go back to South Carolina.' She said that 'these people' were taking her son away."

That night Garnett had walked out of his mother's apartment and had gone to the home of his new friend Billy Taylor. He didn't return for three days.

Taylor was one of "these people" Irby was talking about. He and Garnett had become acquainted on a neighborhood basketball court. Soon, Garnett was often seen in Taylor's company. Garnett said that no one understood him better. He called Taylor "down-to-earth." He said, "He didn't want nothing from me, just wanted to be on my team."

College assistants, ever vigilant to the shifting centers of power and control within families, took note of the change. Soon the best way to reach the nation's No. 1 recruit was to phone Billy Taylor's home. The midwestern college coach admitted that to recruit Garnett that January, he first had to visit "with Billy a couple of times."

Taylor, according to one Big Ten assistant, made "no bones" about the fact that he had won the predictable struggle for Garnett's confidence. He was somehow now Garnett's friend, surrogate parent, and unofficial agent all rolled into one. He accompanied Garnett on visits to schools, once being thrown out of the office by former Illinois assistant and ace recruiter Jimmy Collins.

Even Nelson and Eskridge—the early front-runners in the race to control Garnett's career—were no match for Taylor. When Vaccaro, once a Nike kingpin before a bitter split, persisted in recruiting Garnett for the Magic Johnson Classic, Eskridge and Nelson said, Forget it, Garnett was booked in another all-star game controlled by Nike.

Taylor called Vaccaro and said, "I'll get it done." But then Vaccaro said he found out that Taylor had a price. He called and requested free plane tickets for not only Garnett, but himself and several friends. Vaccaro said he refused and figured that was it for Garnett. But the night before the game, at the pregame dinner and auction at a Marriott fifteen minutes from the Palace, Dick Vitale was deep into one of his earsplitting sermons when Garnett, Taylor, and friends strolled into the back of the banquet room. Dressed in jacket and jeans, Garnett walked straight to the front and plopped himself right next to Vaccaro.

The Man had arrived.

"Well, look who's here," crowed Vitale. *"Ke*-vin Gar-*nett. A diaper dandy!"*

A Billy Taylor special delivery.

But who was this Billy Taylor? Where had he come from? What was his line of work?

No one seemed to have a clue. But they had lots of questions. And shortly after Garnett's announcement to turn pro, the calls began coming in to the Farragut coaches from NBA team officials wanting to know if they need be concerned about the Billy Taylor connection.

The NBA did not have the kind of shared, league-wide security that made NFL rookies and their agents quake with fear. Some NBA officials, such as Chicago Bulls general manager Jerry Krause, were notorious for working in near seclusion, not wanting to share with or trust anyone. Another team vice president said, "I think the Rookie Transition thing lets them know they better be straight." Others weren't going to bank on that. Some teams hired small firms to do background checks. Some just relied on the grapevine, the network of scouts, college connections, and shoe company runners.

The most common question by league and team officials about a player joining the league: "What's his crew like?"

Back in Chicago, Ron Eskridge—who'd seen Taylor around at various neighborhood league games—decided direct confrontation was the best tack he could take:

"I sat up in the stands and told him, 'Billy, if you cannot stand the scrutiny, then get the fuck out of Kevin's life and get into the background.'" Eskridge said he warned Taylor that the NBA would deal only with "legitimate" people, and that team after team was raising the specter of drugs, probing whether Taylor was—or ever had been—a drug dealer. (A check of local police records and law enforcement sources revealed no arrests for any drug-related offenses, and Taylor did not respond to repeated requests for comment.)

"No one ever saw me do anything like that," Eskridge said Taylor replied.

Chris Head, a basketball assistant coach at Westinghouse High who'd once coached at Farragut but had had a falling-out with Nelson, argued in Taylor's behalf. He said that Taylor had for four years helped him coach a local AAU program (ages thirteen to nineteen) called Team Illinois Hawks and blamed Taylor's questionable reputation on intracity hoop wars, on Nelson and Eskridge's "publicly saying to people Billy was a drug dealer and Chris ain't shit."

Then Head said, "I'll tell you this. I've known Billy for a long time. If he was selling drugs . . . I don't know anything about it. Billy's a genuine person for kids who takes time to spend money on them."

Which raised the familiar question of how and where Taylor earned his money.

"He works for . . ." Head paused for five seconds before continuing. "I think he works for a nightclub."

Think?

"His family is into construction," Head continued, starting to sound like Chevy Chase. "His family owns a bar and grill."

By spring, Garnett's college choices were reduced to just three schools—South Carolina, North Carolina, and the heavy favorite, Michigan. But try as he might, he kept missing the qualifying standard on the ACT. College coaches started mentioning junior college, but that sounded like crazy talk to Garnett and Taylor. Junior college for a player whose high school games were being scouted by the NBA, a player whose undeniable skills were making the pro guys drool?

His new mentor, Taylor, was working toward the inevitable. He approached Chris Head, who, as it turned out, had a pipeline to an NBA agent. According to Head, his conversation with Taylor went something like this:

Taylor: "Chris, I really respect you. You know what you're talking about. What about Kevin going to the League?"

Head: "Billy, that's a helluva jump. Nothing like high school."

Taylor: "Can you help me out?"

Head: "If this kid has an opportunity to make millions, I'd tell him to go, if that's what he feels in his heart."

Taylor: "He'd like to give it a shot."

Head: "Well, I have a person who I really respect."

Enter Eric Fleisher.

"I was asked to give Kevin some advice," Fleisher said. "We talked for about two hours, the pros and cons of college, the NBA process. He was exploring different alternatives. . . . Billy was just helping him get through this whole process, giving him some advice. He had a pretty good business sense and really wanted to make sure Kevin made the right decision. He was someone who was very close with Kevin. I really came away with the opinion that Billy was someone who cared about him."

Fleisher also came away with a new client, a prize catch who would ultimately launch his solo career. Eskridge was wrong when he warned Taylor that "NBA people" would deal only with established credentials. Garnett declared himself eligible for the draft on May 15. His mother showed up late and was virtually ignored. Billy Taylor was in charge.

While Eric Fleisher was recruiting Garnett through Taylor, he didn't exactly go out of his way to fill in brother Marc—at the time still his partner—on the details. Once or twice, he mentioned, according to Marc, "this guy named Taylor."

Wherever else Taylor may have worked, he eventually helped get Garnett employment as the fifth lottery slot of the NBA draft. Like Garnett, he was well on his way to being a big-time player. He was out there, roaming the underground network, letting others know he could do for them what he was doing for Garnett.

As far back as the Magic Johnson Roundball Classic, in fact, Taylor had been tunneling elsewhere, into other high school player camps. One very special camp, in particular.

It was at the pregame dinner, while Garnett drew attention from Vitale, that a Louisiana businessman, a close friend of a 6-9 power forward from Baton Rouge named Lester Earl, was approached by Donald Marbury, father of the country's most talked about scholastic point guard, junior Stephon Marbury at Brooklyn's Lincoln High.

"Mr. Marbury thought that Billy Taylor and I should talk," said the businessman.

Soon Donald Marbury, who raised his family in the grinding poverty of the projects in Coney Island and had watched his three older sons fall various levels short of the pros, was talking. Taylor, Marbury told the businessman, was in the construction business, which Marbury also said was his own profession.

"He said that money would not be a problem because Billy and his partner were successful at their trade," the businessman said. "He called several times and said he felt it was an honor for Lester to come to Chicago and line up with Billy. Billy would take care of them. He was adamant about getting him to stay with Billy because he felt Billy had done some great things for Kevin."

According to this businessman, Donald Marbury was close enough to Taylor to let his son, Stephon, travel to Chicago and stay with him. "Mr. Marbury said he would not send his son to someone who he did not think very highly of," said the businessman.

The offer for Earl was declined. "I saw Billy and the element around him," the businessman said. "I didn't think it was a good opportunity for Lester to be involved."

You can't win them all. But Taylor certainly seemed to have won over the Marburys, a relationship that began when Marbury's high school coach at Lincoln, Nike-affiliated Bob Hartstein, arranged for his hot prospect to attend Nike camps in Chicago run by longtime Chicago hoops guru Mac Irvin. There, Marbury met Kevin Garnett, and, quite naturally, Billy Taylor.

By Marbury's senior year—which was also the year Garnett was at Farragut—Taylor was making occasional appearances at Lincoln games.

All through the summer of 1995, Stephon Marbury, on his way to his freshman year at Georgia Tech, flew in and out of Chicago to hang out with Billy Taylor and Kevin Garnett. And hear Taylor and Garnett sing the song of the NBA. By the fall, before he played his first college game, Marbury was saying he might leave school after his freshman year.

Taylor and a couple of his Chicago cronies began hanging around the Tech campus, prompting Marbury's new coach, Bobby Cremins, to ask his freshman, "Who the hell are those guys?"

"Friends of mine from Chicago," Marbury said.

Taylor was also spotted sitting with Stephon's father at Madison Square Garden when Georgia Tech played in the preseason National Invitational Tournament. Atlanta. New York. Who knew where Billy Taylor would next show up? One thing was certain: he and Fleisher had undoubtedly turned up the big winners in the Kevin Garnett Sweepstakes.

Back at Farragut Academy in Chicago, meanwhile, things didn't work out as well for Eskridge, or Ronnie Fields.

A three-time all-state guard, Fields broke two vertebrae in his neck in a February 1996 car crash, while driving a car that was rented by Eskridge. Eight months later, the nineteen-year-old Fields pleaded guilty with two other men to charges of sexually assaulting a twenty-year-old woman the previous July. The attack had occurred in Eskridge's apartment.

Two budding careers may have been aborted, the flip side of the Garnett-Taylor success story, the more predictable side of a system gone awry. Fields did not meet academic requirements to play local Division I ball at DePaul. And Farragut principal Edward Guerra said Eskridge's coaching career at the school was over.

By the end of their week in Orlando, most of the rookies were tired of the lectures, of being stuck indoors, of not playing ball. They were anxious to get on with their first pro season.

One thing at least they were assured of was that there would be no delay in their reporting to training camp. The annual disruption of the top rookies' not signing until late in camp or early in the season had been eliminated by the rookie contract slotting. "The two deals we signed took about fifteen minutes combined," said David Falk, who was representing Vancouver's Bryant Reeves and Cleveland's Bob Sura. "You say, 'Send me a contract for twenty percent above the minimum.' It's automatic."

Kevin Garnett said that knowing there was going to be a rookie slotting system would not have stopped him from coming out. "They're gonna do what they're gonna do," he said, gliding down the Marriott hall toward his room. "And I've gotta do what I've gotta do."

He said he expected his friend Bug Peters to live with him in Minneapolis, as he had for a spell in Chicago. He promised to have no entourage, though, no hangers-on taking bites out of the three-year, $5.6-million contract he would soon sign.

His mother, Shirley Irby, had gone back to South Carolina. "People always thought she was running the show," he said. "We're not that close anymore."

Joe Smith, meanwhile, said his mother was out in the Bay Area, looking for a place for them to live. He, too, had come around to the notion that it was no mistake to leave school after his sophomore year. "I'll be able to renegotiate after my second year," he said. "I'll only be twenty-two."

This was an interesting and ironic by-product of the collective bargaining wars. A league increasingly bedeviled by its rowdy young was sending out a clear but contradictory message: the faster you get here, the faster you'll make your killing.

You could bet that the next Kevin Garnett and the next Stephon Marbury would be hearing exactly that from the next Billy Taylor. And the reality, more than ever, was that most agents would have to deal with the Taylors—or, as the case of Joe Smith would prove, the ambitious relatives—whose power was directly proportionate to their proximity to the "product."

7

Family Ties

I F THE FUNDAMENTAL LESSON OF HIS WEEK AT THE MARRIOTT WORLD Center had been to be wary of the fast lane, to proceed with caution, Joe Smith soon discovered how tantalizingly seductive the life of the NBA player was going to be. Days after lugging notebooks and watching educational films, Smith suddenly found himself making small talk on Broadway with Donald Trump.

He was about to get a crash course in the Art of the Spiel.

The All-Star Cafe wasn't yet open for business—was still under construction, in fact—but a noisy crowd had gathered on a sun-baked but crisp September afternoon in New York's Times Square. The word was out: live celebrities were on the way.

Shaquille O'Neal, part of the new venture that promised yet another trendy sports bar with numerous autographed photos of its famous investors, was coming to promote a one-on-one contest with Hakeem Olajuwon, courtesy of Taco Bell. And Trump, at whose Atlantic City hotel this pay-per-view extravaganza would be taking place.

The Donald, sans Marla, wasn't about to miss an obvious photo opportunity, with gossip-page sure shots such as Olajuwon and O'Neal. But before the serious drawing cards would arrive, fashionably late, a tall, handsome young man would stride confidently across Broadway, continue walking onto Forty-third. He was dressed for success—rust-colored suit, collarless white shirt, polished black shoes.

As he approached the entrance to the building, someone in the crowd turned to a friend and said, "Joe Smith. Number one draft pick." Another person called out, "Yeah, Maryland." Smith, smiling, looked over and gave a little wave.

His companion—shorter, older, and like Smith, fastidiously dressed—stopped for a moment, then nudged the player past the public relations staff greeting guests, up the stairs, and around to the café, which at the moment was very much in skeletal condition.

The main room had an overhead circular balcony. The floor was a sheet of concrete. The ceiling was a mass of beams and wires. While workmen went about their business on the balcony, occasionally pausing to lean over the rail to see who had arrived, formally dressed waiters and waitresses scurried around, offering hors d'oeuvres and glasses of white wine.

The finishing touches were being put on the table that would serve as the dais. Behind it hung a blue curtain, with promotional displays for Taco Bell and SET, the pay-per-view television outlet. There was also a huge banner that read "Congratulations, Shaq and Hakeem."

It wasn't entirely clear what these two NBA Finals combatants were being applauded for, but one possibility was for managing to arrange precisely the kind of event that David Stern loathed. Several years before, a potential Magic Johnson–Michael Jordan pay-per-view showdown was quashed by Stern and the league, for obvious reasons. It promoted gimmickry, not basketball. On a glitzy stage in a gamblers' town, it had an oily ambience. And, of course, the NBA wasn't going to allow the prizes of its talent pool to make money for any promoter willing to produce a wad of up-front cash.

Leonard Armato, the agent for O'Neal, had capitalized on the NBA lockout to create the show with Taco Bell, which had signed the two centers for a series of television spots following Houston's four-game sweep the previous June. As long as the league locked out its players, it had no right to exercise control over what they did. A challenge by Shaquille to Hakeem first appeared in full-page newspaper ads. Then came Hakeem's acceptance. Then the undercard: Kenny Anderson versus Nick Van Exel, a couple of perky southpaw point guards; Joe Smith versus Kevin Garnett, No. 1 pick in the draft against its No. 1 curiosity.

"I kind of leaped through the window of opportunity," said Armato, dark-haired, well-groomed, with a southern-California tan and a quick, engaging smile. "I said to David Stern, 'You've gotta come.'"

He was asked what Stern had replied.

"'I can't be seen at something like that.'"

Armato said he had nonetheless talked Stern into purchasing the pay-per-view. Even if that was true, Armato was still confronted with the more difficult task of getting America to plug in for $19.95 a pop.

For some semblance of broadcasting authenticity, Armato hired Billy Packer. Packer began the press conference by introducing Trump, who stood and announced, with great sincerity, that the one-on-one show would be one of the great events in basketball history.

But it was soon clear whom the real star of this show was going to be. In a brief Q and A with Packer, Garnett said he had no pregame message for his new friend and rival Smith. "I don't talk no trash like Shaq," he said. He flashed a sheepish grin, then looked over at O'Neal, who didn't turn his head.

When Packer suggested that Smith's deep voice could make him the NBA's next best-selling rapper, Smith smiled demurely and rubbed the head of O'Neal, who was sitting to his left. Without looking up, O'Neal yawned.

It was obvious whose attention the rookies wanted, whom they were thrilled to be seen with. When O'Neal stood, towering over Packer, Smith and Garnett turned their heads and looked at him as if he were Olympus. They appeared less infatuated with Olajuwon, the two-time defending champion, devout Muslim, and canny veteran. Olajuwon was no cross-marketing sensation, no transcendent personality. It was tellingly ironic that even at the height of his brilliant career, when it was impossible not to recognize that he was one of the most gifted centers ever, Olajuwon needed teen idol O'Neal, who was all of twenty-three, as his marketing partner.

Only O'Neal, second to Michael Jordan as beneficiary of the hype, sensed the superficiality of it all, understood that neither his menacing size nor his prodigious Q score made him Olajuwon's equal. Not yet. Not without a championship ring on his finger.

Early on in his pro career, O'Neal had been exploited by an unintelligent marketing campaign that featured him bending rims and shattering backboards, presumably a celebration of raw power. Completely ignored was his impressive speed for a three-hundred-pound man, his awesome shot-blocking, array of low-post moves, and passing out of double teams.

Even O'Neal's stepfather, Phillip Harrison, got into the act, slamming the phone down and shattering the glass booth in a spot for a telephone company. When it was pointed out that a wave of imitative kids were hanging from rims and ruining playgrounds all over the country, and that one upstate New York child was buried in his O'Neal jersey after a fatal fall from grabbing onto a rim, Armato defended the campaign. He compared it to psychologists who advise clients to vent their rage by beating on a pillow.

"A new-age thinking," he said. "Don't blow up a building; take it out on the rim."

Eventually, the mere thought of consumer backlash and perhaps a manifestation of good taste sent the Shaq sellers scrambling for another message. A kinder, gentler O'Neal surfaced in ensuing ads, and one even poked fun at his lamentable foul-shooting skills.

To his credit, O'Neal didn't allow Packer to compare him to Wilt Chamberlain and other giants of the game at the All-Star Cafe. Not with Olajuwon a few feet away, O'Neal understood that his record paled next to Olajuwon's, the man who three months earlier had given him low-post lessons on an international stage. And said not one disparaging word or made one disrespectful gesture in the process. O'Neal had not forgotten that.

"I get compared to a lot of players," he rasped, "but if you guys are ever going to compare me to anyone, I'd be honored to be compared to the great Hakeem."

The non–media types applauded. Olajuwon blushed. The press conference dissolved into one-on-one interviews. A small group surrounded Smith, while his companion stepped off to the side, his eyes riveted on Smith.

"Joe looks good," a reporter said to the companion, making small talk. "He's the only player wearing a suit."

"Oh, he wanted to wear sweats, too, but I said, 'No way,' " said the companion. "Appearances count."

That was what Len Elmore would have said, only he might have carried this covenant to another level. He might have argued that Leonard Armato's pay-per-view show was nothing more than basketball's version of a pro wrestling event, bogus and exploitative, not the kind of association Joe Smith wanted to have before he'd played his first NBA game. Not for a $10,000 appearance fee.

This was the part of the job—marketing—that Elmore looked most forward to, derived the most pleasure and gratification (and profit, via Precept's cut of 15 percent per deal) from. Appearances did count, Elmore agreed, and pro basketball players should have an impact in their community. They should be role models. "It's not just about throwing money around and saying that's a job well done, and a solution," he said. "It's about doing something."

He was proud that one of his clients, Sam Cassell, was involved in an immunization program in Baltimore, his hometown, spending hours at hospitals with kids. Another, Walt Williams, had set up a scholarship at the University of Maryland in his father's name. Their money was invested in an African-American–owned bank.

Elmore said he'd been plotting a similar course for Smith, beyond the requisite shoe and card deals, beyond the autograph sessions and donations of corporate merchandise to charitable causes that the player knew nothing about. But that would require a little more of the player's time and, in what was usually the more daunting part, his family's patience. Elmore didn't want Smith to grab for the "cheap" payday. He wanted him to breathe, to establish himself. He wasn't about to attract great attention with his steady demeanor or his unsexy name. Not yet. Elmore, though, foresaw plain old Joe Smith as uncommonly catchy, once he established himself as a blue-chip pro, an All-Star, as a faster, higher-leaping, better-shooting version of Buck Williams. He believed that, in Smith, he finally had a major star to nurture, to guide. A player with whom he could rewrite the rules, allow him to make a difference, too.

That's what he'd envisioned when he left the Brooklyn district attorney's office and jumped feetfirst into the agent game. That's what he'd celebrated in Toronto when Smith turned up No. 1 in the draft. But then there was suddenly a catch, a twist, a reminder that the agent game was just as intense, as unpredictable, as the NBA playoffs. You could play hard. You could play well. But one bad break, one blown call, and despite months of planning, months of effort, you could be done. You could be out.

"I'm Willie Brown," Smith's companion said at the All-Star Cafe, holding out his card. "I'm Joe's uncle. I'm handling his marketing now."

Willie L. Brown lowered his athletic, 6-4 frame into the driver's seat of his Jeep Grand Cherokee, a sturdy black vehicle with the vanity plates Q SHOP 3. The plates had obviously been purchased before Brown added the fourth of his small chain of convenience stores he'd patterned after 7-Eleven, two in Norfolk, two more in nearby Portsmouth.

One unseasonably warm Norfolk autumn morning he pulled the Jeep up to one of his stores, which wasn't exactly out of the mini-mart hall of fame. The words QUICK SHOP were in red script against a yellow background on a sign. A NO LOITERING OR DISORDER sign hung on one outside wall. On the front door, a square yellow sticker was affixed: "Store has less than $30 after dark." Inside, paint was peeling. There was an aroma of fried chicken. The shelves were thinly stocked with panty hose, crackers, soap, detergent. The beer was behind the checkout counter, out of shoplifting range.

Brief business finished, the forty-nine-year-old younger brother of Letha Smith jumped back into his Jeep and headed south down Military Highway, picking up 264 West, while rattling off the credentials he was certain made him qualified to be the guiding force of Joe Smith's promising financial future.

Following a stint in Vietnam, Brown graduated from Norfolk State College with a degree in business administration. He joined a management training program for the Southland Corporation, parent company of 7-Eleven, and eventually became a district manager for forty-nine stores and three hundred employees. He bought a 5,500-square-foot house—"Own my own home," he said with more than a trace of pride—and was the president of the Norfolk State Alumni Association.

And now, his latest and most exciting venture: MSB Marketing & Consulting, Ltd., a new, three-person company, with one client, Joe Smith, and grandiose plans for more.

The *M* represented Celestine McFarland, one of Joe Smith's sisters and an employee of NationsBank. The *S* was for Sharon Smith, another of Smith's sisters and a master sergeant in the army. The *B*, obviously, was for Brown, who wasn't about to compare his résumé to Len Elmore's but wanted to be perfectly clear about a couple of things:

One, he had learned the same lessons from his hardworking father, Jasper, that had filtered through Letha down to Joe. Two, he was nobody's financial fool.

"I've been in sales all my life," he said with a striking self-assurance.

He was dressed, at least, for the part, *GQ* cool in a brown-black custom coat, caramel-colored slacks, and matching pocket hankie, offset by a white collarless shirt. He wore a beeper on his waist, which he would repeatedly touch after feeling the buzz. A gold chain dangled loosely from his neck. His mustache was trim, hair receding, but his most arresting feature were his eyes. They were deep, dark, and penetrating, locking in as if to punctuate the point he wanted to make. Willie Brown had the proverbial "look" down, a game face that could certainly be daunting for a young man with no father in his life.

"My relationship with Joe and his sisters is that they basically came from a one-parent family," Brown said. "I was there for them. Financially and more."

He said it was not as if he'd just walked into Smith's basketball life the minute he landed No. 1 in the draft. Brown said he had assisted Letha in entertaining the coaches who recruited Joe for college. He helped choose Elmore as his nephew's agent after conducting many interviews with others, including the conglomerate IMG and the industry superstar David Falk.

Brown, a successful black businessman, admitted that he'd initially wondered if Joe would be better off with a more entrenched white agent.

"That has been a question, whether a black agent could be as productive for us as a white agent," he said. "We found they could. Len talked about some of the things we wanted to hear, which was taking care of Joe. Not just on the court, but off. We hired Len, not because he's black, but because he could do the job."

Now, in effect, Joe Smith's family was unwittingly saying that he couldn't. Or at least it could do the job without him.

Brown claimed that his presence in Smith's career was not his idea, and that MSB would be no family convenience store. No one, he said, was trying to live off the very talented baby in the family without earning every penny. "We have not drawn a dime off Joe," he said. "When he gets paid, we get paid."

Off the highway, he steered through the streets of a neighborhood called Lamberts Point, on the edge of the Old Dominion University campus. The area appeared to be spiraling downward, NO LOITERING signs were tacked to the sides of several vacant buildings. Brown pulled up to 1327 Forty-first Street, to a single-family brick home accented by rust-colored wood and a large picture window. On one side stood a beige brick apartment building. On the other, a yellow pillbox.

"This is it, where Joe grew up with his mom," he said. The house was dark inside. Letha had already moved out, and had gone to the West Coast to look for a place to live with Joe. A For Sale sign was in front, the contact name of the broker being Willie Brown.

Brown howled as his visitor in the passenger seat wondered if he was also in the real estate business.

"That's my ex-wife," he said. "Believe it or not, her name is Willie Brown. Willie Ricks, when I married her."

Letha Smith, he said, would eventually be shopping for a new house near the Virginia shore. Uncle Willie and sisters Sharon and Celestine would remain in Norfolk, running the family marketing business. And the former Willie Ricks had the exclusive selling rights to the old house with a $60,000 price tag. Ronald Reagan would have applauded this shining example of trickle-down economics.

Brown traced his own involvement in Joe's management to a card-deal promotion engineered by Elmore in New York the previous spring. Joe took along some of his friends and, according to Brown, paid for five hotel rooms, and everyone's food and entertainment. When the credit card bill arrived at the family home in Norfolk, the woman who had never charged anything but her children's shoes became alarmed. She called her brother and said, "Willie, come over to the house." Brown said Letha thought it was a mistake. She was upset, which concerned Willie, whose sister had suffered a mild heart attack months before the draft.

To Brown, the credit card fiasco was an obvious example of what he could bring to Smith's management that Elmore did not. He was family. He was power. "I mean, he's nineteen, you can tell him no," Brown said.

Hell, when Brown was nineteen, he was on his way to the killing fields of Vietnam, snapping to attention at his officers' commands. That was 1965. He was with the airborne defensive unit, replacing another unit that had been in so many gunfights it had lost half its men.

Hands on the steering wheel of his Jeep, Brown looked across the front seat, his eyes locking in again, his voice on the rise. He couldn't let the credit card bill go, not just yet. "I mean," he said, "you can really tell him *no!*"

That's what Letha had wanted to say when Joe, after leaving Maryland and signing with Nike, wanted to trade in his old car for a Mercedes-Benz. It was too much, too soon, she said. But Joe got the car. And one day on Memorial Day weekend, Smith was driving home to Norfolk after workouts and scrimmages conducted by Elmore's group in the D.C. area when he was cut off on a slick highway and skidded off the road. The car flipped over, but Smith was not seriously hurt. "That car probably saved his life," said Elmore. But Letha didn't see it that way. She didn't understand why Joe should have to work out that far from home. From a mother's point of view, Elmore had unnecessarily dragged her son away. And then Joe nearly got himself killed.

From that time on, Letha began to draw Joe back home, away from Elmore, to the family. And when Joe did have to travel, better it should be his uncle who was out there, making sure Joe's interests were taken care of, making sure someone was around to tell him "No!"

For his part, Brown said he'd realized how malleable, how vulnerable, his nephew was when they were promoting the O'Neal-Olajuwon pay-per-view show for the West Coast media. While in Los Angeles, they had stopped off at the Warner Brothers studio where Michael Jordan was filming *Space Jam* and, courtesy of Warner Brothers, hosting star-studded pickup games on a court constructed just for him. Joe, he said, was starry eyed, almost tongue-tied.

"God, these kids," he said, shaking his head. "My son is twenty-two. He's older than them, and they're multimillionaires. Who's really looking out for them?"

An equally relevant question, of course, was who was better equipped to look out for their money? Naturally, in Smith's case, Elmore believed it was him. But he was respectful of the family, of the player's relationships and wishes. He had to be. "I know they all love him and they all want what's best," he said. But he said it more with resignation than with acceptance.

Elmore, of course, was still Smith's official agent for negotiating his contract with Golden State. He was ready and hoping to do more eventually. But Letha Smith, her daughters, and now Willie Brown were the disciplinary forces in Joe's life. His sisters had diapered and fed him when his mother was out working, keeping a roof over his head. How could he say no to them?

"Oh, Len called Joe," Brown said when asked how Elmore had taken the news. "He wanted to make sure Joe knew what was going on. After we talked, Len understood the direction we wanted to carry Joe's future. The ultimate decision was Joe's. We made a pitch. He said, 'Fine, if you can do it, go do it.' I could say anything I wanted to do, but if Joe said, 'No, no, Len's who I want,' then that's that."

But the chances of Joe Smith holding his family at arm's length, at least at this time in his life, were remote. This was a young man whose mother was going to be his rookie roommate. What was he going to say? And how much could Elmore really say? How could Elmore, who had put Smith's money in the African-American–owned bank, tell him not to transfer it to NationsBank, where his sister worked, because Nations had a reputation—and, in fact, was the target of a major lawsuit—for not approving loans to minority applicants? He couldn't. He could only shake his head when Brown would tell him that his own attorney, David Delpierre, would be handling such and such. Elmore called Delpierre, a Norfolk guy, "a wanna-be who's been hanging around since it became obvious that Joe was going to be an NBA player."

To Elmore, Delpierre was just another member of a chorus line of excessive representation. Elmore had learned early on that Smith's family was just not going to let him do his job. The Smiths, he said, made their displeasure obvious when Joe wasn't chosen for a role in *Eddie*, the Whoopi Goldberg NBA satire that Derrick Coleman, a real live NBA head case, might've critiqued with his infamous "Whoop-de-damn-do." Then the first deal Elmore struck after Smith entered the draft was with Nike, four years, for $5 million, plus incentives. The money was offered well before the draft. Reebok and Adidas, he claimed, didn't want to match the offer. Fila, represented by Jap Trimble, a high school and college teammate of Elmore's and one of his best friends, offered a deal that would tie Smith's money to the sale of his shoe.

For Elmore, the decision came down to risk versus solid money and the proven long-term, star-making capability of Nike. He feared the effect of Smith's being drafted by a bad team like the Los Angeles Clippers or into an isolated market like Minnesota. After consulting his industry sources, including Jap Trimble, he flew with Smith out to Nike headquarters outside Portland, Oregon. Smith, whose family was apprised of the details by Elmore, agreed to the deal, though the contract, not yet drawn, was not signed.

It wasn't long before Brown took over Smith's marketing, with his own ideas and his desire to make an immediate impact and demonstrate to Letha and Joe that he could handle the job. Brown was now traveling with his nephew, making new friends, networking the way any industry newcomer would. He quickly became convinced that Joe had been shortchanged by Nike. He contacted the company and said that, as Smith's family adviser at the time the deal was signed, he had not been fully consulted. The family, Brown said, was upset when it learned that Jerry Stackhouse, despite being drafted two slots lower than Joe and by lowly Philadelphia, signed for five years and $15 million with Fila, the deal including Stackhouse's name-brand shoe.

Stackhouse, in fact, was the rookie in greatest demand, the target of a bidding war by Nike, Reebok, Converse, and emerging Fila. Being close to Jap Trimble, Elmore understood that Smith, even as No. 1, could not match the appeal of Stackhouse, taken third. Smith—and for that matter, Antonio McDyess at No. 2— were unsexy big forwards to the shoe companies. A big man had better be able to do more than dunk. If he could tear down the rim like Shaq, well, that's a start. But Stackhouse was another creative, high-flying, midsize player from Dean Smith's North Carolina program, a marketing rep's Michael Jordan wet dream. He had a colorful name. The 76ers were already referring to their new arena, rising across the street from the outdated Spectrum, as "Stack's House."

Still, Willie Brown was determined to do better for his nephew, to demonstrate to his sister that he could play with the big boys. After he did his own market research, he said, "I was in there." He meant he was out at Nike headquarters, to finalize the deal. Nike eventually plugged some extra money into the back end, at which time, Brown argued, the company's stars—Jordan, Charles Barkley, and Scottie Pippen—would be on the way down, if not gone altogether. Brown thought this was proof that he could handle himself in an industry so unforgiving that even the brothers Fleisher could be at each other's throats. By cementing the deal, Brown also claimed entitlement to the 15 percent agent's fee, which Elmore said he might eventually be forced to contest legally.

Uncle Willie was indeed learning fast, though at times he still sounded very much like a student-agent. He said that Armato, whom he had become acquainted with during the one-on-one promotions, seemed quite amenable to sharing his trade secrets.

"I can call him anytime," Brown said. "I have his home number."

He didn't mention the possibility that Armato might very well have been considering another number, the amount in millions Smith would be commanding when it came time to negotiate his next contract with Golden State. From Armato's point of view—or any other agent's—how bad an idea could it be to cozy up to Joe Smith's uncle, just in case?

There were no guarantees, of course, but there seemed to be no limit to the earnings of that NBA star who struck the right chord, who played his cards right. Willie Brown said he intended for his nephew to do just that.

Driving along Charlotte Street, he slowed his Jeep and pointed to a dull, one-story building, shabby and low-slung. It was the Hunton YMCA, where Joe had honed his youthful skills.

"You will probably see Joe give some money to this YMCA," Brown said. "That's what we're working on, putting together his foundation."

Now Brown was beginning to sound more like Len Elmore. He was selling Joe Smith as decidedly un–Generation X.

"Joe is what the NBA needs today," he said. "A clean-cut, American young man. When you have a corporation, a product, you need someone to help you move, an image you want to present. Grant Hill is one. We have a young man in Joe with that unique smile, who is quiet, who listens, who performs.

"Two years from now, a year and a half, whenever the negotiating power comes, it'll be time for Len to start saying, 'Okay, this is what we expect in his next contract.' Like Alonzo Mourning. He had one year left on his contract and he said, 'Give up the thirteen million.'"

Willie Brown laughed, but this was no joking matter. This was about a dream becoming a plan, an inevitability. As if to hold on to that thought and not let go, he was silent for a few moments, hands tight on the wheel, eyes fixed on the road. Then he repeated himself, a little softer this time, rhythmically nodding his head, almost as if he were humming a tune.

"Give up the thirteen million," Willie Brown said. "Give up the thirteen million."

By sheer fate, and the continued run of David Stern's good fortune, Leonard Armato's one-on-one showdown never took place. Two days after the players appeared at the All-Star Cafe, the event was canceled, after Olajuwon wrenched his back and wisely backed out. Ahead was a long season, another championship to defend. Taco Bell, thankfully, was not the highest priority on his list.

Willie Brown was disappointed his nephew would not get the chance to be part of the three-ring promotion. But he was impressed with the way Armato had put it together. Hell, Donald Trump was involved. Not bad indeed. Before they parted ways, Brown decided to ask Armato if he was interested in a percentage of Joe Smith's marketing rights. It would certainly be a coup for Brown to hook up with the agent who had crafted the market for Shaquille O'Neal.

Armato, though, sensed trouble, too many people involved, too many players obstructing direct contact between himself and the client. He thought Letha Smith was a sincere woman. He loved Joe. But the truth was what Elmore had been saying: Joe Smith was not sexy enough to be an instant sell. He needed to play a couple of years, become the unquestioned star of his team, grow into the role of basketball's boy next door. Armato said he politely declined.

Soon, Brown would, through a mutual acquaintance back in Norfolk, be introduced to a man named Ernest Ruffin, a former marketing representative for NCR and AT&T. Ruffin, a Newark, New Jersey, native, had recently formed the East Coast Sports Management Group in Charlotte, his most recent AT&T outpost. He held the marketing rights for two NBA clients, both rookies, Boston's Eric Williams and Miami's Kurt Thomas. He was thinking of becoming certified by the union, in order to do contracts.

And now, suddenly, he was taking on marketing the No. 1 pick in the draft.

As for Joe, he would have his showdown with draft rival Kevin Garnett under more conventional circumstances. His summer as the star of the 1995 college draft was ended. On October 4, he signed his $8.5 million, three-year contract, then reported to St. Mary's College for the final day of the Warriors' rookie/free-agent camp.

Some of the players and reporters in the gym that day remarked how skinny Smith was for a player who was penciled in by Rick Adelman to start at power forward. But Smith also quickly showed a passion to go after the ball, and the skills to beat the opposition to it.

Twice, he missed medium-range jump shots, but followed them up with put back baskets. He also played the entire sixty-minute scrimmage, and though he became noticeably tired, he never asked to be removed. Adelman was impressed, even somewhat surprised. He should not have been, though. Smith was no complainer, not afraid of a hard day's work, and certainly not with his mother watching.

Letha Smith had made good on her vow. At courtside, she sat quietly in a folding chair, watching proudly as her Joe earned his first day's pay.

All around the NBA, less poignant but similarly hopeful scenes were taking place. For now, the labor battle was forgotten. It was time to go to work, to search for that rare, elusive chemistry, to determine which teams had a future and which did not.

In suburban Detroit, Doug Collins was setting out to build more of a bridge to the past. Back to the Bad Boys. Back to when T-E-A-M was much more than an acronym for Turmoil, Ego, Attitude, and Money.

8

Bad Boys

SIXTY MINUTES BEFORE THE OFFICIAL OPENING OF THE DOUG COLLINS Era, traffic outside The Palace of Auburn Hills breezed along. The magnificent brick arena, marked by a distinctive diamond swirl, shimmered in the soft evening light. The vision was marred only by the scaffolding rising against the arena's southwest side—a telltale sign of prosperity and growth.

Unfortunately, these were the rewards of another time, another team. The Pistons of recent years were not Bad Boys, just bad, with all the hallmarks of your typical NBA loser. Overpaid, indifferent players. Coaches resigned to their fate. Attendance dwindling from the halcyon days of the automatic sellout. Forty-four-year-old Doug Collins had been hired to change all that, to infuse the franchise with his trademark energy.

Collins had been a statement hire by the longtime Pistons managing partner, William Davidson. He had coached—however unremarkably—Michael Jordan in Chicago. He had been an exciting NBA analyst on TNT. He had visibility, celebrity, and to many, this was the best thing a coach could have going for him in the New NBA. The only thing that might make the young millionaires put down their cellular phones and open up their playbooks.

"As I was driving in today," Collins said, stretched out on a silver-blue couch in his office, "I told [my son] Chris this is the first time I've been nervous before a game since I went to his games at Duke. Not knowing what to expect. How guys are going to react."

He looked cool and casual in a black turtleneck and charcoal slacks. A twenty-ounce bottle of diet Coke was pressed between his legs. It was Friday, October 13, 1995, truly a special day. Not only was this exhibition opener against Philadelphia a coming-out party, but daughter Kelly had just been named high school homecoming queen in Northbrook, Illinois, and Chris was in town for the game.

It was going to be an interesting year, that much was certain. Despite criticism in Chicago that he was too high-strung, too gung ho, Collins had resolved to be himself. To get his love for the game to rub off on his players. He believed it was the rare coach who was fortunate enough to count simply on the professionalism of his players. Those days, sadly, were long gone. The coach now had to bend the will of the team to match his own. He couldn't count on his star player anymore. Hell, his star was Grant Hill, a terrific kid but a kid nonetheless.

No, it was Collins' job to set the mood and establish the goals. Here, he was going to be tough . . . but fair. Realistic. In his mind, upscale expectations for the young Pistons were at least one year away. The themes this season were learning and growth. "In this business, I always equate building a team with raising a child," he said. "It's a natural process. When you let a team play itself out to the end, get every bit of it you can, and then you start over."

All during the pre-exhibition training camp—Camp Collins— he coddled and coached, coached and coddled. He installed new sets on both ends of the floor. He ran his players ragged. "With Grant [Hill] and Allan [Houston] we have the nucleus to do some wonderful things, but, also, it's about a state of mind," he decided. "There's a toughness you have to bring every single day, and you pay a price for that. That's the one thing these guys have heard from me over and over: change is painful. But the rewards are off the charts."

So Collins and his cadre of bright young assistants—Alvin Gentry, Brian James, and John Hammond—offered the young Pistons an NBA degree in T-E-A-M-work. Teaching them what it meant to be a pro. What it takes to earn respect. How to play with urgency. Collins was watching to see who was unselfish, who wanted to compete, who felt sorry for himself, and who wanted no part of the words written on a locker room board: "THAT'S WHY WE PLAY ALL 82."

"I'm a fighter," Collins said, Marine-like. "I'll be in wars with them."

When push came to shove, Collins hoped all he would have to do was walk down the hall, enter the arena, and point straight up to the white-and-black banners hanging high above the court. To the championship flags commemorating a team—the Bad Boys—pro basketball fans outside the Motor City loved to hate.

"No matter how the game went or how they were feeling, they gave you the same effort, and they played defense," Collins said, having known the displeasure of getting his ass kicked repeatedly by those Pistons while coaching the Bulls. "They were a coach's dream."

Thomas, Laimbeer, Dumars, Vinnie, Mahorn, Dantley, Aguirre, Rodman, Salley, and Edwards. As odd a collection of talent and egos as you'll find. But when push came to shove for them, they pummeled their way to back-to-back titles in 1989 and 1990.

Pistons. A perfect name for a team that left its mark—black-and-blue—on NBA legend and lore. A team that NBA Entertainment first dubbed Bad Boys in one of those set-to-music (in this case, the rock song "Bad to the Bone") videos before the Pistons actually won a title. The marketing backfired, as critics of the increasingly streetlike NBA blamed the Bad Boys for everything from hand-checking to trash talking, from coach-baiting to ego anarchy.

"A Piston was a basketball player totally dedicated to the cause, and by cause I mean the logo, the Pistons logo," said William J. Laimbeer Jr., president and CEO of Laimbeer Packaging, a corrugated-box company.

Big Bad Bill was traded to Detroit in the winter of 1982 by the abysmal Cleveland Cavaliers, one of the poster teams for the league's sorry state. "Cleveland was a running joke, and it just deteriorated into chaos," he said.

He went to a team that was just rising off a canvas bloodied by 127 losses and just 37 wins from 1979 to 1981. But then, in 1981, a nineteen-year-old force of nature left Indiana University and

Bobby Knight after winning an NCAA title. The Pistons wasted no time drafting the 6-1 guard, a college sophomore, second in the draft. Isiah Thomas was already, in the words of Knight, "one of the truly great college basketball players of his era," the toughest kid the toughest coach had ever seen.

Will Robinson, a top Pistons scout, will never forget what he saw. "Let me put it this way," said Robinson, who became a father figure to Thomas. "Frank Sinatra was born to sing. Isiah Thomas was born to play basketball."

So it began. Notre Dame's Kelly Tripucka was selected in that same draft. That November, the Pistons picked up streak-shooting guard Vinnie Johnson from Seattle. Johnson was sitting down to a night of Chinese food and kung fu movies when he got the call from head coach Lenny Wilkens. "Lenny never called me at home," recalled Johnson one afternoon at his own packaging plant, called, quite naturally, Piston Packaging. "I thought maybe he was going to tell me I was going to get more minutes. Before I even take a bite, he said, 'Vin, we just traded you to Detroit.'

"I said, 'Man, why Detroit? Those guys are terrible.' I said, 'I should have kept my mouth shut instead of saying I want more playing time.' Lenny said, 'Don't look at it that way, it could be a blessing in disguise.' And it just turned out to be a blessing in disguise."

Laimbeer arrived three months later, and then, in 1983, journeyman coach Chuck Daly hit town. For all his $1,500 suits, Daly was a lifer, recognizing the bottom line of the NBA: it was a players' game. "Chuck knew how to handle problems without getting his hands dirty," said Robinson. "Whenever we had a problem, Isiah solved it. Chuck didn't solve it. Chuck would say to Isiah, 'Get it straight.'"

The Pistons made the playoffs Daly's first year, the start of nine straight postseason appearances. More pieces began to fit. Dumars was drafted in '85; Mahorn, Salley, and Rodman suited up by '86. All the while GM Jack McCloskey was shuffling the deck, wheeling and dealing. By February 1988, following a trade for center James Edwards, the major players were all in place.

They had their fearless leader (Thomas), their ministers of defense (Laimbeer, Mahorn), and two perfect playmates for Thomas (Dumars and Johnson); they had a rebounder and designated stopper in Rodman, a shot blocker in Salley, a threat to score in or out with Edwards, and a strong low-post player in Adrian Dantley, eventually replaced by Mark Aguirre.

"There were no individuals," said Laimbeer. "If you can do it, do it. We'll feed you, we'll make you successful. If you are The Man, everybody will sacrifice their games for you. It's eighty-two games, forty-eight minutes a game. No letdown, no quitting, no nothing. You're paid to win, not to play."

Bumping and grinding, screening and preening, fouling and brawling, Laimbeer for twelve years in Detroit was willing to do whatever it took. If that meant headlocking Larry Bird in the 1987 playoffs, so be it. "Like him or not," said Lakers VP Jerry West upon Laimbeer's retirement in December 1993 at the age of thirty-six, "he's been a helluva player."

Along the way, the 6-11, 260-pound center totaled more than 10,000 career points and rebounds—one of only nineteen players in league history to reach five figures in both categories. He missed eight games in fourteen years. Two were for fighting.

"I was the enforcement section," Laimbeer said with no smile.

The Pistons' pride and work ethic defined a Detroit of many years ago: A city where the sweat and strain of union men stained assembly lines from Pontiac to River Rouge. The home of men like Henry Ford and Marvin Gaye, the music of Motown and Bob Seger, a city where Walter Reuther and Jimmy Hoffa made a stand, a city struggling to find itself, to rebound, all boarded up, pillaged and plundered for decades by crooked public officials, long divided by race. It was those defiant Pistons clubs of the late 1980s, like the Tigers in '68, that helped hold the city together, if only for an hour or two, forty-one nights a year, when twenty thousand fans would pour into the Pontiac Silverdome, as warm and comforting as an airplane hangar. The Pistons led the NBA in attendance from 1983 to 1988, then from 1988 until 1993 sold every seat in the Palace, averaging 21,454 per game.

"I used to say not only do I risk my body but I risk my mind every day of my job because I was so focused and driven," Laimbeer said. "Isiah used to call it gambling, gambling with your mind, the well-being of your mind."

Gambling with your mind.

"We fought about ways to motivate our teammates, ways to win games," he went on. "Everybody was different. Everybody had, as Chuck used to say, 'the right buttons to push.' Basically, Isiah and I would bounce ideas off of each other. He had part of the team under his . . . I won't say *wing*, that sounds so condescending. I would say he had certain players on the team that were his responsibility to make sure they were prepared."

Such as?

"For Isiah? He had Sal [Salley]. He had a lot of guys, nine or ten. Some guys, Joe [Dumars] pretty much managed himself. I had Vinnie. I had 'Horn . . . Mahorn you had to attack his pride. He was a fat slob when we brought him in. He was a presence, but he came from an organization [that was] every man for himself. He was a worthless guy and turned himself into a fine player for the Pistons.

"Salley was another one, came in with the reputation of a nightclub entertainer. He was in the NBA to get a bunch of money to further his personal life. You always had to stay on John not to let his mind wander."

And Rodman?

"You never had to yell at Dennis. You had to yell at Dennis for the bonehead plays. You never had to motivate him. You never had to question his work ethic. He would just get caught up in his own world at times. Which didn't happen very often. It happens much more now."

Dumars?

"Joe was great, quiet and great. He competed like a son of a bitch. He was mentally tough and smart and came in playing defense first. A perfect fit."

Vinnie?

"Vinnie was a guy you had to pump him up, get him out of the doldrums because unfortunately he was in a position that he was not going to be the star guard because Isiah was there, and then Joe came along. Never an All-Star. Should have been an All-Star."

Edwards?

"Edwards was basically the kind of guy who floated around the league, didn't care. We got him and told him basically, 'Hey, we're playing, you're going to play with us or don't play.' I think a lot of our ability to compete at such a high level rubbed off on the rest of the players, and if they didn't follow, they were embarrassed.

"When Aguirre came in, it was a perfect example. Isiah, myself, and I think Vinnie had dinner with him the first night and just laid it out. 'Hey, this is what we're about. This is where we're going. This is how we operate. You want to play our game, fine, we'll treat you as a teammate, an equal, and look out for you and be your friend. If you don't play that game, we're going to be your worst enemies.' We were very blunt. If somebody got hot, Isiah would say, 'Everybody go screen for Vinnie. I ain't passing you the ball. I'm passing the ball to Vinnie.'"

They gambled with their minds, risked bottomless despair, unspeakable agony in hopes of winning a title. When it came on the night of May 26, 1987, in a hellhole known as Boston Garden, oh, how they suffered. Game five of the Eastern Finals. The night Bird stole the ball, stole what should have been a simple, game-ending inbounds pass by Isiah. Passed it falling out-of-bounds to Dennis Johnson. Layup. Series turned in Boston's favor.

When Laimbeer got home he sat alone on the dock behind his Bloomfield Hills home until sunrise. Dumars stayed up in the dark, lying in bed, staring a hole in the ceiling.

"All the lights were off in my house," recalled Dumars. "It was like I was in mourning. Didn't eat. Didn't drink. I basically stayed up all night. And not only did you have to go through it that night, you had to live with it for an entire summer."

And what about the next season, June 19, 1988, in Los Angeles? Game six of the NBA Finals. Pistons ahead 3–2. No Detroit fan will ever forget the "foul" call on Laimbeer with one second left that put Kareem Abdul-Jabbar on the line. Two free throws later it was 103–102, L.A. Two nights later the margin was three points, 108–105, and the Lakers were champs. Thomas and Laimbeer, the spiritual leaders, grabbed some champagne from the winning locker room, stumbled back to theirs, and headed for the shower where they sat down naked, alone, and cried.

"My mind broke at that point," Laimbeer recalled.

Added Dumars, "Those things shape and form and produce what you see in the end."

Champions. A 15-2 tear through the playoffs in 1989, finishing with a four-game sweep of L.A. A 15-5 playoff run the next season, ending in a five-game pounding of Portland.

"We'll always know we're champions," said Laimbeer. "We

didn't fail. If we had failed, we would hate ourselves. That's the key. We didn't fail."

Isiah Thomas' team went down in history as two-time champs.

On the 8:11 A.M. Metro-North train traveling to New York from Connecticut, the daily ritual unfolds. Most commuters digest the morning paper. A few just stare silently into space. Every so often, a pair of eyes glances up at the face of Isiah Thomas. The first thing that strikes you about it is the right eye, black as coal, boring in like an F-15 fighter. Subtle signs of age are visible in the lines and creases etched across the once-cherubic face. A tiny scar near the left eyelid; another jagged line near the nose. Beyond the eyes, however, the face is difficult to decipher. Only the hint of a smile dances at the corners of the mouth.

Reversed out of a black turtleneck, in thin white type, is the ad copy—pithy and punchy. To summarize the man, like a radio jingle, is a difficult task. But here, the words ring true, and Isiah, the public Isiah, is brought to life:

"Nothing but net. Banging with the big boys. Swishing and dishing. He did whatever it took to bring home two NBA championships. Making up for his lack of size with a towering talent. A keen intellect. Above all, an indomitable will to win. And today these skills make him a star in an even bigger arena. Building a bankrupt printing business into a $170 million winner. Launching a successful NBA franchise, the Toronto Raptors. His winning plays these days are all about creating wealth and opportunity. One-on-one, anybody?"

Below in bold yellow type comes the kicker: Isiah Thomas picked up his first copy of *Forbes* in the Indiana University library in 1979.

Laimbeer on Isiah:

"Fearless. He was fearless. He controlled the ball. He made great decisions. Isiah was way ahead of everybody else, and that's a burden of responsibility that's difficult to carry. It's just mentally demanding because you have to keep certain people happy in the picture of winning the game."

Few did this job any better. During thirteen NBA seasons, Thomas averaged 19 points per game. He retired in 1994 as the

Pistons' all-time leader in eight major categories, including games (979), points (18,822), and assists (9,061). An NBA All-Star twelve straight years, eleven as a starter, he was named All-Star MVP twice and was MVP of the 1990 Finals.

But numbers don't define him as much as memorable achievement, the way this man who shot a respectable 45 percent during his career would be far more dangerous in the fourth quarter, the last minutes of a close game, a big game. In the NBA Finals, he scored 25 in one quarter against the Lakers . . . 16 in the fourth quarter of game one against Portland . . . 16 in ninety-four seconds in the last two minutes of a deciding fifth game in the first round against the Knicks.

The Pistons lost that game in overtime and Thomas was so mad, he stormed out of Joe Louis Arena in downtown Detroit, got into his car, and was halfway to Chicago—still in his uniform—before he thought, "What the hell am I doing?"

Said Daly, "If Isiah were five inches taller, he'd be the best basketball player in NBA history."

With his looks, with his intellect, he should have been a national icon. But he was seldom mentioned in the same breath as Jordan, Magic, and Bird. He has explained that he couldn't afford to be as image conscious as them. He was too busy making up for his size. He had to be tougher, nastier. There were no six-foot franchise players before him. Had he been a nice guy, he would have been Michael Adams.

"I didn't want to be the guy endorsing the products," Thomas once told a *New York Times* reporter. "I wanted to be the guy who owned the company." In other words, he wasn't trying to play the fan-friendly PR game.

As it is, he is headed to the Hall of Fame. The youngest of seven brothers and two sisters, he grew up haunted by hunger, almost living the life of the homeless on Chicago's bleak West Side.

"Abandoned buildings. Nothing to eat. Sleeping on the floor at night," remembers older brother Larry Thomas. "We are taught you only need necessities to survive: food, shelter, and clothing. We never had any food. We never had any clothes. We never had any shelter." He looked down at his hands before speaking again. "I still bite my nails today, and people say that a person who bites his nails is nervous. No, that's not the reason. I started biting my nails because I was hungry."

Hungry?

"At a very young age I would bite my nails, eat my skin," he said. "It was really cannibalistic. I was eating myself to survive and would get me a drink of water to wash it down."

As best she could, Mary Thomas tried to protect her children, especially her baby, but Isiah Lord Thomas III invariably saw crimes no child should ever see. It's not hard to imagine the silent vows to leave that hell forever. "When you're on the bottom, you can't go anywhere but up," brother Larry said.

Today, Isiah is at the top, a millionaire many times over. Despite an unhappy departure from Detroit to run the expansion Toronto Raptors franchise, he remains a hometown hero in Detroit. A savior hailed as much for charity work as his on-court heroics. Pistons fans still recount those championship nights like yesterday, still chuckle at those cute Detroit Edison commercials that ended with mother Mary exclaiming, "Oh, Isiah!"

Still, he complained the media never bought into him, the way it did for the others. It blamed him for leading a walkout off the court after the Pistons were swept by Chicago in the 1991 conference finals, for defending Rodman's "If he were black, he'd be just another good guy" 1987 assessment of Bird after "The Steal" series ended in Boston. It became skeptical of him when his name was splashed across the TV screen and newspapers in reports in June 1990 that his name had surfaced in a federal sports-gambling probe of one of the nation's biggest bookmaking operations. It was the very same day the Bad Boys returned to Detroit to celebrate their second NBA title.

"For thirteen years," Thomas told the *Detroit Free Press,* "I went through lies and innuendos, and much of it was completely untrue."

Much as Thomas would argue otherwise, a big part of his problem was The Other Isiah. One was all sugar and spice who smiled so nice. The other was darker, unpredictable, the cold and calculating twin.

"He's so smart, so devious," said a close friend who has known Thomas since he first came to Detroit. "You can never react to what he's going to do because he already knows how you're going to react, and he's three steps ahead of you. He scares me, he scares the hell out of me because I never know what he's thinking."

Former Detroit TV sports reporter Virg Jacques, now a news

anchor in another city, recalled getting a taste of Thomas' legendary temper in the parking lot after an informal Pistons practice in October 1990. Jacques was walking toward his car with Thomas trailing when Isiah spoke.

"He said something to me as if he wanted to talk," recalled Jacques, a former Big Ten football player who, at 6-2, 195, was more than a match for Thomas.

"Ah, forget it," said Thomas.

"Yeah, forget it," said Jacques.

As Jacques started back toward his car, he saw Thomas walking toward him, staring blankly ahead. Jacques asked Thomas what he was doing.

"The next thing I know, Isiah is choking me," said Jacques. "Then he jumps in his car and starts screaming, 'I'll kill you, I'll ruin your ass,' and takes off at ninety miles per hour."

Jacques filed assault-and-battery charges against Thomas. They were later dropped after Thomas apologized. Two years later, while walking on a beach in Hawaii, Jacques says he ran into a former teammate of Thomas', who mentioned the incident.

"Why didn't you beat the hell out of the son of a bitch?" asked the former teammate.

For all his complexities, a single thread tied the two Isiahs together. From the championships he cherished, to the games he loved to play, Thomas wanted to win—at everything. "Isiah had to have it all, man," said his close friend. "That's his thing."

And to have it all, some say, Thomas sought—and got—access to the Big Boys. Men of wealth and power in the worlds of business, politics, and yes, organized crime.

By the fall of 1995, only the memory of Thomas remained. The current Pistons club had missed the playoffs three years running and combined for a pitiful 48-116 record from 1993 to 1995. Still, Collins believed a resurrection was on its way.

In many ways, Collins was thinking about himself in a similar vein. For much of his life, he had reaped the rewards of a single-minded toughness: in college at Illinois State in the early seventies, he was a human tornado—barreling down the hardcourt, hair flying, all arms and legs, suddenly pulling up to drop a twenty-footer. In three college seasons, Collins averaged a gaudy 29.1 points per game at ISU and was a consensus All-American for Robinson, the first black head coach at the Division I level and now a fixture in the Pistons front office for 20-plus years.

As Collins liked to explain, it was Robinson who taught him three important lessons in life—about courage, toughness, and himself. The first, said Collins, came from climbing a rope to the top of the gym before every practice. The second by boxing a few rounds before he ever put on a uniform. The third? "Will used to make me stand in front of a mirror and look at myself," Collins said. "He'd say, 'How do you think you look?' I didn't look like much, but I'd say, 'Okay, I guess.' Then he'd put a basketball under my arm and say, 'How do you look now?' I smiled every time."

Collins went on to star for the U.S. Olympic team in 1972. He made two free throws to put the U.S. ahead by a point with seconds remaining, only to have the notorious and controversial replay of the Russians' final inbounds sequence result in Aleksandr Belov's layup that handed the Americans their first Olympic defeat in the sport.

Collins went on to the pros, drafted in the first round by Philadelphia. He played for eight seasons, averaging 18 points per game and making the Finals once (a six-game loss to Portland in 1977) before his knees and feet gave out. His was an old-school style of play attached to a new NBA body—a 6-6 guard fully capable of taking you inside or out, tough as a three-day beard.

Now, like his team, Collins was bringing some serious change to his life. In April 1995 he had been lured back into coaching by Davidson with plenty of money and the promise of complete command over all aspects of basketball operations.

To critics, Collins was a risky choice. Three seasons as head coach in Chicago preceding Phil Jackson had ended in his dismissal in 1989, despite a record of 137-109. Rumors as to why ranged from his 13-17 playoff mark, to the inability to get past Detroit, to league-wide whispers that Collins' marriage was in trouble.

Had Collins been able to hold on in Chicago, waited out the development of Scottie Pippen and Horace Grant and the maturation of Michael Jordan, he might not have left. He might have won four championships and been in Jackson's shoes right now, hailed as one of the sport's genius coaches, instead of banging at the door of the elite-coaches club.

There was Jackson. There was Pat Riley, now in Miami. There was the NBA title–less but highly respected Larry Brown in Indiana. There was the low-key but two-time defending champ, Rudy Tomjanovich, in Houston. And Mike Fratello, who, like Collins, benefited from a few seasons telling it like it is on television, in Cleveland.

Without question, though, Jackson and Riley, complete opposites, were at the top of the heap, the role models for Collins. The argument could be made that both built their reputations and crafted their distinct public images on the backs of great players, Jordan and Magic Johnson, without much argument the two best non-centers in the history of the sport. Yet Collins had also coached Jordan, without reaching the NBA Finals. Like them or not, Riley and Jackson had won when they had the talent. And they'd proved capable of winning many games, if not more championships, without those meal tickets.

Riley took over a dispirited Knicks franchise and gave it a new identity, four years of contention, of epic battles against Jordan, of sellouts that allowed management to raise ticket prices every year. The Knicks in 1995 established the $1,000 courtside seat that Spike Lee groused about but shelled out the bucks for anyway. Then Riley, flush with success, drunk with leverage, cashed his own ticket. With another year left on his original Knicks contract, while officially still the Knicks coach, Riley passed along a list of demands to Miami's upstart owner, Micky Arison, through a friend, sports entrepreneur Dick Butura.

The list, a fourteen-point memo, included immediate 10 percent ownership, 10 percent more during a $15-million, five-year contract, plus $300-a-day per diem, housing compensation, and other assorted benefits. Riley also wanted control of the operation. The memo was dated June 5, and Riley resigned from the Knicks ten days later. The Knicks ultimately charged the Heat with tampering, and league sources said David Stern was prepared to boot Riley out of the league for a year until the Knicks realized they were better off dropping the case and taking a first-round draft pick as compensation.

What the Riley case bared was the league's subculture of backroom dealing, little of which adhered to a professional respect for a signed contract. Be it David Falk arranging a trade, or one agent hijacking another's player, this was the way a fair amount of NBA business got done.

As if to demonstrate that to Madison Square Garden president Dave Checketts, the minute it became public knowledge that Riley was gone, his phone began to ring. "Friends" of at least two renowned coaches under contract called to suggest Checketts make a play for their man. One of those men was Atlanta's Lenny Wilkens, holder of the record for most coaching victories and the 1996 Olympic coach. The other was Phil Jackson, the onetime Knick supersub whose friend said he was prepared to desert Jordan for the chance to coach—and cash in with—the Knicks.

Checketts, not wishing to get dragged before Stern, called Atlanta and Chicago and asked if they would negotiate. The answer on both fronts was no.

As Collins prepared to start over in Detroit, Jackson, in the final year of his contract, readied himself for another training camp with the now legendary Bulls. His new book—*Sacred Hoops, Spiritual Lessons of a Hardwood Warrior*—was out, underscoring his philosophical differences with Riley. Whereas Riley preached psychological mind games and extremely tough paternal love— the kind he got from his old man, a failed pro ballplayer turned school janitor—Jackson was a self-described Zen Christian stressing awareness, compassion, and enlightenment. Riley wanted to lead his players to the promised land. Jackson hoped to guide them in the right direction.

For instance, when the insecure Pippen refused to play the final 1.8 seconds of a 1994 playoff game against Riley's Knicks, Jackson said nothing in the locker room. He waited to see what Pippen's teammates would do. Finally, the veteran center, Bill Cartwright, confronted Pippen in front of everyone, demanding to know, with tears in his eyes, how Pippen could cheat his own teammates that way. "That's what a coach hopes, that a team is capable of regulating itself," said Jackson.

For Riley, it was more a matter of law and order, crime and punishment. He set work standards based on his own and expected every player to live by them. He was unwilling to relinquish control. In his last season playing in New York for Riley, Doc Rivers got into it with the coach one day in Riley's office. Rivers, coming back from knee surgery, wanted to be traded to a place where he would play. Riley wanted him to stay with the Knicks as insurance. While the team waited outside on a bus bound for the airport, the two screamed at each other, airing it out until each was out of breath.

"You're like me, stubborn," Riley said, sensing he couldn't bully the veteran. "You're gonna coach in this league."

"I don't know," Rivers said. "I'm a family guy. Look at you, all wound up in this. Working twenty-hour days. You have no friends."

What struck Rivers as he told the story a year later was that Riley didn't even argue with that.

Jackson and Riley couldn't stand each other, or what the other represented. But both were good, damn good, and at no time was it ever more obvious than in 1994. That was the season Jordan sat out completely and everyone figured the Bulls were dead. They still won 55 games, an amazing achievement given the sudden loss of a franchise player. In the second round of the playoffs, in game five in New York, they had the Knicks dead to rights until referee Hue Hollins gift-wrapped the game and the series to the Knicks with an outrageous and flimsy endgame foul against Pippen, who'd barely brushed Hubert Davis during a wild jump shot.

To this day, the call gnaws at Jackson, who might have won the whole thing that year without Jordan. Instead, Riley got to take a flawed Knick team to within a victory of the championship. It only enhanced Riley's reputation more, leading to his precedent-setting arrangement in Miami.

Sitting in a hotel lobby one day in the fall of 1995, after making the morning-show rounds to promote his book, Jackson was explaining why he had signed on to the Bulls' acquisition of Rodman, former Bad Boy and current Wild Man, as the team's power forward. In the previous spring's playoffs, Rodman had subverted San Antonio with an assortment of outrageous acts, including removing his sneakers on the bench in the middle of a game.

Ironically, in his book, Jackson had spoken of a similar incident during his CBA days in the eighties. He was coaching the Albany Patroons during the 1985 playoffs when the team's leading scorer, Frankie Sanders, demanded and received a raise from the team's owner. Wrote Jackson: "Sanders became more audacious after he got his raise, grousing continually about how I distributed playing time. During the first round of the playoffs, I got fed up and took him out. Moments later, I looked down the bench and saw he'd taken off his shoes.

" 'What are you doing?' I screamed. 'Put your shoes back on.'

" 'No,' he said defiantly. 'My foot hurts.'

" 'Your foot doesn't hurt. Put your shoes on. I want you back in the game.'

"Sanders gave me a cold look and walked off."

Disgusted by such behavior, convinced he would never make it to the NBA, Jackson decided one day in 1986 that he'd had enough of coaching and would enroll in law school. The next day, the telephone rang. It was Jerry Krause, the Bulls' portly GM. Would he, Jackson, like to be an assistant in Chicago for Doug Collins?

Jackson jumped at the chance. And for Collins, the sands in the hourglass began to fall. Now, six seasons later, he was getting the chance to refine his act. He would still be a hard-ass, like Riley, but hoped to take something from Jackson, the man who replaced him. He hoped he could back off, if only from time to time.

Asked about his personal state of affairs at the time he left Chicago, Collins carefully settled on "unsettled"—an indirect reference to a separation from his wife and an even more recent breakup with an Olympic gold medalist. TV work had been rewarding, though, but one or two nights a week at Turner, seven months a year, was not enough to quench his thirst. He found himself becoming more and more a stage father, living life through his kids. "Basically, my life was trying to run and see Chris, run and see Kelly," Collins said. "Your kids start providing all the excitement in your life. That puts too much pressure on them to provide the excitement."

Back on the bench, the old energy was returning, as he fueled himself on a mix of caffeine and diet Coke, no fewer than six twenty-ouncers a day, and pure, natural gas. Already thin enough to slip down a laundry chute, Collins still worked out like a madman, measuring weight and body fat like diamonds on a scale. And yet, his handsome, boyish face carried a tennis tan; his eyes were bright and clear.

"This has been a year for me to get to know myself better than

I've ever known myself," he said. "To really pour myself into this, work on every other phase of my life. I'm trying to solidify all the things that represent love in my life; that's what I want at the core." He paused a second. "I've spent a year by myself. I've had no personal life. And you know what? When you really start enjoying time alone, then those times when you're with your wife and loved ones become the greatest, they really do, because they're by choice. There's a sort of contentment."

Such introspection had impressed the team's majority owner. Almost overnight, Collins and Davidson had bonded. "I'm closer to him in a very short period of time than I have been with the other coaches," said Davidson. "Doug is a terrific person. I just admire him."

Davidson knew a thing or two about success. According to the most recent study in *Financial World* magazine, in 1995 the Pistons were the third most valuable club in the NBA ($186 million), generating $28.5 million in operating income. The vast majority of that money ($19.7 million) came from the Palace, far and away the most profitable facility in the league. In the last two years alone, *FW* estimated the value of the Pistons had risen 20 percent, ranking it the twelfth most valuable franchise overall in sports.

Unlike Jerry Jones, the owner of *FW*'s No. 1 rated franchise, the Dallas Cowboys, Davidson is soft-spoken and mediaphobic to a fault. His flagship company, Guardian Industries, is the world's leading producer of "float glass" or "flat glass" used in the construction and automotive industries. Guardian's slogan—"A Company of Vision"—seems cut right from an NBA handbook, and with more than $1 billion in annual sales and facilities in twelve countries, the two have a lot in common.

A University of Michigan graduate, Davidson, a self-made multimillionaire, began rescuing ailing medical companies before taking over Guardian Glass, an automotive glass manufacturer, in 1957. Today, the privately held company owns more than fifty glass, plastics, and fiberglass installation plants around the world, plus Palace Sports & Entertainment, which counts the Detroit Vipers (hockey), Detroit Neon (indoor soccer), and the Pine Knob Music Theatre (the country's top outdoor venue) among its holdings.

A tennis fanatic, Davidson prides himself and his company on old-fashioned values. Loyalty, quality, service, and product development are Guardian staples. One of the league's most powerful and respected voices, a former chairman of the NBA Board of Governors, Davidson has served as David Stern's confidant and sounding board since the early eighties. "I talk to him on a weekly basis," he said.

Guardian's world headquarters rises high above a hill overlooking the Pistons practice facility. It's an architectural marvel, defined by shimmering panes rising from a granite base, and a stairstep array of glass panels peaking just above the lobby entrance. Inside, the mood is soft and elegant. Art Tatum on piano. Sunday morning at a modern-art museum.

"Oh, you must be very lucky," said a stern-faced secretary, greeting a visitor. "Mr. Davidson never speaks to the press. People have worked in this town for more than twenty years and never talked to him."

On this day, Davidson sat in a hard-backed chair, backlit by late-morning light pouring into his spacious first-floor office. Off in the distance, the Palace walls were visible. Davidson attends every home game. Sitting alone along the baseline, a short jumper from the Pistons bench, he rarely meddled and never shouted. He just showed up, invariably in his lucky blue blazer, white shirt, and gray slacks.

"I guess my basic feelings haven't changed because I got into this not as a business venture, which is the wrong approach," he said. "I still look at it as a fun thing, one of the fun things in my life. I try to keep it that way. I stay away, pretty much, not from the business decisions, but the contracts, salary caps. I stay with the basketball and get my enjoyment that way."

For his part, Collins knew he could enjoy the fact that one part of his championship puzzle was already in place. One look at No. 33 was all it took.

If ever an athlete seemed groomed for greatness, it was Hill. He seemed to fit all the NBA-on-NBC demographics. The short, melodic name; the soaring, made-for-TV game; the long, lean GQ style and respectful manner that made mothers blush. Then there was that degree from Duke, the NCAA championship rings, and the perception that he was a superstar everyone wanted to play with and be around. Christian Laettner may have made that miracle shot for Duke back in '92 against Kentucky in the semifinals, but never forget who made the perfect, fifty-foot pass from out-of-bounds. Grant Hill.

"This kid is for real and you'd be foolish to not try and show the world what we've got here," said Pistons president Tom Wilson.

In response to having his face plastered all over town, Hill had drawn back just a bit. "Pretty much I let everyone know what I want them to know," he said. "There are certain things you keep private."

Like the drop-dead black model he was dating. Or showing up late one night at the hottest after-hours club in Detroit, a wild Woodward Avenue haunt. To lower his public profile, Hill purposely skipped every "Do you have a girlfriend?" question posed by fan magazines. "I'm not going to show up anywhere unless it's with Mrs. Hill," he said.

The truth was that Hill's heart belonged to two women, "the two Janets," as he called them. Mother Janet, the celebrated Washington power broker and Wellesley classmate of Hillary Rodham Clinton's. And singer Janet, as in Janet Jackson.

For years, Hill had secretly carried an Olympic-sized torch for the sensuous pop star. He admitted that if he and the lovely Ms. Jackson ever did something of a social duet, it would be *Love Story* all over again. "I think if I see her, I'm asking her to marry me," he said, laughing. "The worst thing she can do is say no."

He was raised as the only child of a "very prissy, very spoiled" New Orleans–born mother and former star NFL running back. To set the record straight about his own family, Hill had already written an absorbing little autobiography called *Change the Game*. In it, he attacked those who dismissed his parents as modern-day Huxtables, TV-sitcom fare. Black families, Hill wrote, can't have two parents with good jobs and respectful children without abuse. "Or at least my family isn't normal for black people," he said. In another section, Hill took a shot at blacks who view clothes, cars, and homes, even a pattern of speech, through the prism of race. "When African-Americans become successful, to some blacks they automatically become white," he wrote. "As a kid, my mom drilled me on the correct use of English, and now I have command of the language. Because of that, I'm not black enough for some members of my race. Well, I've been black all my life. I speak the way I've been taught."

And he was speaking out, defending the way he'd been raised

as the right way. He would not apologize for being a throwback, a young star without the attitude of the street. "You can be a competitor, a gamer, a winner, and you can show some respect, too," said Hill. "That's what 'Changing the Game' is all about."

For Collins, changing the temperament of a team grown accustomed to losing would not be easy.

Up front, veteran Otis Thorpe looked good; he might prove a pillar of a power forward. Then again, maybe not. Houston had a world of God-given talent, but what about his heart? And the rest of the roster, well, it looked iffy at best—journeymen centers Mark West and Eric Leckner, point guard Lindsey Hunter, forward Terry Mills, athletes whose every positive was offset by a serious hole in their game.

"I don't know who Lindsey Hunter is yet," said Collins, picking out one example. "He's got tremendous talent, but I've got to figure out how he fits in." A couple of rookies looked promising. Theo Ratliff, second all-time in the NCAA in blocked shots, could jump through the roof. And the second-round pick, forward Don Reid of Georgetown, played as if his life depended on it, which it did. His $200,000, one-year contract wasn't guaranteed.

Collins at least knew right from the start how he would build. The cornerstones were Hill and Houston. Hill was coming off a sensational first year—Co–Rookie of the Year, a spot on Dream Team III, a season in which he averaged 19.9 points per game and became the first rookie in NBA history to lead the league in All-Star votes. Houston, in his second season, had found himself in the last twenty-four games of the season averaging nearly 25 points per game. That he could score was a given, but did he have the will to play defense, to play without fear?

Did he have it inside? That was the true measure of a champion, as Joe Dumars well knew.

At 7:15 P.M., the Pistons trooped onto the court for their opening exhibition, moving with the benign neglect of a pampered prince. Hill emerged from the tunnel blowing bubbles with his gum, followed by an athlete for the ages, head high, the lone connection to those banners above. Collins knew that, to survive, Dumars had been "forced to detach" himself from the team the past few years. "There were so many people coming in and out, it was hard to get a read on what direction we were going," said

Dumars. "It's tough to lead when you don't know where you're going."

"This is going to be a hard season for Joe," said Collins. "I'm sorry but that's how it is. I need him to lead out on the floor and the dressing room. I have great respect for this man, but he has to show the others what it takes to win."

Few athletes were more suited to the challenge than Joe Dumars III. Few players in any sport engendered more respect than this eleven-year pro. He entered the season the fourth-leading scorer in Pistons history, a four-time All-NBA defensive selection, and the MVP of the club's first championship, when he averaged 27 points in the four-game sweep of the Lakers.

Dumars, from the verdant banks of northwest Louisiana, the all-time leading scorer at McNeese State, the tireless champion of children's causes, wasn't about to brag about himself. "I've always known who I am," he said in his silky voice. "I've always been comfortable with how I am. I've never wanted to change that."

Certainly, he could have sold out, cashed in, woofed his way onto *Arsenio*. Dumars knew better. "For an organization to have success, you have to have diversity," he said. "You can't have all chest-bumping, high-fivin', trash-talkin'. You have to have a mix. I'm part of that mix."

Dumars played it cool. His talk show of choice was *Charlie Rose*. "I'm just going to try to carry myself with a certain amount of class," he said. "I don't expect anybody to be like me."

Joe Dumars II drove an eighteen-wheeler most of his life, leaving a little brick house on Martin Luther King Street in Natchitoches, Louisiana, before dawn and heading out for long cross-country hauls from one Kroger supermarket to another. One by one, when his sons came of age, he delivered a summer "vacation" they would never forget.

"I'm gonna bring you out and let you see what the real world is like," he'd say. "Have an appreciation for what's out there."

"Out there" were long, searing days loading and unloading hundred-pound sacks of rice and flour.

"When I got to about fifteen, it was my turn," Dumars said one afternoon after practice. "When you're fifteen, you want to impress your father. How strong you are. I'm grabbing the bags, just slinging 'em the first two, three stops. He never said a word. Just looked at me and smiled."

At times like these, his arms afire, the words of wisdom would come. "Son, listen," the senior Dumars would begin, "you don't know what kind of hurt you can inflict upon someone just by a look, by looking down on someone. . . ."

"Mom and Pop just tried to be sensitive to everyone they encountered," Dumars said. "They had encountered such discrimination, and I don't mean racial. They encountered that. They encountered social discrimination, *human* discrimination."

Joe and Ophelia Dumars rose above it. They would not allow bitterness into their home, into their children's lives. No fingers were pointed at Southern politicians, at the grim realities for black Americans. Which explained why on Saturday, June 16, 1990, on a picture-perfect day in Natchitoches, more than four hundred friends and neighbors jammed the Ben Johnson Auditorium. A lengthy bout with diabetes had robbed Joe Dumars II of his feet, then his legs. Finally, his life. He died at sixty-six of a stroke.

His son the basketball star was in Portland, one game from a second championship, when Pop died. Bill Davidson's private plane was waiting as Dumars called home. "Stay with the team," his mother said. "Your brothers and sisters are all here. Finish what you have to finish."

In the last game, Dumars felt the power of his influence on his team. "I felt like they were playing for me, to help me get home," he said. And when it was over, when Vinnie Johnson nailed the last-second shot, Joe D went home and buried his dad. At the funeral, everyone from the sheriff to the maid at the Holiday Inn showed up to pay their respects. When Ophelia and the family walked down the aisle, a huge crowd rose up. Later, arms raised, they swayed back and forth as the First Baptist Choir sang "The Lord Is Holy" in honor of her man.

More than two hundred cars—the biggest cortege local police had ever seen—made the trip to the cemetery. As the casket was carried toward the family, an honor guard from nearby Fort Polk held an American flag over the coffin. There was a twenty-one-gun salute before a lone soldier blew taps.

What remains from that steamy summer day for Joe Dumars III are the emotions of championship gain and permanent loss. The championships, alas, stayed with him, too, the sense of sport at its highest level. Blowing downcourt with Isiah on the break, knowing full well what his partner would do next.

"It was scary," he said. "I would just sit there and say, 'He's going left, he's going left.'" He wanted nothing more than to do this again, to pass it on to another frisky band of Pistons before he joined Isiah, Laimbeer, and the others in the history book. He wanted nothing more than to help Collins and Hill bring the Pistons back to life. Back to where they might be considered an NBA asset, a team David Stern wouldn't hesitate to send on one of his celebrated star treks abroad.

Something like the one the two-time defending champion Houston Rockets were about to embark on, in one of the unlikeliest hoop venues of all.

9

King and His Court

Domestic insurrection sufficiently contained, King David Stern soon resumed the entertainment portion of the NBA preseason and the league's manifest destiny abroad. Next conquest: the British Empire.

On the night of October 19, in an arena modified for basketball in London's remote Docklands section, the NBA rolled into town with its two-time defending champion Houston Rockets and the league's assortment of trademark accoutrements. For starters, there was the woolly mascot swinging from the rafters, the ref on stilts, the trampoline dunkers, and the woman lying on her back with spinning basketballs on her knees, elbows, stomach, and fingers and toes. For the more competitively inclined, there was a ring-toss exhibition, featuring the moving target of a bald man with a toilet plunger affixed to his head.

Between earsplitting rock music and circus acts, there were even some fast breaks run, some jump shots made. Welcome to the NBA's international playground, the 1995 McDonald's Championships.

In places such as these the NBA was doing its most difficult but ultimately rewarding work. It was annexing the world, lining its pockets, exporting one of the hottest American products. The globalization of a sport once mired in industrial towns such as Fort Wayne and Syracuse made it feel larger-than-life. Larger, certainly, than American life. And Stern was seldom not in the mood to climb the stage, spread the word.

The official welcoming of the news media to London was made that night by the tournament's ruling triumvirate: Stern, deputy commissioner Russ Granik, and their mysterious partner in global imperialism, Borislav Stankovic, the seventy-year-old European Stern.

Seated between his American allies for the customary state-of-the-sport press conference, the gray-haired, bearish general secretary of the International Basketball Federation (FIBA) opened the floor to questions and was immediately confronted by an angry executive named Pedro Ferrandiz from the longtime Spanish powerhouse Real Madrid. Pausing only to allow a companion to translate Spanish to English, Ferrandiz railed at the injustice of Real Madrid's not being allowed to play all three of its foreign-born players.

"Real Madrid thinks the rules in which FIBA teams have to compete against NBA teams are unfair," Ferrandiz began. "If NBA teams can play with full rosters and FIBA teams cannot, it is conceivable that it will be impossible to beat an NBA club."

(Most FIBA federations allowed their teams two foreigners. Spain allowed three. As a result, it had to sit one of its players for the McDonald's Championships. For its first game against England's Sheffield Sharks, Real defiantly benched American Joe Arlauckas, its best player.)

As Ferrandiz droned on, Stern and Granik began to shift uncomfortably. The press conference, scheduled for thirty minutes, was already one-third over, and no one could get a word in edgewise. The Spaniard seemed capable of talking straight through the weekend, but after proposing that teams be allowed to field full rosters at future NBA/FIBA events, the red-faced Ferrandiz brought his filibuster to a merciful end. But there he stood, waiting for an acceptable response.

Stern looked across the table at Granik. Stankovic looked at Stern. Then the commissioner put his hand on the general secretary's back. "It's all yours, boss!" he said.

This all came across as politically charged slapstick, yet some would also say it was highly symbolic of how Stern had made what his many admirers considered to be his most brilliant coup. While convincing Stankovic to open the door to the stage of his wildest dreams, Stern simply assured him that the NBA was no threat, only a rich relative who wanted to cut him in on the family business.

And that Stankovic was still the ceremonial leader of the global basketball movement.

Certainly, FIBA was better off financially to have Stern's stars and marketing machine behind it. At the 1994 World Championships, for instance, records were set for attendance, and FIBA's net proceeds exceeded $2.5 million. Before its marriage to the NBA, FIBA did not even have enough money to foot the travel expenses for its teams to play in European and world tournaments.

What did the NBA get? Plenty, besides international exposure that had created all kinds of licensing and television breakthroughs. The 1994 World Championships had been scheduled for Belgrade until the Balkan conflict erupted. By no coincidence, it wound up in Toronto one year before the NBA would be launching its Canadian invasion with the Toronto Raptors and Vancouver Grizzlies. In addition, the NBA handled all marketing and sales for the two-week event.

"David was brilliant in the way he basically took over FIBA, the marketing and everything," said Marc Fleisher, who became familiar with the overseas markets by representing several European players. "He sort of made it his toy. David made Boris feel important and powerful, but in reality, the NBA runs European basketball."

He meant abstractly, not day to day. Stern wasn't interested in European expansion. Not yet, anyway. Not when Stankovic's organization was planning to launch its own twenty-four-club, so-called European Super League by September 1996. Stern had enough problems running his league in the States. He knew, as Fleisher said, that he had the best of both continents, given the free exposure the NCAA gave future NBA stars and FIBA's willingness to showcase them on the world stage. The last thing Stern needed was to complicate matters, by trying to manage teams in parts of the world where, as Pedro Ferrandiz had demonstrated, nationalism and ethnic pride could turn a harmless press conference into the worst United Nations free-for-all.

This was a job better left to Stankovic, who had lived all over

Europe, could speak seven languages, and had, by now, developed such a thick skin that even intense assertions that he rigged the 1995 European championships in Athens for his native Yugoslavia with scheduling favors and biased officials were met with a shrug and a plaintive, "What can I do?"

Nothing that time, except watch the bronze-winning Croats walk off the medal stand rather than participate in the crowning of the hated Yugoslavs as champions following their victory over Lithuania, whose team became so incensed by an American official's calls near the end of the game that it walked off the floor.

"I don't know how he does it," said Granik. "Everything is an argument over here."

"There are many, many problems," Stankovic agreed. "The NBA is one league, one country. In Europe, they don't even speak the same language."

Devotion on his part to Serbia was certainly understandable. His family was expelled from its home north of Belgrade during the German occupation in 1941, allowed two suitcases while fleeing to the city. Four years later, his father was seized by the puppet government of Marshal Tito and charged with being a collaborator with Gen. Draza Mihajlovic's Serbian nationalists, guerrilla fighters known as Chetniks. "My father was not so much in the war, but he was more of a politician, a moral supporter of the movement," Stankovic said.

In 1945, the senior Stankovic was rounded up, thrown into prison. "Then he was put on a wall and shot by a firing squad," Stankovic said. "He was forty-five. I was fifteen." He paused and his voice seemed to quiver. "All these years, that never goes away."

Stankovic went on to study veterinary medicine, but played basketball, a popular sport in Serbia. As a coach, he worked in several European countries. By 1972, he was deputy secretary general of FIBA, and four years later, he became its chief administrator.

In those days, FIBA was known as the International Amateur Basketball Federation, a flagrant contradiction since affiliated leagues in Italy, Spain, and elsewhere paid their players. The amateur title was for the sake of maintaining its influence within the Olympic community. The only players who were truly held as professionals were Americans, and they had no interest in international competitions. At least not until David Stern took command of the NBA.

"Sometime in 1986, Stern came to Europe, in Milan, for some games and we met for the first time," Stankovic said, sipping coffee between halves of a Rockets–Perth Wildcats McDonald's semifinal, while all around, his and Stern's well-heeled guests munched on catered food and sipped alcoholic drinks.

According to Stankovic, a willingness to do business, beginning with what was initially called the McDonald's Open, emerged from that first meeting. Two years later, in what he called "a special, extraordinary congress," FIBA voted to open its competitions to all and petition the IOC to correct what he termed "an impossible situation, morally." Two major countries voted against the move, the United States and the Soviet Union. Stern liked to point that out whenever complaints arose about the NBA's Olympic presence. In other words, Americans hadn't forced themselves on anyone. But the truth was that the NBA had worked Stankovic like an unrelenting Washington lobbyist, by making him offers he couldn't refuse.

In keeping with Stern's unofficial social policy of seeking power more than publicity, Granik claimed it was actually Stankovic who made the first move. "We were asked by friends of his if he could come and meet with us," he said. "He came in and said he thought it was time for FIBA to get rid of distinctions of amateur and professional, and that he couldn't do it in one shot, but in his mind, the best way was to start with some kind of tournament. Something officially sanctioned. We said, 'Great. If you can deliver the teams, we'll stage the event.'"

The deal was set, with FIBA to get 20 percent of all net proceeds. "I couldn't see anything wrong with the relationship," Stankovic said. "Maybe in a few years, with the marketing of television rights. But David has told me many, many times that he has no interest in expanding the NBA into Europe. The bottom line is that we are increasing the popularity of basketball. The television, marketing, media. And the most important thing is that the number of people playing basketball is increasing since we have had the NBA in our competitions."

The first was in October 1987. Stern made his maiden international stand with the McDonald's Open, a three-team event staged in Milwaukee that contrived a game between an American pro team, the Bucks, and the Soviet Union powerhouse.

Why tuck such a "historic" occasion into a small, unexciting Midwest market when Stern might have lured the Soviets to the media hotbeds of Los Angeles or New York? The answer was that he was already demonstrating the art of creating a league that could take its hit show anywhere, that could become the Rolling Stones of professional sports. "Here, they were able to establish it as an important, premier event, as opposed to a bigger city where it might have gotten lost," said Milwaukee's longtime public relations director, Bill King.

Stern had already guaranteed national exposure by selling the television rights to ABC. (CBS, his league partner at the time, was committed to college and pro football.) In Milwaukee, the demand was so great that, after the games were sold out, the league blocked off the streets around the old Mecca arena, erected giant viewing screens, and staged a citywide block party with an international ambience. Not bad for Milwaukee, and not lost on its European visitors was how Stern's league could dress up for big occasions.

The Bucks beat the Soviets, 127–100, but the real winner was Stern, who had unlocked a treasure chest of global riches. The McDonald's Open would go from there to Madrid, Rome, Barcelona, Paris, and Munich. By 1995, NBA "global offices" had popped up like McDonald's franchises in Geneva, Hong Kong, Melbourne, Tokyo, Mexico City, and Miami (for South America). The league seemed to be everywhere, and even Stern's most vocal critics were impressed.

"I remember questioning a lot of David's decisions," said Fleisher. "Doing the work in Europe in-house rather than hire European companies that were successful in those markets, for example. He put his own people in there and had them learn every market. To say, 'We're going to go into Europe and put on this McDonald's Open, virtually on our own' doesn't seem like a big thing now, but no one had done anything like that before."

After Milwaukee, there was no turning back for FIBA, for the IOC. When the Soviets defeated the U.S. Olympic team composed of collegians at Seoul in 1988, the movement to have NBA players in the Olympic games gathered steam. Before long, the NBA was planting its flag right in the headquarters of USA Basketball, as its marketing agent. The president of USA Basketball at the time was Dave Gavitt, who also happened to be running the Boston Celtics. Granik was soon elected vice president. In September of 1991, the first Dream Team was announced in a network special produced at the league's spanking new entertainment studio in Secaucus, New Jersey. Magic Johnson would be wearing red, white, and blue in Barcelona during the summer of 1992. Larry Bird. Michael Jordan.

In Monte Carlo, where the Dream Team trained the week before the Games, French kids outside the hotel squealed when they caught a glimpse of the players strolling to the team bus. Barricades held back crowds in Barcelona outside the team's plush downtown hotel, accommodations that did not sit well with many Americans consigned to the spartan athletes' village. To practice and for games, the Dream Team traveled by police motorcade.

The stage was set for what Stern would years later reflect back on as his league's "defining moment."

"Less than a decade after they wrote us off as too black, as drug infested, here we were on the gold medal stand, the whole world looking in," he said.

One summer away from another Olympics, one on home soil, anything seemed possible to him now. Even the notion of conquering the British Empire, where soccer was royalty, virtually untouchable, the way baseball had once been back home.

"No way, never, will basketball ever replace soccer here," Hakeem Olajuwon said in the Rockets' London Arena locker room an hour before they were to play Buckler Bologna for the McDonald's Championship.

To go with his sudden back spasms that killed his pay-per-view special against Shaquille O'Neal, Olajuwon had required minor elbow surgery that prevented him from playing in London. Enjoying his new exalted position as two-time champion and certified basketball ambassador, he amiably chatted his way through interviews and smiled for the photo opportunities at Tower Bridge, Big Ben, and Buckingham Palace. But he wasn't buying the party line that the NBA was an automatic sell wherever it wanted to go. As historically significant invasions go, he was more or less comparing the Rockets' landing in London with the Dave Clark Five's in New York.

Growing up in Lagos, Nigeria, Olajuwon said he spent much of his youth waiting for the television signal to beam in the exploits of "Georgie Best and every other English footballer. They were the kings. Soccer players are still kings. There is nothing like the World Cup. Basketball is a growing sport, yes. But it can never touch soccer. Never."

"In two years, they'll all be wearing the jerseys and loving the game, just like in the States," Robert Horry, the Rockets' lanky forward (traded in the summer of 1996 to Phoenix for Charles Barkley), butted in from a couple of feet away. "There's more happening in basketball. Nothing happens in soccer."

If the rest of Europe was in the NBA's pocket, or vice versa, Britain wasn't the same thing as Europe, as the Tories like to say. To the soccer aficionado, with his appreciation for what it takes to score one goal, the idea of oversized men stuffing balls through defenseless hoops all night was almost a personal affront. And compared to soccer's spartan sensibility and no-frills veneer, the NBA's marketing concepts seemed even dumber than the game.

As opposed to the continental media, which had embraced McDonald's, the London press practically ignored it. Not a word about basketball appeared in the down-market, mass-selling *Sun*. There was no line at London's betting shops. As if to make its own statement about traditions, even American ones, the *Times* of London ran a longer article on the start of the Cleveland-Atlanta World Series than it did on the Rockets' 126–112 victory over Buckler Bologna.

Wrote David Hunn in the *Times* of London:

"Style seldom leaves a mark on sport, but the Americans stamp theirs very clearly. It involves acrobats, jugglers, stilt walkers, a chorus line, a man dressed as a bear and a determination to fill every pause with frenzied music. . . . In a country that seems disinclined to accept basketball as a grown-up sport, it is difficult to appreciate how huge the game is in the States. . . . The whole scene is a whizz, if you can stand the noise."

What drove Stern's blueprint for leveraging the game to become an acquired taste was the presumption that kids could not only stand the noise, but would usually go wherever it was. The packs of logo-laden kids begging Clyde Drexler for his autograph at Big Ben and gyrating to the music during time-outs at London Arena suggested that, as usual, he knew whom he was selling to.

"Anyone over thirty here, they don't know what team we're on, what sport we're playing, what planet we're from," said Kenny Smith, the Rockets' spindly point guard from Queens, New York. "But you walk down the street, and the kids seem to know exactly who you are."

They were the future ticket buyers and cable-television subscribers. Stern would never have been narcissistic enough to honestly believe his sport could dislodge soccer as England's major sporting pastime in his lifetime and probably his children's. But then, how many Americans would have liked his chances to muscle in on baseball the way he had back in the early 1980s? And as long as we were on the subject, he had to point out that the NBA had for the 1995–96 season cracked mainstream British television, completing a deal with Channel 4 to televise regular-season and playoff games. In a market with only four free stations, he considered this to be no small feat.

England's young pro basketball league had also just landed a national sponsor (Budweiser) and a television contract with an all-sports network. The Manchester team was playing in a new state-of-the-art, 19,000-seat arena that was modeled after Phoenix's America West. Jay Goldberg, a former Rockets official who was spending the season in Manchester as a consultant, said certain parallels might one day be drawn regarding basketball's growth at the expense of an entrenched sport of the culture that had a penchant for shooting itself in the foot.

"You talk to anybody over here and they say, 'There's no way I'm going to take my kid to a soccer match,'" he said.

Hooliganism, the unseemly by-product English soccer was notorious for worldwide, had all but killed the traditional Saturday father-son local-match outing. Goldberg was saying that there was now a void in the professional sports community. There was an opportunity for a new, colorfully upbeat game, provided it could reach out through television screens and grab the attention of teenagers, who, in another fifteen years, would be looking for a place to take their own kids.

"This is a traditionalist country," a more cautious Stankovic said. "I would think it would take a lot of time."

Time was one commodity that David Stern had. He had only been on the job as NBA commissioner for twelve years, and look how how far he'd already come. Across an ocean. Across the

Pacific, too, and over to Japan, where regular-season NBA games were now annually played.

At the McDonald's Open, Stern was asked what plans for European expansion he had. He mouthed Stankovic's claim that creating a European division would be a nightmarish endeavor, one beyond the league's current means, or needs. He talked instead about expanding the NBA calendar, the potential for creating summer television programming, for more network partners, via some kind of expanded rookie league. Then he let another little "secret" slip out: the NBA, he said, was seriously studying "growing the sport with regards to the women's game."

What did he mean by that? NBA historians could read between the bottom lines. Stern wasn't blind to the growing popularity of the NCAA women's tournament, to the star-making vehicle that was beginning to accelerate at an impressive revenue-producing pace. The women's Final Four, appearing regularly on ESPN, was making its presence felt in the ratings game. Its recent principals, players such as Sheryl Swoopes and Rebecca Lobo, were far more popular than their predecessors, players such as Carol Blazejowski, who suddenly appeared in 1995 as the NBA's director of women's programs.

The league had already hatched its exploratory beacon, putting NBA Properties on the case of a touring USA national team, in preparation for the summer Olympics in Atlanta. The league had lined up the advertisers, sold the television rights, helped broker a deal where Nike would market a shoe named for Swoopes. Days after the McDonald's Open, Spike Lee would shoot the commercial with Swoopes, Lisa Leslie, and Dawn Staley in a Manhattan playground.

The ball was rolling now, a snowball packing more and more as it carried on. Granik admitted in London that an NBA women's league was on the horizon. It had been tried by others before, with dismal results, but now the NBA machine would be cranking up. The premier women's players knew this would be the best chance they ever got, after years of suffering through months of loneliness and, much worse, playing professionally in Italy, which had the best European league, or in Japan. Most didn't last long abroad and would come home with no place to play except their driveways or local gyms.

"The people who follow basketball eventually will take an interest in the best basketball," Granik reasoned. It was the same thought process that had led to the investment in Europe, in FIBA, in the almost arrogant way the NBA believed that no one could resist it.

All this accomplished—historically speaking—in little more than a blip of time, a decade-plus, during the reign of King David. Perhaps inside the arenas, the bulk of the credit could be given to the Birds, the Johnsons, the Jordans. Outside, in the sparkling team offices throughout the country, in the boardrooms of the companies happily married to the NBA, it was Stern who was the point man with all the moves.

"In the eighties, it was somewhat fortuitous, the whole Bird, Magic, sneaker explosion that brought the focus on individual players," said Stan Kasten, who runs the Atlanta Hawks and Braves for Ted Turner. "But the focus for David was always, as he said, 'growing the business.' In his mind, each piece of the pie could be the same, but its slice of business would be bigger."

Dealing with baseball's comparative Neanderthals, Kasten had a unique frame of reference. In August 1994, he spoke at a joint session of baseball owners and players during stalled labor talks. He suggested that their bargaining table enmity and resulting lack of cooperation and respect were retarding their business. "Right now," he told them, "the NBA players' union is in court with the league to undo the labor agreement and the draft." He added that despite these hotly contested issues that might lead the NBA to civil war—which they did—Stern and his people still promoted the hell out of Dream Team II for the Toronto World Championships and accompanied Patrick Ewing and Alonzo Mourning to South Africa for a goodwill tour.

"Why?" said Kasten. "Because it is about making money. About growing the pie."

About climbing higher and higher, like Michael Jordan in midflight.

10

Michael and Murder

THE LOCAL MEDIA WAS OUT IN FORCE ON THURSDAY, JANUARY 4, AS the Chicago Bulls pulled into the Charlotte Coliseum for a morning shootaround, in preparation for that night's game against the hometown Hornets. On the surface, this was no surprising development, Charlotte being Michael Jordan's homecoming stop on the NBA circuit. That the reenergized Bulls pulled into town with a 26-3 record only made them that much more of an attraction, but there was another reason why Jordan would be besieged from the moment he stepped off the bus.

The trial of the twenty-one-year-old man accused of shooting his father was going on in Lumberton, North Carolina.

Before leaving Chicago, Jordan had admitted to reporters covering the Bulls that it would be difficult to ignore the circus atmosphere surrounding the trial of Daniel Andre Green. He would not get drawn into public discourse, though. He had avoided it for three years, going so far as to claim that he didn't much care if the alleged assailants were spared the death penalty. Nothing would bring James Jordan back. Nothing could restore to life the man he had trusted most.

Jordan promptly laid the ground rules that morning, and he held fast to them right through the Bulls' 117–93 win over the

Hornets, a game in which Jordan scored 27 points in thirty-four minutes. But Scottie Pippen admitted his longtime teammate and mentor was having to work hard to stay focused on his game.

"For him to have to deal with all the media attention has been the toughest part," said Pippen. "He's trying to stay away from it and get it out of his life. He's just trying to remember his father the way that he was."

Some one hundred miles away from Charlotte, outside the Robeson County Courthouse, the only vestige of the Old South is a stone sentry anchored atop a four-story statue honoring "Our Confederate Dead." Inside the sprawling, undistinguished design an intriguing American drama was playing out. Two teenaged friends—one African-American, the other Lumbee Indian—were starring in a murder mystery featuring the father of an athlete whose shoes are worshiped around the world.

Near the halls and stairwells of Judge Gregory Weeks' second-floor courtroom, there were signs of the same media circus that surrounded the dead man's disappearance three years earlier. A man who spent his fifty-seventh birthday submerged in the deep black waters of Gum Swamp Creek, and whose death left his son's life in pieces.

James Jordan wasn't so much a father as he was a friend. That's how it was pictured, at least: the shots of one Jordan or the other laughing and cracking jokes in the locker room; the televised hugs and kisses Michael and his father enjoyed following the Bulls' third consecutive title; the times they shared the limelight on the celebrity golf and banquet circuit.

But late on the night of July 22, 1993, James Jordan was alone. He had left his Mint Hill, North Carolina, home to attend the funeral of Willie Kemp, a friend of twenty-five years and coworker at the General Electric plant in Wilmington. After the funeral, Jordan spent time at the widow Kemp's home in Atkinson, North Carolina, before leaving for Wilmington and a late dinner with friends. Around midnight, Jordan climbed into his 1993 $50,000 cherry-red Lexus 400I for a two-hundred-mile trip west along Highway 74 toward Charlotte. In the morning, he was scheduled to fly to Chicago to attend a charity function with his son. But those plans ended when Jordan decided to pull off the road for a short rest stop, a quick catnap that would close his eyes forever.

For Larry Martin Demery, the morning of July 22 dawned with a dysphoria, the mild anxiety common to criminals who drift in and out of the criminal justice system. At seventeen, Demery was well on his way to becoming a permanent guest of the state. His everyday anxiety stemmed from garden-variety problems: low self-esteem, no money, and pending prison time—in this case, for felony robbery charges. So, for a change, he eased his mind by delivering a birthday present to his girlfriend Angela McLean, pregnant with Demery's daughter. From McLean's, it was off to Lumberton, where lifelong friend and partner-in-crime Daniel Andre Green shared a trailer with his mother and grandmother. Green, eighteen, was another surefire candidate for a guest shot on *Cops*—a deadeye delinquent fresh out of state prison after doing two and a half years of a six-year stretch for armed robbery and assault.

Like two hunters, Green and Demery were back on the prowl. "All day me and Daniel had planned to rob someone," Demery later confessed to police. A July 5 mugging of a Rhode Island couple in a motel parking lot had opened their crime spree, netting some much-needed cash and a video recorder.

One of the victims, Dorothy Tedeschi, said she would never forget Green's face. "I saw his eyes. It was like an unfeeling stare," she said. In a subsequent stickup—a convenience-store job off Route 72 eleven days later—Green shot store clerk Cullis Demary, a former New York security guard, three times and left him for dead. During the robbery, Green swiped Demary's .38-caliber revolver from a drawer in the store.

For Green and Demery, the night of July 22 would be no different. Another tourist rip-off. Nothing fancy. Grab the gun and put the wet in somebody's pants.

By midnight, Demery was wheeling his Ford Tempo back toward the Quality Inn, with Green and the stolen .38 at his side. A Lumbee Indian, Green was part of the statistical majority in Lumberton (41 percent) but was batting a distant third in the local social order behind whites and blacks. Yet in defiance of color and creed, Demery and Green were friends, good friends, since childhood.

Together again on this summer night, cruising down a dark dirt service road hard by a canal. They parked and slowly walked back toward a gas station adjacent to the hotel, ready to prey on some unsuspecting tourist, his or her only crime consisting of being in exactly the wrong place at exactly the wrong time.

Demery first noticed the car. Off the shoulder on Highway 74, right in front of the flea market, parking lights on.

"Looks like a cop car," said Green. "Undercover."

"I don't think so," Demery said. "Let's check it out."

They crisscrossed the highway several times, back and forth in the shadows. A Lexus, they thought. Some special kind of plates.

Still they weren't quite sure. So they dipped back into the darkness surrounding the service station, standing silent for nearly an hour, eyeing the hotel lot, waiting as the night wore thin, along with their patience. In time, their attention turned back to the car, and they sneaked close enough to notice, for the first time, the "UNC" tag on a plate. A University of North Carolina student, they said. Easy pickin's. Somebody looked asleep inside; the passenger window was down, offering a breath of night air. The front seat was pushed all the way back.

Green and Demery reached the car just as the man inside rumbled softly from sleep.

"What's going on?" he asked.

What's going on?—the last three words James Jordan would utter.

"As soon as the words were out of his mouth, Daniel cut him off," Demery told a jury in the spring of 1996. "By that I mean he shot him, Daniel just shot him. We both stood there and watched the man die."

Now they had a fast car, a dark road, and a dead man riding shotgun. They lit out on Highway 301, turning onto a dirt road and into a cornfield near Rowland. Under the harsh, eerie indoor light, they stripped the body of his Gucci shoes, wallet, watch, and ring. As Green grabbed the jewelry, he caught a clue to the man they had just murdered.

"Damn," he said. "I believe we killed Michael Jordan's daddy."

"No, we didn't," said Demery.

"Yes, we did."

"Why'd you say that?"

Green held up an NBA ring with the initials *MJ* on one side, marked by the phrase *All-Star 86*. The watch was embossed *90–91 World Champions* and had the letters *MVP* on its face. If that didn't clinch it, the name on the driver's license did.

Green climbed into the driver's side, pushing the dead man

across the console as Demery scrambled into the back. The two headed off into the night trying to decide what to do with the body. The water-treatment plant, thought Green. That's it. Dump the body and let the chemicals go to work.

But the front gate was locked. So the Lexus roamed the grounds, searching for another entrance. Demery's shirt was soon showered in sweat.

"Let's get out of here," he said.

"You got a better idea?" demanded Green.

"Yeah. I do."

Now it was Demery's turn behind the wheel, rolling south on 501, the clock creeping toward dawn when he crossed the state line into South Carolina and rolled up near a small bridge fifty yards south of the border. The cool, murky waters of Gum Swamp Creek rumbled below. As Green and Demery lifted the body from the car, it made a gurgling, gaseous sound. "A sound scared me so bad I almost dropped the body," Demery told police investigators.

Instead they tossed the body off the bridge. The black waters shook and churned, the sound drifting out into the night.

At First Union Bank in Laurinburg, the two ex-cons went for a quick withdrawal—courtesy of Jordan's ATM card—but struck out sticking various PINs into the cash machine. So they dug out $10 of the $63 Jordan had in his money clip, for gas. From there, it was on to Green's trailer for a couple hours of sleep.

Midmorning. Back on the move. At a deserted canal, they got down to business, tossing blank checks and assorted papers into the drink. On the way back to Green's, the teenage killers began punching out the electronic beeps that would help put them behind bars—cell calls, one after another, lined up like tiny little cops, carefully marking time, date, and place. The calls continued all day Friday and Saturday, two small-town hoods suddenly riding high, cruising with a couple of chicks, dialing up friends and relatives in Philadelphia and New York, hunting for some place to dump a high-priced car for cash. They used the video cam from the earlier job to record a little history: Green dancing and rapping, playing Mr. Big, showing off in James Jordan's jewelry and clothes.

By Monday the twenty-sixth, there was still no deal, and the circle of friends attempting to peddle the car had doubled from Green and Demery fourfold—to "David" to "Eric" to "Rick" to

"Joe." But still no buyers. That was the end of the Lexus, they decided. It had been four days of strutting their stuff, and local folks were starting to talk, getting a mite curious about how these two boys got their hands on $50,000 worth of wheels.

In a remote wooded area near Fayetteville, Green and Demery dumped the car, but not before grabbing a final stash of CDs, golf clubs, and clothes. Green took the MVP watch and All-Star ring. Demery got $30 and the wedding ring, the same band of gold that sat on a dusty shelf in a dumpy trailer when Larry Demery decided to rat out his lifelong friend two weeks later in hopes of saving his life.

Wandering in the woods on private property on August 2, sixteen-year-old high school dropout Chris Thomas discovered the abandoned Lexus. By now, James Jordan had been missing for eleven days. Missing from his flight out of Charlotte, and at his son's foundation dinner. He had not checked in with his wife or any member of his family and failed to show for a fifty-seventh-birthday celebration. James Jordan had pulled disappearing acts before . . . but eleven days?

In Chicago, Michael had long since passed into worry. His father, for all his TV smiles and solid, soothing influence on his son, was no stranger to trouble. In 1985, James Jordan had pleaded guilty to a felony charge of "aiding and abetting in commission of false pretense." As part of a larger fraud case, he and a coworker at the GE plant in Wilmington had been found guilty of embezzlement for accepting a $7,000 kickback from a private contractor. He was sentenced to three years in prison (suspended) and five years' probation.

There had been recent trouble as well. According to newspaper reports, JVL Enterprises Inc., James Jordan's T-shirt and clothing company based in Rock Hill, South Carolina, was the subject of several lawsuits involving unpaid bills, and Jordan owed money to the company. On top of this, Michael was once again being dogged by reports of high-stakes gambling. So he called Risk Prevention Group, a private security firm in his employ since 1989, and asked that it try to locate his father.

"Privately, they were looking for James," recalled a close family friend.

Looking. But not finding.

Meanwhile, Chris Thomas, who had stumbled upon the Lexus, was pondering some serious reward money. Somehow, the killers, in a frantic cover-up effort, and four Fayetteville juveniles arrested for stripping the car of its tires and stereo equipment, had missed papers connecting the car to the World's Richest Athlete, which was why Thomas spent several days playing detective, calling every Jordan he could find in the North Carolina phone book before giving up and making one last call—to the Cumberland County Sheriff's Office. It was Thursday, August 5.

Two days earlier, back in South Carolina, Hal Locklear, a construction worker and avid fisherman, had made a discovery of his own, a grisly finding not far from his favorite fishing hole. Right there in Gum Swamp Creek, a hoot and a holler from the Pea Road Bridge, Locklear saw a body, a black man, hooked around a tree.

Marlboro County coroner Tim Brown took the call about the floater. Like most small-town Southern coroners, Brown worked part-time. But he'd been at the job for nine years and took more than a small measure of pride in his work. He arrived on the scene with a no-nonsense county sheriff named Chuck Foley. A cursory exam at the scene revealed a male, dressed in short-sleeved shirt with red-blue and black stripes and designer jeans, between twenty-five and fifty years old, approximately six feet tall, 175–190 pounds.

The floater was in sorry shape, unrecognizable. He was shoeless and carried no ID. But there were distinguishing marks, which Brown filed away for future reference. Before starting his own construction company, Brown had owned and operated a dental lab. He knew a set of expensive teeth when he saw one. Guy must be a drug dealer, thought the coroner, who had examined nearly a dozen dead men pulled from South Carolina waters during his career.

By the time the body arrived at Newberry (S.C.) Memorial Hospital, two forensic pathologists were on hand to conduct a formal autopsy. Determining the cause of death posed no problem: a single gunshot wound to the chest. According to Brown, the bullet had traveled downward and lodged in the chest, leaving no exit wound.

After the phone call from Chris Thomas, the high school dropout, Cumberland deputy Scott Williams became involved; so did North Carolina State Police trooper Ray Battle, a grizzled thirteen-year veteran, who had happened to pick up the call over his scanner. Today, Battle is very clear about what Thomas showed him and Williams that day—establishing a direct link between the car and Michael Jordan. Yet right before Battle's eyes, Williams, at his superior's direction, was telling the owner of the property the car was not stolen and could be towed and placed in storage. By not having the car impounded, Battle felt they were cutting off an important avenue of investigation.

"I was astounded," said Battle. "What I wanted to know was, how did the car get there? Where's the owner?"

Battle intended to find out. Running the car's VIN (vehicle ID) number through DMV, he got a hit—a vanity UNC license plate with the numbers 0023—23, for those just in from another planet, was Jordan's number in college and virtually his entire career in Chicago. Battle tried calling every Jordan listed in the North Carolina phone book but drew a blank.

By now, Tim Brown, the Marlboro County coroner, was getting nervous. Without proper refrigeration, the body was deteriorating. He called the state attorney general's office and laid out the news: One body. One bullet. No ID. No freezer. No clue as to who it may be. Little did Brown know Risk Prevention was combing the South, searching for MJ's daddy; little did he know Trooper Battle was working the phones, searching for some link to the Lexus.

Brown wanted the body cremated, but not before ordering the jawbone cut away and held in Newberry, the hands removed and sent to the South Carolina Law Enforcement Department Laboratory in Columbia, South Carolina (for a possible fingerprint match), and the rest of the body reduced to dust and sent to a funeral home in Lexington, South Carolina, about ten miles south of Columbia.

On August 6, with the funeral director breathing down his neck, Brown called the attorney general's office, demanding a decision on the body. "It's your call," he was told.

"I did a lot of soul-searching," Brown would say three years later. But with no refrigeration, he had no choice. He told the funeral director to cremate the body. It was done the next day, a Saturday.

By August 10, Officer Ray Battle was living up to his name. After five days of work, he located a Lexus dealer in Glenview, Illinois, an affluent suburb about fifteen miles north of downtown Chicago.

The owner, Martin Bredemann, confirmed Michael Jordan had purchased the car for his father. But Bredemann refused to give out the Jordan family number. "Customer privacy," he said.

The next day, Jerry Brandt, head of Risk Prevention, called trooper Battle, telling him not, under any circumstances, to notify the press. Strangely, Battle says, Brandt never asked Battle if he had seen or heard from James Jordan. Asked no questions about the circumstances surrounding the discovery of the vehicle. Said Battle, "All Brandt wanted to know was what I found in the car and its location. They said they [Risk Prevention] were leaving Chicago immediately and wanted me available to talk to them."

Battle said he never heard from Brandt or Risk Prevention again. But Cumberland County Sheriff Morris Bedsole certainly did.

Today, Battle suspects Bedsole might have already spoken to Risk Prevention Group and informed Brandt of young Chris Thomas' discovery of the car. Then, at Brandt's request, he kept the information away from the press so Risk could quietly continue its search. Battle bases this belief on a conversation he said he and 1st Sgt. Ralph Price had at Bedsole's home when they challenged the sheriff about his "investigation"—admonishing him for not going public.

"Why are you sitting on this?" Battle said they asked the sheriff.

"I'll take care of it," said Bedsole.

The very next day, homicide detectives Cliff Massengill and Ray Wood, who had been out of town at a conference, felt equally uneasy after Bedsole called them into his office to report the discovery of the Jordan vehicle. Said Massengill, "He told us it was very hush-hush, to keep a low profile. We have a lot of work to do on this and to keep it confidential."

But keeping it confidential was becoming a problem. Battle had put the pressure on by calling the Lexus dealer and confronting Bedsole in his own home. If Bedsole didn't go public, chances were Battle would.

So on August 12, Sheriff Morris Bedsole decided to call a press conference, with the apparent blessing, it turned out, of Risk Prevention. Though Risk was not part of any criminal investigation, it had been in constant contact with Bedsole and had gone as far as to assist in ground and air searches with sheriff's department personnel prior to the press conference.

Finally, Bedsole stepped before the cameras and announced

that a late-model luxury car owned by James Jordan had been found in his jurisdiction, stripped of its tires, license plates, and other parts. He told of how James Jordan, after attending his friend's funeral, had not been seen or heard from since departing Wilmington the night of July 22. He told of how, supposedly, he had not been reported missing for three weeks.

Tim Brown was home watching the *CBS Evening News* when Connie Chung described the discovery of Jordan's car in Fayetteville, North Carolina. The father of a worldwide icon was missing. Brown bolted upright in his chair. "That looks like our man," he said, turning to tell his wife. Eventually, Brown reached Bedsole's office in Cumberland County. "Get me James Jordan's dental records," he said. "We may have your missing man."

By three-thirty in the morning they had a match from the jaw Brown had been smart enough to save. Further proof came from Jordan's hands, since the fingerprints were on file with the feds from the embezzlement case. From that moment on, the James Jordan story was destined to roar through the public eye like a hurricane, feeding the twisting gambling travails already doing damage to Michael's reputation.

The first winds had blown earlier in the year, during nine minutes of testimony in a North Carolina courtroom. There, Jordan was forced to admit under oath that a $57,000 check he wrote to a convicted cocaine dealer named Slim Bouler was not, as he had long insisted, a loan to help Bouler build a driving range but rather payment on a gambling debt. More wind: a late-night jaunt down to Atlantic City for some gaming on the eve of a playoff game against the Knicks. Then the big blow: in a self-published book, San Diego businessman Richard Esquinas claimed that Jordan had lost $1.25 million to him on the golf course and that he still owed Esquinas several hundred thousand dollars from the matches. Esquinas backed up his claims with a string of canceled checks and letters that he said supported his story. So intense was the heat that Jordan broke a self-imposed media boycott to issue a statement denouncing Esquinas and the book:

"I have played golf with Richard Esquinas with wagers made between us," he said. "Because I did not keep records, I cannot verify how much I won or lost. I can assure you the level of our wagers was substantially less than the preposterous amounts that have been reported.

"It is extremely disappointing to me that an individual whom I caused no harm and who held himself out as my friend would shamelessly exploit my name for selfish gain. It is equally disappointing that my off-court activities are receiving more attention in the midst of the NBA Championship than my on-court activities."

Nevertheless, there was no stopping the story now, no slowing the media from hightailing it to Fayetteville. Meanwhile, Risk Prevention called Coroner Brown with a request. Could he round up what was left of Mr. Jordan and deliver the remains to a funeral home in Wilmington in time for a burial in two days?

Brown called Robert Stewart, director of the South Carolina Law Enforcement Department (SLED), and asked for help, and Stewart did what people do when Michael Jordan needs anything.

He said yes.

The next day, Brown went about picking up the pieces of James Jordan's life. It was a day, he said, he'll never forget, being chauffeured around two states by helicopter, car, and airplane. Traveling five hundred miles in a single day, picking up Jordan's jaw in Newberry, his hands in Columbia, and finally over to the funeral parlor in Lexington, where the jaw and hands joined the cremated ashes. Next, Brown then flew on to Wilmington, offering the remains to a funeral director before heading home to Bennettsville.

The next day, the son whose tears had warmed the world championship trophy he'd shared with his dad, two months earlier, cried again.

While the Jordan family mourned, Sheriff Hubert Stone's office on the outskirts of Lumberton was abuzz with activity. In the early-morning hours, a young black male had been brought in and fingerprinted. By 2 A.M., Larry Demery had also been arrested; soon after, he'd dictated, read, and signed a seventeen page confession naming Green the killer. A search warrant executed by sheriff's investigator Mark Locklear and state investigator Barry Lea at the trailer of Daniel Green had uncovered a .38-caliber revolver concealed in a vacuum cleaner. Green was arrested and brought to a deserted jail complex shrouded in a moorish mist of sodium light and fog.

Only two *Sports Illustrated* staffers were present at the time, one a writer, the other a top criminal investigator who remembered calling Stone over to a window overlooking the parking lot before offering some advice.

"Sheriff, go home and spruce up," he said. "Get a clean shirt and tie and get ready to do about one hundred interviews, because when you call Fayetteville and tell them you've got two guys in custody who shot and killed James Jordan, there will be a mad rush down I-95, and that parking lot will be full of news trucks, satellite dishes, you name it."

Sure enough, by 11 A.M., the lot looked like a satellite convention, jammed with dishes and trucks from ABC, CBS, NBC, ESPN, CNN, and a small battalion of print and electronic reporters. By now, Stone was in shirt, coat, and tie.

"Hey, you were right," he yelled to the *SI* investigator. "I just gave my twenty-third interview."

While Stone fed the media what it wanted for breakfast, and Demery and Green were being arraigned in county court, charged with first-degree murder, armed robbery, and conspiracy to commit murder, civil rights leader Jesse Jackson and local NAACP officials were having coroner Tim Brown for lunch. Jackson blasted Brown—wrongly, it turned out—for allowing the body to be cremated before identification was final. Said Jackson, "The instant cremation without contacting the family looks to be part of an organized cover-up, and attempt to destroy evidence."

"There is no doubt I would do the same thing tomorrow and make the same decision," Brown told the *Amsterdam News*, a leading African-American newspaper based in New York. "I like to think of myself as a practical person. We had no facility to keep the body. Down here, we have a lot of respect for anyone who loses someone. We're not trying to capitalize off this. All of the Chicago Bulls fans are not in Chicago. Hindsight is a somewhat treacherous perch to reflect from."

Yes, it is. But it sometimes offers a far more expansive view. For instance, if Bedsole had gone public with the discovery of James Jordan's car immediately, chances are Brown would have made the connection forty-eight hours *before* the cremation and James Jordan's body would never have been cut up and spread out over three cities. Jesse Jackson's divisive comments would never have aired. And Trooper Ray Battle would not have been brought up on charges, instigated by Bedsole no less, of interfering with the sheriff's investigation. (As it was, Battle was completely exonerated in a State Police investigation. In fact, he received a letter of commendation lauding his efforts in the Jordan case.)

And Michael Jordan would have been spared days of frantic worry before discovering the grisly truth.

Both Green and Demery went on trial facing the death penalty. Green's trial went first—and it was treated by the media as Must-See TV, while Jordan's family wisely stayed away. In prison, Green converted to Islam and wanted to be known as As-Saddiq-Al-Amin Sallam U'Allah. By any name, the results were the same. In February 1996, with Demery serving as the prosecution's star witness, Green/U'Allah was convicted of murder during the commission of a robbery and sentenced to life imprisonment.

By May, when Demery's trial was drawing to a close, the scene was starkly different. Demery had long since lost the look of a teenage hoodlum. He instead took on the air of a well-groomed law-office clerk or newspaper reporter (not counting the ponytail). Only ten spectators dotted Judge Weeks' courtroom, including Demery's fiancée and mother, as Demery looked lovingly at his baby daughter while his attorney told the twelve-member jury of his model conduct in jail, displaying diplomas and letters of support.

There was one macabre moment: the time prosecutor Luther Johnson Britt III asked about a pair of James Jordan's pants.

"When is the last time you saw this article of clothing?" said Britt.

"When I saw Green wearing them in court during his trial," replied Demery.

On May 20, 1996, at the ripe old age of twenty, Larry Martin Demery was sentenced to life in prison for first-degree murder. After 1,010 days of confinement, he was remanded to the North Carolina prison system, but not before Judge Weeks issued an order that seemed a million days away from the night of July 22, 1993.

"Larry Martin Demery is not to be housed at any unit with Daniel Andre Green, A.K.A. U'Allah, unless active protective measures are taken. The court ORDERS that protection be given to Larry Martin Demery while housed within the Department of Correction."

Oddly, sadly, on the same day Demery went to prison, Michael Jordan—who had quit the NBA months after his father's murder, played baseball (the game his father loved most), and then

returned to rededicate himself in the memory of James Jordan—
was named the league's Most Valuable Player for the fourth time.

There were many unanswered questions regarding Jordan's
shocking "retirement," an element of mystery, just as there had
been surrounding his father's murder. Not surprisingly, imagina-
tions ran wild, with speculation that James Jordan's murder was
not the type of random crime that has torn apart so many families
in a gun-wracked society.

The lack of an exit wound, and thus the lack of blood in the
Lexus, was seized upon by some media members who postulated
that Jordan's murder may well have been a mob hit, a message
from gamblers associated with Michael. The *New York Post* plastered this baseless theory all over its front page before the Jordan
family could even conduct a proper funeral service. The report
made David Stern livid. Even now, league officials use it as a
means of attacking the media for its treatment of the entire Jordan
story. "A black day for journalists," Brian McIntyre, the league's
communications VP, said.

He was right about that, but it had become much too easy for the
NBA to saddle up and climb aboard its high horse about fairness
and accuracy. Not after how the league conducted itself in its own
"investigations" of Jordan's gambling, how it attempted to pass off
his high-stakes golf and card games as little more than pedestrian
recklessness, a series of boys-will-be-boys lapses of judgment.

It was much more than that, a far more dangerous game that
Jordan became involved in, with drug dealers and gamblers, one
of whom would meet the same fate as his father. It was a shocking
example of how easy it was for the criminal element to gain access
to the NBA's most prized possession, and that was no bull.

11

MJ's Secret Life

IMAGINE THE IMPOSSIBLE POSITION DAVID STERN FOUND HIMSELF IN during the late summer and early autumn months of 1993, when it suddenly became all too clear that the greatest player in NBA history was entangled in a web of decadence and deceit, playing fast and furious with drug dealers, money launderers, and the like. Indeed—as any investigator with standard knowledge of underworld infiltration practices would readily attest—putting himself in a position to be potentially controlled by forces of criminality in ways that would stagger the mind and floor a league.

Michael Jordan was at the height of his professional basketball career and the personal low of his thirty-year life. Three-time champion and devastated son of a murdered man. What was the CEO of a wildly successful but suddenly most vulnerable corporation supposed to do?

The greatest mystery of modern NBA history invariably begins with an interrogative. Why did Jordan quit the NBA days before training camp for the 1993–94 season? Did he, as he claimed, simply want a chance to move on with his life, get closer to his family, and take a swing at becoming a major league baseball player? Was some clandestine deal cut between Stern and Jordan to allow the stench of Jordan's gambling sprees to go away? Or did Jordan, knowing he would soon be suspended if only for the sake of the league's saving face, decide to show Stern who was calling the shots and walk away on his own?

Years later, there is enough backroom whispering and public discomfort to lend some credence to the latter scenario. Other details of this fascinating drama have proved to be more easily unearthed, putting a more serious and disturbing spin on the Jordan gambling story than the NBA—for obvious reasons— wanted out.

For one thing, when it came to Michael Jordan's "secret life," the high and mighty NBA was, not surprisingly, among the last to know. And when it came to investigating the details of Jordan's gambling, the league—as it has made an obvious pattern of doing in such situations—took the path of least resistance.

A long list of central characters in the Jordan saga including law enforcement agencies with jurisdiction in the matter—were contacted in the researching of this book. One after another, they said they had never been questioned by the NBA. Had the league done its homework—as it has time and again insisted it had it might have realized that Jordan's associations with men of unacceptable repute were hardly of a chance, fly-by-night nature; how cocaine dealer/golf hustler Slim Bouler and the boys were said to have plucked the world's most famous athlete like a pigeon; or come across a previously unreported cache of correspondence and checks allegedly involving Jordan's high-stakes golf losses to Richard Esquinas.

According to Esquinas, two cashier's checks, totaling $75,000, had been sent in May and June of 1992 by Michael Jordan's wife, Juanita, to Esquinas in care of a company called E & S Marketing.

Also discovered during research of this book were two letters sent by a Jordan attorney to Esquinas. Both were accompanied by $100,000 checks, which Esquinas says were partial payoffs on Jordan's huge golf-course gambling debt to Esquinas. Yet neither golf nor gambling was ever mentioned in either letter. Instead they were both written in legalese, discussing the consummation of a curious "arrangement" between the two men. The same kind of arrangement, perhaps, that Jordan had with Bouler when Jordan publicly declared a $57,000 check had been a "loan" to help Bouler purchase a driving range.

As it was, Jordan was forced to admit under oath he had lied in the Bouler deal to "save the embarrassment or pain from people knowing that was gambling." The same way he'd lied to *Chicago Tribune* columnist Bob Greene in *Hang Time,* and when he had told Frederick Lacey, who headed the NBA investigation, that there were no more checks, no more heavy gambling losses, no more bombshells. And in doing so, failed to mention one previously unreported check for $22,500 in the original episode in North and South Carolina, as well as several hundred thousand dollars in gambling debts to Esquinas.

Careful observers noted how, once Jordan announced his retirement, he and the league neatly managed to lay the gambling issue to rest. How Jordan skirted the subject during his "good-bye" press conference and was never questioned about it by the attending press. For his part, Stern publicly—and often heatedly—dismissed any deal. He told *Sports Illustrated* the mere notion was "scurrilous and disgusting." He went so far as to say he was certain Jordan never had a gambling problem and had never bet on NBA games.

Was October 6, 1993, just one more well-scripted event? Jordan-ologists searching for clues looked at the tone and tenor of his stunning press conference at the Bulls training facility and saw a calculated, professional performance. No tears, no sorrow. They saw forty-five minutes of simmering hostility, mixed with remarks about having nothing left to accomplish in basketball and about the laudable desire to spend more time with his family.

"I have nothing more to prove in basketball," said Jordan that day. "I have no more challenges that I felt I could get motivated for. It doesn't have anything to do with my father's passing or media pressure or anything other than I have achieved everything in basketball I could. And when that happened, I felt it was time to call it a career."

Still, something felt wrong. Maybe it was the twenty-one references to "you guys" in the media, the way MJ went out of his way to tell the press, "You did not drive me out of the game." Or all that talk of family commitment, only to see him leave for an instructional camp in Arizona, the beginning of a failed attempt to make the major leagues as an outfielder. And why had Chicago Bulls owner Jerry Reinsdorf, notoriously stingy even in his dealings with Jordan, agreed to pay Jordan $4 million and left a small contractual window open for him despite the fact that No. 23 claimed to be leaving basketball forever?

Then he made a strange reference to Stern. Had it slipped out? "Five years down the road, if that urge comes back, if the Bulls have me, if David Stern lets me back in the league, I may come back," Jordan said.

"If David Stern lets me back"? A curious phrasing, considering the NBA's gambling "investigation" headed by Lacey, a former federal judge, was coming to a head. Esquinas, former part-owner and general manager of the San Diego Sports Arena, had claimed in his controversial book that the Bulls star had lost $1.25 million on the golf course. (Even more seriously, he says he had told Lacey of a betting-related remark Jordan had made into a telephone with Esquinas present in March 1992.) And Stern had publicly said the probe would end before the 1993–94 season began.

If Jordan was walking away on his own rather than accepting even cursory punishment from Stern, he would have been following a pattern of self-rule he had pursued, under David Falk's tutelage, for years. Jordan had challenged and broken the NBA's ability to control totally its players' merchandising earnings. He refused to acquiesce even when it involved feel-good Olympic participation. He settled a dispute at the 1992 Olympics involving the wearing of a Reebok-made medal-stand suit by crassly draping a huge American flag over the corporate logo and acting as if it were an act of patriotism.

Like Falk (and Stern, for that matter), Jordan had demonstrated a fondness for flaunting his power, using it as his best defense. Though the press accepted the lies he told regarding the Bouler "loan" and did no further investigating until the next series of checks surfaced, Jordan persisted in casting himself as the victim of a media witch-hunt. In a society far more willing to bring down a politician than a sports hero who could turn on the town, Jordan was arguably the most globally transcendent athlete since Muhammad Ali. He was used to doing things his way.

It was all enough to make Esquinas' attorney Costello's account of Jordan's retirement quite plausible, his claim that he had heard from someone in the league office that "Jordan or Jordan's people" had been told a week before the retirement that the league was going to take action against him. Lacey's investigation was beginning its fifth month. It had been nearly three months since Lacey had interviewed Esquinas. Jordan had yet to be interviewed. Come in, Costello said Jordan was allegedly told. The league needed some explanations. And a deadline was set.

As the story goes, instead of meeting with Stern, the world's wealthiest athlete decided to take a proactive hike. Reached by phone, a midlevel league executive, who Costello claimed had knowledge of the situation, was asked directly about a deal. With a hint of panic in his voice, the man said, "I have heard those allegations before. Let me, you know, let me talk, let me clarify this with some people."

He made clear those "people" were not members of the league's public relations staff, who normally handle interview requests. "I don't . . . I don't think I will be able to help you," he said. "I have to tread lightly for a lot of reasons. I'll get back to you as soon as I can."

The next day he called back. His tone had changed.

"I have no information to back up those allegations," he said. "I would be shocked if that happened." Yet during this conversation, the executive said something odd in the face of his sudden denial. He allowed how "my involvement was minimal" in the Jordan matter and that he had "a little bit of involvement on the back end."

The whole unseemly story, chronicled ahead, was enough to draw the conclusion that Jordan had defiantly dragged the NBA into a mess it simply couldn't afford to be in, and had to get out of, as fast and efficiently as it could.

January 30, 1990: On this day, attorney Horace M. DuBose III of Gastonia, North Carolina, wrote a pointed letter to Jordan's agent, whom he called David Folk, regarding "Eddie Dow, Dean Chapman & Mark Rollinson vs. Michael Jordan and Al Wood." In the letter, DuBose pressed Falk to approve a mutual release drawn up to settle a dispute between Jordan and Wood, on the one hand, and the three men on the other. DuBose reminded Falk that he had yet to receive a response to an earlier fax, and that efforts to contact Jordan's longtime agent had been unsuccessful.

Wrote DuBose: "It was, after all, Mr. Miller's [another attorney] request that Michael Jordan would require assurance that the

$22,500 would end this matter. . . . Neither I nor my clients require this Mutual Release. As far as we are concerned, you may forward the $22,500 today *and forget* the Mutual Release. If we do not have approval of the release by February 9, 1990, we shall be in the position where you have failed to accept our offer and we will no longer consider ourselves bound to the $22,500 figure."

The release was eventually signed by all five parties. The terms called for Jordan to pay Dow, Chapman, and Rollinson $22,500 for what DuBose says were gambling losses by Wood and Jordan. In exchange, the three men would release and discharge Jordan of any claims for money owed or loaned to the parties through January 1, 1990. The money was eventually paid to DuBose, who, after taking 10 percent, distributed $20,000 to Dow in three checks.

To understand how it was that Bouler, Dow, Chapman, Rollinson, Wood, and Jordan ended up together in Hilton Head Island, we begin with James L. "Slim" Bouler.

Bouler, forty-one, was a golf hustler from Monroe, North Carolina, and owner of the Golf-Tech Driving Range and Pro Shop in town. He had been convicted of cocaine trafficking in 1986, about the same time he met Jordan through Wood, a former University of North Carolina star and NBA player whose close friendship with Jordan eventually broke up over gambling losses.

Through Bouler and Wood, Jordan ended up in Gastonia, a textile town, where Dow and Chapman held court. Several sources painted Gastonia as two towns in one: a place known for the most incredible kindness, as well as headquarters for a ruthless band of drug dealers and gamblers. "If I wanted to bring in ten full-time cardplayers, gamblers, I could in about thirty minutes," said one local attorney. "It's just like Atlantic City or Reno. If you want to do some serious gambling, you can do it." Said another attorney, "There are parts of Gaston County where you'll find the most vicious acts of violence you can imagine."

Dow, forty-seven, a tall, gregarious bail bondsman, seemed to symbolize that dichotomy. Although active in the community, where he donated time and money to various charities, there was clearly a seedy side to him. According to court records, he had been charged and found not guilty of assault with a deadly weapon and indecent exposure. Tammy Powell, a former office manager for Dow, said that Dow and Bouler had business dealings together. She also said local drug kingpins regularly brought hundreds of thousands of dollars into Dow's office to launder. The money piled up faster than Dow could spend, invest, or fritter it away, Powell said, so much so that her boss gave his employees big wads every week as advances against salaries and lent cash to people who wanted to buy businesses, in exchange for a percentage of profit.

Convicted drug dealer Kenny Ray Hyleman Jr. was also part of the Gastonia crowd. In sworn testimony in the February 1992 drug trial of Bouler, Hyleman described Eddie Dow as a major drug dealer, gambler, and associate of Bouler's. Hyleman further testified that he dealt drugs for Dow in Gastonia, and that he, Dow, and Bouler played high-stakes card games all over the Charlotte area in 1988 and 1989, with anywhere from $5,000 to $60,000 in a pot.

It was Bouler who introduced Jordan to Dow. Dow then introduced Jordan to Chapman, a local contractor who, in March 1977, had been charged with "operating a gaming table" only to have it dismissed three weeks later. So at one point, Jordan's little gambling club included a convicted drug dealer (Bouler), a cardsharp accused of running an illegal gaming table (Chapman), and a money-laundering bail bondsman accused of drug dealing.

Years later, Dow's brother speculated a ringer had been brought in—a stakes golfer recruited specifically for the Hilton Head matches against Jordan. "I think that's the guy Eddie heard was a good golfer," said Flip Dow. "I remember him saying, 'We want to have fun, but we also want to win.'"

Flip Dow was not the only person who believed Jordan had been set up in golf and cards. Roy Tidwell, the owner of the Shrimp Boat restaurant on Franklin Boulevard, Gastonia's main drag, pleaded guilty to operating an illegal gambling enterprise and tax evasion. The twenty-four-count indictment accused Tidwell of money laundering and possession with the intent to distribute more than one hundred pounds of marijuana, a charge prosecutors dropped in exchange for a guilty plea to a lesser charge and forfeiture of $200,000 in ill-gotten gains. Tidwell described himself as a close friend of both Dow and Chapman. It was his opinion Jordan was set up during card games with Dow and others.

"I think they were setting Jordan up and taking him for a sleigh ride," Tidwell said.

As for Chapman, he issued statements through his lawyers saying his "dealings with Jordan were of a private nature." He has refused further comment.

September 1991: At golf courses all over San Diego County, Jordan and Esquinas went head-to-head in a series of gut-wrenching matches. In one wild stretch of bets and presses, Esquinas says he went from $98,000 down to winning more than $1.2 million.

October 1, 1991: During a long weekend of golf and poker-playing at Jordan's Hilton Head Island vacation retreat, Bouler, Dow, and Chapman took His Airness to the cleaner's. Total winnings: at least $130,000. Jordan promised to send them checks.

October 4, 1991: Bouler was picked up, on a court-authorized wiretap, talking to a man named George. The tap came courtesy of a local drug investigation in which Bouler was a suspected cocaine courier. In a transcript of the phone call, Bouler said he "bet a motherfucker out of about two hundred thousand dollars." He said he had three separate cashier's checks in his hands and was looking for a way not to pay taxes. When George asked if he wanted to avoid paying taxes, Bouler replied, "Hell, yeah."

Bouler had an idea. He would tell "the motherfucker that it was a personal loan. . . . 'Cause, you know, I'm fixin' to buy this other driving range, right? So he loaned me the money to get the driving range."

"Well, there you go," said the friend. "That might work."

October 7, 1991: According to court records, Bouler contacted the Monroe Mall branch of a local bank and asked whether it could cash a check for $57,000. He was told that the bank does not normally keep $57,000 in cash on hand.

October 17, 1991: A $57,000 cashier's check drawn from the Sovran bank in Washington, D.C., was sent via certified mail to Bouler.

October 17, 1991: A $77,000 cashier's check drawn from the same bank was sent to Dean Chapman.

October 21, 1991: Seventeen days after his original phone conversation with "George" and others about the three cashier's checks, the $200,000, and the idea of having "the motherfucker" say the money was a loan for a driving range, Bouler received and deposited into the Golf-Tech Driving Range account the $57,000 check. Unknown to Bouler, the bank had notified the IRS about the pending deposit, believing the funds may have been obtained illegally. At the time, Bouler was under investigation as a suspected cocaine courier for various drug organizations in the Charlotte and Monroe area (as a result of this investigation, he was later convicted of money laundering and gun-related violations). The next day, a U.S. magistrate issued a seizure warrant for the money.

December 1991: The *Gaston Gazette* and *Charlotte Observer* broke the story about the October 1 gambling spree, reporting that Jordan called the $57,000 check a loan to help Bouler build a driving range. "It's totally true. It's a loan," Jordan said, adding, "I have the right to associate with whoever I choose."

In the wake of those press reports, Jordan told the *Chicago Tribune* the same story. He offered no support material, no contracts, no loan papers, as evidence. The Chicago media basically passed on the story. "It was virtually ignored," Sam Smith, the *Tribune* reporter and author of *The Jordan Rules*, later told *USA Today*. "Remember, Michael has been so good for Chicago. Until the Bulls won the [NBA] championship, it was a city of losers."

January 4, 1992: The first of many letters and calls was exchanged between Esquinas and Jordan. The tone at this time was reverent. Three months had passed since their supposed million-dollar match. It's time, Esquinas wrote, to "inch" toward settlement. To that end, he offered a five-point plan asking for complete payment by October 1992. At the very least, he wanted 15 percent ($180,000) immediately.

He ended the letter thusly: "Listen World Champ, I know you need to focus on this season. I'm watching you on cable nitely [*sic*]. I just want you to know I'm pulling for you. Send my [enclosed] envelope back with check and you won't have to give our situation an 'iota' of consideration."

February 19, 1992: Gastonia bail bondsman Eddie Dow was brutally slain and robbed by four men who entered his heavily secured backwoods home and gunned him down in his carport. The intruders pried open Dow's stainless steel briefcase, which served as a movable cash register, and grabbed an estimated

$20,000 in cash, leaving assorted papers and documents. Police found three photocopies of checks totaling $108,000—$11,000, $20,000, and $77,000. The two smaller checks were written on August 22, 1991, from Jordan's personal checking account. The larger check was a Sovran Bank cashier's check written on October 17, 1991, payable to Dean Chapman. The two checks to Chapman totaled $97,000; the other was made out to "Pay."

March 6, 1992: U.S. District Court Judge Graham C. Mullen ruled that the IRS violated Bouler's rights in seizing the $57,000 check. In his opinion, Mullen stated, "Michael Jordan confirmed that this check was a loan made by him to the Petitioner." Subsequently, when questioned by *Sports Illustrated*, Judge Mullen admitted he based his statement on a *Charlotte Observer* newspaper clip filed by Bouler's attorney. It had quoted the *Chicago Tribune* saying Jordan had given Bouler money as a loan. Under the Federal Rules of Evidence, the newspaper clip would normally not be considered admissible evidence. Judge Mullen confirmed he never questioned Jordan. Neither did U.S. Attorney Tom Ashcraft.

March 10, 1992: A federal grand jury in Charlotte, North Carolina, indicted Bouler on charges of conspiracy and money laundering.

March 19, 1992: Commissioner Stern called the Jordan gambling allegations a "very serious matter" and announced that Lacey would head the NBA investigation.

March 20, 1992: U.S. Attorney Ashcraft issued a statement that said, in part, "This office does not have an investigation under way on Michael Jordan."

March 31, 1992: After its own two-week investigation, the NBA warned Jordan about his associations but did nothing else. It had no idea—as Jordan surely did—that he was receiving letters from Esquinas seeking settlement of the gambling debt.

"This situation has been investigated with complete cooperation of Michael and his attorneys and Judge Lacey has assured us that there appears to be no reason for the NBA to take action against Michael," said Stern. "Michael has advised us he understands the gravity of the situation, and that if he is not more careful about his associations, it can reflect adversely on his fellow players and the NBA. He has assured us he will be more careful about those associations in the future."

That night, before a Bulls-Knicks game in New York, Jordan addressed a surprisingly sparse group of reporters. "I wasn't worried," he said. "I was very aware of the whole situation. I was anxious to see what their points of view were. I was gracious [grateful] to see that it was really what it was and that I could help clarify it and move on. Once again, I appreciate the NBA doing it. They did what they had to do. I'm glad to put this behind me. I hope I've learned my lesson."

In retrospect, it is easy to see how Lacey and the league would have found "no reason" to take action against Jordan. They never contacted or questioned:

Slim Bouler
Dean Chapman
Flip Dow, Eddie Dow's brother and executor of his estate
The Monroe, North Carolina, police department, in Bouler's hometown
The Union County Sheriff's Department
The Police Department in Gastonia, North Carolina, home to Chapman and Dow
The Hilton Head (S.C.) Police Department, site of many of the high-stakes games
The clerk of U.S. District Court in Charlotte to review or retrieve any documents from the Bouler case
U.S. Attorney Tom Ashcraft
IRS or FBI agents assigned to the case.

May 1992: A Citibank $25,000 counter check payable to "E and S Marketing" was sent to Esquinas.

June 24, 1992: A second check for $50,000 was sent from a Citibank account to "E and S Marketing." It carried the accompanying note: "Richard this is from Michael. Take Care, Juanita."

Late October–early November 1992: "Dear MJ," wrote Esquinas in what would quickly become a string of increasingly demanding letters. "I'm writing to grab your attention for a few minutes and urge you to please call me to settle our 'monies issue' over the past year. Let me assure you I want to be fair and reasonable and allow for you to make a prompt and somewhat painless transaction. We must put closure on this issue so both of us can continue without having this unresolved." Esquinas ended by writing, "I know you're honorable and I know we can resolve this but I must have your attention and desire to close."

October 20, 1992: U.S. District Court House, Charlotte, North Carolina. The drug trial of Slim Bouler. Under questioning, Bouler admitted playing stakes matches with Jordan over several years and receiving the $57,000 from Jordan. After a recess for lunch, amid extraordinary security, a tight-lipped Michael Jeffrey Jordan took the witness stand, impeccably dressed in a gray-green suit. Jordan was questioned by Bouler's attorney, James F. Wyatt III, then by Assistant U.S. Attorney Frank Whitney. He said he had played golf with Bouler "eight to ten times" with stakes from "anywhere from twenty dollars to one thousand dollars a hole."

November 13, 1992: Another letter from Esquinas to Jordan. This one was more urgent and put a number on the remaining debt, $902,000:

"Dear MJ: Thanks for the message. I still haven't received your check but I'm certain it will be here. I'm writing to urge you to settle with me, so we can both put behind us this unsolved issue. We sit here today having to either A. Settle or B. Agree to carry forward for another year an unsettled debt of 902 (after forthcoming payment).

"*You prefer to carry forward full amount of 902 until June.

"*I prefer to settle.

"*We need a compromise and I'm willing to be overly accommodating."

With that, Esquinas offered a proposal, Plan A or B. In Plan A, he said he would settle for $300,000 if Jordan paid that week. "Done! Done! Done! No more thoughts, energy, etc.," he wrote.

Plan B was far more complicated, offering a $100,000 payment in exchange for a debt reduction to $600,000. "I prefer Plan A," Esquinas wrote, "just to end this madness."

November 23, 1992: Another letter from Esquinas to Jordan refers to Esquinas' receipt of a FedEx package containing a $50,000 check from Jordan. The San Diego businessman was not happy:

"Your note stated 'I am sure the enclosed is a sufficient number to put this thing behind us.' I want to point out this was an overdue payment from our last golf outing," Esquinas wrote back.

"MJ, I have been flexible with time, and I've offered a substantive reduction in your debt owed to me. I get the impression, you want to delay. . . . I know you're honorable, I know you want this behind us, but please don't try and turn your back on your responsibilities. I want this behind me *soon,* and you do too. I must insist on full settlement by Dec. 15, a reduction by 2/3 to 300. You can afford it, it's overdue. . . ."

November 25, 1992: Jordan called. According to notes by Esquinas dated that day, Jordan's "opening remark" was an attack.

"I hope this isn't a threat," Jordan said.

"Of course not, MJ," Esquinas answered. "I simply want [to be] paid."

"I thought we could carry this," Jordan told Esquinas. "I thought you would be more understanding. Do you need the money?"

"We all need money, MJ," said Esquinas. "More than that, I want to resolve this issue and get this behind us."

"If you want to put our friendship on the line," Jordan said, "fine, I'll settle for the three hundred."

"MJ," said Esquinas, "I'm trying to help you. You need to get this behind you, as well. Look, I think you should at least send fifty, and I'll give you a three-to-one discount."

At the bottom of the notes was a notation: "Jordan Agrees to 300,000."

November 26, 1992: Thanksgiving Day. Esquinas wrote Jordan another letter hoping to clarify what he called the "Friendship vs. Payment" issue:

"After our discussion, I reflected on many of the things we talked about and I had the distinct impression you questioned my friendship because I was asking for payment. MJ, YOU HAVE ALWAYS STATED YOU WILL PAY ME. I believe you, I've given you time, and I've offered you a steeply discounted 'out' so you can put this behind. . . ."

February 8, 1993: Esquinas had lost all patience. He wanted his money and he wanted it now.

"MJ, the last time we spoke you promised a partial payment by Dec. 15 (50)," he wrote. "Again, you did not deliver on a promise of payment. And, it finally struck me that neither one of us is doing 'the right thing' on this issue. You're negotiating for unfair lengths of time and steep discounts and I've been too 'easy' regarding payment schedule.

"We have been in a cat and mouse situation for over 16 months. MJ, my patience has simply run out!! Your not delivering on this last promise just made me realize the insaneness of our situation."

March 26, 1993: In a letter marked "Personal & Confidential," Chicago attorney Wayne A. McCoy, who later said he was representing Jordan, sent by Express Mail a $100,000 check payable to Esquinas. The cover letter read as follows: "In furtherance of assisting our client in consummating his arrangements with you, I am enclosing a cashier's check in the amount of $100,000 payable to your order. Thank you for the prompt return of your notarized affidavit confirming the necessary representations."

April 5, 1993: Esquinas acknowledged McCoy's "prompt and efficient handling" of his client's "arrangement to consummate his agreement with me." Then Esquinas went one step further, laying out a payment schedule for another $100,000 by June 1, 1993, and the final $100,000 between January 1 and January 10, 1994. It was the $300,000 he believed Jordan had agreed to back in November.

April 14, 1993: McCoy responded. In lawyerese, he informed Esquinas that his April 5 correspondence "goes further and purports to memorialize certain additional details of our client's arrangements with you. Since we lack familiarity with the details which you set forth, you should contact our client's representative with whom you exchanged previous communications." In other words, McCoy knew nothing until Jordan authorized another check.

May 26, 1993: Jordan and his father gambled in an Atlantic City casino the night before a playoff game against the Knicks in New York.

May 27, 1993: Another letter from McCoy to Esquinas. Another $100,000 payment. Same "in furtherance of assisting our client in consummating his arrangements" cover letter.

June 3, 1993: The story broke that Esquinas had self-published a book entitled *Michael & Me: Our Gambling Addiction . . . My Cry for Help!* In it, he extracted no small measure of revenge for all the failed attempts at settlement. He alleged Jordan still owed him $900,000 from bets on the golf course. The NBA launched a second investigation into charges, with Lacey again in the lead.

June 9, 1993: Jordan told NBC reporter Ahmad Rashad, "If I had a [gambling] problem, I'd be starving. I'd be hocking this watch, my championship rings, I would sell my house. My kids would be starving. I do not have a problem. I enjoy gambling."

July 12, 1993: Lacey and an associate interviewed Esquinas for more than two hours in New York. Costello was also present. A league spokesman emphasized that the investigative focus was narrow, on whether Jordan had "broken any rules" and whom "Michael was associating with."

During an interview with Lacey, Costello said, Esquinas raised a red flag about Jordan and illegal sports betting. He told Lacey that on March 29, 1992, while at Jordan's home in Highland Park, Illinois, he overheard Jordan utter the phrase, "So you say the line is seven points," while speaking on the telephone to an unknown person.

"He turned his head and made reference to the line," Esquinas said he told Lacey. "He had the kinda look that, 'You're not listening to this call.'" Added Esquinas, "My clear impression was of a point spread, wagering, but I did not hear a bet being placed."

On that particular day, a Sunday, one college game—an NCAA tournament game between Cincinnati and Memphis—had a published national line of six points. Three NBA games that night had national lines of nine points. That's as close to a seven-point spread as could be found.

Esquinas says he told Lacey two other people were present in the room—Jordan's young son Jeffrey, and Jordan's limo driver, George. Only George, said Esquinas, was close enough to hear. Both Esquinas and Costello recalled that Lacey showed a great interest in the betting remark.

"Now, Rich, can you repeat what you heard," Esquinas recalled Lacey asking. "He wanted me to recite in detail, word for word, how I heard what he said."

Esquinas also said Lacey peppered him about his background. "He asked me about my activities, insinuating other vices," Esquinas said. "I told him I had no connection to the mob or organized crime. That my wagering was limited to the Super Bowl and golf courses, and that I bet on basketball games in college."

Following that meeting, Costello says, neither he nor Esquinas heard from the judge again. No memos, no phone calls, no follow-up, no review of notes. Costello said it was only after he fired off two letters to Lacey that he finally responded. "Ulti-mately," Lacey wrote back, "I have to submit a report to the commissioner." Contacted about his investigation, Lacey had no comment.

July 23, 1993: James Jordan was murdered.

August 1, 1993: In a compelling *Washington Post* story by investigative reporter Bill Brubaker, Bouler spoke out for the first time. "I gambled and played golf with Michael Jordan for six summers, but the NBA hasn't even called me," he told Brubaker. "What kind of investigation is that?"

During a four-hour interview at a minimum-security facility in Texas, Bouler said he played golf with Jordan as many as fifty times from 1986 until 1991 and loaned him thousands of dollars to play.

While working at the range one day, Bouler was told by some friends that Jordan was down at the local golf course. "I said, 'So what?'" Bouler told Brubaker while Bouler was serving a nine-year sentence for money laundering and gun-related violations. "I mean it wasn't no big deal because I'd been around celebrities all the time in different golf tournaments.

"But when they said, 'Jordan's playing with hundred-dollar bills,' that drew my attention because I make a living by playing golf. I said, 'Go in and get my equipment.' So we played and there was chemistry between me and Michael. Michael likes golf and I like golf. Michael likes to gamble and I like to gamble."

September 1993: As the 1993–94 season approached, Stern said the Jordan investigation would end before training camps opened on October 8.

October 6, 1993: Jordan retired. The gambling investigation was "continuing," a league spokesman said.

October 8, 1993: The Jordan investigation ended. The same league spokesman explained that Lacey had "finished his work," although, when pressed, the spokesman admitted neither Lacey, Stern, or anyone else associated with the league had ever inter-viewed the principal subject of the investigation. Said the spokes-man: "Lacey was going to meet with Michael and David [Stern] but never did . . . but Michael and David agreed to meet some-time in the future."

Asked why the league closed its investigation without talking to Jordan, why it chose not to release any portion of Lacey's report, the spokesman replied, "Those are valid points. What the answers are I'm not sure."

Later, he said that Jordan was never interviewed because Esquinas "wasn't considered very credible." The spokesman made it a point to question why Esquinas didn't put the betting reference in his "tell-all" book.

"Why? Because it wasn't a tell-all book and I sure as hell didn't tell it all," responded Esquinas. "It wasn't like I was trying to take down Michael Jordan. Bob [Costello] told me to tell them everything, so there were no problems later on."

Which left Costello with just one conclusion about the NBA investigation. "A gigantic cover-up," he said. "There was no investigation. Lacey told me everything Esquinas said was, quote, 'irrefutable' because he had the checks to back it up. How, suddenly, is the betting remark not credible? How can you not ask Michael Jordan about the phone conversation? Lacey clearly told us he wanted to interview Jordan. He was upset Jordan had played him for a fool because of the results of his previous investigation. He wanted an answer as to who Jordan was talking to on the telephone. But he got called off.

"We wanted to give Lacey testimony under oath, on the record. Lacey declined a lie detector, said there was no need for a court reporter. He wanted no part of it. The only investigation the league did was to try and intimidate Esquinas to make him go away.

"Listen, Michael Jordan is clearly the greatest basketball player of all time, but just as clearly this NBA investigation was an insult to the American people."

March 10, 1995: The official announcement comes that Jordan had given up on a baseball career, after hitting .202 at Class AA Birmingham.

March 20, 1995: In a two-word press release—"I'm back"— Jordan confirmed widespread speculation that, after a seventeen-month absence, he would return to the NBA.

March 21, 1995: A league spokesman said Jordan and Commissioner Stern had finally talked, prior to Jordan's return to basketball.

"They have had a conversation," said the spokesman. "They talked several times during his retirement. It was private between the two of them."

Was gambling discussed?

"It was a private conversation," said the spokesman.

When Michael Jordan returned to the Bulls, he remarked that he had done so, in part, to restore his own behavorial standard to a league overrun by the anarchists of Generation X. He certainly did. Weeks later, in a playoff series against Orlando that was the NBA's most anticipated event since Jordan's departure, Jordan first defied unwritten league policy by changing his jersey number back to 23 from the 45 he wore upon his return. Then he drew the ire of the media by not speaking after practices or games. It didn't take long before the other stars in the series, including Shaquille O'Neal, followed Jordan's lead.

One Sunday in Chicago, Stern walked through the tunnel of the spanking new United Center following a Bulls victory over the Magic and spotted Brian McIntyre, his PR guru.

"What's going on?" Stern asked McIntyre, who filled him in.

Stern tried to play some late-game defense for the NBA, if not for Jordan.

After joking that he hoped O'Neal didn't show up for the next game wearing No. 99, he said the jersey issue would be dealt with later (the Bulls were eventually nominally fined). As for the media boycott, Stern said with a sigh, "Our guys have always been the best at this. No Steve Carltons here."

Then Stern walked off, leaving crabby reporters to chase after cooperative scrubs such as Steve Kerr and Will Purdue.

While a long way from its attitudes regarding gamblers and drug dealers, this was yet another symbolic nonact and example of the league's ultimate powerlessness—or its sense of it, anyway—when dealing with its meal tickets. "It's a difficult issue to draw a distinction between whether a player is doing something that's maybe not in his best interests and the NBA's," Russ Granik told *The Washington Post* after the Jordan gambling debacle. "But we don't feel we're in a position to interfere in every player's private life and to [require him] to live up to certain standards that somebody else might set."

The question remained: What standards did NBA stars have to live up to at all? Then–baseball commissioner Fay Vincent placed the Philadelphia Phillies' Len Dykstra on one-year probation in 1991 after the outfielder piled up $78,000 in debts to a gambler in

Mississippi. In contrast, Bulls general manager Jerry Krause repeatedly said he didn't give a damn about Jordan's gambling because the player had broken no team rules.

That hear-no-evil denial after so many unmistakable alarms only made NBA stars feel less beholden to their employers. The great ones, those who had come to have it all, didn't really feel as if they worked for the NBA as much as they believed the NBA— and a whole lot of others—worked for them.

As Stern's machine pushed on with the sneaker sellers and the rest of the marketeers, pro basketball icons were feeling more and more untouchable, invincible. In a way, Jordan had been lucky that fate had intervened. Evidence of his "secret life" had slipped out, forcing him to at least acknowledge it, put the right spin on it, before his $40-million-a-year endorsement haul was threatened. Before he got pulled in too deep, as another NBA superstar in another championship city was said to have already done.

Jordan came back and became bigger than ever. By the time 1995 was giving way to 1996, he was again at the wheel of his sport, driving hard, though he was about to pull over to pick up a familiar and fan-friendly face, a once-magical man who desperately wanted one more ride in the NBA fast lane.

12

Mr. Smith Goes to Hollywood

THERE WASN'T A WHOLE LOT OF MAGIC, JUST MANY SIGNS OF unusual maturity, in Joe Smith's rookie season. Not until Earvin Johnson Jr. stepped out of the poster on Smith's bedroom wall for a little Showtime one-on-one.

The basketball world had been waiting for this moment for four and a half years. Smith had been fantasizing for almost all his life.

He was at the rented home he shared with his mother and his twenty-three-year-old cousin, Keith Sharp, in Oakland's Blackhawk section the last week in January when the stunning news spread quickly around the globe. After false starts and dashed hopes, Magic Johnson was returning to the Lakers. As league rules dictated, Johnson was selling back his 5 percent ownership stake to Jerry Buss (for $12 million, or $1 million more than he'd paid in on June 27, 1994). He would play his first game at the Great Western Forum on January 30 against Golden State, at his new position, power forward. The global legend would match up against a player sixteen years his junior, the twenty-year-old No. 1 pick in the 1995 college draft.

The phone calls began coming in, from Smith's former Maryland teammates such as Exree Hipp, and some of the guys from the Norfolk playgrounds. One of them told Smith, "Don't get used. You'll be on *SportsCenter*."

That was a nineties mentality, Generation X talk, and Smith, the more time he had to think, wasn't buying into it. Who was he to worry about getting "used" on national television by his own boyhood hero? It was only about a year before that he'd practically begged to stand next to Johnson and have their picture taken together.

His Maryland team had been in Maui for a holiday tournament, and Johnson, who owns a home there, was scouting for the Lakers. "We were at the pool in the hotel, and all of a sudden, there's Magic. One of the guys had a camera, so I just jumped up and said, 'Do you mind?'"

Of course he didn't. There was seldom a photo opportunity, an interview on the run, a chance to celebrate celebrityhood, that Johnson could pass up. It was what made him the smiling face of American sports in the 1980s, the standard-bearer for the decade in which television, via the cable explosion, the coming of specialization, became more entwined than ever with sports.

As Magic himself once said, explaining how he and Laker teammate Michael Cooper repeatedly teamed up for fast-break lobs to the rim, "It's kind of like we have ESPN."

The remarkable growth of the NBA as prime sports television in the eighties created a division between the modern game and the less popular version that had preceded it. So driven to survive, then grow, was the NBA that it didn't have baseball's obsession to connect its generations, to retain as much old-time flavor. The NBA, with no golden era to fondly recall, did not really want to look like its past.

It wasn't until 1981 that David Stern convinced his teams to drop what today would be money to cater an All-Star breakfast buffet, $140,000, on videocassette recorders so all league games could be taped and archived. Considering most games were not televised in the pre-cable era, that left the NBA with precious little footage of yesterday's heroes.

So for players such as Smith, the kids with the endorsement deals and droopy shirts, it was as if nothing had happened before 1980, when Johnson flamboyantly led the Lakers to the NBA championship. He was, back then, an affirmation of what they wanted to be now. An instant success, a kid who stepped from his sophomore year at Michigan State, where he won an NCAA title, right into the NBA Finals. He was the best player there, too.

At 6-9, with the skills of the most diminutive point-guard wizards, Johnson, with a hefty assist from Larry Bird, changed the way players were perceived, the way they were typically consigned to position by size. He was a player for all positions, and all seasons. You could make the argument that he had become, given the unfortunate circumstances that caused his retirement, basketball's Joe DiMaggio, superstar athlete turned social statement. All he lacked was Paul Simon putting him to verse.

Smith was four years old when Johnson won the first of his five NBA championships. And even at the height of the Magic-Bird rivalry, the mid-eighties, he was a ten-year-old kid imitating Johnson's loping dribble and signature no-look pass. And when Smith reached high school, he still was one major growth spurt away from taking his game down low. "I was only six-two," he said. "I played guard. I tried to do whatever he did."

Johnson's poster was on the wall overlooking Smith's bed. He wore his number, 32. And that terrible night, November 7, 1991, when Johnson, still fantastically poised under pressure, still fracturing the English language with what was now a sad and fateful ignorance, told the world that he had "attained" HIV infection, Smith stared at the pictures coming out of Los Angeles in utter disbelief. He went to practice at Maury High School the next day and stumbled around the gym in a fog.

"He couldn't believe that this could happen to somebody like Magic," said the Maury coach, Jack Baker. "We used to sit around all the time, talking about Magic. He was a big part of Joe's life. He worshiped the guy."

Johnson's contracting HIV laid bare the indulgent lifestyle of the contemporary NBA star. Not all, but many. Too many. And some of the coaches weren't much better, with little black books and clandestine meetings all over the NBA map. In the era of global basketball celebrity, in the age of AIDS, too many NBA people were revealed to be anywhere between high risk and, as Johnson would admit, out of control.

"Today, because of the money and the fame, all you have to be is an athlete," said Walt Frazier, the handsome, urbane New York Knicks icon of the 1970s and admitted champion partyer of his generation. "That lifestyle will find you. I'm not saying it's wrong.

Sex is a human need. But the rules have changed now. These guys need to use their heads."

Frazier left the sport for almost ten years before returning to broadcast Knicks games on radio. He couldn't believe what he saw, and had missed. "In my day, you at least had to go to parties, and you had to have a rap to pick up women," he said. "Now you see them lining up against the wall after the game. The stars just take their pick and the other guys get the leftovers."

In the firestorm caused by the revelation of Johnson's aberrant lifestyle and the predictable cry of the high-handed moralists, Johnson never did get enough credit for at least bringing the AIDS debate and the message of safe sex into the locker room, where most athletes—indeed most heterosexual men—preferred to believe AIDS was not something they could get. Johnson could have said nothing and played on. Though his attempts to be an AIDS educator were usually clumsy, halfhearted, and ill-informed, he was one of the first mainstream celebrities at least to admit what he had.

The question of whether Johnson's shocking story encouraged NBA players, athletes, and men in general to practice safe sex was another story. Most players, agents, and league officials said they believed the use of condoms became more widespread post-Magic, though one former agent who left the industry but remained close to several players said, "The smarter guys use condoms, but, by and large, there's still too many guys out there who think what they want to think. Some question how Magic really got the virus, some just don't think it can happen to them, and some just don't think period."

This former agent said the one way to determine if players were using condoms was to gauge the number of children being conceived by unmarried players. "Look at the college kids, half of them come into the league now with kids," he said. "Stephon Marbury had a kid before he got to Georgia Tech. Ray Allen. What does that tell you about condom use?"

One day following Magic's latest comeback, Karl Malone, whose anti–Magic comeback statements in November 1992 to the *New York Times* contributed to Johnson's scurrying for the sidelines again, was asked if the sexual habits of players had changed at all in the last four years.

An honest-to-a-fault, self-described country boy from backwater Summerfield, Louisiana, Malone tilted his head, offered an incredulous sneer, and said cryptically, "Nothing's changed, and you'd be surprised who's out there."

Malone, by now, said he had no problems playing against Johnson. Actually, he never said that he personally did. His comments had been more of a biting indictment of the rosy prognosis the media was putting on Johnson's post–Dream Team comeback. Malone said players were lying because they were scared to speak their minds. He, meanwhile, worried that his teammates would instinctively hold back against Johnson, and that would tarnish the competition.

This hysterical fear of HIV came at the league like Magic on the break. "We spent weeks closeted around here," said David Stern. "How do we respond to this? What do we do? Who the hell knows?"

In the end, even Stern didn't know how to put the right spin on this daunting crisis. Charles Grantham hastily commissioned a Johns Hopkins expert, Michael P. Johnson, to create an educational program for the Players' Association. But more than clinical talk about "infinitesimal" odds, the players needed "family" assurances. They needed people they knew to bring the whispering in the locker rooms and on the team buses to a more open forum. Utah's Malone beat them all to it, saying he was unconvinced there was almost no risk of transmission playing against an HIV-infected player. He said most players were scared but more afraid to admit it.

Johnson, not used to rejection, picked up his ball and went home. At the time, he could at least rationalize the players' fears much better than Stern's flaccid support. Where was the great NBA public relations machine when he, for a change, really needed it? "We all could have dealt with it better, myself included," Johnson said.

As the years passed, Johnson realized more and more that he should have held his ground, played on. Now, after more than 370 missed regular-season games, with twenty-seven new pounds of muscle packed into his arms, chest, and neck, his stomach no longer the washboard it once was, Johnson was back with some advice for those who remained unenlightened: "Everybody's going to have to deal with it."

That included Jerry West, the Lakers' astute general manager, their other legend-in-residence. From the time Johnson retired, West had been trying to rebuild the team, but always confronting Johnson's unyielding presence as a possible player, an interim coach, a minority owner, a scout, and Buss' confidant. A serious and straightforward man, West respected Johnson's greatness and popularity, but he was weary of his constant distractions. West had managed to keep the Lakers more than competitive with a series of clever personnel moves. The Lakers, while not yet contenders, were headed beyond the Johnson era. Thanks to West, they were the one dominant team from the 1980s that had not fallen on dreadful times, such as Philadelphia, Boston, and Detroit.

Now Johnson was back and the fragile young egos on the team would have to, as Johnson said, deal with it. Privately, West wasn't sure they could. And for how long was Johnson back? How could West plan for next year or the year after that when Johnson, he feared, was almost week-to-week?

Asked for a comment in the Lakers' offices the day of the Golden State game, West seemed far removed from the festive spirit that had overtaken L.A. to the point where Johnson was being hailed for reuniting a region racially torn by Rodney King and the O.J. trial. The mayor, Richard J. Riordan, was in the newspapers comparing Johnson to Franklin Roosevelt.

"I've already said what I have to say," West said, waving off three reporters, and familiar ones at that. "No comment."

Ninety minutes before game time, Joe Smith stood in front of his dressing stall in the visitors' locker room at the Great Western Forum, admitting he had had trouble sleeping the previous night. He had Magic on his mind. "It's been real nerve-racking," he said, pulling his blue-and-gold No. 32 jersey over his head. He sat down, still wearing his underwear briefs. He tapped his bare feet rhythmically, obviously not able to contain his excitement. This was going to be a happening, and he, by luck of the draw, would happen to be right in the middle of it.

"I never thought I would get a chance to play against him," Smith said. "Maybe against a team he was coaching. But not against him. This is like . . . a dream."

Smith was only nine days removed from the best night of his young pro career. Matched against Larry Johnson, Smith had outscored the $84-million man 21–12 and outrebounded him 20–8 in a Golden State victory at the Charlotte Coliseum, where Smith had played both of his Atlantic Coast Conference tournaments.

So that, someone said, must be the highlight of the season.

"No," Smith answered, shaking his head and producing his own made-for-TV smile. "This is. Tonight."

In the stall next door, an eavesdropping Chris Mullin couldn't help but chuckle. This was typical Smith, he said, a refreshing kid in a man's world not trying to make believe he was all grown-up.

"He's a real good listener," said Mullin. "The coaches mention it once, he does it every time."

An eleven-year veteran whose brilliant career was nearly annulled early on by a drinking problem, Mullin still had his trademark buzz cut and severe Flatbush accent, though years of arresting alcoholism borne of family dysfunction had helped make him an introspective and eloquent voice in a locker room that too often seemed like a poorly supervised reform school. Back at the Oakland Coliseum, it was no coincidence that Smith was given the stall right next to Mullin's.

Mullin said he wasn't into comparing Smith with anyone else, especially anyone named Webber, but left no doubt that the Warriors could not have reversed their young-power-forward fortunes from the previous disastrous season any better than they had.

"With most young players, you get thirty, you start to think it's easy," Mullin said. "You don't get it, you think it'll never happen. The best thing about Joe is that you can't tell what happened the night before."

Mullin said he'd seen that unflappable quality in Smith several times already. The first was during a preseason game in San Diego against Denver and Antonio McDyess, the No. 2 pick in the draft. Carrying at least an extra twenty-five pounds of bulk, McDyess manhandled Smith, outscoring him 19–2 and outrebounding him 9–2. During one stretch, McDyess powered a tomahawk dunk over Smith, then swatted his layup into the stands. By late in the game, a smirking McDyess was posting Smith up, calling for the ball.

The expression on Smith's face, Mullin recalled, never changed, which was truly remarkable, given that McDyess, No. 2, was out there making a show of trying to embarrass No. 1. These days, a kid could get killed in a city playground for doing that. Smith, Mullin said, swallowed his medicine and took nothing personally. But not two weeks later, the Nuggets showed up for a regular-season game in Oakland, and this time, Smith scored several clutch baskets in a 13-point, 8-rebound game that went the Warriors' way. McDyess, on the bench for most of the fourth quarter, had 6 points and 4 rebounds. Smith didn't run off with one finger wagging, didn't talk about how he'd got even.

Such performances had moved Jon Barry, the backup Warriors guard and son of former Golden State star Rick Barry, to nickname Smith "Simba." As Barry explained, "Joe has the heart of a lion."

In the Bay Area, he was already generating a wave of positive press that was priceless to the franchise after the Webber-Nelson debacle. Sportswriter after sportswriter made the pilgrimage to Joe and Letha's house, for a sampling of motherly love and her son's favorite meat-loaf dinner. Sometimes the press followed Letha and Joe to Oakland's Allen Temple Baptist Church on Sunday morning. The party line was that these were the values the NBA needed more of. And veterans, at least the intelligent ones, weren't doing double takes when they watched Smith stride into the Coliseum, his mother struggling to keep up.

"Too many rookies come in here with their chests sticking way out like they know every damn thing," said Karl Malone. "I don't see any of that in him."

But there was also much material evidence that times and fortunes had changed for Joe and Letha. For the first time in their lives, wads of cash were being spent. In December, three days before Christmas, she came home one day to find a champagne-colored Lexus in the garage. The sight of her first new car, she said, made her knees weak. Joe had also kept his promise and bought her a home. It wasn't on the Virginia shore but on Lake Whitehurst in the Norfolk area. This way, the now-retired Jasper Smith could come over to fish.

For Christmas, Joe was named December's NBA Rookie of the Month. The first month's honor had gone to Toronto's Isiah Thomas wanna-be point guard, Damon Stoudamire. Now Smith seemed to be coming on in the early race for Rookie of the Year. The Warriors weren't winning enough. They had internal problems that were about to induce the dealing of longtime point guard Tim Hardaway to Miami. But Smith couldn't complain, particularly on January 30, as he lined up for the Warriors' pregame layup drill, sneaking glances to the other side of the court, where Magic and the Lakers were warming up to the familiar beat and lyrics of Randy Newman's "I Love L.A."

The long wait for Magic would soon be over. At 9:39 of the first quarter, the Lakers' starting power forward, Elden Campbell, picked up his second foul. To a resounding ovation, Johnson peeled off his warm-ups. On the Lakers' next possession, he headed straight for right post, turned, and stuck his rear into Smith's waist. Up went his right arm, the signal that he wanted the ball. The guard, Nick Van Exel, obediently delivered it. Johnson dribbled, threw up a baby hook with his right hand. It missed. But Magic was back.

And, as the courtside photographers flash-recorded the moment for posterity, Smith was right there with him, forever linked with his hero, in a moment he would savor for the rest of his days.

Smith fouled out of the game late in the fourth quarter, trying to guard Johnson. With the Warriors mounting a late rally, Johnson got the ball, this time on the left post, and spun off Smith's hip, to the baseline. The official, Eddie F. Rush, blew his whistle. Two free throws. Money in the bank. Lakers win, 128–118.

No one was going to remember that Smith, who had 23 points and 10 rebounds, had more than held his own against the returning and—for this night, anyway—conquering hero. He didn't care. Even in defeat, there was a postgame giddiness in Smith that was more than understandable. It was charming. "When he came on the court, I wanted to clap, too," Smith said.

For most NBA fans, it was a night out of a storybook, a game televised nationally by TNT that would not soon be forgotten. Johnson played as if he'd never left. He had 19 points, 10 assists, 8 rebounds. The Lakers accumulated a season high in points, a league season high in assists.

And as it turned out, it wasn't Smith who got "used," who wound on the clip that would be rewound and reshown for days. The "honor" went to Latrell Sprewell, the lanky guard with the big offensive game and the even bigger head.

It was a moment that not only symbolically served as Johnson's reintroductory statement but also as a brainy commentary on basketball's generational divide. In the first quarter, Johnson missed one of his patented shot-puts that passed for jump shots from the right wing. When Smith failed to box him out, he followed his shot and was in perfect position to catch a pass from center Vlade Divac, who rebounded the ball in the lane.

Sprewell, an active defender, was between Johnson and the basket. Not for long. Johnson gave a head feint, faked a shovel pass right, and presto, a path to the basket magically appeared. It was only fair to ask what one of the Generation Xers, having faked his opponent right out of his way, would have done with that space between himself and the basket. The answer was obvious. He would have power-dunked, sneered at the vanquished defender, and suggested he keep his pitiful ass out of the way.

Johnson laid the ball gently in and jogged downcourt. Different approach. Same effect.

"He got me," said Sprewell, a Chris Webber supporter in the Nelson feud—he'd scrawled Webber's number on his sneakers—and then at odds with Hardaway over who deserved the ball more. "That was a sweet move."

Not enough for Sprewell to change his position in the debate he'd had with Smith a few days before in Salt Lake City, though. With the anticipation of Magic's return growing, it was Sprewell's contention that while Magic could come back and make the whole Western Conference disappear, he still wasn't going to be Michael Jordan.

"Mike's the man," Sprewell lectured the rookie.

"No, Magic's the man," said Smith.

"He was the man."

"No, he is the man."

Jordan, as it turned out, was on his way to Los Angeles, to settle this issue, once and for all.

The Bulls arrived in Los Angeles late on Thursday night, February 1, immediately after disposing of the Kings in Sacramento. It was their eighteenth straight win, their forty-first of the season against a ridiculous three losses. They were destroying the league, openly discussing their prospects of shattering the 1971–72 Lakers' all-time regular-season record of sixty-nine wins. Before the game, in fact, Jordan referred to the Bulls as being "on the brink of winning seventy."

He said it to warn the media not to blow the Bulls-Lakers confrontation—being touted by Johnson as a "see-where-we're-at game"—out of proportion.

"Everyone sees Michael Jordan versus Magic Johnson, not the standings and the situation," Jordan said. "This is going to be a real game, not no barnstorming tour."

Jordan, in other words, was more or less discounting the Golden State game as a barometer of where Johnson and the Lakers were. He said he hadn't watched, only heard that the defense was not quite up to Chicago's imperial standards. Or to put it in his own coldly candid way: "Joe Smith had twenty-five and ten." After having added two points to the rookie's total, he added, "There are a lot of good teams out here. Golden State's not one of them."

Jordan maintained the appearance of a friendship with Johnson, but they were not particularly close. Jordan, far more private than Johnson, far more selective in choosing members for his entourage, was never completely comfortable with the way Johnson suddenly touted the two as contemporary allies, not coincidentally just as Larry Bird's back woes were removing him and the Celtics from prominence.

Among Jordan's best friends in the game were Charles Barkley and Patrick Ewing, his contemporaries if not his equals. In his mind, Johnson and Bird were an entry, from the league's historical perspective, having entered the league five years before Jordan did. He stood alone, in his very own era. And if Johnson had been a loyal friend to any player, it was to Isiah Thomas, whom Jordan despised and still believed to be the ringleader of a plan to keep the ball away from him during his first All-Star Game in 1985 due to resentment over his benchmark Nike contract. Years later, after his own falling-out with Thomas, Johnson called Jordan to assure him he had not been part of any boycott, which Thomas always claimed never existed. During the 1991 Finals, Johnson's last hurrah before HIV, he finally engaged Jordan on the championship stage. The Lakers lost the title, Jordan's first, in a decisive five-game rebuke.

"Our friendship is our friendship," Jordan said, when asked, in the moments before they would renew their on-court relationship, how close they were.

On the other hand, he genuinely respected Johnson, what he'd meant to the game, and to him. "I used him as a driving force," he said. "Bird, too. They were the best. Magic, Larry, myself, we earned what we have. Nothing was given to us. Magic Johnson didn't have to be marketed to become marketable."

Here, Jordan was taking one sure-handed swipe at the over-hyped, under-accomplished Generation X superstars, whom he, by virtue of being the first player championed by corporate America, had ironically opened the gates for. He resented the notion that Shaquille O'Neal was as marketable—or as worthy of the hype—as him.

"It's sort of like Jordan was this incredible stereo and Shaq comes along and he's in the digital age and he's multimedia," said the ever-expressive Shaq-seller and L.A.-based Leonard Armato, whose greatest wish was for O'Neal to bolt Orlando when his contract expired following the '95–96 season and join him in Los Angeles, with the Lakers. "Shaq's almost a superhero who doesn't need special effects."

Jordan, however, was saying, Get real, that's exactly what O'Neal does need. In his subtle, calm way, he was arguing that Shaq Fu—not to mention Larry Johnson's Grandmama and Anfernee Hardaway's Li'l Penny—were nothing more than bogus boardroom creations, whose marketing campaigns were not based on skills, on performance. It was just phony celebrity.

One only had to witness Jordan's performance against Jerry Stackhouse in Philadelphia on January 12 to understand his disdain for Fast Food Stardom. Early in the season, the rookie had anointed himself a Money Player, saying he did not find the league all that tough and it was just a matter of time before he got the calls, like Michael. Uh-oh. Jordan heard that. He beat up on Stackhouse so bad that night Stackhouse should have immediately called Dean Smith to find out what the reenrollment policy was. Final score of the Tar Heel Classic: Jordan 48, Stackhouse 13.

The morning after, ESPN's *SportsCenter* would repeatedly show Jordan ball-faking Stackhouse as if he were a traffic light and his eyes were flashing green. Let Fila put that one into its promotional tapes. Case closed.

Magic, Larry, and Michael—the Originals—didn't need anyone to dream up a playful alter ego for them. While Jordan entertained the press in the locker room, Magic was on the floor, soaking in the pregame flavor, not missing a beat. He was so excited that he'd arrived three hours before tip-off. Before long he was out challenging Frankie King, a rookie Laker guard, to some long-distance shooting. He bantered with local television reporters, stepping over to embrace the females. He chatted with early-arriving courtside regulars. He invited the freshman cable analyst and former Celtic obstructionist Danny Ainge out in his shirt and tie for a couple of three-point flings. He summoned his friend and longtime nightlife collaborator Arsenio Hall for a hug and a chat.

"Everyone's coming tonight," Magic yelled out, shooting a three. Denzel Washington. Charlie Sheen. John Cusack. Jack Nicholson, shooting *Blood and Wine* in Miami, hopped right on a plane as soon as he heard that the director, Bob Rafelson, was ill and had called off filming for the day.

They were all coming to see Michael and Magic, and Magic was here to be seen. The photographers and camera crews recorded every move, while Johnson smiled through it all. This more than anything illustrated the difference in the public personas of Michael Jordan and Magic Johnson. For Jordan, it had always been about the raw competition, along with the extraordinary cash. For Johnson, it was the attention, too. The love of the life.

Once, when the original Dream Team trained in Monte Carlo for the Barcelona Games and the crowd started to chant Johnson's name during an exhibition against France—"Ma-jeek! . . . Ma-jeek!"—he stopped the game to take a bow and even climbed up to the royal box to share the moment with Prince Albert. When the fans began a similar chant for Jordan—"Mike-el! . . . Mike-el!"—Jordan, on the bench, put a towel over his head until they stopped.

On the court, it was all basketball, all business. And this was Jordan's time, as he had reminded Johnson that same week in Monte Carlo during a riotous practice game between the Jordans and the Johnsons.

Johnson's team had taken the early lead, and he couldn't stop himself from teasing Jordan each time his team notched another basket. Finally, Jordan got mad. These were the best players in the game on the court, with the country's premier basketball writers sitting in the stands. In a matter of minutes, the score was tied. In the waning seconds, one of the officials hired by USA Basketball to police these celebrity scrimmages called what seemed to be a cheap foul on Johnson, sending Jordan to the line.

"Man, oh, man," Johnson whined, playing to the crowd. "This may as well be Chicago Stadium."

At which point Jordan, holding the ball at the free-throw line, turned to Johnson and deadpanned, "No, Magic. This is the nineties."

And now it was the mid-nineties, as Johnson was about to be painfully reminded in a game that was such a stunning reversal from the one seventy-two hours before, it already made Johnson's comeback temporarily sag around the eyes.

Playing without their starting center (Australian Luc Longley) and versatile sixth man (Croatian Toni Kukoc), and on what should have been tired legs, the Bulls held the Lakers to their season low in points, crushing them 99–84, seemingly punishing them for having even acted as if this were a showdown of significant magnitude. They showed no sympathy for Johnson. He was bounced around in the pivot by Dennis Rodman, knocked down half a dozen times, and had to hold himself back on two occasions from jumping in Rodman's face. He had a few moments, but none as telling as his most unflattering attempt to be the Magic of old.

It came in the third quarter as Johnson drove the right side, guarded by Rodman, blond for the occasion. Johnson, in the lane, was suddenly confronted by Scottie Pippen, with Rodman a step to the side. For an instant, it looked as if both players were going to try to block Johnson's shot, setting Johnson's mind on making the pass, as he had all his playing life, to the open man. But both defenders suddenly dropped back, forcing Johnson to double-clutch, to improvise, which his bulked-up body wasn't prepared to do. He looked positively George Foreman–esque, throwing up a roundhouse layup that didn't reach the rim.

Later, drawing from his own unpleasurable experience of not being able to defy the laws of gravity, at least not up to his onetime standards, during his own impromptu comeback the previous spring, Jordan said, "Because of your competitive nature, you think you can come back and do what you want to do. But the game teaches you not to take it for granted."

Jordan's comeback season had been rudely ended by youthful Orlando in the second round of the 1994–95 playoffs. In the fourth quarters of the games Chicago lost, Jordan missed jumpers, couldn't get to the rim, and lost the ball. It infuriated him that he'd lost to O'Neal's team, and suggestions that greatness was gone from him for good sent him to the gym like Rocky before a climactic fight. At thirty-six, given the whimsical way he seemed to make these life-altering decisions, it didn't seem likely that Johnson could recapture enough old Magic. His comeback, even to Jordan, already seemed more about retiring again, only this time on his own terms.

"I think it bothered him that he didn't go out the way he wanted to," Jordan said.

He had gone right over to Johnson when the game ended, and they walked off together. Soon they shared an unusual but charming postgame press conference, an NBA version of *Late Night with Leno and Letterman.* It was also the third time Johnson and Jordan were interviewed that day. First, after the teams had their morning shoot-arounds. Then, before the game. And finally, here, in the bowels of the Forum, in a makeshift area blocked off by barriers and curtains.

It was a lesson in how the media-savvy NBA and its marketable stars used to do up a big event. By being available, talkative, irresistible. Now, most of the young stars and many of the veterans refused to talk at all on game days, until after the game, when they often were rushing to catch a plane or dine with their agent or meet up with a date. Even Jordan, after years of enjoying the pregame banter, was usually off-limits in the weight room. And whereas once most teams had open practices for the regulars on the beat, they were now closed, with windows covered up so no one could so much as peek, an NFL policy introduced by Pat Riley.

But not this night, when Johnson wanted to tell the world that "it was a thrill playing with Michael again," when Jordan graciously slid into the chair next to Johnson. He wore an exquisite olive suit, perfectly tailored compared to Johnson's baggy blue jacket and matching pants. There was one microphone on the table, which the two megastars traded, as the questions came fast and furious.

Jordan: "I'm planning on playing a couple more years and I hope he'll stay around, too. I'd hate to see it end on this note because we'd like to have a better game."

Wicked smile, at which point Johnson pulled the microphone away.

Johnson: "That's for sure. You know he'll be dogging me all summer about this."

Jordan: "He don't have Jabbar to throw the ball to. He doesn't have James Worthy."

Johnson: "When I saw him walk out, he's looking at me, and I know he's got the firepower behind him."

While this was probably nothing more than an acknowledgment of the team with the best record in basketball, now winners of nineteen straight, it was easy to understand how Johnson's sensitive or insecure teammates might have misconstrued what was being said. While Johnson was up on that pedestal with Jordan, Van Exel, Cedric Ceballos, and some of the other young Lakers were way off to the side, looking on.

They didn't seem to be soaking up the festivities as giddily as the reporters were. They had to wonder legitimately if Johnson had returned to run with them or stand with Jordan. To play for the Lakers or get back into central casting for special events like the upcoming All-Star Weekend. Magic's comeback was only two games old, but it wasn't too soon to wonder how long the honeymoon would last. To remember that not every young NBA millionaire was as deferential, respectful, and well behaved as the one Letha Smith had raised in Norfolk.

The master showman who
masterminded the global
rise of the NBA.
(Allen Einstein Photo)

David Stern: The picture of
success at Teaneck (NJ)
High School.

Joe Smith: The number-one draft pick who actually lived up to the hype. *(Nick Lammers/*The *Oakland* Tribune)

Joe and Letha Smith: Mom watched her son's back on the dock of the family's new lakefront home. *(Huy Nguyen)*

Len Elmore: The All-American turned Harvard lawyer turned player agent who was disillusioned by a guy named Joe.
(Courtesy of ESPN)

Kevin Garnett: Everyone wanted a piece of this high school phenom, who proved he was ready for the pros. (Chicago Tribune/*Photo by Charles Cherney*)

Buck Williams: the sturdy power forward and—unlike so many young bucks—a stand-up guy. *(Courtesy of the Portland Trail Blazers)*

Doug Collins: At peace with himself, the fiery coach taught his young team what winning was all about. *(Allen Einstein Photo)*

Joe Dumars: Detached during the fall of a franchise, the consummate pro returned to lead the rebirth of the Pistons. *(Allen Einstein Photo)*

Allan Houston:
grew up into a
major Money
Player, then
left the Pistons
to cash in with
the Knicks.
*(Allen Einstein
Photo)*

Grant Hill: After a brilliant regular season, the league's Air Apparent learned a lesson in playoff hoops. *(Allen Einstein Photo)*

James Jordan (left) and Michael Jordan (being hugged by his mother): The mysterious murder of his father seemed to symbolize the secret life of the famous son. (Chicago Tribune/ *Photo by John Bartley)*

Larry Martin Demery: The shooting of James Jordan with a stolen .38 put Demery and lifelong friend Daniel Green behind bars for life. *(Photos by Martin F. Dardis)*

Dick Ebersol: The brains behind NBC Sports' rise to power and the perfect TV marriage to the NBA. *(NBC/Maryanne Russell)*

Bill Laimbeer (right): The Baddest Boy believed being a Piston was something special. *(Allen Einstein Photo)*

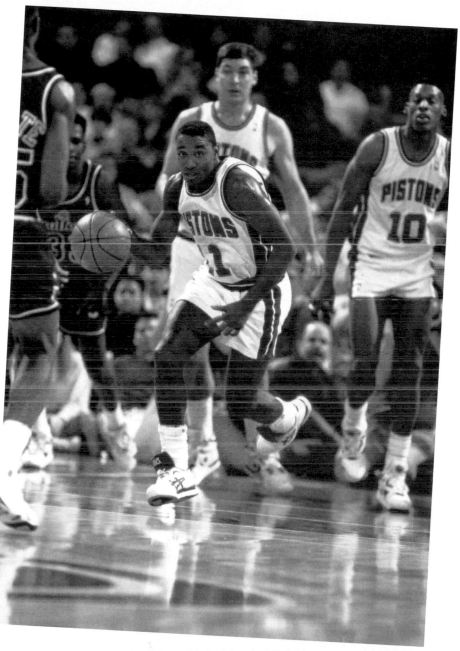

Isiah Thomas: The Best Little Man in NBA history gambled with his mind to win NBA titles, but lost so much more along the way. *(Allen Einstein Photo)*

James Edwards: The sweet-shooting center was said to have found himself at the center of questions about high-stakes dice games. *(Allen Einstein Photo)*

The Thomas family was finally all smiles as Isiah's No. 11 was raised to the rafters. *(Allen Einstein Photo)*

13

Star Gazing

SATURDAY NIGHT IN ALAMO CITY HAD NEVER LOOKED ANYTHING like it did on the night of February 10, when Planet Hollywood staged a gala opening for an intimate gathering of fifteen hundred, including some of the best basketball players on earth and the biggest sports star in the universe

The crowd of celebrity worshipers was, appropriately, Texas-sized.

By late afternoon, it had swelled to what local authorities would later estimate as 110,000, swamping Commerce Street and the surrounding area along San Antonio's magnificent Riverwalk, to the point where all available San Antonio police, including some from surrounding military bases, were called in. Nearby, at the posh St. Anthony Hotel, security was so airtight that welterweight boxing champion Pernell "Sweet Pea" Whitaker was arrested and accused of punching a police officer who wouldn't let him in.

Upstairs, Arnold Schwarzenegger, Maria Shriver, and their three children were nestled in the tenth-floor Presidential Suite. Two floors below, in the John Wayne Suite, were Bruce Willis, Demi Moore, and their three kids. These were Planet Hollywood shareholders, hosts of the gala opening that just happened to coincide with another cozy gathering of thousands on this particular weekend, the NBA All-Star Game, David Stern's annual showpiece.

Willis and Moore brought in the movie stars; Stern summoned his megastars. Together, they turned this funky Tex-Mex city into Celebrity Central, USA. In the early evening, Willis' blues band, the Accelerators, warmed up the crowd with a raucous eight-song set. Then the guests began to arrive: Dan Aykroyd, Jimmy Smits, Luke Perry, Julia Roberts, Tom Arnold, Chuck Norris, Patrick Swayze, Charlie Sheen. Schwarzenegger, Maria at his side, broke away to perform an impromptu Mexican hat dance. Willis and Moore blew kisses as Moore paraded in a tight, low-cut black dress she could have worn onstage in *Striptease*. Her hair pulled back in an elegant topknot, she smiled and yelled out, "Thanks for having us."

To decidedly fewer hoots and hollers, Stern arrived with his wife, Dianne, stopped to pose for the snapshot-starved fans, and spared them his Kennedy impersonation. "The biggest and best All-Star Weekend ever," he said, smiling. "Thank you, San Antonio."

Yeah, sure. But Stern's appreciation was not exactly what these fans were waiting for.

"Where's Michael?" someone called out.

"He's coming, I think," said Stern, ducking inside.

Arriving first, to predictable cheers, were local heroes David Robinson and Sean Elliott of the hometown Spurs. Then Hakeem Olajuwon. Shaquille O'Neal. Much later, just in time for a much smaller and more private party, Jordan, His Airness, made his way along the yards of ceremonial red carpet. A near mob scene broke out, police pushing the crowd back. And the following day, a San Antonio media personality assigned to cover the event agreed that it wasn't much different inside.

"The most interesting thing was the celebrity pecking order," said Debora Daniels of KMOL. "Michael Jordan was clearly the king."

One day earlier, when the guest list was merely fourteen hundred media types, Jordan decided not to show up at all. He went golfing at Steve Wynn's Mirage Hotel in Las Vegas and took along his good buddy Charles Barkley.

The amount of the fine they each received for skipping the traditional All-Star Weekend media soiree: $10,000, not enough to make a dent in Jordan's weekly recreation allowance.

"Obviously we would prefer Michael were here," sighed Russ Granik. "But it's not something we'll lose sleep over."

That's because there was nothing they could do about it, anyway. Jordan was beyond league obligation. He contributed what he wished, and such were the spoils for those who ruled the television airwaves.

"We do want to tell you that business looks pretty good right now since we sat for this in Phoenix," Granik said, alluding to the previous year's midseason bash in Jerry Colangelo's desert sports province. "Because since that time, a couple of guys named Michael and Magic came back."

One had merely to survey the previous week's television ratings to understand their impact. Johnson's comeback game against Golden State had rated a 4.4 on TNT, which was the league's season cable high until Jordan roared into L.A. three days later and produced a cable regular-season record 7.1. What made these ratings even more remarkable were that they were generated from West Coast night games, starting at ten-thirty back East, when much of the potential audience was dozing off.

Flush with Nielsen pleasure, Stern and Granik, smiling and relaxed, in sport jackets with open-collar shirts, began their traditional weekend-opening press conference by running through the familiar inventory of impressive domestic and global achievement: season's attendance was up 3.5 percent, not including expansionist Toronto and Vancouver; television ratings were up on all three network carriers; 145 countries would be showing the All-Star Game; 277 international credentials had been issued representing 38 countries, including broadcast teams from 22 countries.

In addition, Johnson, who had returned too late to be placed on the Western Conference team (though he was in town, hosting his own Saturday-night party), was on the covers of that week's *Time* and *Newsweek* magazines.

"Questions?" Stern asked, smiling benevolently at the audience in a ballroom of the Marriott Riverwalk Hotel.

Soon enough, a hand went up. It was Phil Jasner, the veteran, no-nonsense reporter from the *Philadelphia Daily News*.

"How much did you need Michael and Magic back?" Jasner asked.

Stern frowned, probably wishing about this time that he'd stopped off in Vegas for a round or two himself.

"The question is unfair," he snapped, his demeanor changing from sunny to scrappy. "You would expect that two of the greatest players ever to play the game would supercharge the league. But that doesn't diminish the extraordinary state of the sport."

In a large sense, and judging by the mob scene that the Marriott Riverwalk lobby became that weekend, Stern was right. At this point, no sports league seemed more in tune with its audience. Nobody could blend the rhythms of day and night, of popular culture, the way the NBA could. All-Star Weekend was now some monster hybrid, Disney World meets *As the World Turns*.

"All right, folks, move it back!" barked a security guard inside the Marriott, ordering fans off the ropes. No sooner were those words spoken than another roar erupted near the entrance, signaling the arrival of the Grammy Award–winning group Boyz II Men. High above their heads hung more signs of the league's locomotive marketing power that was spread out around the twenty-two San Antonio hotels housing NBA players, officials, and guests: bright blue and orange mobiles, cowboy-boot cutouts bearing the names of the individual All-Stars, and on every level, a stand where one could drop $250 for an authentic autographed All-Star ball, among other outlandishly priced merchandise.

The league's happy sponsors permeated the Fleer Jam Session. From the Foot Locker Million Dollar Shot to the American Express Autograph Stage to the media dining (sponsored by Schick), no promotional stone seemed to go unturned. In San Antonio, more than one hundred thousand fans would attend the three-day Jam Session inside the 300,000-square-foot Henry Gonzalez Convention Center, featuring a wide range of family activities, exhibits, and seminars. Elsewhere, McDonald's—another Stern ticket to Kid's World—was hyping its NBA 2Ball program, a youth skill competition to take place in nine league cities following All-Star Weekend.

"McDonald's 2Ball builds on our long-term global relationship with the NBA," said David Green, senior vice president of marketing for McDonald's. This was all music to Stern's ears.

And what this corporate orgy meant for "basketball people"

was more opportunities, more jobs, perhaps even a chance to rise from the dead. Back in the lobby, former Players' Association kingpin Charles Grantham worked the crowd, still unemployed and looking for an opening, any opening, to get himself back into this most exotic life. Other various agents and hustlers mingled with beautiful and short-skirted women, balancing gingerly on spiked heels. Suddenly, a burly seven-footer was pushing to the elevators, amid the familiar sounds and shrieks. "When it's George Zidek," said one league official of the Czech-born rookie center from UCLA's national 1995 champion, "you know you have a popular league."

But the levels of fame were all relative, many of these players becoming attractions simply because they belonged to the club graced by a transcendent, chosen few. And even at the top, it was easy to confuse one of the true winners with a wanna-be, or a pretender with a contender. The amount of attention, of noise, didn't necessarily tell the more complete tale.

Outside, for instance, the noise was beginning to swell to old Boston Garden decibel levels as Jason Kidd, the stylish Dallas point guard, walked through the crowd and slipped into the back of a waiting white stretch limo. The din quieted for a moment— until Kidd reappeared. Oops. Wrong limo. Within seconds, a black one arrived, and Kidd and his compatriots were off to the private Magic Johnson party.

It was only fitting that Kidd be invited, for among the All-Stars gathered in San Antonio, he was most revered for his breathtaking creativity with the ball. "A young Magic" was how his agent, Aaron Goodwin, generously described him. "He's larger-than-life right now. He's like a rock star."

The only question was whether he would merely be the kind who would score with a string of disparate singles, or if he could achieve the rare collection that would make him golden, then platinum, the kind of NBA-brand superstar the league wanted desperately to cultivate—though more carefully two years after the horror show in Toronto—for long-playing prosperity and fame.

Money certainly wasn't an issue. Kidd already had a $16-million, four-year Nike deal that included hats, outerwear, and a Nike-Kidd basketball. There was a deal to market multicolored rubber bands for the wrist, the latest NBA fashion statement.

"And," said Goodwin, "if I got a deal with Hanes to do under-wear, Nike has the option to make underwear as opposed to Hanes."

It was clear that Goodwin, who had zeroed in on Kidd when he was a real kid, eight years old, had honed his client's marketing pitch to breathless elevation. Whereas Grant Hill was being sold as Mr. Clean, Kidd was being pushed as the nouveau melting-pot man—an athlete from a mixed-marriage, middle-class family whose game was honed in urban Oakland playgrounds and whose persona transcended black and white. "African-Americans follow Jason, white Americans follow Jason," said Goodwin. And of course, this being San Antonio, Goodwin wasn't about to exclude Hispanics from Jason Kidd's Big Tent. "He has a huge Mexican-American following," he said. "J is a hard worker more interested in passing the ball. Middle America can relate to this kid."

On a roll, Goodwin added that nine major corporations were lined up waiting to do deals, including Pepsi, Pizza Hut, 7UP, and Frito-Lay. Also, a multimillion-dollar deal was in the works for Kidd to endorse Trojan condoms, plus a two-year, $2-million deal with a wireless-pager concern. Goodwin was holding off, though. "All Dream Teamers must sign a marketing agreement that says they can't do deals with nonleague Olympic sponsors," he said. Meaning Kidd, up for one of the two remaining spots on Dream Team III for the Atlanta Olympics, could only sign with sponsors such as Coke and AT&T.

The question was whether Kidd would be picked by the Olympic selection committee, which just happened to be chaired by the NBA's Rod Thorn. Or, more to the point, why he wasn't one of the ten original selections the previous September, after having won Co–Rookie of the Year with Hill, who was picked, along with Milwaukee's Glenn Robinson, a prolific scorer but no one's idea yet of a marketing sensation.

That less-flattering answer wouldn't come from Goodwin. For all his talent, for all his appeal, the league remained skeptical of Kidd. It was trying to step back from its disastrous attempt to bestow instantaneous star blessing on young players by virtue of their statistics and the size of their contracts. No more Derrick Colemans and Larry Johnsons, not if the NBA could help it. Even

Seattle's Shawn Kemp and Gary Payton, two of the best pure young talents around, were not original Dream Team III selections. To prevent embarrassment on home soil, Coach Lenny Wilkens had a roster laden with veteran returnees of the original Dream Team, including Utah's pick-and-roll legends Karl Malone and John Stockton, Scottie Pippen, and David Robinson. Reggie Miller was back from Dream Team II; Hakeem Olajuwon was a shoo-in after becoming a U.S. citizen. That left room for Orlando's Shaquille O'Neal and Penny Hardaway, both of whom, while unpolished, had no record of being big trouble and had already taken the Magic to the NBA Finals.

Kidd, on the other hand, was only a year removed from college off-court incidents that nearly crippled his Q score forever. In May 1994, misdemeanor hit-and-run charges were filed when Kidd's Toyota Land Cruiser, traveling at high speed, clipped another car and careened out of control at 2:50 A.M. In the car with Kidd were Joe Davis, twenty-five, of Hayward, California, and Milton Jackson, twenty-seven, of Washington State. The three had been returning from San Francisco 49er great Ronnie Lott's nightclub in nearby Emeryville, California. According to police, Jackson acted "belligerent" at the scene and was arrested for drunkenness. He later kicked out the window of the police car. Subsequent reports showed both Davis and Jackson had criminal records for possession of cocaine for sale.

"It's being portrayed," Kidd said at the time, "that I knew these things about my passengers and that I condone these actions. I did not then, and I do not now."

Less than a month later, Kidd was the subject of a civil suit from an eighteen-year-old woman who claimed that Kidd physically abused her in the wee hours after he turned twenty-one on March 24, also the day he decided to turn pro after his sophomore year at Cal-Berkeley. (Kidd denied the claims.) Soon after, another woman sued Kidd for child support in San Francisco Superior Court, claiming he was the father of then seven-month-old Jason Kidd, Jr. Her suit sought a house, $10,000 in furnishings, a $25,000 automobile, and medical insurance.

By now, more than a year and a half later, these legal troubles were long gone, and Kidd hit San Antonio having been voted the Western Conference's starting point guard by the fans and having just torched Stockton and Utah for 25 assists, a performance he described as being "in a zone passing the ball." Yet the NBA remained suspicious of him, as did Grant Hill, of all people.

Hill admitted concern about what he perceived to be Kidd's attempts to draft on Hill's spotless image, which this season had earned him more All-Star votes than even Jordan. He'd heard that Kidd was making noise in public about Hill's being his "campaign manager" in gaining one of those last two spots on Dream Team III, which Hill denied and made clear he didn't like.

"He says we're friends," Hill said one day around All-Star Weekend. "He's not my friend. I barely see him."

A year ago, with Michael Jordan and Magic Johnson out of the sport and Charles Barkley making his annual threat to join them, Hill had been thrust into the position of Most Valuable Product, the envy of all other young players, except maybe O'Neal. At the 1995 All-Star Game in Phoenix, the league and its media myth-makers latched onto the rookie Hill as if he'd been in the league ten years and won six titles. He attended all the functions, shook all the hands, did all the "in-depth" interviews, which predictably portrayed him as the Everything Man, a great player with the additional benefits of a Duke degree, a Yalie, football-hero father, and attorney mom. African-American upper crust. When GQ magazine churned out a special issue titled "The Future of Sports," Hill was its cover boy, smartly dressed in light brown suit, passing a ball between his legs while the headline above his left shoulder asked, "Can Grant Hill Save Sports?"

The NBA had granted an audience to Calvin and Janet Hill to discuss plans for their son, but by the end of that Phoenix weekend, with Letterman set up for the following day in New York, Hill was already wondering what he had gotten himself into. "I have to learn how to say no," he said.

The danger in creating Saint Hill was that the NBA, in its haste to quell the Generation X uproar, was running the risk of going too far to the other extreme, sounding like a Republican Party platform. Hill was certainly a treasure, but he had enjoyed every material and social benefit, contrary to, say, the sweet-tempered and doe-eyed Penny Hardaway, who was raised by his grand-mother in a Memphis shanty, and survived being shot as a youth.

The massive buildup even had its social downside for Hill, a young man who was used to thinking before acting and began to worry that maybe now he was thinking too much. He confided to a close friend that even though he was The Man in Detroit, single and just twenty-three years old, and couldn't "just (----)" a woman because he was afraid they'd think his clean-cut reputation would preclude having a night of sex and that he would surely be up for a relationship or marriage. By the start of his third season in the league, Hill was talking more, referring to himself as the most mature player on the Dream Team. Fila would be running a promotional campaign starring Hill lightheartedly breaking away from his Mr. Nice Guy persona by attending Camp Toughguys, where counselors such as Bill Laimbeer and wrestler George "the Animal" Steele teach him to growl, throw elbows, talk back to the ref, trip opposing players, and wear lots of jewelry.

Move over, Dennis Rodman.

Hill never said he didn't want any part of the Big Sell as the Future Savior, or that he was afraid of its burdensome side. He just didn't want to become a cliché. "We're not poets, philosophers, or statesmen," he said. "I shoot a ball through a hoop for a living. But a lot of people, and especially kids, will listen to someone like me before they listen to their local congressman. It's unbelievable power. I'd like to make positive change. I'd like to be a role model. I'd like to inspire people like Arthur Ashe or Julius Erving or even Magic did. Not everyone gets this opportunity."

At least now, with Jordan back, presumably for a while, Hill could settle back some, adjust more accordingly to the demands of wealth and fame, as well as the needs of Madison Avenue and the NBA. As long as Jordan was around, he would be The Man at All-Star games and wherever else he showed up. "I'm just a star in his galaxy" is the way Hill put it. He could focus on players his own age now, be one of the gang. "Do you know who the league is looking at?" he asked innocently, regarding Jordan heirs. "How are Shaq and Penny getting along?" He wondered what it was like with two superstars on one team.

In San Antonio, he said the league was again leaning on him, and now Hardaway, O'Neal, and to a lesser extent, Kidd and Joe Smith. "Sponsor stuff, MTV, media," said Hill. "Myself and Hardaway, it's our job to sort of carry that, what the guys have done before. That comes with playing great, conducting ourselves a certain way off the court, representing our teams, our families, the NBA in a good way.

"They work us to death, have us doing everything. Michael and Charles don't do that sort of thing. We are the new generation. No one has actually come out and said it, but you can feel it, sense it."

But even what the most earnest young players, including Hill, were willing to do reflected the enormous changes in the league since the 1980s. For instance, when Stern borrowed from the old ABA and adopted marketing guru Rick Welts' brainstorm for All-Star Saturday in 1984, he could count on Jordan and Dominique Wilkins to grace the high-flying dunk contest, on Larry Bird to lend his brilliant touch to the Long Distance Shootout. These days, other than the global benefits derived from being on the Dream Team, most of the young stars weren't angling for temporary exposure that might earn them an endorsement contract. Like Jason Kidd, they came into the league prepackaged. Stern couldn't get Shaq or Shawn Kemp up on the glass, or Reggie Miller out on the three-point line, if he promised to join them in a tutu.

"It's just not worth it, and that's what we tell our players," said one of the leading agents. "A guy could hurt himself trying some crazy dunk. Or if he does poorly, then he doesn't do himself any favors as far as his endorsement deals. That's just the way it is."

Hill, bucking the trend, originally entered the dunk contest but bailed out the week of the game, much to the relief of Doug Collins, with a sore right wrist. That left no veteran marquee names for the Nestlé-sponsored event. The AT&T Long Distance Shootout was won by Washington Bullets journeyman forward Tim Legler. All-Star Saturday also featured an abbreviated exhibition featuring the league's top rookies (sponsor: Schick), which in recent years had replaced the Legends Game, a torturous exercise featuring flabbed-out old-timers demonstrating how much basketball is truly a young man's endeavor. The rookies played a spirited and close game, with Damon Stoudamire leading the East team to a 94–92 lead. On the West's last possession, Joe Smith hit a long three-pointer left of the key, but it was waved off as after the buzzer. Stoudamire, who had 19 points and 11 assists, was named MVP.

"Point guards love All-Star Games," Smith said back in the locker room, looking over his $3,000 losers' check. "They always get the ball." He said he hoped he'd have better luck come springtime, in the voting for Rookie of the Year.

The dunkers did produce the biggest and most startling news of the weekend, a white man not only entering but winning. Not once, but twice, did 6-6, 185-pound rookie Brent Barry, son of Rick, run the floor and take off from the free-throw line to execute the signature dunks of Julius Erving and Jordan. In the finals, Barry, having already done the foul-line routine, needed one last burst to beat Phoenix rookie power dunker Michael Finley. He looked over to the sideline, to what he called "the thousand-dollar-suit section," and there were Alonzo Mourning, Miller, and Hill frantically waving him toward the backcourt.

Barry, brash as his famous father but blessed with a sense of humor, complied, elevated off his left foot as he reached the free-throw line, and scored a perfect fifty. The stars erupted. Mourning bowed. And one could imagine some bright marketing executive filming Barry slamming on Woody Harrelson someday soon, selling a sneaker with the ebullient chant of "Yes, we can!"

"A touchy subject," said Barry. "I was going to wear a T-shirt that said 'White Men Can Jump,' but I didn't want to burst anyone's bubble."

He already had.

If the likes of O'Neal and Hill were worried about breaking a bone in something as gratuitous as a dunking competition, the NBA, in its everlasting pursuit of determining new ways to sell itself, was happy to oblige them with the latest in communal expression. No physical exertion required, other than making the drive across the league's ever-expanding information super-highway.

In a small, sterile meeting room on the second floor of the Marriott Rivercenter, directly across the street from the Marriott Riverwalk, Cory Schwartz sat hunched over his laptop computer. A small, wiry point man on the NBA's new World Wide Web site (http://www.nba.com), Schwartz bubbled over with excitement about the three thousand "pages" of schedules, scores, polls, stats, news, and views.

Since November, up-to-the-minute info on all twenty-nine teams and several European leagues was as close as the click of a computer mouse, which Schwartz at this moment was working to death. "The advantage is this is a twenty-four-hour global medium," he said, sounding like a mad scientist at work in the David Stern Laboratory.

Schwartz's actual business card read Assistant Interactive Programming. "From any part of the world, anytime, you can find out what's going on," he said. "For the fans who can't come to San Antonio, we're trying to make it as real for them as possible."

Already this week, he said, fans from outposts in Australia, Israel, Germany, Indonesia, Belgium, Holland, Lithuania, Greece, Slovenia, Korea, Brazil, and even Aurora, Illinois, had checked out league-inspired chat sessions with the likes of Stern, legendary Celtic John Havlicek ("He'd never used a computer before, loved it," said Schwartz), Joe Smith, and Sonics coach George Karl.

With a couple of quick clicks, Schwartz took a visitor on a guided tour of the Web site that had debuted three months earlier, a partnership among the league, Portland Trail Blazer owner Paul Allen's cutting-edge Starwave Corporation, and ESPNET Sports-Zone, one of the hottest Web sites on-line. On this day, it was well on its way to setting another record for "hits," or requests for specific files.

During All-Star week, nba.com was averaging thirty thousand users a day, generating about 1.5 million hits, up from the twenty-five thousand and 1 million marks the league was doing during the regular season. In typical NBA style, the Interactive group was searching for innovative ways to wire its way into the hearts and minds of fans, especially those in the eighteen-to-thirty-five demographic group courted by Stern and his advertisers.

"While we respect the history of the league, our main emphasis is on where we're going," said Jamie Rosenberg, the manager of the Interactive group, who had quietly entered the room and was now peering over Schwartz's shoulder. "We're always trying to push the envelope."

Here were a few examples of what he meant:

Click, click: A Pick the Weekend Winners poll, forecasting results of the Slam Dunk, Three Point Shooting, Rookie, and All-Star games.

Click, click: An All-Star Saturday quotebook featuring players and coaches.

Click, click: "The Life & Times of Juwan Howard," diary of a first-time All-Star.

Click, click: Q & A with David Robinson.

Click, click: A visit to NBA Theater. "This is cool," said Schwartz, downloading Harold Miner's winning dunk from a year ago in Phoenix. Next came the Top 10 plays of the week. Want an archival dip into clips featuring the greatest plays, games, and moments in league history? All there, in full color.

Click, click: A "home court" report on every team, complete with game schedules, statistical and biographical info, feature articles, historical data, and multimedia events, updates at 5 A.M. (EST) each and every day, along with league leaders, records, and game-by-game results. Have a nice life, *USA Today*.

Click, click: A Global Game section listing Americans playing internationally plus NBA news, with special sections translated into Spanish and French. There are also weekly reports from leagues in England, France, Germany, Greece, Italy, and Spain. "We even get E-mail from fans in Europe correcting stats," said Schwartz.

Click, click: "What's Up Doc?" A Jam Session Journey, starring Doc Rivers and two kids named Casey and Samantha. NBA photographers had followed the trip around the amusement area taking digital photos. Three hours later, the pics and story of the trip—including some serious dunking on seven- and eight-foot baskets—showed up on-line.

Click, click: 12th Man saga starring Sonics forward Steve Scheffler, who took a laptop on the road for a thirteen-day trip. Most of the musings were tame, even lame: excitement at finding Q-Tips and cotton balls in a Miami luxury-hotel bathroom, tips for hoarding $80-per-diem meal money ("Go to the grocery store and pack a suitcase in munchies"). Buried in the diary, however, were a couple of gems: how five Sonic players paid their own way to Atlanta—a city that African-American players felt more welcome in—for New Year's Eve rather than hang around in Phoenix, and Scheffler's Letterman-like experience digging out an Indian cabdriver during the Blizzard of '96 that shut down New York.

Of course, this was more than everything the NBA freak wanted to know and nothing that he or she had to. It was also expanding the reach of partners like Schick, the first major sponsor to ante up cash in exchange for signage rights on five of nba.com's most heavily trafficked pages.

"It gives us something else to offer when they buy league-wide sponsorship," said Schwartz.

Click, click: The bottom line.

For its 46th All-Star Game, the NBA had made its usual meticulous arrangements to guarantee a finely tuned show, right on down to the pregame introductions, which featured a stage manager—in headset wired to the game producer—stooping down behind both team benches. One by one, before each player's name was announced, the stage manager would grab the back of the player's warm-up jacket, and when—and only when—word arrived from the producer the hand would release and the player be literally pushed onto the floor.

Timing is everything with these matters, as Michael Jordan surely realized. And when Penny Hardaway's turn to be introduced to the Alamodome crowd of 36,037 arose, Jordan placed his firm hand on the back of the young Magic guard's warm-up pants and held on tight. The snaps on the pants came undone as a blushing Hardaway trotted out. More evidence of the Jordan Rules. He was back at the All-Star Game, upstaging the field.

Actually, the most electric performer in the game, at least the early part, was Aaron Goodwin's Kidd, young Jason. Point guards, as Joe Smith had correctly pointed out, traditionally dominated All-Star competitions. In the best games of the 1980s, Magic Johnson and Isiah Thomas were playing tit for tat, no-look for no-look. And with Johnson and Thomas watching from the stands, Kidd showed that he was a passer without peer, teaching team-mates and opponents geometry lessons they surely didn't learn in college. On one play, Kidd caught an outlet pass at midcourt looking right at the player who'd thrown him the ball. In one motion, he caught the pass and sent it back over his head, right into the hands of Kemp, who streaked in for a dunk.

It was a demonstration of visionary art that belied Kidd's Marine boot-camp buzz cut. He controlled the first quarter despite taking just one shot. But two other point guards were also on George Karl's roster: Stockton, the league's all-time assist leader, and Payton, Karl's own temperamental Seattle star (another Aaron Goodwin client), whom Karl had already said deserved to start ahead of Kidd, prompting a response from Kidd along the lines that Karl could go fuck himself. Kidd never regained control of the game after the first quarter.

Jordan and O'Neal powered the East to a 41–22, third-quarter run that ultimately was the difference. Jordan sat down at that point with 20 points in twenty-two minutes and never returned. O'Neal went on to finish with 25 points (and 10 rebounds) in twenty-eight minutes, including a ferocious dunk right over David Robinson as the game wound down. O'Neal, who went to high school in San Antonio, enjoyed giving this facial to Mr. Robinson in his own neighborhood. He didn't respect Robinson the way he did Hakeem Olajuwon. He recalled Robinson's once commenting that young players such as O'Neal were getting too much attention, making too much money. This was O'Neal's way of explaining why. "What was he thinking?" O'Neal sneered when asked for his reaction to Robinson's trying to block him.

O'Neal could have brought the backboard down on Robinson, and it would still have been too late to win him MVP. The ballots had been collected from the league-chosen media panel early in the fourth quarter. In a clearly outlined contest between what Leonard Armato had described as "stereo" and "digital," the voters went with the golden oldie. Around the pressroom, there was a palpable sense of satisfaction from knowing that, on this rare occasion, sportswriters and broadcasters could unspin the corporate spin, restore proper pecking order to the basketball universe.

As Jordan had said in Los Angeles, Shaquille O'Neal was more marketing sensation than basketball phenomenon. "I'm shocked I won," Jordan said diplomatically. "I might go right into the locker room and give Shaq the trophy." He didn't, of course, because, if nothing else, the trophy was affirmation that he alone usually lived up to the hype.

From the mob scene that engulfed Jordan after he was presented the trophy by Stern, the commissioner slipped away coolly and began walking away from the court. He had more personal matters on his mind.

Stern was on his way to San Antonio's University Hospital, where his good friend and partner-in-profit, NBC Sports President Dick Ebersol, was laid up, after suffering chest pains the previous Thursday and undergoing angioplasty to free a blocked artery.

Ebersol, forty-eight, was the seven-year architect of NBC's increasing dominance of network sports. He was as driven as Stern, though not terribly smart about it. He admitted eating badly, smoked too much, and didn't get enough sleep. He and Stern had more than ambition in common, though. He, too, was a lifelong basketball fan.

Ebersol had his own history with the NBA, working the 1969 Finals, Boston against L.A., when he was just starting in television. He said that is when he fell in love with the sport, with its brash and colorful cast. "The producer-director was Chet Forte," he said. "The assistant director was Don Ohlmeyer, and the stage manager–production assistant was me. That was it, the entire crew."

Now, almost three decades later, he delighted in calling Ohlmeyer, his mentor and boss, and comparing those days to now, to the 120-plus staffers on a contemporary NBA Finals. More than that, he reveled in knowing that his instincts had been right in 1989, when he went after the NBA like a pit bull, when he believed the league had not peaked, as some industry analysts thought. Then he came up with a plan that helped Stern ease out of an expiring deal in which CBS had specific renewal language at a time when it had lost its cornerstone baseball deal.

"The second day I got the job, I had breakfast with David," Ebersol said. "I had never met him, but I told him this was what I wanted more than any other part to begin to build NBC. He explained how difficult it would be. He had to give CBS a figure, and if CBS accepted the figure, that was it.

"But in that breakfast, he told me about a program they had been developing, a half-hour syndicated show they were going to take to the air in the winter of '89–90. I said, 'Wait a minute, wait a minute, wait a minute. . . . I think I can deliver you a time period on the network, which is what you want more than anything else.'"

At the time, he said, the other networks were much more successful with Saturday-morning cartoons than NBC. So Stern went into negotiations with CBS in September 1989. The contract figure he eventually presented a month later was $600 million for four years (way up from the previous four-year, $188-million deal) plus the Saturday-morning show, to be carried from the first of November until the first of July. By early November, CBS had passed, and Stern—after calling ABC, which had just lost a bundle on the "Earthquake World Series" and didn't have the stomach to shell out another $600 million—called Ebersol.

"I'll never forget the day," he said. "It was late in the afternoon, about five o'clock. He said, 'Do you want to make a deal?' I said, 'I'll be there in five minutes.'"

Ebersol had his favorite sport to show, and sell, and a new Saturday-morning show called *Inside Stuff*. And a new best friend with whom to get rich.

It also wasn't long before Ebersol learned that Stern was no mere dealmaker. He was hands-on, and more. The telephone rang every day, and soon Ebersol was in the habit of calling first. They began to talk, he guessed, as many as 350 days a year, to the point where, as Ebersol said, "sometimes our wives think we're more attached to each other."

Their synergy helped the NBA on NBC become a more symbiotic relationship than business partnership. Two years into the contract, they set a practice of weekly meetings. "Twelve to fourteen of us for lunch, once our season starts up, to discuss how we're promoting, how we're producing, what we're doing with features in the pregame, at halftime, what *Inside Stuff* is doing, our thoughts about the previous weekend," Ebersol said. "And if he [Stern] feels that something may have been lightly treated or not enough . . . he'll go right in the face of the producer or director or promo person and it will be a tough one minute."

It wasn't just the big picture that Stern wished to draw. It was also the lines television people were allowed to cross. "They ask, 'Why are you doing that story?'" said one network announcer of NBA games. "They want to know when we're doing something controversial."

For example, days before TNT was to have Dennis Rodman on its halftime show, just as his popularity with the Bulls was starting to sizzle, a Turner Sports producer says Turner honcho Harvey Schiller got a call from Stern. The NBA had already shot itself in the foot by promoting the Bad Boys of Detroit, so there would be no shots of Rodman's antics. If TNT wanted to deal with the Bulls' pursuit of seventy wins, fine. No controversy.

"It violates everything I believe in journalistically," the broadcaster said. "But at the same time, the NBA is our biggest property." He paused, preparing his justification: survival. "ESPN's got an NBA nightly show. The message is clear. They're ready to take it away from us. You don't want anything to fuck up your relationship."

When NBC moved Bill Walton out of the studio to game coverage, it auditioned several candidates to join Bob Costas and Peter Vecsey on the pregame and halftime reports. Former Portland and L.A. Laker center Mychal Thompson, articulate and funny, claimed he was told the job was his, only to be told by the network that Stern had stepped in and pushed Julius Erving—for whom he wanted a more visible role in the sport—into the slot.

Only the most leveraged industry superstar reporters could afford to challenge Stern, who bristled when Costas grilled him about his handling of Jordan's gambling habits during an NBC interview at the 1993 Finals in Phoenix. Costas and Marv Albert were too big to bully, but everyone else was on notice. Leave investigative journalism to nonpartners.

Long before Woody and Mia and the O.J. trial, Stern sensed how television could blur the differences between news and entertainment, how the NBA could deliver its own undistilled message. Fans would not remember if they read it in the newspaper or heard it from Ahmad Rashad and Willow Bay on the league-produced NBA Inside Stuff.

These weren't exactly the principles great journalism was founded on, negotiating with or being dictated to by the subject. But the notion that networks that paid rights fees to sports leagues should cover them objectively (apart from their news divisions, of course) was always something of a reach. They were in business together, and nobody worked in concert better than the NBA on NBC.

"What makes our relationship so unique was that we talked all year long," Ebersol said. "For example, we started talking where we could take the promotion to last November. Maybe promote more on soap operas, because you've got all the men you're ever going to want. We were talking about it in a quantitative way, when it suddenly dawned on me one day there was even a better way.

"I went to Don Ohlmeyer and said, 'Do you think we could get the biggest stars to sit down and do promos?' I mean, there is no amount of money that is going to get Seinfeld. Don said, 'Oh, yeah, almost all of them would love it.' And they came back within a week and said they'd do it. So over the next six weeks, the casts of *Friends, Mad About You, 3rd Rock From the Sun,* and *Seinfeld* did it, all at no expense. They were shot on their own sets, the normal shooting day of their show.''

His conservative estimate on the cost to produce and televise such a promotional campaign, which debuted during the 1996 Super Bowl, was $45 to $50 million. But in this case, all it had cost was shooting the spots. "It was another division of our company so caught up in the NBA thing," he said. And such were the promotional spoils to the sports league that didn't spread its games across competing networks, as did baseball and football. The NBA knew how to maximize its television leverage in more creative and ultimately more rewarding ways. The message continued to go out that NBA stars were part of America's celebrity elite.

NBC was not going to have Seinfeld hawking a product that CBS or Fox also made money on. Ebersol knew that much. So, of course, did Stern. And both loved the mix of celebrity and glitz the league had become. They were constantly together during the big NBA events. During a 1995 Finals party, they rode around like vacationing kids at Universal Studios in Orlando in the Back to the Future–mobile.

But all that hype was forgotten as Stern left the floor in San Antonio. Even the unprecedented eight-year contract, longest in General Electric and NBC history, that NBC head Bob Wright had offered Ebersol while walking around the Alamo the day before his heart attack, as a reward for negotiating $4.1 billion worth of Olympic deals, plus the NFL, U.S. Open golf, and above all, his visionary work on the NBA, was on hold.

"He's going to be okay," Stern said. "It's been a tough weekend. I've had to act normal at several functions while I knew what Dick was going through."

Even as Stern's own fortunes were rising to unimagined heights. For, as fate would have it, the word was out that Stern's paycheck would also soon reflect the dramatic escalation of NBA revenues. A committee headed by Pistons owner Bill Davidson had agreed to present to the Board of Governors for rubber-stamping a new five-year contract for Stern that would pay him $7 million a year plus incentives that would swell the package to over $40 million.

Stern acknowledged that a deal was done, and consistent with his anti-agent rant, he had negotiated it himself. "Contrary to unfounded rumors, I plan to continue doing what I'm doing for many years to come," he said.

Since he'd brought it up, there had been whispers that Stern was being wooed by ITT, co-owner of Madison Square Garden and the Knicks. Even Stern admitted that he got as many as "six or eight" feelers a year but said whatever notions he had of leaving were as rare as they were brief. "Yes, it comes to mind, but usually more in moments of great frustration and despair rather than seeing other spectacular opportunities," he said.

What else would he do? "Make widgets? Something that's considered more important?" he asked. In his mind, professional basketball had become so entwined in the social fabric that it had become a way to engage the country—the world—in meaningful ways. In recent years, Stern had toured South Africa with Nelson Mandela. He'd talked politics in Israel with Natan Scharansky. He was no stranger to the heads of Fortune 500 companies. No, Stern was not going to capriciously walk away from this gig, from a league he freely admitted was like his "baby." Not when it was still growing, when things seemed so much under his control.

Davidson, an old-guard owner whose low-profile values and style were similar to Stern's, said Stern never discussed the possibility of going elsewhere while negotiating the contract. "Did he have leverage? Sure," said Davidson. "With what you see in both Hollywood and the media in New York, he certainly could go to a number of very, very important posts. But I can say this: he expressed to me the fact that he considers this his life's work."

The contract was not only ratified by the owners at a meeting in New York later that month, but it was decided that Stern would have the right to impose fines of up to $5 million per team, as opposed to the previous limit of $1 million, and issue additional penalties of multiple first-round draft picks instead of one. Miami's Pat Riley heist had embarrassed Stern. He'd made a case for broader powers and won it.

New deal in hand, stronger than ever, there was one only piece to the puzzle left for Stern—a signed collective bargaining agreement from the Players' Association. From September on, the union had dragged its feet in expanding the thirteen-page overview that settled the lockout into a detailed and completed collective bargaining agreement.

The trouble, from Stern's point of view, was the issue of who was in control of the union, or who wasn't. "Simon had to spend all his time trying to save his job," Stern said. Even then, the storm clouds seemed far off. Stern said most deals with the union were sketchy documents that eventually reached comprehensive finality.

But just a couple of weeks before San Antonio, Gourdine had been unceremoniously dumped in what amounted to a dissident-inspired revolt.

Buck Williams, still supporting Gourdine, had floated an $800,000-a-year, six-year commitment for Gourdine but was shot down. Williams realized that Gourdine had taken too serious a pounding from Falk/Fleisher and Jordan/Ewing in the wake of the contract ratification vote from the previous summer and did not have popular support. But firing Gourdine would have been, in Williams' mind, an act of disloyalty, of punishing an ally to appease men like Falk, whom he resented more each day. He decided the best tack would be a short-term extension for Gourdine, two years, and the hiring of a new general counsel who would be primed to take over as executive director. He announced the extension, then put in a call to Len Elmore, asking if he might consider coming aboard.

Falk, however, wanted no part of this. He made his move through Patrick Ewing, who circulated a petition denouncing Gourdine's contract, forcing a vote of the twenty-nine player representatives that amounted to a referendum on Gourdine's job. "The player reps made it clear they didn't want Simon," Williams said.

Gourdine's ouster resulted in Alex English assuming the role of acting director, along with the rehiring of the law firm Weil Gotshal & Manges to represent the union in the difficult finalizing of the language of the contract with the league. In effect, it meant that the leader of the decertification movement, Jeffrey Kessler, was now the de facto union leader, until another director could be hired.

Stern was so furious that, according to the union people, he refused for months to meet with Kessler over the contract language, setting the stage for another early-summer showdown. Stern wanted to know how the man whose program of confrontation was roundly defeated could suddenly be back at a time when peace was supposedly at hand. The answer was that the players had never really embraced the framework of the deal, much less the intricate language the league was now trying to write. Back in September, they had merely voted to play and get paid.

To succeed Gourdine, Williams and the board produced a list of six candidates: Elmore; Paul Silas; Charles Bennett, former financial adviser to Charles Grantham; Washington, D.C., agent and onetime Falk associate Bill Strickland; former U.S. attorney Bill Hunter; and Providence attorney Dennis Coleman, who represented the NBA's retired players.

Behind the gala festivities during the weekend, the candidates—all African-American—were brought before the board, one by one. By the end of the weekend, no decision had been made, the process began to drift, and only one thing was clear: Jeffrey Kessler had not been brought back to walk the path Gourdine had.

It wasn't long before negotiations on contract language broke down, and the NBA mounted a legal assault to rescue the process. Howard Ganz, representing Proskauer Rose Goetz & Mendelsohn, filed a complaint in U.S. District Court in Newark against the Players' Association, and agents Frank Catapano, David Falk, Marc Fleisher, Ron Grinker, Steve Kauffman, Arn Tellem, and John Does #1 through #10. In typical NBA "Big Brother is watching" fashion, a warning was being sent to any others who might aid and abet the Kessler cause.

Poker-faced David Stern, now making at least $4 million more in salary than Michael Jordan drew from the Bulls, was setting out to prove all over again that he could defend his deal as well as he could make the big score. Ironically, the next big event of the season following All-Star Weekend brought the spotlight on the Palace of Auburn Hills, and the man who helped fan the flames of union discontent, along with a much hotter story than that.

14

Raising Isiah

As the clock struck midnight on Isiah Thomas Night, the packed invitation-only reception high above the Palace grounds was in high gear. The leading man of this and several hundred other nights in this building stood center stage in the dark, festive swirl, flashing a three-hundred-watt smile as highlights of a brilliant career danced on closed-circuit TV screens around the room.

Fresh off a 13-point win over Toronto, Joe Dumars and Grant Hill entered the room. Slowly, through a crush of season-ticket holders and dozens of Thomas family and friends, they made their way to the bar for a soda. Both had come up big against the Raptors (14 assists for Dumars, 27 points for Hill), and a few moments passed before Dumars broke free, glided across the room, and wrapped his arms around Thomas.

"Congratulations, this is a great night for you," Dumars said softly in Thomas' ear.

"I love you," replied the onetime fearless leader.

"I love you, too," said Dumars.

So many nights during their remarkable careers, Zeke and Joe D did play the perfect duet. When they were at what Dumars described as "our highest point of consciousness," what you watched was backcourt basketball as an art form. "Flawless basketball," Dumars declared one day.

But for all their on-court syncopation, their off-court marriage was more a matter of convenience. In college, Dumars had idolized Thomas, but in the words of one front-office executive, their friendship was "all cosmetic." The big reason: Dumars had little use for Thomas' salacious personal life. But this was Isiah's night, and Dumars, in memory of battles fought, won, and lost, had answered the call. So had the alluring Anita Baker, the diminutive pop diva who had wrapped more than a little Motown around the national anthem. "Why am I here?" she asked. "Because he [Thomas] asked me. His secretary called and said, 'Do you want to sing?'" Baker laughed and, with her voice moving up an octave, added, "If he wants me to sing, I sing. This is hometown boy makes good . . . makes great . . . makes history!"

A few feet away, a team photographer was busy capturing it, frame by frame. He snapped shots of those who had come to congratulate Thomas. Near the back of the room, Chuck Daly stood deep in conversation with Hill; every so often he popped his index finger into the young man's chest. Head down, Hill listened. A while later, another invited guest, a reporter, sidled up to the star of the show.

"Call me if you want to talk about the truth," said Isiah Thomas. "Not this."

Earlier in the evening, a portion of it had leaked out from a member of the Thomas family. During a taped halftime interview, Larry Thomas had called the tribute "a charade," charging the Pistons had waited far too long to honor his youngest brother.

"It was something they really didn't want to do," he said. "It was, like, hurry up and get out and, you know, let's close the chapter on Isiah Thomas."

Larry Thomas revealed that that very morning his brother had broken down—"cried like a baby"—in front of the family. Upset and confused after giving his "heart and soul" to the franchise, he had never received his proper due.

"His heart is broken," said Larry Thomas. "He gave them everything and he got his heart broken. The house he built, he can't get in."

Informed of these comments a few nights later, a senior member of Pistons management rolled his eyes.

"I'm so happy we've written the last page on this guy," he said.

Still, as Isiah Thomas Night opened at the Palace, the unmistakable signs of an NBA happening were everywhere. Looking presidential in a black, custom-made suit, Thomas arrived fashionably late, with wife Lynn and children Joshua and Lauren at his side. Flashbulbs fired and Minicams whirred before Lynn, a stunning but tightly wound woman, split straight for the dressing room door marked THOMAS FAMILY. Meanwhile, out in the corridor stood the living chapters of Isiah Thomas' life. Mother Mary. Brothers Larry, Gregory, Lord Henry, and Mark. David Stern. Bobby Knight. Bill Davidson. Jack McCloskey. Tom Wilson. Will Robinson. Former teammates Laimbeer, Johnson, and Kelly Tripucka. And, of course, Daly, coach of the Bad Boys.

"As great a player as he was, what he does best is lead," Daly told one TV reporter after another.

"He had a heart as big as a giant," Tripucka said in another TV interview. "He just wanted to win. That's what separated him from everyone else."

Lost in the star-studded crowd was a high school coach Thomas himself credited for helping him separate from West Side Chicago neighborhoods infested with gangs, drugs, and trouble. It was November 1975 when Gene Pingatore, the controversial coach from the movie Hoop Dreams, first saw Thomas dominate an eighth-grade tournament at St. Joseph's High.

"Even then Isiah knew exactly how good he was," said Pingatore. "Even then, he knew exactly where he wanted to go."

Where he wanted to go, at least short term, was St. Joseph's, a perennial Catholic League power, which Pingatore discovered after he "accidentally" bumped into Thomas outside St. Joe's gym.

"Nice game, Isiah," he said. "How'd you like to come to St. Joe's High School?"

Thomas just looked up and flashed that angelic smile. "That would be great," he said.

The following summer, Pingatore saw how special Thomas would be. In a park league filled with top nineteen- and twenty-year-olds, Pingatore's club, consisting mostly of sophomores, juniors, and one recent eighth-grade grad, won game after game. "He totally dominated," said Pingatore.

To help his star guard, Pingatore said, many a night after practice ended, he drove Thomas to the nearest bus stop or all the way home. Pingatore knew some of Thomas' brothers had problems with drugs, including Lord Henry, who once led the Catholic League in scoring as a sophomore. It was on those rides home that Pingatore said young Isiah opened up. About his fears, getting caught by gangs as he raced home from the bus. About food. Oh, how he loved to talk about food.

"When you get home, what do you eat?" Pingatore would ask.

"Probably nothing," came the quiet answer. "Whosever there first, eats. When it's gone, it's gone."

It was the same sad story with socks. Just because you had a pair yesterday didn't guarantee you one today. "The first one up puts them on," Thomas said.

By the time Thomas became a senior, his name was on the lips of every top recruiter in the country, and St. Joe's opened the basketball season ranked No. 1 in the state. The first three games, Pingatore said, Thomas scored about 40 points per game, but the team dropped two of three. "I told him we can't win if you score forty. So instead he averaged about twenty-four and put out about ten, twelve assists a game. We never lost again until De La Salle beat us."

De La Salle was St. Joe's archrival and had tagged one loss on Pingatore's team early in the year. This time, with just a few ticks left in overtime and a state title on the line, St. Joe's was up by one. Thomas had fouled out after a brilliant effort; the game was out of his control now. Which made the shock all the more real when a sub just off the De La Salle bench hit a desperation heave as the buzzer rang out. Thomas started crying and wouldn't stop for thirty minutes. "He once told me it was the hardest loss he ever took, harder than the pass he threw that Larry Bird intercepted," Pingatore said.

Rightly so, on Isiah Thomas Night in Detroit, that infamous inbounds pass was nowhere to be found on the highlight film that played high above the Palace floor. Six minutes of vintage Isiah, to a pounding Elton John beat. Six minutes of amazing coast-to-coast drives, sleight-of-hand magic, speed dribbles, change-of-pace spins, jaw-dropping jumpers. A blind pass from a sitting position for a layup. Spewing in some Celtics' face during the playoffs. Kissing Stern while hugging the world championship trophy. Images from the late great days of "Sweet Repeat," headlines and champagne spray.

Finally, the lights were dimmed and the sellout crowd was ready. As a full-throated roar ripped through the arena, the voice of longtime Pistons play-by-play announcer George Blaha took a trip back in time . . .

"At six-one, from Indiana University, the captain of your Detroit Pistons, Number Eleven . . . *Iiiii–siah Thomas!*"

At this moment, Thomas and family emerged from a tunnel and out into an explosion of light and sound. The 21,454 fans transported an entire building back to the glory days of the late 1980s. For seventy seconds, the cheering continued. Issuing a smart salute of thanks, Thomas strolled across the floor, his floor, into the arms of McCloskey, Bing, Lanier, and the ubiquitous commissioner, David Stern.

"What a historic evening," Blaha bellowed. "Tonight we are honoring the Pistons' version of Gordie Howe. The Pistons' version of Bobby Layne. Ty Cobb. Al Kaline. *The greatest Piston of all time . . .*"

The final words got lost in another wild ovation, before the crowd quieted and listened while Blaha ticked off the list of honored guests, then the first speaker.

By nature, Bill Davidson is a very, very private man. But what happened next was shocking, even by his tight-lipped standards.

"In 1981," he said, "we drafted Isiah Thomas. And I had a dream and Isiah fulfilled it. Thank you very much."

Nineteen words.

In twenty-seven seconds.

Almost as little time as it takes to say: "So long, farewell."

Davidson's "speech" spoke volumes, as did the frown on Lynn Thomas' face. And the fact that excluding those ex-teammates required to attend as part of either the Pistons (Dumars), their radio-TV package (Johnson and Tripucka), or the opposing team (Salley), Laimbeer was the only former Piston to show. All part of a night where what wasn't said turned out to be just as important as what was. As one team official later put it, "It was a bittersweet night for me. You notice I didn't say anything because I couldn't afford to talk. I knew the hypocrisy of what was going on."

But the crowd didn't. And as the NBA Commissioner stepped to the mike, he spoke for the paying public:

"Isiah, I get to represent hundreds of millions of fans around the world in saying thank you. Thank you for being a spectacular competitor. Thank you for the thrills and the championships. Thank you for the Hall of Fame career. But most of all, thank you for setting the standard with your community service. Your working with the kids of Detroit, of Michigan, leading the way now with the kids of Toronto. You have been one of the great . . ."

What followed was lost, swallowed up in another deafening roar. Stern was forced to shout his final words. "We'll see you in the Hall of Fame."

Now it was Bobby Knight's time. Decked out in Indiana red, the cantankerous coach got a big laugh when he admonished the Pistons' owner for taking his star two years early. "Mr. Davidson, you had your dream in 1981. Goddamn it, you took my dream away from me."

Then Knight got, for him, downright misty. "I always use Isiah as an example of what competitiveness is all about. I've never been around a player in any sport that had the absolute determination just to win that Isiah had."

As the impact of those words echoed, Pistons president Tom Wilson was introduced. Gesturing around the arena, Wilson noted how the Palace "probably wouldn't be here" if it were not for Thomas. Probably? And how fitting it was for his jersey to hang inside. Then Wilson announced the North Entrance to the arena had officially been renamed Isiah Thomas Drive.

For Piston insiders, the irony of Wilson's bestowing gifts on Thomas was almost too much. For years, they said, Wilson and Thomas had been viewed as powerful rivals, dutiful sons vying for Davidson's affection and, ultimately, control of his team. It appeared Wilson had won. Depending on the version of the story, Wilson had either seized on a major Thomas mistake to oust his archrival from the organization, a charge Wilson flatly denied, or Thomas had sliced his own throat by leaking details to *Free Press* columnist Charlie Vincent of Davidson's very private offer to sell Thomas a piece of the club, a charge Thomas flatly denied.

Something of a golden boy, Wilson had a whizbang marketing mind, the long, lean body of an athlete, an actor's looks, and the mind-set of a Marine. In fact, Wilson had once been a bit player at Universal, surviving on what he described as "schmucky little roles." A cabdriver on *McCloud*. A small part on *The Partridge Family*. A student in *Room 222*. Ironically, he was filming a *Barnaby Jones* episode at the Forum about fixing basketball games when he learned a job in the marketing department had opened, which at the time was a little like getting stock advice from Warren Buffett.

"If the Lakers got on your résumé, that was pretty good," Wilson said. So good he got hired in his hometown, Detroit, and over the next nineteen years worked his way up the corporate ladder from the Pistons' season-ticket salesman to Employee of the Year in 1990, for Guardian Industries, Davidson's company.

During the mid-1980s, Wilson spent the better part of three years traveling North America, studying various arenas before the Palace was built. Now the Palace and Pine Knob Music Theatre are annually rated among the top indoor and outdoor arenas in the country, and last year ranked No. 1 in revenue. The rewards for Wilson have been enormous: he not only monitors all basketball operations, but supervises the Palace, Pine Knob Music Theatre, and several other Davidson businesses. "He's a great mentor," said Wilson. "He's got tremendous vision. For the most part, he trusts you, and he views me as an alter ego, I guess."

According to team sources, Wilson was never much of a threat to Thomas until it became clear, by 1992, that this young executive had become Davidson's right-hand man. At the time, he was elevated to team president where he would oversee all basketball-related decisions, including the draft, player trades, and salary negotiations. "Isiah had no clue who Wilson was until, all of a sudden, he becomes competition in year nine or ten," said a Pistons official. "He cared when it counted."

Yet everything still seemed in place when Thomas called a press conference in early 1994 to announce it was official: he had forgone the chance to finish his career elsewhere, most notably with Pat Riley's New York Knicks. He planned on being a Piston for life. But when he retired a few months later, his final season cut short by an Achilles tendon tear, it was a completely different story.

"I won't have a future role in the Pistons' organization," he announced. "There were no jobs. All the jobs were full."

Thomas later described those last few months of his career as his darkest time in Detroit. "A misunderstanding," he said, offering nothing more.

For his part, Davidson insisted he still enjoys a "special relationship" with Thomas. But when asked directly about the circumstances surrounding Thomas' departure, he shook his head from side to side. "No reason to provide that," he said.

Thomas spoke of a misunderstanding. What was that all about?

"I'm not going to speculate," Davidson said.

"We sort of all agree that we're not going to talk about it anymore," Wilson said one night in the privacy of an empty locker room. "I think you can suffice it to say that Isiah had certain things that he really wanted, most of which he received in Toronto. Ownership, control, et cetera, et cetera. Things that maybe were here in the future, but were not here in the present. Maybe things got pushed a little too much. I don't want to be too blunt about that."

Others, however, were.

According to a top Pistons official, Davidson went ballistic following the *Free Press* story, which soon took on a life of its own. The team found itself holding press conferences to discuss press conferences. Several people within the organization said they tried to repair the damage done by the leak, but Davidson was no longer listening. Some argue that's because Wilson was doing the talking.

"I think it was used as a wedge to put him in power and Isiah out of power," said a high-ranking team official. "Tom knew Davidson's weakness, which was he didn't want publicity about his personal life."

Or as another longtime supporter noted, "That was the end of Isiah."

Close. But not quite. Nobody outthinks or outsmarts Isiah Thomas. Nobody gets the best of him. For days, Thomas is said to have begged and badgered Davidson for compensation—if not a slice of the club, then a bonus, a fat reward for all the money now flowing into "The House That Isiah Built." The kind other franchise players were typically getting. Championshipless players like Patrick Ewing in New York, for instance. Finally, Davidson agreed.

And when Thomas was sure that the money—somewhere between $3 million and $13 million, said a club source—had been wired safely into his account, the source said, he called a press conference that very same day to proudly announce he had just been hired as part owner and vice president of basketball operations for the Toronto Raptors.

The owner of the new team, John Bitove, had been a student at Indiana when Thomas was the Little Big Man on campus, and a longtime admirer with business interests in Windsor, Ontario, across the river from Detroit. So, as it turned out, Thomas' last move as a Piston was a breathtaking crossover dribble right on out of town.

Later, asked about any payment and his departure from Detroit, Thomas declined to speak directly about any compensation he may have received, adding, "It's fair to say I love the Detroit Pistons. A lot of things were said about Tom Wilson doing this and that. I don't know. I don't have any hard feelings against any of those people."

The end of the Bad Boys had come two seasons before. By then, the architect of those back-to-back championships was on his way to Minnesota to rebuild a reputation badly damaged by several bizarre personnel decisions. Laimbeer, for one, had roasted the general manager in print, charged that he had destroyed a roster it had taken years to build. But on this night, all the acrimony was lost in the cheers for the next speaker.

"This is like old times, happy times," said Jack McCloskey.

The wise man still wearing the uniform later explained what went wrong, in his own thoughtfully sensitive, less-bitter way. "When you have a tremendous amount of success, there are certain things that happen," said Joe Dumars. "There's a lot of credit that's given out. There's a lot of credit that's being sought after. I think we became so enamored with our success that we lost a bit of the edge. To be a champion you have to keep that edge, and our edge was being tough, blue-collar *Detroit* guys. And I think we lost that *edge*."

The enduring symbol of the Pistons' demise was an overpriced, underachieving, smart-ass center from Memphis State. If ever a player didn't fit Laimbeer's description of a Piston, it was 7-1

William Bedford. Traded to Detroit for a first-round draft pick in June 1987 following the Phoenix drug scandal, Bedford earned immediate and universal disdain for his wretched work habits and deplorable personal life, including twenty-two separate traffic offenses in four years.

After missing about half of the '87–88 season and all of '88–89 for violations of the league's drug policy, Bedford contributed little to Detroit's second title, averaging 3 points and 1 rebound a game. Will Robinson had worked religiously with Bedford, but nothing moved him. Robinson hated what he saw, especially for someone making $800,000 a year. "A dog of dogs," Robinson calls him today. "I told Jack we got to get rid of him because he had no heart and he was not trustworthy. Jack said he was our player of the future."

Toward the tail end of the '90 season, Daly and his staff had told McCloskey the same thing. Bedford's attitude and personality were a cancer on the club. He had to be removed. Instead, on April 3, the *Detroit Free Press* writer Corky Meinecke broke the news that McCloskey had secretly signed Bedford to a conditional three-year contract extension at an estimated $1 million per year. "It's no great deal," McCloskey insisted at the time. "We're just looking to the future."

"That's the kind of stuff that tore this franchise apart," said PR director Matt Dobek. "Nobody could figure out what Jack was thinking. Chuck's theory was Jack looked at Bedford as a son he could save."

"Our biggest mistake," added Robinson. "It caused us to lose esprit de corps. Chuck didn't want him. The players didn't appreciate him. But Jack was a stubborn guy. And always before that he had been right."

Robinson took a deep breath and then spoke again.

"That was the beginning of the end."

Actually, the very beginning started a year earlier when Mahorn, a warrior throughout the first championship run, was left unprotected in the expansion draft and was selected by Minnesota. "That was an emotional piece for us because he was a very good presence in the locker room, so that hurt," said Laimbeer. "But we overcame that." Overcame it the only way they knew how, by closing ranks. But after the second title, management faced the familiar problem confronting all aging championship teams. Hold your aces and go for the gold one more time? Or wheel and deal while the assets are hot, before it's too late? The Pistons had always been big on loyalty. So Johnson was re-signed and the Bad Boys went for a three-peat.

They took a great shot in 1990–91, winning fifty games and the division, pushing as far as the conference finals before getting blown out by the Bulls. That was the famous series in which Thomas, playing with a bum foot, accused Dumars of essentially collaborating with the enemy, charging he had been played for a fool by a suddenly friendly Jordan. And much was made of the infamous "walk out" following a four-game sweep.

It was over, Chicago's time. The phrase *youth movement* began to work its way into the Detroit papers. Piston by Piston, the team was torn apart. The unselfish play, the finding the third and fourth option on offense, went by the wayside. "It was a tremendous high," said Vinnie Johnson. "It wasn't like one guy was going to carry the team. We executed our offense. We took what was there." But soon Johnson—along with his hot hand and that steady "15" pick-and-roll play he loved to run with Laimbeer— was gone. Waived. Then in one red-letter day, August 13, 1991, center James Edwards was traded to the L.A. Clippers for somebody named Jeff Martin, and Orlando Woolridge, a talented but troubled scoring forward, was acquired from Denver. The Bad Boys nearly choked when the Woolridge package went public: two years, $5.2 million. Today, Laimbeer's voice takes on a loud, nasty ring when discussing that deal:

"Bringing Orlando Woolridge in and paying him more than the rest of us—for what? I mean we busted our ass. Our salary structure was you earn it. You don't give it away. They never, ever gave money away; that was their trademark. We understood that. When you earn it, you can hold your hand out and say, Okay, I deserve some more. A new airplane. A new building. We all earned that. When they started giving somebody money, and then we saw what that individual was like, it caused major problems."

Problems compounded by the third and final blow. The disappearance of Dennis Rodman.

Not physically. But by the summer of '92, the seeds of the *Bad As I Wanna Be*, cross-dressing, anything-goes boy toy were beginning to bloom. Rodman had arrived in Detroit as a second-round pick in 1986, a big-time talent from a small-time school (Southeast Oklahoma State), and early on, had gone virtually unnoticed around town. Teammates loved Rodman's relentless work ethic, the way he practiced and listened and learned. Thomas and Laimbeer invested hours tutoring the rebounding genius, fully believing he would prove to be the competitive link between champions of today and tomorrow. "He got the torch," said Laimbeer.

But by then the NBA had turned the Bad Boys into big business, and the stars, Rodman included, were getting mobbed in malls, offered free suits and cars from sponsors. To make matters worse, much worse, Daly departed following the 1992 season; he had been, without doubt, the single biggest influence in Rodman's life, a father figure. Daly would not easily be replaced, certainly not by the commando-style coaching of his replacement, Hubie Brown–disciple Ron Rothstein. With Daly gone, Rodman went off the deep end. He boycotted training camp, showing up for a preseason game in Lansing against Daly's new team, New Jersey, and sat defiantly in the stands. Daly took him inside a spare room for a quiet halftime chat, or personal plea. Rodman listened because he loved Daly. But he was on his own now. To the Pistons, he was a lost cause.

Said Wilson, "When we lost Dennis, we lost everything. We lost our heart, our willingness to compete, and our confidence at the same time."

Said Laimbeer, "When Dennis went south, the franchise was mortally wounded."

What followed was a merry-go-round of front-office hirings and firings, dubious trades and transactions. By the beginning of the 1993 season, McCloskey was the GM in Minnesota. Salley was gone, Rodman was playing in San Antonio, and Mark Aguirre had been placed on waivers. Mahorn. Johnson. Edwards. Salley. Rodman. Aguirre. McCloskey and Daly. All that remained of the Bad Boys, that eight-cylinder beast, were Dumars, Thomas, and Laimbeer.

In 1992, Detroit lost more games than they won (40-42) and missed the playoffs for the first time in ten seasons. By the time Collins took over, they'd lost 116 more.

* * *

Finally, on Isiah Thomas Night, it was the players' turn to speak. First Tripucka, followed by Hall of Famers Dave Bing and Bob Lanier. The crowd sensed closure, the circle drawing ever closer around Thomas. Soon, Stern stood and the fans followed, as Dumars looked up to the stands and spoke. When Joe D talked, Detroit listened.

"A night like this is not deserved more by anyone than Isiah Thomas," he said. "We hear people step up here and say that this place wouldn't be here, these banners wouldn't be here. You just don't know how true that is. So many nights and so many days we would come in here and practice, and sit down and talk and talk how we were going to win the championship, and the leader of all that was definitely Isiah Thomas. Make no mistake about that."

The stone-cold look on Lynn Thomas' face was still in place a few moments later when Vinnie Johnson told the crowd what an "honor" it had been to play ten years with Thomas in Detroit, how much he appreciated the sacrifices both Thomas and Dumars had made in their minutes. "Oh, and one more thing," said Johnson, coyly setting up his last-second championship shot. "Thanks for passing me that ball in Portland."

Now it was time for Blaha to bring the tribute home. He brought out Laimbeer, the man Isiah—late in their careers—sucker punched in the back of the head during one stormy practice. But that was rationalized as Isiah just being Isiah, being a Bad Boy to the bitter end.

"I'm not going to stand up here and butter you up like everybody else has," Laimbeer said. "All I can say is you know how much you mean to me—and your family. And I'm always going to love you. I'm always going to respect you because you're almost like a brother to me."

Daly opened with a cute little story about running into Thomas during All-Star Weekend. "Last Saturday I was in San Antonio for the Shootout, walking back to my hotel with Dave Checketts and Ernie Grunfeld. We got as far as the Marriott when this window rolls down and Isiah is laughing at me. I said, 'What the hell else is new? I'm walking and you're riding in a limo.'

"I have a personal debt because he is responsible for me, and all the other players that we have mentioned, to have the success I did as a basketball coach. We were able to forge something that will take a long time to replace. Everywhere I go, I see Detroit people on planes, it doesn't matter what city, they come up to me and all want to shake hands and thank you for what you did for the city of Detroit. None of this would have transpired without your leadership. Of all the players I've had in my career, and there have been hundreds, there are only a couple that have this kind of leadership. Even though they're retiring this number tonight, they will never retire your spirit in the city of Detroit."

What followed was the gift portion of the program. After the obligatory trips (Hawaii), scholarships (St. Joe's), posters, and paintings, finally, at 8:22 P.M., the object of all the affection stood silent before the faithful, head down, soaking up the sound. There was a cry of "We love you, Zeke!"

Standing there, indeed, were the two Isiahs. The Good Isiah who anonymously purchased rims and nets for eight Detroit parks, who played with a heart as wide as the Michigan sky. The Bad Isiah was there, too, bubbling beneath the surface. The Isiah who "saw red," as one friend put it, and was fully capable of exploding into a wild, choking rage; the man with the angelic smile and the devilish bent who gambled with far more than his mind.

"Tonight is not an individual honor," he said. "It's not an individual accomplishment. I had a lot of great teammates. A lot of great friends. But most of all, I had a lot of great fans. The cheers that have inspired me, the cheers that inspired our team to do great things, and as you get ready to raise my number to the rafters, just remember how important a part you played in my number being up there. It was not solely me that did those wonderful things. I had great teammates. I had great coaching. And also played for a great organization. I'd like to thank Bill Davidson and the Pistons organization for giving me the chance and opportunity to come into the NBA and play thirteen wonderful years here in Detroit."

Soon Thomas pulled a piece of paper from his pocket.

"I'd also like to thank the most important people—my wife, my two kids, my mother, my mother-in-law, my brothers and sisters. You know they say behind every great man is a strong woman. Well, I'm a fortunate guy. I was standing behind a great woman. I'd like to thank my wife for making my career possible. I'd like to thank my wife for making this family we have possible. I'd like to thank my wife, Lynn, for being the single most important person

in the world, influence-wise [pause] next to my mom . . .
[laughs]."

It was here Thomas decided to send the first of many messages.

"I don't think all of you realize when I came to Detroit, I was
nineteen years old. You watched me grow up. You watched my
bad parts. You watched my good parts. You saw my sins, my bad
parts; you watched a young man grow into an adult. And you got
to see that right before your eyes. Not only did you get to see it,
you got to judge it and critique it. That was very tough for me on
an individual basis. At night when I would go home, and none of
you were there, none of you were in that room, I would crawl into
bed and lay there next to my wife and cry. It was her, it was her
hand that guided me through the night."

As the crowd erupted in cheers, Lynn Thomas never budged.
Never moved a muscle in her still-silent face.

"When I first came to this organization to play for the Detroit
Pistons, my goal was to make sure my family was okay. We
weren't born with silver spoons in our mouth. We didn't have the
greatest of things. You watched me grow up here, the problems my
brothers had. The reason I came to the NBA was to give them a
better life. So I'd like to introduce them to you tonight. Gregory
Thomas, Larry Thomas, Lord Henry Thomas, Mark Thomas, you
all come out here." As the brothers made their way toward center
court, their youngest brother continued on his family-values
theme, though some people in the building would have called that
another charade.

"I want you to look at those players on the Toronto bench, the
Pistons bench. You see us run up and down the court and
entertain you, right? We have families. We have families. The
things you whisper about us, spread rumors about us, you talk
about us, we have families. This is my family. My wife and two
kids, that is my proudest accomplishment."

Now Thomas and family stood alone, in front of a black curtain
draped high from above. As the drapes swept back, and No. 11
was revealed and carried up to its proper place in the rafters, Lynn
Thomas finally smiled. As if to say that of all the tributes, only the
actual No. 11 was the real thing. The player himself.

Much later, as the clock worked toward one, the photographer
at the party was still firing away, dozens and dozens of people to
shoot from an amazing, thirteen-year journey. The next night, one

photo would quietly surface. It would show Thomas with his arm around a good-looking, olive-skinned man in his midforties, wearing a black T-shirt under an expensive black leather jacket.

This was no athlete, but, like Isiah, a man with two distinct sides. He was also the man at the heart of what was said to be the most thrilling, yet dangerous chapter in Isiah Thomas' life.

15

Bad to the Bones

IT WAS CLOSING DOWN TO MIDNIGHT AS A COTERIE OF GAMBLERS swarmed around a table in the heavily guarded home of world-champion boxer Tommy Hearns. The game was dice. High-stakes dice. A single roll, one quick flick of the wrist, worth ten or twenty grand. "Make your bet!" someone shouted, and in seconds a blizzard of fifty- and hundred-dollar bills hit the table, peppered by wild, macho chatter. The stage was set. Everything was perfect. And right on schedule, a new "player" arrived.

"Let's go, boys," he called out to the crowd. "Let's bust them bones."

Isiah Thomas was ready to roll.

"Isiah was on fire that night," recalled a man who years later said he watched Thomas gamble all night. "He was like a fucking kid in a candy store. When he got the dice, he got hot, on a roll. Gamblers like to intimidate people when they're hot; Isiah was no different. He was funny, Gumby-like, the way he moved his body, making his moves."

Betting like a man in heat, Thomas is said to have soon burned several men out of the game, including a man named Walid, a bitter rival who would eventually tell his story to a federal grand jury. Deep into the night the dice danced without stopping. A mountain of money rose higher and higher, like an office tower in the foreshadows of No. 11's face. Finally, it was over. "Follow me," whispered a businessman, scooping up some cash. Together he and Thomas moved to a nearby bedroom.

A man says that once inside the room he watched as Thomas and the businessman quietly counted a pile of largely $50 and $100 bills. When they had finished, the point guard wrapped his stash in a bedsheet and slipped out into the night. It was 5 A.M., and Isiah Thomas had $56,000 in his hands, winnings from a game he swore he never played, a game the NBA wanted to know as little about as possible.

Mull this scenario over in your mind. The most valuable and visible player of an NBA championship team, said to be deeply in debt from dice games, making himself vulnerable to leaders of a nationwide multimillion-dollar sports-betting syndicate involving organized crime figures. Hard to believe, but as it turned out, NBA security actually examined the seeds of this scandal in late 1989 . . . only to drop the ball.

"The league washed their hands of it," admitted one Pistons executive. "Why, I don't know. They never got involved. They never lifted a finger. Not one."

Actually, the league, in the person of security chief Horace Balmer, did lift a finger—to call a league-appointed security representative in Detroit and order him to conduct an investigation. Balmer also spoke to the lawyer representing Thomas, whose name would surface in a sports-betting case in June 1990, the day after the Pistons won their second-straight NBA title. But after the local U.S. Attorney publicly declared that Thomas was not a target of the investigation, it became a "dead issue" for the league.

"I was told I would be contacted by the league, and I never was," said one of the most obvious interview subjects, an ex-FBI agent named Ned Timmons.

The Pistons were two time zones away when the call came into *Roundball One*, the club's plush private plane. It was June 15, 1990, and in a matter of hours, Channel 2 News investigative reporter Vince Wade would drop the first bomb. He would report that as part of a probe into a huge sports-gambling and money-laundering operation, a series of checks written by Thomas had been subpoenaed by a federal grand jury in Detroit. Wade went on to report that Thomas had participated in what Wade described as "high-stakes" dice games and had cashed some $100,000 worth of checks through a grocery store owned by Emmet Denha, forty, a former neighbor of Thomas and the godfather of his only son. Wade added that Pistons' forward Mark Aguirre had met with Timmons, the ex–FBI agent, just prior to the Pistons' playing the Chicago Bulls in the Eastern Conference Finals, Aguirre reportedly worried about Thomas' gambling, and that Denha had been identified through court-ordered wiretaps as a money-laundering suspect connected to a major bookmaker named Henry Allen Hilf.

While the TV story stated Thomas was not the target of the investigation, that fact got buried a bit in an explosion that landed on the front page of every major newspaper in the state. ("WEL-COME HOME, CHAMPS—Pistons' return marred by gambling probe, violence," read one headline.)

Thomas' response was a campaign designed to clear his name. From his lawyer's office in Bloomfield Hills on Saturday, Thomas gave one emotional interview after another. For nearly twelve hours he angrily denied involvement in "high-stakes" dice games or any unsavory connection to Denha or illegal sports-betting rings, at one point adding, "I don't gamble any more than the next guy."

"I don't deserve this," Thomas said. "I think gambling is one of the stupidest things you can do. . . . I know in my heart; I know in my mind [I have done nothing wrong]. More importantly, the FBI knows. People just made stuff up."

In addition, Thomas told reporters:

- The checks he had cashed with Denha over a three-year period were nothing more than his regular $4,000 monthly allowance. "The reason why I cashed these checks at Imhad's [Emmet's] store is because it's easier for me to cash them with him than to go to the bank and stand in line and sign autographs," he said. "It's perfectly legal."
- He had participated in three "low-stakes" dice games in the last nine years, including one at Denha's house. "We had a barbecue at Emmet's house one day, and just like how some people may play cards or poker or whatever, we bet five dollars or ten dollars," Thomas said. "But it wasn't

hundreds and hundreds of dollars like what's being reported. And it wasn't like this happened seven, nine, or ten times. It was maybe once or twice over the seven years I've known the guy."

By Monday morning, as Thomas and the Pistons had hoped and planned, the media tide had turned. An interview with Bill Bonds, the No. 1 anchor in Detroit for decades, helped; so did the words of *Free Press* columnist Mitch Albom, who penned a typically powerful essay. While noting he and Thomas had had differences in the past, Albom said it was clear, at least for now, the Pistons' captain had been accused of absolutely nothing wrong. "Except, perhaps," wrote Albom, "not having the greatest luck in choosing friends."

Another of Thomas' friends was Detroit's Teflon-coated mayor, Coleman Young, who throughout his long, contentious reign had seen the city overrun with crack cocaine, and damaged by a string of police and public corruption scandals involving officials in his administration. One of those officials was longtime police chief William Hart. In August 1992, Hart was sentenced to ten years in federal prison for embezzlement and tax evasion after being convicted of stealing more than $2.5 million of taxpayer money from a secret police fund set up to catch drug dealers. During fifty-one days of sometimes tawdry testimony, it was disclosed that Hart, sixty-eight, a decorated undercover cop who spent nearly forty years in the department, had lavished cash, furs, and lottery tickets on a succession of girlfriends while narcotics operations went begging for money. He also hid bundles of cash at home; one stash, in his kitchen ceiling, came tumbling down during a remodeling project.

Newspapers reported how U.S. District Court Judge Paul Gadola, in a ninety-minute sentencing, lashed out at city officials—including the mayor by inference. Without naming Young, Gadola noted that when Hart was convicted, the mayor had said there was no "smoking gun" and described the case as a bookkeeping exercise. Gadola said the city's "executive level" had displayed hostility and resistance in the face of the scandal. One paper noted that as part of his defense, Hart told federal authorities a portion of the missing money—the feds found only about $100,000— went to protect the mayor's relatives. One such relative was

Young's niece, Cathy Volsan Curry, who for three and a half years, the papers said, got special police protection—as many as four officers working twenty-four hours a day, seven days a week—while she was dating drug kingpin Richard (White Boy Rick) Wershe, who ran one of the city's largest cocaine rings. Curry had begun dating Wershe when her husband, another drug lord and former partner of Wershe, was in federal prison awaiting trial on drug charges. Both men received long prison sentences.

Yet here was Young, along with other local politicians, unleashing a scathing attack against Wade.

"The lowest blow to hit the city," charged City Councilman David Eberhard. "You can pick on elected officials, but a natural hero, I think this is an absolute sin."

"Whoever leaked that story out of the FBI should be prosecuted," Young charged, "and so should Vince Wade."

But Wade wasn't some blow-dried Ken doll looking to make a name for himself; he already had one. In more than twenty years of Detroit radio and TV reporting, the forty-three-year-old Wade had earned a reputation as a hard-nosed, fair-minded journalist. In the past, he had locked horns with the Mafia, Chaldean racketeers, crooked cops, and even Mayor Young, and had escaped unscathed. This time, Wade and his TV station had tracked the story for months, making charts, doing interviews, working a number of sources, including federal and local law enforcement officials frustrated by the government's reluctance to fully investigate the gambling conspiracy.

"I feel I was fair to Isiah on this story," Wade said at the time. "I felt like it before we went on the air. I feel it today.

"When is it a good time to go after a hero?" he asked. "Do you wait until after the parade? Do you wait until the White House ceremony? Do you wait until after the MVP award? Do you wait until after his NBA career is over?"

Like hundreds of thousands of Iraqi Catholics, Emmet Denha, the man in the black leather jacket on Isiah Thomas night, had immigrated to the Detroit area from the Middle East with his parents at an early age. According to court papers, after arriving in Detroit he dropped out of school in the ninth grade to help support his family, working in various grocery stores and supermarkets in the greater Detroit area. By the time he was twenty-one, he had leveraged his life savings and loans facilitated through Chaldean bank connections to purchase a small grocery store of his own; four years later Denha bought another, larger store. By the time the gambling story broke, he owned several grocery stores, including two large Shopper's Market supermarkets, a video store, and management and development companies. A handsome man with jet-black hair and a confident air, he carried a reputation among the ever-expanding Chaldean populace as a shrewd, heavy-tipping, community-minded businessman with a Midas touch.

Indeed, for much of the 1980s Denha was living the American dream. He and his family had moved into an exclusive area of Bloomfield Hills, the moneyed enclave of old-line advertising and auto executives and nouveau-riche sports stars. Over time, Denha and Thomas had grown from next-door neighbors to fast friends, tight enough that Denha said he would often drive Thomas to the airport before road trips. Thomas himself described Denha as one of his two closest friends.

What Thomas didn't know was that for much of the 1980s and into the '90s his onetime next-door neighbor and Joshua's god-father was essentially married to the mob—deeply involved in a scheme that laundered more than $6 million in illegal gambling money for Henry Allen Hilf, "the director and supervisor" of what the government called a bookmaking operation of "national significance involving extremely large-scale illegal sports betting." An operation, the government charged, under control of organized crime.

As it turned out, a federal strike force and the Criminal Division of the IRS had been investigating Hilf and several of his associates for more than two years through court-ordered wiretaps. The indictments came down in May 1991 and proved very bad news for Hilf, Denha, and eighteen others. Together they were charged with ninety-nine counts of racketeering (RICO), illegal gambling, conspiracy, and money laundering. According to the hefty indictment, Hilf, fifty-two, a massive man nicknamed the General, was the Midwest boss of a ring that stretched from Brooklyn, New York, to Miami, Las Vegas, Chicago, and Detroit. The indictment charged that Hilf was "engaged in the business of betting and wagering on sports events" with no less than five other illegal sports books, the biggest in alliance with Joseph John Costa of

Brooklyn, New York, Alan Denkenson of Queens, New York, and Louis Mark Cohen of Miami.

The scope of "The Enterprise" was evident in the staggering amounts of money the government said had been passed among the principals. In just one month, November 1987, for example, the government charged Costa had collected some $250,000 from Hilf; a month later, another $300,000. One bettor, William E. Rosenbalm Jr. of Las Vegas, known as Airplane Bill for his former ownership of an air charter company, was said to have lost several million dollars in wagers. (Rosenbalm, who was not indicted, had no comment.)

In court papers, Denha admitted that in or about 1984 he began cashing Rosenbalm's checks to Hilf. The indictment charged that in just one fifteen-month period, October 1986 through January 1988, Denha laundered thirty checks totaling more than $6 million. *Six million dollars.* No checks less than $46,000 and some as high as $420,000 had been washed through Denha's Shopper's Market account at Michigan National Bank.

In a lengthy Monday, June 18, 1990, interview with the *Detroit Free Press*, Thomas painted a poignant scene. To a reporter he described how shortly after landing at the airport the previous Friday from Portland, he had rushed home to find Lynn, his wife, standing in front of a television set watching the evening news in tears.

"I said, 'What wrong with you?' " he told the newspaper.

"She said, 'Well, they just reported on television that you were involved in some sort of gambling ring.'

"And I'm like, 'What?' "

There was only one problem: the sweet little scene he had created was only half true.

The full truth was that Thomas knew Wade's report was coming well before it aired; certainly well before his wife ever mentioned it. At the very least, the first hints of trouble came while the team plane was flying over Denver early on Friday. "We knew something was coming down," confirmed a Pistons official. "We knew there was going to be a problem in Detroit. We had a couple of hours to react."

But that timetable didn't fit into Thomas' damage-control campaign. No, this one was better: the hero returning home to find a tearful wife unglued by baseless charges against her husband. Baseless, of course, because Thomas had heatedly denied each and every charge in Wade's report. Never played dice more than three times in his entire life, he said. Only once during a barbecue at Denha's house, he said. Always five- and ten-dollar bets, he said.

But now four eyewitnesses—including the man who watched Thomas win $56,000 that night at Tommy Hearns'—have said otherwise. Independent of one another, they cited a number of occasions on which they said they watched Thomas gamble large sums of money. Two men who attended a barbecue at Denha's house, for example, insisted the stakes at that dice game were ten times higher than Thomas told the press.

"They were gambling with stacks of hundreds," one said. "It was thousands [of dollars], definitely in the thousands."

Another eyewitness recalled how one minute Denha's pool table was vacant, the next, covered over and transformed into a craps table complete with a fancy bunting wrapped around the sides.

How stiff were the stakes?

Sitting in his office, the man stretched the thumb and middle finger on his right hand as far apart as they could possibly go.

"They had wads of cash in their hands that thick," he said.

Still, as heavy as this action could be, with cash-rich Chaldeans tossing Franklins and Jacksons around like Saudi sheikhs would, these games proved peanuts compared to the invitation-only affairs at Tommy's.

To many Detroiters, Thomas "Hit Man" Hearns was another Motown hero—a ghetto warrior with dynamite in his fists who had battled his way off the streets and into ring history. Hagler-Hearns. Leonard-Hearns. Those epic bouts, along with six title belts, had made millions for Hearns, enough for a yacht and several homes, including—according to court papers filed in a wrongful-death suit involving Hearns—a sprawling, well-guarded estate in the Detroit suburb of Southfield loaded with guns, rifles, Uzis, even an exotic pistol crossbow. It was at that home that on the night of June 10, 1989, Hearns' brother Henry used one of those weapons—a rare Smith & Wesson .41 Magnum handgun—to kill girlfriend Nancy Ann Barile during an argument. Henry Hearns eventually went to prison, but back on the second Monday of December 1991, brother Tommy was in a lawyer's office giving a deposition as part of that wrongful-death suit filed by the family of Barile. Plaintiffs' attorney Marietta S. Robinson was deep into the questioning of Hearns, a defendant in the lawsuit, when Robinson began to explore the area of parties at Hearns' house.

What follows comes from an official transcript of Tommy Hearns' deposition.

Robinson asked the boxer if Pistons center James Edwards had ever been to Hearns' house.

"Not that I recall, no," said Hearns.

"Isiah Thomas a friend of yours?"

"Yes."

"Has he been to your house?"

"Yes, he has."

"On several occasions?"

"Probably just a couple of occasions."

Later, Robinson asked this series of questions.

Robinson: "Have you ever had a group of gentlemen at your house, where you engaged in high stakes dice games?"

Hearns: "I have done that in my house."

Robinson: "And Henry has not been the doorman for those events?"

Hearns: "No, No."

Robinson: "In those dice games, am I correct that you have had bets as high as five, ten, twenty thousand dollars?"

At this point, the transcript indicates, Hearns' attorney objected to the line of questioning and instructed his client not to answer any more questions about the dice games. Robinson plunged ahead anyway, asking Hearns about the dice games.

Hearns: "Only had a couple of games."

Eyewitnesses who said they attended such games pinpoint several occasions from late 1988 to late 1989 on which they said Thomas, Edwards, and occasionally other Pistons participated in the gambling. Most of the games, they said, were run by Hilf, Denha, or a big-time gambler and reputed race fixer named Imad Samouna. Nicknamed Skinny Eddie for his slight, fallow frame, Samouna and two close friends, Charles "Stosh" Maloney and Freddie "the Saint" Salem, were arrested in September 1990 for running a notorious after-hours gambling joint. According to an investigator assigned to the case, the club specialized in all-night craps games, 2:30 to 8 A.M., seven days a week, and was routinely frequented by drug dealers, bookmakers, and professional athletes. It was a place, said the investigator, where "serious, professional" gamblers hung out, twenty to thirty at a time, often betting more than $100,000 in a half hour.

In May 1991, after pleading guilty of violating state felony gambling laws, Samouna, Maloney, and Salem were "ejected and excluded" from all Michigan race tracks "until further order of the Racing Commissioner."

Said one law enforcement source: "They have a very direct financial interest in how races turn out. There is a total potential for corruption, fixed races, when they are around the track." Although suspected by Michigan racing investigators of fixing races at Hazel Park Harness Raceway near Detroit, Samouna, Maloney, and Salem were never charged.

Samouna and Salem are said to have been major money players in the action at Hearns'. The scene described is something out of a Scorsese film—a smoky menagerie of swarthy, motor-mouthed Chaldeans, mobsters, bookmakers, drug dealers, race-fixers, boxers, managers, bodyguards, power brokers, politicians, judges, bad boys one and all, crowded around a craps table, ready to bust them bones.

"Thirty to forty-five people, mostly a Black-Arab crowd, including some damn good-looking hookers," recalled a defense attorney who said he saw Thomas and Edwards gamble at least twice. "I went with a guy now in federal prison, a dope guy," said the man. "With him I was accepted. The first time I left at six A.M., the second time four A.M. Denha was there. A lot of Chaldeans with big, big bucks . . . betting ten to twenty thousand a pop."

The stakes were mind-boggling at times, nights when ego and balls and credit lines ran wild. When monumental amounts of cash—$200,000, $300,000, $400,000—were said to be won or lost by a single man, stakes so steep they are said to have driven other players quickly out of the game. But not Thomas. Or Edwards. One night the attorney said he watched Thomas win what he estimated was $250,000; another night he said he saw Thomas and Edwards take a severe financial beating.

"Yeah," he said, "they were big, big losers."

How big? By late 1989, several sources say, the dice games had worn a huge hole in Thomas' and Edwards' wallets. Thomas' markers alone to the Chaldean crowd are said to have exceeded six figures. "He owed them a lot of money," said a source with direct knowledge of the alleged losses. "A lot of money."

One November day a few years ago, another man, the one who said he saw Thomas win that $56,000, sat in the front seat of a rental car, a black baseball cap pulled down over his face. There he talked for more than an hour about his background, the dice games, and Thomas. "He plays people," the man said at one point. "He's two-faced."

In time, the man described a second night he said he watched Thomas gamble at Hearns' mansion. This time Aguirre came, too.

"I don't think he won a lot of money when Aguirre was there," said the man. "Aguirre was just fucking around. He didn't play. That's when he figured he [Isiah] had a problem, when he went to Ned shortly after that."

Three years later Ned Timmons sat behind a paper-and-photograph-strewn desk in his sleek Sylvan Lake office. By his own admission, he hardly fit the profile of an ex-FBI agent, certainly not on this day, dressed as he was in snappy red suspenders and sun-bleached hair trailing down toward his shoulders. During a nine-year stretch with the Bureau during the 1980s, Timmons said he specialized in undercover work, often in dangerous locales. He left the Bureau in '89, tired of trying to survive on a $50,000-a-year cap. At the age of forty-seven, he was co-owner of a booming high-tech security company, Legal & Security Strategies Consulting, Inc., or L.S.S., which specializes in executive protection and crisis management. A write-up in *Crain's Detroit Business* reported that revenues exceeded $4 million in 1995, thanks in no small part to a former colleague at the Detroit FBI who helped L.S.S. land the job of providing security for Detroit newspaper executives during the perilous strike at the city's two major dailies, the *Free Press* and the *News.*

When the gambling story broke, Timmons was in Central America, where he had been on and off for two years, working for an import-export company he owned called Caribe Pacific, which had a helluva lot more to do with guns and the Contras than it did with shrimp and snapper. During more than a dozen interviews

Timmons said he got thrust into the center of the story purely by accident. He said that out of the "clear blue" one day he was contacted by a Chaldean businessman asking for help. "Chaldeans had come to me with a lot of problems—what to do with this, what to do with that," said Timmons. "This guy was a friend. He said, 'You have to talk to this guy, he's in trouble.' That individual turned out to be Emmet Denha. Emmet had some problems legally and he asked me for advice."

The biggest problem: Timmons said Denha was petrified he was about to be indicted by a federal grand jury. "He was totally out of control, extremely nervous, afraid. Stated he couldn't go to prison, he couldn't do the time," recalled Timmons. "He was terrified. He felt he had a severe problem and didn't know where to turn."

Over the next three weeks, during a dozen different meetings and calls, the story spilled out: Timmons said Denha explained how he had slowly been sucked into the money-laundering scheme by Hilf; how it had started with small checks at first, $30,000 or so, but after a bacchanal in Vegas, Denha said he was blackmailed to cash larger checks or face public exposure on what happened in Vegas. So the checks got bigger (as did, incidentally, Denha's 10-percent commission on everything he washed). But now the IRS was crawling up his ass, and he was scared.

Timmons said he told Denha to hire the best attorney he could find, get in prior to the indictment, and try to work something out with the government. At Denha's behest, Timmons said, he also acted as a liaison with the Detroit FBI office. "Emmet was aware I was relating information to the Bureau at his request," said Timmons.

As it turned out, according to Timmons, Denha had some interesting information to relate.

"Emmet seemed to feel that Isiah had a great deal of exposure in the situation," Timmons said during a long videotaped interview. "Emmet advised me personally that Isiah had cashed several checks with him."

Thomas told the local press those checks were for $4,000. Monthly allowance money.

"I recall the checks were much higher," Timmons said. "I don't recall exactly, but they were large numbers."

As Denha waited for the feds to act, Timmons said, he got

another surprise call. A Chaldean named John Oram, a close friend of both Timmons and Denha, was on the line. Oram was another Iraqi immigrant turned multimillionaire thanks to a string of Jam Sound electronics stores, including one outlet that was particularly popular with several Pistons players. Timmons said he had no idea what Oram, who refused comment, wanted as he drove over to the Jam Sound store on Woodward Avenue. No idea he was about to meet Aguirre, whose Pistons had just whipped the New York Knicks in the second round of the playoffs. Timmons said that once introductions were made in front of several eyewitnesses—"I didn't know the guy"—he and Aguirre talked alone for about forty minutes in Oram's private office, and that Aguirre conducted himself in both a "professional and gentlemanly" manner.

Yet, Timmons said, fear was written all over the face of perhaps Isiah Thomas' closest friend since childhood, an NBA All-Star Thomas had helped bring to Detroit, working behind the scenes to dump forward Adrian Dantley in favor of his man Mark.

"He was very serious, very concerned, and extremely intense over the situation," said Timmons of Aguirre. "His greatest concern was for his friend Isiah Thomas, the Pistons, and the entire situation. He was extremely concerned as a senior individual on the team that Isiah might have some exposure in this gambling probe. Aguirre never said he didn't or never said he did. Mark Aguirre was looking out for his friend.

"We discussed the different degrees of exposure that Isiah might have in a situation. If Isiah's gambling, it's one thing. If he was gambling on sporting events, I think it increases his exposure. If, in fact, he was betting on basketball games that he participated in, I think that took him to a different level. Aguirre and I discussed these various levels, and again, Aguirre never said that he [Thomas] had participated in anything. The discussion was: what if he was at one of these levels, what should be done?"

Timmons said he advised Aguirre to get the best attorney possible, go to the FBI, tell the truth, and hope for the best. Timmons said he also told Aguirre their conversation would be passed downtown, to the Detroit FBI.

Timmons said he never saw or heard from Aguirre again, and that he was out of town when Wade's story broke. The night before, WJBK sports anchor Virg Jacques, who had been in Portland covering the championship series, said he confronted Aguirre outside the team's private postgame party, looking for comment to balance Wade's pending report.

"He denied any conversation [with Timmons] took place," said Jacques. "He kept looking at the ground. He never looked me in the face."

When the story broke, both Thomas and Aguirre vigorously denied the latter had ever talked to an FBI agent, and technically Timmons couldn't argue with them; he was an *ex*–FBI agent. In the last seven years Aguirre has said virtually nothing about his meeting with Timmons or his role in the entire episode.

Contacted by one of the authors of this book, Aguirre, now a member of the Dallas Mavericks front office, initially indicated an interest in talking about the team and Thomas. He subsequently failed to return a series of phone calls.

One person who did receive a call from league security director Balmer was Bloomfield Hills attorney John Caponigro, whose firm represented Thomas from 1987 through 1992.

"We were in touch with the league," Caponigro said. "The league was in touch with us. They asked a lot of questions. I think, generally, they wanted to know if we were on top of it, handling the problem. I had a feeling they were as concerned with facts as with image. They wanted to make sure Isiah was in capable hands."

The NBA's investigation began in late '89, sparked by club concern over rumors of gambling by Thomas, Edwards, and others. According to one top Pistons official, league security also investigated the possibility of point shaving by one or more team members in late 1989. "There was some hinky stuff," said the official. "It always became secondary information."

Acting on those concerns, league security chief Balmer assigned his newly hired Detroit Pistons security rep, a man named Harold Johnson Jr., to supervise an NBA probe. A tall, dark-skinned black, he had been a member of the Detroit Police Department for twenty-five years, ultimately rising to the rank of inspector. Within the department Johnson was known for his military mien and close ties to controversial police chief William Hart. From

1985 to 1987, Johnson had been loaned to the neighboring city of Highland Park, where he became director of public safety, supervising both the police and fire departments. In 1988 he was named police chief for the city of Ecorse.

It was during Johnson's days in Ecorse that he conducted a brief investigation into the gambling/point-shaving allegations with the help of some Detroit police officers. (Despite repeated efforts, Johnson could not be reached for comment.) As best as can be determined, neither Johnson nor his investigators talked to any of the principals in the case, and by the end of the year, their inquiry was over.

"They found nothing, nothing," said the Pistons official. "They never, I think they ignored . . . They didn't want to know what they would find."

NBA Vice President of Communications Brian McIntyre said the league was "made aware" of the situation, but when "law enforcement people" told NBA security they had "found nothing," the league ended its investigation.

"It became a dead issue for us," said McIntyre.

Exactly, said one cop involved in the so-called investigation. "We were told to squash it," he said. "It was over before it began."

(However, in February 1997 the authors learned that the league began to reinvestigate allegations of gambling and point shaving.)

Yet in local gambling and law enforcement circles and right down into the Pistons' locker room, the hard questions the NBA never seemed to want to consider were being asked. Could the unthinkable have occurred? Just as in any case, much like Michael Jordan, when an athlete plays around with criminals, a natural concern is to question how deep his involvement might go.

A few years ago while standing outside an elevator in a downtown Boston hotel, a former Piston expressed such concern when he was asked a very direct question. It focused on Thomas' alleged involvement in high-stakes dice games. In low, direct tones, the player did not duck or deny the query. Instead, after a bit of a pause, he whispered: "Listen, I hate the guy, but there are other people involved."

Later, that same ex-Piston acknowledged within the locker room word had spread about dice games, that somebody "had won big" at Hearns' house. "We were all trying to figure out: Is this true?" he said. "The talk was somebody had won a lot of money, $300,000 in a shoebox."

Even more ominously, the same player admitted he and some of his teammates discussed the possibility that there had been point shaving in two specific Pistons games in late 1989.

"Golden State and Milwaukee," he said.

The Golden State game proved both odd and interesting. It had been played in Oakland on Saturday night, December 16. The night before, in Utah, Thomas had played thirty-eight minutes and scored 18 points on 6-of-17 shooting. In the first half, while going up for a jumper, Thomas took an errant elbow from Utah guard John Stockton. Once the bleeding stopped, he was taken to the locker room. Five minutes later he returned and resumed playing.

After the game Thomas said he felt fine, but according to news reports, on the plane to Oakland later that night, he experienced dizziness and numbness in the legs. When the team plane landed, Thomas was reportedly taken directly from the airport to a local hospital, where he was kept overnight for observation. A precautionary CAT scan reportedly taken the next day was negative.

Thomas' injury was kept quiet until game time against the Warriors. The official game notes reflect Thomas was "not with the team—concussion [sic]." Because the injury occurred on a weekend West Coast game, the NBA front office was not notified of Thomas' injury until well after the fact. That meant Las Vegas oddsmakers had no idea the Pistons star guard would not be in the lineup. With Thomas sidelined, the Pistons lost. The score: 104–92. Detroit had been favored by 3 points. While Aguirre had a season-high 31 points, and Laimbeer (11), Dumars (14), and Rodman (11), scored in double figures, Edwards shot just 1-5 and scored 4 points. Vinnie Johnson was 1-7 and scored 3 points.

It wasn't until Monday morning that the news of Thomas' injury found its way into the Detroit papers. The Warriors team physician is quoted as saying Thomas "was a badly hurt young man. He had a headache and was confused and disorientated." The initial estimate was Thomas would be sidelined a week to ten days. He played the following night at home against Seattle.

Some six years later, a top Pistons official put the circumstances surrounding Thomas's "injury" in a far different light. "I don't know where concussion came from," he said. "Supposedly, Isiah punched a hole in a wall in his hotel room in Oakland and hurt his hand. We put concussion down. We even sent him to the hospital for precautionary X rays to make it look good."

The Milwaukee date was December 29, a Friday-night encounter between the 17-10 Pistons, third in the Central Division, and the sixth-place Bucks (13-13). The Vegas line read Detroit by 10. Playing before a sold-out Palace crowd, the two teams were tied 72-72 at the end of three quarters. But in the final twelve minutes, Milwaukee outscored Detroit 27-13 to roll to an easy 14-point victory, 99-85. While Aguirre (19 points), Edwards (17), Dumars (16), Laimbeer (11), and Rodman (10) all scored in double figures, Thomas did not. He shot just 1 for 8 from the field and did not attempt a free throw in thirty-four minutes. He scored 2 points, committed 4 turnovers, and tallied 2 assists.

Fast-forward to the spring of 1990. It was playoff time and the Pistons were gunning for a second-straight NBA title. It was also the time two people say that Thomas told them he was receiving threats related to his gambling activities.

"He said the crowd he was hanging with, the Chaldean crowd, there were threats because he had won money, because he had won money from these guys," said a close friend of Thomas.

The second person, independent of the first, not only confirmed Thomas had talked about threats, but added that Thomas said he was in fear for his personal well-being.

"What I heard, I heard from him," said the person.

The man responsible for prosecuting the Hilf case was U.S. Attorney Stephen Markman. From the very beginning Markman made it clear that Thomas was never, had never been, and would never be, a target of his investigation. As it was when Thomas was called before the federal grand jury, he was whisked in and out of the federal courthouse through a private entrance. In public, Markman went out of his way to calm any fears about Thomas' testimony. "He was certainly helpful in his willingness to repeatedly state Isiah was not a suspect," said Thomas' attorney, John Caponigro. "When he [Isiah] testified before the grand jury, Markman tried his best to remove the stigma from Isiah, saying he was simply doing his duty as a citizen of the United States."

In retrospect, it's simple to see why Markman decided not to pursue a gambling/point-shaving investigation. The evidence he presumably had consisted of the results of the grand jury investigation, Thomas' checks to Denha, plus Denha's and Aguirre's revelations to Timmons. Wherever that evidence might have led him, he also had a very nervous potential witness in Denha, who was facing multiple counts of racketeering and "illegal monetary transactions" stemming from Hilf's money-laundering activities. But Markman was no political novice—nor were the Justice Department officials increasingly interested in the growing power of the Chaldean Mafia. A source with ties to the federal investigation confirmed that the government was after "bigger fish" than any individual gamblers or any illegal outgrowth of that gambling. Plus, pursuing an investigation against members of a world championship team could be disastrous. There was a chance that Detroit would go up in flames, as it had during the 1967 riots, and that Markman would be a marked man forever.

So, for whatever reason, Markman made clear that Thomas was not a target of his investigation. The league could not have been happier, even after Denha was indicted for his part in Hilf's scheme to launder at least $6 million in illegal sports-gambling money for the mob.

"In our handling of the matter, it finally went away," said Caponigro. "They [the NBA] were happy with [that], I would suspect."

The man who headed that investigation for the NBA—Harold Johnson Jr.—went away as well. On January 9, 1990, just days after completing his investigation, Johnson left the Ecorse Police Department to become police chief in Mobile, Alabama, where he remained until last year.

James Edwards was traded by Detroit to the Los Angeles Clippers on August 13, 1991, and is now out of the NBA. He categorically denied any involvement in high-stakes dice games or point shaving.

Asked about the dice games at Hearns', Edwards said, "I've never been to Tommy Hearns' house."

A more complete picture was painted of the games, featuring Isiah, Hilf, Denha, and "Skinny Eddie" Samouna.

"I don't know any of those guys at all, except Isiah," he said. "I don't know how to play dice."

So just to make sure, Edwards was asked, as a result of any substantial losses you are said to have sustained in those games, did you shave points in any games during the 1989–90 season?

"No, not at all," said Edwards, who paused a bit before speaking. "Not at all. We were too busy trying to beat people, the Bad Boys were, to worry about that stuff."

Stephen Markman, meanwhile, left the U.S. Attorney's office in April 1993. He was subsequently hired by arguably the most powerful—and politically connected—law firm in the state, where he worked until December 1994. At that time, he was appointed to be a judge on the State Court of Appeals in Michigan. Asked about the appointment, Markman replied, "I went through the process and the governor [John Engler] appointed me."

As for Emmet Denha, after a succession of attorneys, he ultimately hired Albert J. Krieger to handle his lengthy plea-bargain negotiations with the government. A heavyweight lawyer out of Miami, Krieger had unsuccessfully defended John Gotti, the so-called Dapper Don and former head of the powerful Gambino Crime Family in New York. Gotti is now serving a life sentence in federal prison in Illinois.

Denha, who declined comment through two of his attorneys, was convicted of a single count of racketeering. In November 1993 he became the last of twenty defendants to be sentenced. He received six months in prison and was ordered to pay a $62,000 fine and $275,000 in restitution—by far the lightest sentence of any major defendant. (By comparison, Hilf received five years in prison.)

"We were delighted by the sentence," said Krieger.

Did the NBA ever contact his client?

"No," said Krieger. "Definitely not. I would have known."

The phone call came on a dark, dismal January afternoon, from Michigan to New York, two days after a personal and confidential Express Mail letter had arrived in the Raptors offices in Toronto.

"Isiah Thomas," said the caller.

In reaction to a letter from one of the authors requesting comment, Thomas' response was unequivocal.

"I've never, ever been involved in point shaving, betting on games," he said. "Now, I have from time to time, in college, high school, and sometimes in the pros, yeah, you know, you play cards, you know, you shoot dice. But I have never, ever point-shaved, or gambled or bet on games."

From there a forty-minute talk—part mutually agreed upon tape-recorded interview, part private discussion—ensued. The first question dealt with several eyewitness accounts of Thomas' participating in high-stakes dice games at the home of Tommy Hearns and at Emmet Denha's house. Ten and twenty thousand dollars a roll. Up to fifty-thousand-dollar pots. Were you at those games? And did you participate in them?

"Yes, I was there," said Thomas.

How did you do?

"I don't recall those games being what you guys are alluding to, or what has been alluded to," he said. "It was a fun-type atmosphere, where there were a lot of people there. I got invited to Tommy's house. And those type of activities took place, but I was never involved in fifty-, sixty-, seventy-, eighty-thousand-dollar card games, dice games, or no other kind of games."

What was the most that you played for, to your recollection?

"I don't remember," he said. "It was quite a while ago. But I was never involved in the type of activity that you're explaining in terms of this type of money, gambled or bet."

Just so we're clear, these types of games were not five- and ten-dollar pots talked about in the Detroit papers.

"I never participated in any of those type of things," Thomas said.

But you just said you were at those games at Tommy's, and you were involved in those games, but not at those stakes? What kind of stakes were you playing? Because those were the stakes at those games, without question. We need some kind of range of the amount of money you won or lost at those games. Some people have said you won as much as $250,000 at those games. And some people have said you lost as much as $200,000.

"That never happened," said Thomas. "I can honestly tell you that kind of money was never bet by me. Gambled by me. Or won by me. In no way, shape, or form."

I'm confused, said the interviewer. If you were at those games and participating, they were lower-stakes dice games?

"I went there with the assumption there was a party at Tommy

Hearns' house," said Thomas. "When I got there, other activities started taking place. And friendly card games, blackjack games, and dice games that went from five bucks to ten bucks, maybe you had a hundred-dollar pot at some point in time. If there was any other activity going on there, betting and all this other stuff, of that money being bet, I, in no way, ever bet that kind of money, lost that type of money, or won that type of money."

The conversation shifted to the checks, how Denha had told someone the checks cashed by him for Thomas were not for $4,000 but for much larger amounts.

"That is not true. I have every check," said Thomas. "Balanced bankbook, accountants, legal work, and when all that stuff was went through, I had every check documented."

Why then, he was asked, would someone make such specific allegations?

"I can only speak for my actions, for Isiah Thomas," he said. "Every dime that was ever spent, money out of my account was documented, and every single dollar was followed. And the largest check I was cashing, I was paying out of my corporation, I was giving myself a monthly allowance. Those checks ranged from $3,000 to $5,000."

Has your life ever been threatened?

"No," he said.

Last question. Back to Oakland. To the Golden State game Thomas missed because of a reported concussion. Do you remember what hospital you went to, whether you checked in under your own name?

"No, I don't at this time," he said, "but I'm sure I can go and find out, wouldn't be hard to do."

Do you remember the concussion? You didn't play against Golden State. You were disorientated on the plane. It was a Saturday-night game. December 16, 1989.

Ten seconds of silence.

"No, but I'm sure if I look back, any of this stuff won't be too hard to find."

(An employee of Merritt Hospital, now called Summit Medical Center, said that the Center has no record of an Isiah Thomas, birthdate 4/30/61, ever having been admitted.)

At this point, Thomas requested the two men speak privately. During that twenty-minute conversation Thomas once again said he would never do anything to disrespect the game of basketball, the Pistons, or his family.

Time and time again, he told the other man on the phone, one who had spent many hours reporting this chapter of Isiah Thomas' life, to go out and find the truth. Find the truth. Find the truth.

What Isiah Thomas believed that truth might be, he would, or could, not say. And neither could the NBA.

16

College Games

THE MORNING METROLINER RUMBLED ALONG THE EASTERN INDUStrial corridor, from Penn Station below Madison Square Garden, through Newark and Philadelphia, on toward Washington, D.C. It was mid-February, but the sun reflected brilliantly off the banks of snow and patches of ice along the tracks, and Len Elmore found himself in quite the chipper mood, as he folded the jacket from his dark blue suit onto the seat next to him, placing it neatly above his briefcase. Then he sat down to stretch his long left leg into the aisle.

He was planning a busy, productive day, after kissing his wife, Gail Segal, and five-year-old Stephon and three-year-old Matthew good-bye at their high-rise Broadway apartment on Manhattan's Upper West Side. The first stop after leaving the train at the Maryland Beltway station would be his home in the nearby suburb of Highland. Then Elmore would shoot over to Columbia, to the office of Precept Sports, and spend the afternoon huddling with staff, checking in with his people on the college circuit. Finally, after dinner, he would be out to play the field himself.

Wake Forest was in College Park to play Maryland that night, giving Elmore the perfect opportunity to drop by Cole Field House and take a close look at Wake's 6-10 sensation, Tim

Duncan. The prize of the 1996 college draft, as far as Elmore was concerned.

That's if Duncan, a junior, came out a year early, which at the time seemed likely, in that three years of college was starting to look like a lifetime for the typical future pro.

Despite being clearly outplayed by Massachusetts' Marcus Camby earlier in the season, Duncan was a lock to be No. 1 if he came out. Unlike Camby, a lanky, finesse player whose position was undefined, Duncan clearly had superior low-post skills. With experience, with upper-body development, he was exactly what two-thirds of the NBA did not have: a highly skilled post player. Elmore didn't have to be a former center to know that.

Of all the potential lottery picks, Elmore had to best like his chances with Duncan after landing Randolph Childress, Wake's high-scoring guard and Duncan's good friend, in the previous draft. When Childress was a junior, frail and unheralded, Elmore had thrown out the possibility that he could benefit from staying another year in school. Childress did and, as a senior, gained in stature by lighting up the ACC Tournament. Appreciative for the objective advice, Childress' family came right back to Elmore before he was drafted nineteenth in the first round by Portland.

It was a good example of Elmore's argument that agents did not have to bullshit players and their families to recruit them. "Some of them you'll tell the truth and they'll shut you right out," he said. "You hope to get the ones who want the advice in the first place."

What attracted Elmore to Duncan was that he was not going to decide to give up his senior season without serious deliberation. He was not the stereotypical urban kid harboring the NBA-at-the-end-of-the-rainbow dream. Duncan, from St. Croix in the Virgin Islands, was an aspiring Olympic swimmer until Hurricane Hugo devastated the island, destroying the pool he'd trained in. When he started to grow, reaching 6-1 by the ninth grade, he began playing basketball, finally auditioning for Wake coach Dave Odom on the recommendation of a scout in 1992.

Duncan was a serious psychology student and an avid computer junkie, often browsing the chat rooms on America Online. Once, early in the season, a *New York Times* reporter off on his own expedition through cyberspace came upon Duncan. The reporter asked if Duncan would be a pro the following season. Duncan said he was racked with stress about the decision. His mother had not long ago died of cancer. "She took treatments in a tent," Duncan said. "It was terrible." And he'd promised her that he would get his degree.

So intriguing a player was Duncan that he would have been the first pick in 1995 as well. "Wasn't mature enough," he said, a once-logical refrain that was now more of a contradiction in the era of Kevin Garnett. Whatever, the result had opened the door for Joe Smith, and Elmore's first big catch.

Pointing out that Duncan was an underclassman, Elmore wasn't planning on approaching Duncan in College Park. He had never actually met Duncan, but he wasn't about to deny that he had Childress, among others, on the case. He was a dead duck, he realized, if he didn't network.

Only in the last two weeks had Elmore refocused on Precept business after what had proved to be a most unsavory experience with the NBA Players' Association and its satellite politicos. He'd been intrigued, first when Williams called him about becoming Gourdine's general counsel with the executive directorship in his future, and then when his name was included on the list of candidates to be interviewed at the All-Star Game. He was also wary, with every right to be.

Whose agenda was being pursued? Alex English's? Jeffrey Kessler's? David Falk's? Where did the majority of players who voted for decertification stand? Michael Jordan? The new director would have to somehow have the support of all the special-interest groups or the job could be, as Elmore put it, "occupational suicide."

Credential-wise, Elmore was a natural candidate, or at least Buck Williams thought so. "I would have loved to have Lenny come in," Williams said. "You want an attorney and the smartest one you can get. Look at what the NBA brings to these negotiations, a Dream Team of lawyers, a machine.

"It's sad what this became, everybody wanting to elect their own man. First people said I negotiated a good deal for the owners because I wanted a management job. Then they said I wanted the union job for myself. Then Paul Silas, who's been a friend, got mad at me because I campaigned to hire someone with a law degree. So I guess I didn't really want the job after all."

As for Elmore, Williams added, "Lenny's a Harvard lawyer, a former player. I thought a lot of people would agree with me."

The first sign that few in power shared Williams' vision, that Elmore's candidacy was not even going to get out of the gate, came with the sudden emergence of a recruiting letter Elmore had written to Sam Cassell while the Houston Rockets' guard was still at Florida State. Elmore addressed the issue of players who were conditioned to think that an entrenched white agent would get them better deals than a black one, writing Cassell that, to have the right connections in the league, he was not "obligated" to sign with a white agent.

In a telephone conversation with one reporter, when Elmore's name casually came up, one well-known agent had the letter at his fingertips, quoting from the passage regarding black and white agents, and commenting that it was a disgrace.

How had this letter, three years later, fallen into the hands of Elmore's rivals? There were several possibilities—college coaches, athletic directors, someone with a relationship with any one of the agents. Elmore said he didn't know and didn't care. "I will never back away from that," he said. "These guys are circulating the letter as if there's something in it that I should be embarrassed about. Their own players are saying they want a black director of the union. Why is that okay?"

The answer, Elmore believed, was fear. With the unmistakable conceit of a Harvard man, he contended that he was the "worst nightmare to some of these people." Paraphrasing Eddie Murphy in *48HRS.*, he said, "I'm a brother with an education."

That is why, he was convinced, there was even a campaign, however arbitrary, to quash his candidacy, the superficial excuse being that he, as "Buck Williams' candidate," was part of the Gourdine/Williams faction that had negotiated a terrible deal.

The truth, as Williams acknowledged, was that Elmore had been squarely in the dissident camp. David Falk surely knew that, as did Marc Fleisher, who, according to Elmore, told him in a telephone conversation, "You stepped up in the decertification thing."

There seemed to be more credence to Elmore's assertion that he was suspiciously viewed as an unallied quantity, as an unpredictable and creative thinker. No one really could say where Elmore would try to lead the union. And certainly the NBA wasn't going to want him empowered, after he'd authored the *New York Times* article advocating—however whimsically—the formation of a breakaway league.

Still, one league official said Stern had once referred to Elmore as a "black power guy," though if it meant wanting to be recognized as being capable of doing the same job as his white rivals, then Elmore wasn't going to dispute that label. Even Willie Brown had admitted that the Smith family had wondered if a black agent could get for them what a white one could, and perhaps that partially explained the lack of professional respect the Smiths gave Elmore. To Elmore, it was no different than members of an African-American community shunning black-owned businesses and believing that white proprietors would service them better. He believed it was this kind of thinking that explained why "black leaders are never able to build a strong enough consensus" within the NBA, as Charles Grantham had found out, as Buck Williams was finding out.

Yet to even broach this issue was to set oneself up for predictable retaliation. Circulation of the Cassell letter was a means for others to try to portray Elmore as someone who would use race to promote himself, but as an African-American, he had an antithetical view: he just didn't want race to be a handicap.

"Am I racist?" he asked. "With my wife and kids?"

His wife, white and Jewish, worked as a managing director for the Bank of America. When their boys reached nursery school age, she enrolled them in one of New York's prominent yeshivas. Elmore, not a religious man and certainly not a practicing Jew, had no objections. "I want them to have a cultural understanding of their heritage," he said.

He didn't sound like Louis Farrakhan, but on the subject of the Million Man March, he again demonstrated a knack for looking beyond the surface. "I don't buy that stuff about Farrakhan being a terrible messenger because I don't give a damn," he said. "I am not a Farrakhan supporter, but if anything he says or anyone else up on the podium is taken in by those four hundred thousand to one million who were there and brought it back to those communities and increased the awareness of respect between men and women, then I don't care who said it.

"People continue to think that black Americans are either here or there, not in the middle, which is where most white Americans are. It's like Malcolm X and Martin Luther King. Malcolm was necessary because he allowed Martin to be viewed in a more positive way. Farrakhan is a necessary evil, in order to make the moderate voices more effective. People rush to the Arafats and Rabins because they sound so moderate compared to the alternative."

If Elmore were a "black power guy" in the radical sense, he might have been shouting from the mountaintop about all the Jewish lawyers hoarding power over the sport played predominantly by young black men. Instead, he considered most of them, on the sides of management and labor, to want the best for the sport and the players, as well as themselves. "But it's in a paternalistic way, the old ACLU thinking that 'we know what's best for you poor, undereducated people,'" he said. He couldn't resist a more strident term: "puppet masters."

Elmore got a taste of the marionette show during his forty-five-minute interview for the union's executive directorship. Among the board members were Williams, Patrick Ewing, Dikembe Mutombo, Ken Gattison, Jim McIlvaine, and A. C. Green. Elmore spoke for about fifteen minutes, mainly in generalities, of promoting a vision to create the model union in sports. "I told them that, deep down, their members didn't believe in their own bargaining position anymore but that they had tremendous potential because they are irreplaceable," Elmore said.

Board members, on the other hand, were not when they decided to leave. When Elmore finished his opening statement, Ewing and Mutombo, 7-foot clients of David Falk's, suddenly stood up and walked out, a Machiavellian dis. And during the ensuing interview, it was A. C. Green, a client of Marc Fleisher's, who had the most to ask, though little of it related to Elmore's game plan. Green, who wrote a book preaching abstinence from premarital sex, couldn't resist grilling Elmore about his onetime fling with booze.

Elmore, who never went around broadcasting news about that unhappy chapter of his life and his longtime sobriety, was stunned. "Not because I felt it was some dark secret, but because I realized how much effort someone had to go to not only know about all that but make an issue of it with Green," he said.

Seething that he had to explain to this highly moral jury the extreme emotional conditions of that time in his life, he answered

Green's questions but clearly got the picture. He realized this was a job he could consider only under optimum conditions, which didn't exist. Elmore concluded by saying that he believed the only way the union would again be effective against the power of Stern and his minions was to make a strong financial and emotional investment in a new executive director. And if the union wasn't prepared to do that, then he would prefer that his name be withdrawn from consideration.

"So that's what they did," he said. "Withdrew my name."

The treatment of Elmore at Cole Field House, if not befitting an actual celebrity, was respectful and warm. A seat was reserved for him in the VIP section behind the basket near the Maryland bench. Here was a basketball alumnus the school could flaunt as the very best example of college athletics. Elmore was a success story who even stayed close to home, serving on the board of the University of Maryland Foundation, caretakers of private contributions and endowments.

His Maryland number graced the row of All-Americans on red banners with white lettering that hung high above the floor. Elmore's 41 was seventh from the left, starting with Walt Williams' 42, Len Bias' 34, Albert King's 55, Buck Williams' 52, John Lucas' 15, Tom McMillen's 54, Elmore, Gene Shue's 25, and Louis Berger's 6.

Apart from the tragedy that the Bias name brought to mind, the school, with no national championships, could at least be proud of its surviving basketball elite. In addition to Elmore, McMillen was a former congressman, Buck Williams the NBA Players' Association president, and Lucas, after years of substance abuse, was accomplished in the field of recovery.

Still, trouble always seemed to be lurking near the program. "I call it the Maryland jinx," said Elmore when the latest gossip reached him as he settled into his seat and cracked open a diet Coke.

It seemed that the starting Terrapin point guard, senior Duane Simpkins, had just been suspended for three games by the NCAA for accepting an unauthorized loan from a man described as a "former AAU coach" to pay off $8,000 in campus parking violations. Elmore shook his head and rolled his eyes. The obvious question was why the coaches and athletic department officials, who had to know about the parking tickets, didn't help the player somehow settle his debt so he wouldn't have to accept an "unauthorized loan." The story, at face value, didn't make much sense.

Not much about big-time college basketball did, except for the obvious financial inducements for the schools and their entrenched power brokers. Cole had all the familiar trappings, including Billy Packer, Mr. ACC, slipping into his headset for the cable telecast on ESPN. Commercial sightings were everywhere, signs on the scorer's table for Geico Insurance, Coca-Cola, Powerade, *The Washington Post.* The players' seats bore the sponsorship of USAir.

While the Maryland band pounded out bad fight songs, the overwhelmingly white student crowd—short-haired males with their baseball caps turned back—booed the visitors when they trotted out. The home team followed, then Coach Gary Williams, who approached the bench, looked up in the stands, and began wildly punching the air, sending the Maryland kids into euphoric spasms. It was all part of the show, part of the deal. Campus entertainment for the middle- and upper-class kids, direct from the teeming heart of urban America.

Elmore did not count himself among those who believed the college game was being jeopardized by the mass defection of star underclassmen to the NBA. Maybe it wasn't good for Packer, for Dick Vitale, and ultimately the big-salaried coaches, because the networks would have less to sell and would ultimately pay less for the privilege. But each player was an individual with a choice to make, and with many options beyond the decision to stay for however many years.

"Joe came out after two years and people here said, 'Oh, too soon,'" said Elmore. "But for whom? After his fourth double-double in the NBA, I didn't hear anyone say Joe isn't ready. The thing is, it's not the Joe Smiths and Allen Iversons who you have to worry about. If they screw up a ten-million-dollar deal, shame on them. It's the kids who are vulnerable to the ego stroking, the ones who aren't ready or may never be. But it always comes back to choice and responsibility. It's almost insulting when people said, 'Oh, he won't go back and get his degree.'"

Smith was about to return to Maryland, but it wasn't for his degree. Two weeks after the Wake Forest game, another packed house of 14,500 jammed Cole to salute the Warrior rookie as 32 officially became the school's tenth retired number. Smith presented the school's athletic department with a check for $10,000, and the ovation was thunderous as the banner was hoisted.

As for his degree, Joe said he was keeping his promise to Letha, with one slight variation on the theme. He was taking correspondence courses not from Maryland, but from Norfolk State, Uncle Willie's school. Not to speak disparagingly of that school, but Elmore couldn't help but wonder, given the Willie connection, how much work Joe was going to have to do to get that degree.

There was nothing he could do about that now, though. And after watching Tim Duncan destroy Maryland on February 15 with a career-high 33 points, making 12 of 14 shots in a stunning display of low-post dexterity, Elmore made the rounds, though he carefully avoided the locker-room area. It was a sore point with him that Williams, after finding Falk in the locker room the previous season hovering around Smith, made it plain that he didn't want any agents back there. No exemptions, not even for Elmore, a familiar and popular campus figure. Elmore smirked that he was sure John Thompson similarly restricted Falk, his own agent, at Georgetown games.

The night growing late, Elmore climbed the steps from the court to street level and walked out into the cold February night. He lit a cigarette and began walking toward his car.

"Duncan," he said admiringly, "is the real deal."

At this moment, his deal with Smith as fuzzy as the smoke rings he blew into the frosty, late-night air, Elmore was trying to concentrate harder on forging ahead than looking back.

Tim Duncan's junior season came to an unceremonious conclusion one wintry Saturday in Minneapolis against a buzz saw known as the Kentucky Wildcats. Back in Lexington, Jodi DiRaimo sat at the bar of his restaurant, sipping a beer, looking up at the screen as his close friend Rick Pitino, cheeks rosy red, jumped around and barked out commands like a drill sergeant on speed.

The downtown mall in which the restaurant, Bravo's of Lexington, was located was a virtual ghost town, an almost unfathomable weekend American development. The only noise apart from the television screen, DiRaimo, three visitors, and a couple of bored waitresses were occasional muffled whoops of joy from other shopkeepers watching the game.

When the local CBS affiliate broke for a commercial, the spots were mostly from car dealerships featuring Pitino (who else?) and updates for the evening news with anchors sporting huge blue GO WILDCATS buttons. DiRaimo, with a grizzled face that bespoke many a New England winter, shook his head in disbelief. "Sometimes you have to wonder about these fucking people," he said.

After a half dozen years in Lexington, he still couldn't believe the UK basketball phenomenon. Pitino—whom he'd met in Providence when the now forty-four-year-old steered a nowhere Big East program to the 1987 Final Four and became a national star—invited him to Kentucky to invest in and operate an establishment that would provide edible Italian food to Denny's-endowed Lexington.

Now, after Pitino had restored prominence to the scandal-racked UK program, DiRaimo feared that the city, much more interested in tasting the title than a good pasta sauce, would drive the sensitive Pitino out of town if the favored Cats didn't win it all. When the postgame interviews turned into a wake for the ACC school, DiRaimo said, "There's still very good teams left." And the one DiRaimo feared most, John Calipari's Massachusetts team, was about to come on and pound the hell out of John Thompson's rugged Georgetown Hoyas.

UMass was one of two teams to have beaten Kentucky, albeit much earlier in the season. But their Final Four rematch at the New Jersey Meadowlands was not only perfectly scripted but one that would help produce extraordinary fallout later in the spring: it was No. 1 versus No. 2. It was Pitino versus Calipari, a Pitino clone and protégé. From a short distance, you almost couldn't tell the difference, as both were dark haired, boyishly handsome, smartly dressed, unfailingly buoyant.

Pitino, in fact, had helped Calipari get what would become his breakthrough job at UMass, where Pitino once ran the point alongside a budding legend named Julius Erving. The story went that Pitino, by then raking it in, even chipped in a few bucks so the cash-starved UMass program could offer Calipari a decent contract.

That's the way it went in the coaching fraternity. That is how

Pitino had come through the ranks, with more than a little help from his friends. The fraternity was about being connected, and for much of the sixties, all of the seventies, and on into the eighties, the most powerful pledge master was a man named Howard Garfinkel, better known in the business simply as Garf.

The summer of 1990 marked the twenty-fifth anniversary of the highly respected Five-Star Basketball Camp, once a rustic little camp in the Poconos, now seven different sessions at three separate sites. That summer, on sun-baked asphalt courts at Robert Morris College near Pittsburgh, 350 teenaged boys of varying size and ability had paid $330 each for the privilege of being drilled by some of the best basketball minds in the country.

"Five-Star," Garf proclaimed time and time again, "is where the teaching never stops." And over the years, Michael Jordan, Moses Malone, Isiah Thomas, Patrick Ewing, Dominique Wilkins, Alonzo Mourning, and Grant Hill were among the neophyte future milionaires to breathe in Five-Star's fresh-air fundamentals.

Garfinkel played the role of headmaster as scripted by Damon Runyon. Pacing five steps one way, five steps back, reaching back to the glory days of his native New York youth, between drags of a smoke, there were bons mots about his latest backcourt find. Pithy points that made Garf and later his HSBI scouting report a must-read on high school talent.

But as any king attests, his power flowed from his seemingly limitless connections, the direct lines into athletic directors' offices around the country. The immediate access to coaches who knew coaches who knew more coaches. And like a great point guard, he created opportunity for others. Habitually, he promised and produced what ambitious coaches wanted most: a job.

Over the years, hundreds of Five-Star campers became counselors and, finally, coaches. The pro list of coaches who traced their roots to Five-Star included Chuck Daly and Hubie Brown. And the kids who assisted them as counselors knew whom to hang with. Brown's influence spawned a whole generation of younger coaches, including Mike Fratello, Brian Hill, Ron Rothstein, Richie Adubato, and finally, Pitino. Calipari, in turn, was a Pitino guy. Bobby Cremins, Pete Gillen, came out of Five-Star. Tim Duncan's coach at Wake Forest, Dave Odom. On and on.

"My family," said Garf, who never married. And by the

summer of 1990, Garf's "family" had sent, by his count, at least 134 men into the college and pro coaching ranks.

"It's in the Guinness book," he barked at the time. "And if it's not, it should be."

Six months earlier, in January 1990, a New Jersey State Police criminal investigator noticed Howard Garfinkel's name, address, and phone number in two other, less-flattering books. They showed up twice in telephone books belonging to a major East Coast bookmaker by the name of Gary Latawiec; twice more in phone books of John Laffman, a runner who made his living hustling bets and collecting debts for New York bookies.

In March 1992, Latawiec, fifty, was convicted in Ocean County (N.J.) Superior Court of five counts of gambling and income tax–related charges, the most serious being Count No. 1—"a leader of organized crime." Latawiec was sentenced to fourteen years in prison, before skipping off to Costa Rica. (He was eventually arrested and extradited to the United States.)

"A very significant bookmaker in New York and New Jersey," recalled John J. Mercun, the Ocean County assistant prosecutor who helped put Latawiec away. "During the period we investigated, he made two million dollars, from the records we were able to get."

Laffman was also arrested by Mercun's office, in January 1989, along with three other men. He was charged with promoting gambling and possession of gambling records. That indictment was dismissed four years later after Laffman was found dead at a friend's house, at the ripe old age of thirty-three.

During a joint investigation by the New Jersey State Police and the Manhattan District Attorney's Office, a call from one of Latawiec's many "wire" rooms was traced to Garfinkel's Manhattan apartment. According to a New Jersey state police investigator, several others were traced from the Bronx apartment of another gambling figure, from whom cops seized $325,000 in cash and bonds and who was taking upward of two thousand calls a day on six phone lines, to a Central Park South apartment owned by Garfinkel's mother.

"We figured it [the Central Park South apartment] was a layoff joint," said a cop involved in the case. "So we hit it."

That they did, on October 21, 1992, when a public morals

squad, assisted by the N.J. State Police, executed a search warrant at 210 Central Park South, Apt. 12D. According to the report, present in the apartment were Merrill A. Garfinkel, Howard M. Garfinkel, and [their mother] Eva Garfinkel.

Quoting from the report: "At the time of the Search Warrant, the investigation discovered that Merrill Garfinkel was providing a betting line—however, same could not be implicated in any further gambling conspiracy."

Despite their suspicions, the cops never arrested either brother, since making a betting line is not illegal. But with Howard's name popping up in gamblers' phone books, the consistent calls from their Bronx wire room, and the raid, one New Jersey intelligence officer decided it was time to notify the NCAA.

"With all the college coaches this guy knows and all the kids, you've got a potential problem," said the officer, reflecting on the Garfinkel connection.

He was asked how the NCAA responded to his report.

"They didn't want to hear it," he said. "They didn't give a fuck."

For his part, Garfinkel said he had "never heard" of either Latawiec or Laffman. "I don't know any bookmakers," he said. "I don't deal with bookmakers."

At first, Garfinkel said he didn't "know anything" about a search warrant executed at his mother's house, but when specific details were given, he said, "I remember that. That was a mistake of some kind. What my brother does, I don't do. I'm not involved with what my brother did or does. It was very minor what he did.

"I'm not involved in anything. I just work on my camp, play horses once in a while. As far as betting, bookmakers, I don't know anything about that. I try to help the game, not hurt the game. I don't gamble."

Asked if he had ever called a college coach on game day, Garfinkel said, "They all call me. I don't call college coaches to ask about a game. They call me. We talk about scouting reports, strategy."

Had he ever placed a bet on a college basketball game? "In my life? I can't say that. But not in the last ten years. I don't call college coaches. They call me. No one can tell you I called and asked about a game—it never happens."

Not unlike the NBA, the NCAA may not have been so quick to

embrace law enforcement information that might lead to embarrassing situations and costly potential scandal, but it certainly was not averse to discussing means of prevention. Thus the first order of business when the Final Four hit metropolitan New York in 1996 was a "Gambling and College Sports" panel discussion on March 28 at the Marriott Marquis just up the block from the All-Star Cafe at Times Square.

Moderating was Gene Policinski, then the sports editor for *USA Today*. Others on the panel included Bob Frederick, chairman of the Men's Basketball Committee for Division I, NBA Security Chief Horace Balmer, and C. M. Newton, athletic director at the University of Kentucky. The discussion opened with Frederick tweaking Policinski for printing betting lines and other gambling information in his newspaper and on-line service. Balmer, for his part, lauded his league's Rookie Transition Program and suggested education was lacking at the high school and college levels.

But the most refreshing candor came from a man with the least to gain, or lose. Arnie Wexler, a onetime gambling addict who didn't even mind explaining how gambling interfered with his marital rate of sexual intercourse, stood up, looked his fellow panelists in the eye, and said, "The gambling is going on. The next general thing that's going to happen is a major point-shaving scandal. It's right around the corner, guys. And when it happens, you're going to see college administrators say, 'How could this have been in our school?'"

Wexler, more than most, knew the score. For years, this Peter Boyle look-alike ran the New Jersey Council on Compulsive Gambling, taking on the powerful Atlantic City casinos with a tiny budget from a cramped basement apartment in Trenton. Wexler said he generally received far more interest in the subject from newspaper reporters than from college sports administrators.

"I've had four articles on compulsive gambling that the NCAA was nice enough to let me write the last five years," he said. "And I've never, ever gotten a call from a college administrator, coach, or director who said, 'Hey, this looks interesting. Come to our school and speak.' I've gotten calls from athletic directors who tell me, 'Nobody in my school gambles on sporting events, they only play cards.'"

Wexler paused, obviously for effect.

"You talk about having your head in the sand."

(Less than one year later, this very issue exploded when Boston College suspended thirteen football players for betting on a variety of sports, including football and the World Series. Two of the players were accused of betting against their own team.)

Even as the NCAA planned its well-intentioned panel, the insidious nature of gambling was lurking in the shadows of one of the country's most prestigious basketball programs. The case of Georgetown coach John Thompson was a prime example of how easily—how quietly—personal and business relationships could create the appearance of impropriety. Even if intentions were absolutely pure.

The Thompson story broke two days before Georgetown arrived in the East Regionals for its fatal showdown with UMass. Within hours, *The Washington Post* and ABC News reported Thompson had applied for a Nevada gaming license in July 1995, the first regulatory step in becoming a 10 percent partner in a Las Vegas company holding operating rights through 2002 to the slot machines at McCarran International Airport. Thompson's proposed business partner was a longtime friend—Las Vegas casino operator Michael Gaughan (pronounced "Gone").

NCAA leaders were dumbstruck. The timing could not have been worse. Here, during its showcase tournament, was arguably the most powerful coach in the game taking a machete to its incontrovertible antigambling stance. In Overland Park, Kansas, home of the NCAA, one top official groaned repeatedly as the Thompson story was laid out by an ABC reporter over the phone.

- According to figures compiled by the Clark County Department of Aviation, partners with Gaughan in the airport slots, the estimated one thousand machines generated $23,594,775 in revenue during fiscal 1994–95. That money was split between the county (86.5 percent) and Gaughan's Airport Slot Concession (13.5). Gaughan's company received nearly $3.2 million, from which it was responsible for buying and servicing the machines. Given these figures, Thompson's proposed 10 percent cut, excluding expenses, was worth $318,000.

- In addition to the airport slots, Gaughan owned both the Barbary Coast and Gold Coast casinos and several other resorts. Both the Barbary Coast and Gold Coast feature popular sports books where millions of dollars are legally bet on pro and college sports, including Georgetown games, every year.
- Brendan Gaughan, Michael's son, happened to be a junior walk-on on Thompson's Georgetown team.

The younger Gaughan stood out for several reasons. He was 5-9. He was pudgy. He was white. Add it all up and you had a hustling player far more suited to intramurals than a Final Four contender, and one that had for years been overwhelmingly black. There was no conceivable way to explain his presence other than as a token of one man's friendship to another.

Obviously, at face value, there was no impropriety in that. But all the factors, as one NCAA official said, put Thompson "on dangerous ground." Added the official, "This sends absolutely the wrong kind of message. It's not about the applicant's personal integrity, but you have to draw a line somewhere. Gambling is a huge problem and this creates a huge question mark."

The most obvious, the possibility of proprietary information—the status of star guard Allen Iverson, to cite an obvious example—passing from Thompson to Michael Gaughan. Or from son to father. And eventually on to oddsmakers.

"In gambling, relationships are everything," said the NCAA official, acknowledging what the NCAA didn't want to know about in the Garfinkel case.

Still, the official conceded there was no evidence that Thompson had been responsible for any leaks of information, so the NCAA was "wrestling" with what, if any, action it could take. "The question is, can we legally prevent this kind of thing?" he asked.

To his credit, NCAA Executive Director Ced Dempsey did not react meekly. "I do have strong concerns about the image statement this makes about the sport and about him as a coach," he said. "Your team competes and doesn't play to the caliber which it's capable of, there's going to be questions whether or not the game had been fixed."

Thompson, not surprisingly, argued in terms of African-

American business opportunity, not to mention equal opportunity. "Ced Dempsey is a little late," he told the *Post*. "We didn't tell Adolph Rupp [Kentucky legend and champion of the preblack college basketball era] that . . . I think this is going to be a very interesting journey."

It sounded like an accepted challenge until Thompson said any final decision would rest with Georgetown president Rev. Leo O'Donovan. The following day, O'Donovan issued a statement that said in part: "Our position is that it is inappropriate for an active Georgetown coach to have investments in the gaming industry." The next day, Thompson backed down. After several talks with O'Donovan, who'd hired him twenty-four years earlier, the coach said he'd drop his license bid (he hadn't by the middle of the 1996–97 school year). But not before hoisting up a few shots of his own.

"My only problem is with people who get religious or sanctimonious about it and don't get that way about other things," Thompson said. "I didn't introduce gaming into this sport and I had no intention to. Maybe we need to redefine what's real or not real. Anybody who hasn't played a slot machine, get up and leave this room. Anyone who works for a newspaper that doesn't carry point spreads, get up and leave. All of us are struggling to define what this is."

Not really. For all his rationalization, Thompson seemed to be missing—or ignoring—the point privately expressed by his peers. To wit, is he kidding? Playing the slots was one thing, as Thompson routinely has during his trips to a second home in Vegas. A point spread in a newspaper was yet another. But the slots deal, the $300,000, the son on his team, and the sports books were all a little bit much. As was, it seemed, another, unpublicized relationship Thompson was said to be involved in.

The day the story broke, a Georgetown University spokeswoman was asked about another close friend of the coach's. Simply, why was a man named Steve Delmont, a close friend of Thompson's and the Director of Foods at the Barbary Coast, listed on the Hoyas' travel roster during the Big East Tournament in New York? According to the hotel's accounting department, Delmont's name was on the official travel and rooming list supplied by academic adviser Mary Fenlon, and he received a reduced rate at the Guest Quarters Suites.

The spokeswoman declared Delmont's presence was no big deal. A variety of names go on the travel list, she said.

Through Georgetown's lawyers Thompson claimed to have no knowledge of Delmont's appearance on the team travel roster or the details of his travel arrangements.

But in a world where every scrap of solid information is grist for crafting a line or pushing a bet, Thompson's dealings with the Gaughans and Delmont cast him, his team, his school, and his sport in a most unflattering light. To think that nothing Thompson might say in the company of Gaughan or Delmont might find its way into a betting line or bet was unrealistic. No one claims that Thompson had intentionally or unintentionally passed information regarding the team to anyone. But, at best he was playing with fire, thumbing his nose at an NCAA ethical conduct rule that stated: "Staff members of the athletics department of a member institution and student-athletes shall not knowingly provide information to individuals involved in organized gambling activities."

The week before the NCAA tournament, Len Elmore drove to a Hyatt Hotel in Baltimore on a Friday morning to address an NCAA special committee on agents and amateurs studying the fast-changing landscape of college basketball and football. Elmore wasn't going to deny that his own industry was culpable for many of the problems, but to blame everything on agents had become too much a cliché, an exercise, according to Elmore, in "intellectual dishonesty."

He had a few other targets to point fingers at, starting with the source of his worst heartburn this particular season.

"The families who see their sons as breadwinners," Elmore said.

He would also cite the shoe companies who cultivate relationships with the players when they are still children. And last, but certainly not least, the college basketball Division I coaches.

"In too many cases," Elmore told the NCAA people, "the dynamic includes the coaches who will keep some agents away from their locker rooms but look the other way while the shoe companies and an agent they favor walk right in."

Somehow, the name of John Thompson happened to come to mind again.

Thompson for years had been thundering about the basketball world's needing to offer more opportunities to African-Americans. Yet whenever his program seemed to burp up another first-round draft pick, he inevitably landed right in the lap of Thompson's own Nike hot line, David Falk. "You don't want a chicken to guard the henhouse," Thompson liked to say in defense of the Falk connection.

Elmore, wondering if it was much better to hire a fox, acknowledged that Falk had enormous power and appeal. First and foremost, he was Michael Jordan's guy, and the average young player might choose him just to be on any team that included His Airness.

But he was not without critics, among them James Worthy, who left him, and Adrian Dantley, who sued him. And what Elmore asked was why, as a college educator, Thompson didn't seem to encourage his players to make their own choices. When Jerry Stackhouse left North Carolina, for instance, Dean Smith arranged for agencies to make ninety-minute presentations to Stackhouse and his family. Why wouldn't Thompson "teach" choice, especially since Thompson had been criticized for sending so many of his players Falk's way?

Not that Elmore believed for a second that the process would be different for Allen Iverson, but he said he diligently mailed his material to the Georgetown athletic department, in the event Iverson left after his spectacular sophomore year. "Just to prove a point, see what happened," he said.

Nothing happened.

"Never heard from them," he said.

One of Elmore's assistants said he had heard that Thompson had discouraged Iverson from playing in games that Elmore organized around the D.C. area. For weeks following Georgetown's elimination from the tournament, Thompson insisted that Iverson had not reached a decision. He went so far as to say Iverson would not leave school unless he, Thompson, told him to. Yet on the day Iverson did declare himself eligible for the NBA draft, there, smiling broadly on the dais, was David Falk. Amazing how quickly an agent had been selected once Iverson decided to turn pro.

This press conference was strikingly similar to the one that kicked off a veritable storming of the NBA draft gates. Two days after the Final Four, to the surprise of no one, Stephon Marbury stood in front of assorted family, friends, and sycophants at Junior's Restaurant in downtown Brooklyn and announced, with tears in his eyes, "It's official. I'm going to the NBA."

Flanking Marbury on the dais were his parents and four brothers, along with the man who was already his former coach, Bobby Cremins. In front of them were a half dozen Junior's famous cheesecakes, all with No. 3 candles in the middle. After much whooping by the crowd, Marbury had one more announcement. Actually, it was an introduction. Would his agent, Eric Fleisher, please step forward?

No surprise here. It was another coup, courtesy of Fleisher's Kevin Garnett/Billy Taylor connection. While still legally embroiled with his brother, the younger Fleisher was undoubtedly becoming quite the Money Player out on his own. Yet back in Stamford, Connecticut, Marc was lamenting, much in the manner of Elmore, how revolting the entire recruiting process had become. He didn't mention his brother by name. He didn't have to. "It's awful what's going on out there," Marc said.

The playground was more of a pickup scene than ever, and nowhere was this better illustrated than in the case of Marcus Camby. Long after Kentucky had held off Camby, Calipari, and UMass in the semifinals, then wasted Syracuse in the final to put Pitino on top of the heap, Camby was on his way to a predraft camp in Chicago in June when the *Hartford Courant* broke a blockbuster: Camby and friends had for months allegedly been accepting cash and gifts from a Hartford trial attorney and another man who wished to become Camby's agent.

One of Camby's friends, Tamia Murray, said Wesley S. Spears had given Murray as much as $300 a week since January. Camby reportedly admitted he'd accepted gifts from his friends, including a diamond necklace he'd even flaunted in a CBS interview during the tournament. "At first, when I looked at it, I thought it was homemade," said the school's athletic director, Bob Marcum, in arguably the quote of the year. However, Murray insisted that Camby had not been told that the gifts were paid for with money from Spears.

Out in Chicago, agents waited in the lobby for prospective clients to emerge from the elevator, trying to look busy with a newspaper or a drink at the bar. "Look around this hotel, the agents shaking hands with everybody," Rory Sparrow, the former NBA guard and now on the NBA team responsible for helping players make the adjustment from college, told the *New York Times.* "They've got runners; their friends, people who have hung on to this guy since he was a freshman. . . . It's just an ugly cycle."

The agent Camby did choose, IMG's James Sears Bryant (of Richard Dumas note), wound up doing damage control. Meanwhile, the underclassmen were leaving college as if they were taking the last chopper out of Saigon. Included were two high schoolers, Philadelphia sensation Kobe Bryant and South Carolinian Jermaine O'Neal. The predictable moral debate ensued, with David Stern, sounding like Elmore when it suited his purpose, wondering why few lamented the lack of college and high school education pursued by white tennis players. Sure enough, days later, Justin Gimelstob, ranked No. 1 in NCAA singles, blew out of UCLA after three semesters to join the ATP tour—but not before signing a lucrative Nike deal.

Not every star basketball underclassman left, though. As Elmore's luck would have it, Tim Duncan turned out to be a rare exception. After reaching his decision, Duncan met up with his *New York Times* cyber buddy one night and punched in the words of an era past its time: "The money will come," Duncan said.

Elmore, meanwhile, was left to wonder where all the clients had gone. Not only would there be no back-to-back No. 1's, but he would not land a single player from the first round. Falk, meanwhile, had a field day, signing Kentucky's Antoine Walker and Walter McCarty, Villanova's Kerry Kittles, plus some of the wave of international talent. He'd make a pittance off them compared with his take on his crop of summer free agents: Jordan, Mutombo, Alonzo Mourning, Juwan Howard. Counting rookies, Falk now had thirty-six NBA players in his stable, fifteen of whom were already earning more than $2 million.

Falk, most assuredly, could afford to tell a rookie that he would waive the fee for negotiating his first contract, which, of course, would require little or no actual negotiating. Len Elmore could not afford to lose his 3 percent. Not if he intended to make the quick plane trips, help with the personal struggles, the sudden parental needs, do more than examine the fine print. "The truth is, despite what he's telling them, it's not free," Elmore said. "They'll wind up paying one percent of the gross to his financial manager." And then, of course, there would be the bigger marketing fees. (A spokesman for Falk declined to comment specifically on his clients' fees, but said the contract and financial fees are "not related," and that, in any event, the one percent figure was "too high.")

It was, no question, a disheartening comedown for Elmore, who, in Toronto, had delighted in announcing, "We are *here!*" But that was moments after Joe Smith became No. 1. Now Smith, to be sure, was Elmore's No. 1 heartache.

In early May, the other sneaker dropped, in the form of a letter from Smith that officially severed his ties with Precept Sports. Elmore was not shocked. How could he be? Weeks before, Letha Smith had not even invited him to a Planet Hollywood charity bash for Joe in San Francisco. She let it slip in a phone conversation, and Elmore, seeing his commitment to the bitter end, shelled out the airfare for the occasion. He felt like an outsider, another spectator at the $100-a-plate event.

He said that Joe called the office after the letter was sent. He wanted to know if the guys were angry with him. He mouthed respectful clichés—"Things didn't work out"—and said he'd put off signing the letter for weeks. Elmore realized that Joe was still only twenty. But there would come a point, sooner than later, where the responsibility would blur, where his family would be no excuse.

"He should have blue skies ahead regardless, but he's going to have to start taking responsibility," Elmore said. "Otherwise, even what should be a sure thing could get screwed up. Listen, when we'd first talked about marketing, I told them that it takes time to cultivate an image. They were impatient as hell. It was 'Stackhouse got this.'" He paused, out of frustration. "We were talking to an electronics company last year, and all the family cared about was if they'd name a game after Joe."

As much as he tried to rationalize the story, he had to fight his bitterness over the deal. He was only human. "I guess," he said finally, "they just never got over the Nike thing."

Deep down, he knew it would have been one thing or another. He was still left with his reality. He had lost No. 1. He was wounded. The sharks were out there circling.

"I wasn't willing to do what some do and wasn't able to do what some did," he said. He meant pay money to recruits or promise them everything in return for nothing. "Yeah," he conceded, "it wasn't my year."

As spring drifted into summer, he legitimately wondered if this was his calling, what he was doing knee-deep in the mud of the sports-agent business in the first place. He drifted back to a comment his brother-in-law had made the year before, even as Precept appeared on course to succeed. "You're an attorney who wants to make a difference," his brother-in-law said. "Why do you want to do this shit?"

"I laughed it off at the time," Elmore said. "But certain things happen, and sometimes you begin to believe there are no coincidences."

Joe Smith should have been his ticket to establish himself in the business, a bridge to more big names, as Kevin Garnett had been for Eric Fleisher. Instead, the bridge had collapsed and Elmore's company and its message that the process didn't have to be a cesspool had dropped to the bottom of the ocean floor. He still had Walt Williams, Randolph Childress, Greg Minor, Terry Dehere, but his best remaining player, Cassell, was already sending out ominous vibes of going someplace else. The football experiment with Kellen Winslow had been a flop, and he was long gone. There were financial inconsistencies in the company that Elmore was looking into, and a cash flow problem.

Elmore wasn't the first agent to take a few on the chin, but he couldn't escape the feeling that the whole sport had somehow ganged up on him. There was a good argument to make that, in some ways, it had. Sad evidence that perhaps the NBA wasn't so ready to welcome one of its most highly credentialed graduates as an entrenched Money Player.

By midsummer, Elmore was home in Maryland, plotting a new career course, starting with selling off the company assets. No one answered the phone anymore at Precept's Columbia office. The machine at Elmore's Manhattan apartment, formerly Precept's "New York office," contained only his taped personal message.

The notion of hanging his own shingle, or catching on with a law firm in the D.C. area, was beginning to sound more attractive to him. He could bring his sports practice, the players who wanted to stay with him. He could keep his eye out for that rare player who didn't come with the baggage that Joe Smith had. Maybe that player would be Tim Duncan. Maybe not.

"I'd like to be the guy in the firm who does the pro bono work, the stuff most lawyers don't want to do," Elmore said. "I'd still like to work with players, but I don't think I'm cut out to be out there, desperately trying to get four guys a year."

Then he said, "I'm a firm believer in intuition."

A voice in the back of his head, be it his or his brother-in-law's, was asking, "Why do you want to do this shit?"

He didn't have the answer.

He knew only that the likes of Joe Smith's problems were no longer his, just when it turned out that Smith could use his wisdom more than ever.

17

The Long Season

THE CARS STREAMED OFF INTERSTATE 80 INTO THE OAKLAND COLISE-
um sports complex, Bay Area fans having come to offer a belated
hello to baseball's Athletics and a likely farewell to basketball's
Warriors. It was a warm Friday evening, the reddish sun looking
like a large, fiery ball dropping in the late-April sky. The perfect
symbolism for the setting of Joe Smith's rookie season.

And, as it would sadly turn out, his unblemished reputation as
the NBA antidote for Generation X.

Coming out of the parking lot, the fans holding baseball tickets
headed left, toward the ballpark, a renovation project in progress
that had sent the A's scurrying to open their home season in Las
Vegas. The hoop fans, 15,025 sellout-strong, proceeded right,
knowing the Warriors needed a final weekend "double" to make
the playoffs.

The mission, unlikely if not impossible, was simply enough
explained: beat the surging Portland Trail Blazers, then board the
bus, steam along Interstate 80 into Sacramento, and knock off the
Kings the following night. Then eighth place in the Western
Conference and an unenviable first-round, best-of-five playoff
engagement against the 64-win Seattle SuperSonics would go to
Golden State.

This is what usually passed for late-regular-season NBA excitement, survival of the weakest, though only days had passed since the Bulls had gone into Milwaukee and imprinted their world-renowned logo on the mantel of the greatest regular-season team ever by winning No. 70. But by now, fourteen of the sixteen playoff teams were determined. Only the Warriors and Charlotte in the East had nominal chances to rewrite their brackets, salvage pride plus a game or two of critical playoff gate receipts.

The Warriors would not have been in such dire straits if not for one lousy break back on March 10, when they held a 2-point lead in Sacramento with 3.2 seconds left. The Kings got the ball to their star, Mitch Richmond, way out on the right side, behind the three-point line, guarded by Latrell Sprewell. "Spre was right in his face," moaned Julie Marvel, the Warriors' public relations director. No matter. Richmond, a former Warrior in the so-called Run TMC days (Tim Hardaway/Mitch Richmond/Chris Mullin), fired up a prayer that was answered with the sound of a swish. "Everyone said then that the playoff race was going down to the end and that'll be the shot everyone remembers as the difference," Marvel said.

They were right, and this was exactly the kind of painful memory that deflated dedicated employees such as Marvel for weeks. Players, on the other hand, usually moved on about a half hour after the game. They had to. The next one was twenty-four to forty-eight hours away. The inner voice of the typical player told him there were always more games, more shots, more seasons. Being so young, so gifted, they tended not to be cognizant of limited opportunities, not to mention their own limitations.

"It would be good for the young guys on the team—me, Spre—if we get in," Smith said in the pregame locker room. It was revealing that he'd stopped after two names, for the Warriors were finishing up another sub-.500 season more a collection of disparate journeymen than of rising stars. Center Rony Seikaly, habitually injured, was out of sight and out of mind. Seven-foot Kevin Willis, acquired from Miami in the Tim Hardaway deal, was in one of his trademark funks. B. J. Armstrong, holder of three championship rings, was dealing with the shock of being with a perennial loser. Jerome Kersey, once a Rick Adelman mainstay up in Portland, was just trying to figure out how to stay in the league. Even Smith wasn't exactly going out with a rush, seeming to have lost the momentum he generated around All-Star Weekend. Right after leaving San Antonio, in fact, Smith had welcomed the Bulls and Dennis Rodman into the Coliseum with a stunning 20-rebound outburst, which included 14 offensive boards. "No, that's not me," Smith said, breaking up, when asked if he'd considered coloring his hair after taking Rodman, of all people, to boarding school.

But the season dragged on, past the NCAA tournament, on into April, and so did Smith. He denied he was tired, but his slender frame had taken a beating, in the opinion of those who observed him every day. He'd had a solid rookie season, no question, stirring at times, especially for a comparatively thin twenty-year-old playing power forward. He had appeared in all 82 games, averaging 15 points and almost 9 rebounds. His coaches and teammates loved his work ethic. But there was much work ahead of Smith in the training room. And more than anything, like most young players, he needed time.

"I'm patient, I think things will be better next season, hopefully for me and the team," he said that night, flashing the smile that Willie Brown was so certain would earn millions. They hadn't come yet either and were nowhere in sight. The process of Smith's becoming one of the NBA's chosen seemed to be going much slower than Smith's family believed it would. He had been No. 1 in the draft, yet the mega-deals had not followed, not the way they had for Jerry Stackhouse. Not even close.

"As far as major endorsements, we're still working," Ernest Ruffin said late in the season. He said there had been some discussion with Coke for a major endorsement deal, but nothing of a national scope was imminent. Smith had finally made the family happy by landing a movie role, a cameo as Connie Hawkins in an HBO production on the life of a New York City playground legend, Earl Manigault, and Smith was the subject of a TNT piece on his returning to school at Norfolk State. But the best Ruffin could report was a deal he'd made with his former employer, AT&T, for Joe to be a celebrity chat host for the company's World Internet Service.

He said that the NBA's marketing guru Rick Welts had showed up at the AT&T press conference in New York and come away impressed. But before he left, Welts invited Ruffin over to the league office to discuss Smith's marketing and financial situation.

He confided that the word was out; there was disarray in the Smith camp, and it had, not surprisingly, reached the highest echelons of Olympic Tower.

Ruffin didn't deny that he was in precisely the situation Elmore had been in the previous summer, trying to forge a sensible, long-term strategy while navigating the Smith-family minefield. By this point, Celestine McFarland was as influential in MSB Ltd. as—if not more so than—Willie Brown. And Letha Smith was as proactive as ever. Ruffin was understandably reluctant to protest too loudly, but at one time during the season he wondered if he was even part of the process anymore. "You can't market by committee," he said. "If you have too many people in the way, too many saying, 'Do it this way, do it that way,' it gets very, very hard."

Finally, he put the onus squarely on the twenty-year-old. "I said, 'Joe, what do you want me to do?'"

"Oh, you're the man," Joe told him. But little, if anything, changed.

Ruffin made a familiar appeal and case: They all had to understand that Joe was not the kind of player and personality who became an overnight sensation. They had to stop the yearlong fixation on what was happening for Jerry Stackhouse and even Kevin Garnett. But they had heard all this before, from Elmore, from Leonard Armato. It all seemed to be falling on deaf ears.

In February, when the *Wall Street Journal* in a lengthy feature marveled over the success that the Advantage International had had marketing Stackhouse to Fila and Pepsi, among others, the Smiths, according to one person close to the family, "were beside themselves." They decided that Joe's problem was his not getting enough national attention. Especially back East, three time zones away, on Madison Avenue. Soon a public relations specialist named Sandra Varner was hired, except that she worked out of Oakland and was yet another addition to Smith's expanding payroll. According to Ruffin and Elmore, she had Hollywood connections and was instrumental in landing actor Danny Glover to lend star appeal to the April 9, $100-a-plate Planet Hollywood charity benefit.

The proceeds, it was announced, were going to the East Oakland Youth Development Center, a couple of other Bay Area charities, and as Willie Brown had mused all those months before, the Hunton YMCA in Norfolk. But others close to Smith and within the Warriors organization wondered about the high cost of raising this money—the plane fares for several members of Joe's family, the fees for Glover and an actor from the hit TV show *Martin*. If Smith wanted to donate money, why not call a press conference and present a check at the facilities themselves? Why not let the organizations spread the word of Smith's generosity and put him above potential charges of self-aggrandizement?

The sheer extravagance of the night was not the impression young Joe Smith needed to be making. That's what Elmore said he would have argued. Michael Jordan could get away with it. Jason Kidd. But it made the Smiths appear to be way ahead of themselves, playacting, trying to be something they were not.

Damon Stoudamire, the rookie who controlled the ball for a porous expansion team, seemed to be headed for Rookie of the Year, though Stackhouse was clearly the class glamour boy and Kevin Garnett the most intriguing player in terms of future growth. But by April, the rookie playing the best ball in the NBA was Portland center Arvidas Sabonis, and it wasn't even close.

Sabonis, a Lithuanian seven-footer with feet so chronically sore that he could barely jump, was once considered the European Bill Walton as he burst through the old Soviet Union system under Alexsandr Gomelsky, the Russian patriarch. He was the hub of the 1988 gold medal–winning Olympic team in Seoul and spent many lucrative years dominating European leagues.

At thirty-one, past his prime, he had finally taken the Trail Blazers up on their long-standing offer to sample the life of the American pro. They drafted him with the last pick on the first round in 1986. Now, a decade later, Sabonis was not only a rookie but the best player in the league from that most notoriously tragic first round.

He was a bulky man with a feathery shooting touch from as far out as three-point range, and he was the best-passing center in the league from the minute he walked through the door into Portland's training camp. Due to his fragile feet, he couldn't play much more than half a game. But when Sabonis lifted his imposing presence off the bench, replacing an offensively comical shot-blocker out of Yale named Chris Dudley, the Blazers seemed immediately blessed by the basketball gods. Everything he did with the ball seemed to have the purpose most of his teammates sorely lacked.

Not that Portland was without complementary talent. Its point guard, New York City product Rod Strickland, was at once one of the league's most thrilling and troubling players. From the time the quiet but moody Strickland was drafted by the Knicks out of DePaul in 1988, almost no one could contain his dribble penetration and variety of body-contorting shots. At the same time, no coach could harmoniously coexist with him. Rick Pitino had tried. Stu Jackson. Larry Brown. P. J. Carlesimo, in his second year with Portland after signing a five-year, $7.5-million deal to leave Seton Hall, had the worst relationship with Strickland of all, almost from the day Carlesimo showed up to coach.

One day during the winter, with Strickland on a grumbling mission to get himself traded, Carlesimo insisted he had no idea what he'd done to alienate his best player. "Do I yell? Sure I yell," he said. "How many coaches don't? But what made it such a personal thing, I honestly can't say. That's not to say he doesn't have valid reasons in his mind, but I can't say I have a clear sense of what those reasons are."

Eventually, Strickland's unhappiness reached the showdown stage. After the All-Star break passed without completion of a rumored deal, Strickland went AWOL on February 22 and was immediately suspended. He missed six games, losing $27,805 for each, or $166,830 of his $2.28 million salary. The Blazers lost nine of eleven after the break, dropping to ninth place, out of playoff standing, in the West. Tensions rose. A locker-room fight broke out between another unhappy star, Clifford Robinson, and reserve guard James Robinson. Normally dedicated Portland fans booed in owner Paul Allen's spanking-new Rose Garden, and all of this was enough to make Buck Williams start to think that he'd finally had enough. He'd been here before, a very long time ago.

The effect of the Strickland mess on the team was, with obviously different circumstances, the Micheal Ray Richardson syndrome all over again. Williams, at thirty-six, was too old for this, too easily able to convince himself that it wasn't worth his effort to get up on the glass, the staple of his game. The Blazers had an option on him for the following season, but he knew it was time for them to get younger, to start over. They had acquired him from New Jersey with the hope that he was the final, stabilizing piece to a championship puzzle, and he had almost been. Portland had lost two championship series, in 1990 to Detroit and in 1992 to Chicago. But the mainstays of those teams—Clyde Drexler, Jerome Kersey, Terry Porter—had moved on. Soon it would be Williams' turn.

There had, ironically, been talk around the Warriors that Adelman, a great fan when Williams played for him in Portland, wanted him to come south and teach Joe Smith the tricks of the power-forward trade. "Joe doesn't play like a rookie," Williams said before the game in Oakland. "He just seems to bring more intensity to basketball than most of these other kids. Offensively, he's more versatile and aggressive than I ever was, but in a lot of other ways—especially the way he approaches the game—he reminds me of when I broke in."

By April, however, Williams had already abandoned his plans to quit. His zest for rebounding, for the game, had returned. The Blazers had done a stunning 180-degree turn after Strickland was lured back with verbal assurances that he would be traded after the season. About the same time, Carlesimo inserted Sabonis into the starting lineup and increased his minutes from twenty-four a game to about twenty-eight to thirty. The results were dramatic, 19 wins in 22 games, putting the team back on firm playoff ground.

Williams wasn't kidding himself, though. The Blazers' first-round opponent was going to be Utah, with the Jazz holding the home-court advantage. Williams couldn't remember the last time Portland had won in Karl Malone and John Stockton's house. Nor was he deluding himself that the inner hostilities that had almost destroyed the Blazers in February were not bubbling beneath the surface. Rod Strickland, first and foremost Portland's lifeline beyond mediocrity, managed to look calm and cool. Williams knew better. He could spot a team going nowhere a mile away. He was on one, and so was Joe Smith.

The notion of tutoring Smith sounded appealing, he said, but not likely. If he was going to base next season's decision on that, he might as well retire and get into coaching. Deep inside him, he still burned to win, the old-fashioned way. The Warriors weren't the kind of team he'd be looking at if, as he expected, the Blazers cut him loose when the season was over.

"Look what playing with Michael has done for Rodman," Williams said before going out to do battle with Smith. Maybe it was time, he said, to hitch himself to the kind of star who could help get him his ring before it was too late.

By four o'clock on the afternoon of April 16, the downstairs bar at Michael Jordan's restaurant at 500 North LaSalle Street in downtown Chicago was packed to capacity, with a line of about five hundred stretched all the way down North LaSalle to Illinois Street. Inside, the bar was decorated in a seventies motif, the jukebox played songs from that decade, employees wore jean jackets and leisure suits, and seventy-cent drink specials flowed from the taps.

Up in Milwaukee, the Bulls were going for win No. 70, and Chicago was ready to party.

Milwaukee being not more than an hour's ride from the Bulls' practice facility in the northwest suburb of Deerfield, the team bused its way toward history, and what a ride it was.

"We were trying to keep it normal," Phil Jackson said of the ride up the Tri-State Tollway. "But when kids are hanging from the overpasses with signs, and people at the tollbooths are taking your picture and not charging you tolls along 294, it makes it a little different."

The countdown to 70 had proceeded smoothly, almost like a perfectly timed clock ticking its way to midnight. Even Rodman's six-game suspension for head-butting referee Ted Bernhardt in New Jersey on March 16 had not slowed the Jordan Express. Rodman seemed, in fact, somewhat remorseful, perhaps realizing what a lucrative deal he'd jeopardized with that foolish and self-destructive outburst. And Jordan, unlike the reticent David Robinson in San Antonio, had pulled no public punches when discussing Rodman's foibles. He made it clear that he was pissed.

Naturally, the debates of how the Bulls stacked up against the NBA's greatest teams were beginning to rage. The Bulls didn't seem to want any part of that. Not yet.

When Jackson was asked if he had a sense of making history, he responded with his trademark bemused grin and head-tilted look, as he sat cross-legged on the bench before the game.

"Somebody does out there," he said. "But not me particularly."

Jackson and Jordan knew that only the championship would

eventually matter. The ring. Seventy wins would be a milestone to think about down the road, long after the fury of the playoffs had subsided, win or lose. This had become a distraction to the physical and mental playoff preparation, a night to get over with.

That was how the Bulls would play the game against the lowly Bucks, too. The Bulls had lost 9 games all season. The Bucks had dropped 54. Yet the Bulls were sluggish most of the night. They scored 12 points in the second quarter. They shot under 40 percent for the game. But after trailing most of the way, they were hanging on to an 82–80 lead with just less than five minutes left. Then neither team scored until Luc Longley dropped in two free throws with twenty-one seconds left. Fittingly, a team with the greatest offensive star in the history of the sport clinched the game and the record on a defensive play—by Jordan, who blocked Johnny Newman's three-pointer, and that was the Bucks' dying gasp.

Soon, the Bulls' bench players were standing, counting down the final seconds. Three . . . two . . . one. Over. Michael Jordan's team had won more regular-season games than anyone else's. More than Magic's. More than Bird's. More than Kareem's. More than Russell's.

Jordan, knowing what the consequences would be of failing to win the championship after such a feat, recognizing whose psyche would most benefit down the playoff road from an impromptu massage, decided to do a little player-coaching. He walked right up to embrace Rodman before he acknowledged anyone else, even Scottie Pippen or Jackson, the only Bulls left from the three-peat teams.

"Great season," he whispered in Rodman's ear.

"It's not over," Rodman shouted back. "But it has been a great season."

Jackson—his job, as always, made easier by Jordan—sat on the bench, legs still crossed, and let the players celebrate. He rose slowly, waved to his wife, June, in the stands. He walked slowly to the locker room. Once there, Jackson lit a cigar, Red Auerbach style, and contentedly puffed away.

And back in Chicago, minutes after the horn, retailers all over Chicago were busily preparing for the next day's rush. The "70" caps, T-shirts, jackets, and sweatshirts were going right up on the shelves. Over at the United Center, Bismarck Enterprises' Fandemonium, the team merchandise store, was setting up more displays for the exclusive "seventysomething" caps and shirts.

There were, after all, three more regular-season games to play.

The third quarter was over; the Warriors had given up the lead to Portland, and Joe Smith seemed to be running out of gas. Buck Williams' punishing body blows, administered whenever Smith would step into the lane, were taking their toll. The man who as union president had helped prevent Smith from making a huge rookie score was now shoving him right out of a playoff share.

While the teams huddled up for the start of the last twelve minutes, longtime Warriors player, coach, and now front-office handyman Al Attles stepped to the middle of the court and grabbed a microphone. Attles had come to extend a thank-you to the fans for their support, to ask that they follow the team to San Jose next season while the Coliseum underwent a face-lift. Or, more to the point, had luxury suites added so the team could better compete in the NBA's era of mind-numbing revenue.

"I need you to give this team and the coach a big hand because they need you these last twelve minutes to make it back to the playoffs," Attles said. The fans, on cue, stood and cheered.

Attles would have been laughed out of Madison Square Garden, or the Great Western Forum, with this hokey act. But this was the Bay Area, and the Warriors, a longtime consistent also-ran, were treated more as a novelty, the creation of their onetime idiosyncratic owner, Franklin Mieuli, a small, stout man whose trademark was a deerstalker cap he always wore.

Mieuli was exactly the kind of owner the league had outgrown, an irascible, passionate sportsman the average fan could identify with. As the balance of power shifted to the players more and more, Mieuli sensed he was being forced out. He would battle with David Stern and the other owners at board meetings over the rising costs of doing business, the increasing risk. He would storm out of meetings, come back, and storm out again. By the late 1980s, he couldn't afford to come back and let the Warriors go.

He still attended most home games, and this one was no different; Mieuli was seated across from the scorer's table, center court. Under the basket closest to the Portland bench, meanwhile, sat Paul Allen, Bill Gates's former Microsoft partner whose fortune was estimated by *Forbes* magazine in 1996 to be $7.5

billion. Allen was so rich that he often said there were times he didn't know what to do with his money, but he was dressed no fancier than Mieuli, in droopy flannel pants and a plain denim jacket. A bottle of Coke dangled from his right hand as he yelled encouragement to his team as the game entered the final minutes.

Even with Strickland back in Portland nursing a hamstring injury for the playoffs and with Sabonis sitting out the fourth quarter, it looked inevitable that the Blazers would win. The Warriors, on the way to a 38-point second half, just couldn't score. Sprewell was their only player who could create off the dribble. Armstrong had no Jordan to get him the ball for the spot-up jumper. Donyell Marshall came into the game and could barely get a shot off. Smith had the moves, but his legs looked tired and his jump shot was flat.

Buck Williams had playfully loped through most of his thirty-two minutes, but now, as the Blazers protected a small lead in the closing minutes, he was charged. He blocked a baseline drive by Marshall. He knocked Smith down when the rookie tried a jump hook in the lane. He went into the stands after a loose ball to make a back-pass and save a possession.

That particular play, a Williams specialty that would not show up in the box score, led to a free throw by Aaron McKie that gave Portland an 86–79 lead. The Warriors got no closer and the fans began to file out. Smith, shooting 6 for 17 in his last home game, was soon dressing quietly in the locker room while outside in the hall the usual postgame crowd of family and friends began to form.

Letha Smith waited for her son, standing against the wall opposite the locker-room door. She wore a teal, matching jacket-and-pants outfit. In her arms was a small bouquet of flowers. All around her were younger women, wives and girlfriends of the players, most of whom seemed to know her quite well.

When Joe appeared, sunglasses resting on top of his head, holding a can of Orange Crush, a half-dozen kids rushed to ask for his autograph. He signed them all, then walked up to his mother and put his arm around her waist.

"Joe, turn around," another woman said. When he did, he found himself posing for snapshots. Soon a few more amateur photographers joined in, snapping away at Joe and Letha's final Coliseum appearance as the Warriors' first family.

As the Smiths and their entourage of about twenty began to move down the corridor and toward the ramp leading to the parking lot, it was clear that Letha was no mere supporting actress. In her one season with Joe, she had become a star in her own right, Meat Loaf Mom. She was, ironically, the most identifiable aspect to Joe's young career, which helped explain why the endorsement deals had not yet come his way.

As Letha made her way up the ramp, still surrounded by her friends and fans, a huge throng of kids holding out programs and pens from behind a barricade recognized her. They began chanting, "We want Joe Smith. We want Joe Smith." But Joe, nowhere in sight, was still down at the bottom of the ramp.

Walking with his cousin Keith Sharp, he was stopped by a casually attired but well-dressed man, about thirty-five, good-looking, his short hair slicked back. They spoke for several minutes, the man getting close to Joe, almost whispering. When he was finished talking, the man patted Joe on the shoulder. As Joe headed up the ramp, the man moved over to Sharp. They spoke for about thirty seconds, and then Sharp was accepting a business card.

"Call anytime," the man said, walking away.

"Who was that?" Sharp was asked as he followed his cousin up the ramp.

"Oh, Robert Carrol, he's Chris Gatling's agent," Sharp said, referring to the reserve big man traded by the Warriors to Miami in February.

At the time, Elmore was still Smith's agent of record, but in the world of sharks and their prey, it was open season on Joe Smith. He may as well have still been in college, twenty years old, and like Marcus Camby, vulnerable to anyone with a card and a pitch. And who was really looking out for his best interests, filling his head with what he needed to hear? Who in his inner circle understood what this industry was all about?

Those were the questions Elmore had been asking as he moved farther and farther from the center of Joe's circle, and finally out. The answer would within months become painfully clear, although there were hints that night in Oakland. After signing her own autographs in the parking lot, Letha Smith left the Coliseum in her own car, while Smith climbed into a white Toyota Land Cruiser with Maryland plates, accompanied by Sharp and a few friends. He would soon be headed back East, toward the kind of national attention no one believed he was capable of getting.

On the night of Friday, July 26, smack-dab in the middle of the Atlanta Olympics, Joe Smith and about ten of his friends went out in Chesapeake, Virginia, to celebrate his twenty-first birthday at a place called Ridley's Restaurant and Lounge at 711 Twenty-second Street. Ridley's, with a predominantly black clientele in a working-class section of town, twice a week featured male exotic dancers.

Such a show happened to be going on when Smith, dressed in a beige shirt and casual slacks, arrived with his group. Being a local celebrity, he was soon spotted and introduced to the small crowd. He stood and smiled, happy to be recognized. But as the night wore on, Smith and his friends reportedly tired of the dancers. They wanted to party. They wanted the floor. Joe Smith was an important man in these parts, an NBA star. It was his birthday. He had a right to dance.

Witnesses at the club said Smith and his friends became loud, unruly, and obscene. According to the police report that would later be filed by Officer J. J. Brown, Smith shortly before 1 A.M. "threw an ashtray and a beer can onto the dance floor, then told the dancers, all black males, to get off the floor." Soon one of the dancers, twenty-five-year-old Carlton Coney of Norfolk, confronted Smith about the ashtray and beer can. Another of the dancers, David Turner, said that when he and Coney tried to talk to Smith, Smith's friends began pummeling Coney.

A fight broke out involving the dancers and Smith and his friends. Coney, while being held over a railing, was hit with a broken beer bottle between the shoulder blades, just below the neck. Coney, bleeding from two open wounds that would require twenty-two stitches at Chesapeake General Hospital, staggered out the back door, where he was found a few minutes after one o'clock by police and medics.

Smith, the dancers said, fled the club, but the damage was done. Two of the dancers, Turner (no age given) of Chesapeake and Martin Curtis, twenty-nine, of Newport News, fingered him as the man who'd struck Coney with the bottle. His demeanor was described as "angry, irrational, and violent." And though Smith had indeed been introduced, police ran a check on all area subjects by the name of Joe Smith in the twenty-to-twenty-three age range with a possible date of birth of July 26. Ten Joe Smiths came up in the computer, but only one with the birthdate. That subject was Joseph Leynard Smith of Leafwood Drive, Norfolk.

A warrant for Smith's arrest was issued the following night, charging him with malicious wounding, a Class II felony. On Sunday the twenty-eighth, accompanied by attorney David Delpierre, Smith turned himself in. He was arraigned in Chesapeake General District Court four days later and released on his own recognizance.

In Virginia, a conviction on the charge carried a potential penalty of five to twenty years in prison. In a similar case several years before, Allen Iverson wound up serving less than four months in prison for his part in a bowling-alley brawl before being fortunate enough to receive a pardon from the governor.

Predictably, those who at least thought they knew Smith best—and had the most to lose if the charges stuck—rushed to his defense. The Warriors' general manager, Dave Twardzik, said Smith had insisted to him that he had not hit Coney. "You look at his past and he's never been in any kind of trouble," Twardzik said.

"Joe did not do that," Letha Smith told the *Virginian-Pilot* newspaper. How did she know? "I know my Joe."

The calls to Len Elmore's home in Highland, Maryland, began coming in almost immediately from reporters. After informing them that he was no longer Smith's representative, he sounded much like Twardzik and Letha Smith. "This doesn't sound like something Joe Smith would do," he told the reporters.

Privately, he didn't know what to believe anymore.

"You kept hearing things, that he was running with the wrong crowd, becoming a runaway child," Elmore said. He'd heard from sources he'd developed in Norfolk that Joe was running with a fast crowd. There was even word on the grapevine that he had a cash-flow problem.

Elmore took no comfort in what had happened. He called Smith's sudden misfortune "a crying shame." He was also not surprised. "To a certain extent, he's surrounded by people who are manipulating him, and in the process, he's able to manipulate them."

In the end, the malicious-wounding charge was dismissed on

September 16 when Judge S. Bernard Goodwyn said the prosecution had failed to prove that Smith had struck Coney, and that despite inconsistencies in the testimony of six defense witnesses, they all agreed that Smith had not been the culprit. That the defense witnesses could agree on that one thing and almost nothing else was something of a miracle, according to Nancy Parr, the Commonwealth prosecutor. "The defense witnesses . . . it was like they were in six different bars," she said.

Joe cried at the judge's decision. Letha shouted, "Hallelujah!" She later added, "Justice has prevailed, by the glory of God."

And, one source added, perhaps by the Commonwealth's lack of enthusiasm for pursuing a local sports hero on behalf of a few male dancers. But enough damage to Smith's reputation had already been done.

It was safe to assume that the Smith family's yearlong obsession with marketing their prize had at least come to a temporary halt. Smith wouldn't be packaged and sold any time soon by the mythmakers as the boy next door. He was no longer the sweet-smiling kid who'd danced with his sisters in the old house at 1327 Forty-first Street on the night he turned twenty. Even while maintaining his innocence of the malicious-wounding charge, the twenty-one-year-old Smith admitted to the police and the press that he'd been drinking and had been somewhat unruly.

"I'd never even seen him have a drink," Elmore said.

It was awkward for Elmore, at his own career crossroads, to say where Smith would have been—and conversely, Precept as well—had the family given Elmore his chance. If Smith had been working out in Washington the way he had the previous summer. Impossible to say. Maybe exactly where he wound up. Bad things happen to good people, that much Elmore, of all people, surely knew.

He knew another thing. Smith had obviously forgotten what he'd heard at the Rookie Transition Program and what Elmore had preached from the time he'd signed him.

"You warn these guys all the time: don't even put yourself in the position," he said. "But this is where the family situation, with its certain level of self-interest, gets in the way."

Smith was still a good kid, might still wind up with everything his loved ones wished for him, and themselves. Jason Kidd was making a mint, but no one had ever tried to sell him as a choirboy.

Smith didn't have the flair, the margin of error, to compensate for critical missteps.

Elmore knew that it didn't take much for it all to go bad. He knew that big things go wrong when small signs are ignored. How many times had he seen this during his forty-four years? At least twice when it hit home, when it took away his breath, his peace of mind, both his brothers. It may have been easy for society to stereotype Cliff and Rob Elmore as dead junkies. To Len, they were the kids he had wrestled with, played ball with, loved, mourned, and missed.

He had tried to watch over this likable fellow Maryland alumnus with the most common name, but this time, he was not going to blame himself. He believed he had made the right moves, said the right things, warned of the system's greed-inducing temptations and its parasitic character flaws.

"Sometimes," Elmore would say, "you feel like the unheeded prophet."

18

Playoff Lessons

AT FIRST SIGHT, THERE WERE SMILES AND SNICKERING ALONG PRESS row. As the head coach neared the home-team bench, a woman's voice from the power-broker seats carved through the pregame clatter like a buzz saw through cream.

"Hey, Doug!" came the voice. "What's with the tie?"

Ah, yes, the tie. From the opening tip of the season, Collins had set a sartorial standard, carefully mixing and matching an ever-changing array of crew, collarless, and turtleneck shirts with an equally impressive collection of designer suits and sport coats. A tie? Hah, Collins would rather do a Rodman. But here he was, looking like some kind of investment banker lost on the way home from Wall Street.

"Just trying to change our luck," he yelled back to fans delighted to be paid attention to.

Ah, yes, the luck. At the moment it looked as if it had all run out. The Pistons' season hung by, well, a thread. Detroit was down 0-2 in the best-of-five first round of the playoffs to the Orlando Magic, a deep, talented team with one purpose in mind.

"We're at opposite ends of the spectrum," Collins said. "Our goal is to try and find a way to win a playoff game. Their goal is to win the NBA title."

Truth be told, tie or not, Collins was more relaxed, less manic, than he had been in months, and with good reason. When the season began, he had hoped to change the Pistons' losing attitude, to teach young and impressionable players to compete unselfishly each and every night. And he had. When all was said and done, the Pistons had finished the regular season ten games over .500 (46-36), good enough for a fourth-place tie in the Central Division. The 18-game turnaround from the 28-win season a year earlier had tied a team record, set in 1981–82. Overall, Detroit had finished No. 2 in team defense (92.9 points allowed per game), climbing a mountain their coach could once merely pray his players would.

"I wanted to give our guys a chance to taste what it's like to be in a playoff game," Collins said, reflecting before game three as if he realized the Pistons were about to exit, stage left. "The intensity. The preparation. The atmosphere in the building. How everything changes. How good teams screw it down, crank it down on you. How they go right for your weakness."

In the first two games of the playoff series, Orlando had defined "crank it down" for Grant Hill and Co. Fresh from a franchise-record 60 regular-season wins, the Magic blew Detroit away in the second half of both games one and two in Orlando. It was obvious that the Pistons were too young, too inexperienced, and too thin to stop Orlando from its date with destiny. Thus the pregame talk at the Palace centered on the pros and cons of getting swept: the booster shot of confidence tied to a playoff win versus the long-term benefits of the broom.

But as Pistons PR Director Matt Dobek said, "Even if the Magic sweep, it won't downplay the season we've had. It's more than any of us could have imagined."

Mere weeks before.

Atlanta. Saturday. The third weekend in March. The same night Georgetown and UMass were clashing in the Georgia Dome in the NCAA East Regionals Finals, the Pistons prepared to meet the Hawks at the Omni, a game with major playoff implications. Just a half game separated Atlanta, Detroit, and the Cleveland Cavaliers in a scramble for the coveted fourth seed in the Central Division (a seed ensuring home-court advantage against the fifth-best team in the first round of the playoffs). On this day, it appeared Detroit had the best shot at grabbing it. The Pistons, plain and simple, were on fire. So much so that a Turner Sports film crew was on hand to feature a team that had won 12 of 16 and, improbable as it may have sounded six months before, was now considered by some to be one big man away from being a serious contender.

In his TBS interview, Collins' television experience was obvious, as he spoke with conviction, with passion, about coming to training camp hoping to change the "comfort zone" of certain players. How he had pushed and tested Allan Houston to determine how good he wanted to be. Why Grant Hill was the most improved player in the league ("Because of the impact he's had on this team"). That Joe Dumars was a symbol of what "this franchise was about, and where it would like to go, a bridge to the good times again."

From the very first day, Collins said he had acted as "an electric cattle prod," pushing and prodding his players to improve. He knew of the inherent dangers in this strategy; one shock too many and the player goes numb, stops listening. He knew he'd come dangerously close to that level with Hill, Houston, Terry Mills, and Lindsey Hunter. Fact was, he didn't know any other way. But he, too, was trying to learn.

"I just want the guys to respect me," Collins insisted. "Respect the fact that I love the game. What it stands for. What it meant to me in my life, what it does for them. I think deep in their hearts, guys know I care about them."

Whether they cared or not—and at least on the surface it seemed most did—the team had turned it around. The crucial point, at least in Collins' mind, had come a few weeks earlier, in Minnesota, the first game of that pivotal nine-day, six-game road trip out West. At the time, the Pistons were two games over .500. Expecting to find the same dispirited Timberwolves team they'd waxed by 30 points five days earlier at the Palace, the Pistons showed up cocky and bored. But the trade of the self-centered Christian Laettner and arrival of role-playing Andrew Lang and Spud Webb from Atlanta had changed the Wolves' molecular structure just enough to inject some fire into them. And believe it or not, the heart of their team already was the string-bean forward known as Teen Wolf.

Kevin Garnett.

"He's been the one bright spot this whole season," said Minnesota's assistant coach, Jerry Sichting, a valuable spare part on the champion Larry Bird Celtics of 1985–86. "But we have to make sure he doesn't fall in with all the other stuff that's going around. We have to give him some hope that this is not what he's going to go through his whole career. The biggest challenge for us is to improve so he wants to be a Timberwolf his whole life."

The race was on, with free agency two years away, thanks to the new collective bargaining agreement. Right about the time Michael Jordan might be checking out of Chicago for good, Garnett might be in position to pick up the pieces in his adopted hometown.

There was no question that the notion of him as a pretend player was dead. Not that it had been a bed of roses from the start. Early on, he had looked clumsy, out of his element. Taking wild shots, losing the ball, a child among men, a Lone Wolf who couldn't even accompany teammates to bars on the road. He wished he had been able to go to college. "This isn't as much fun as I thought it would be," he confided once to teammate Doug West.

Sensing his rookie needed a boost, Kevin McHale pulled Garnett aside one day and showed him Scottie Pippen's first-year stats. They weren't as good as the relatively modest ones Garnett was posting.

Pippen, of course, didn't enter the league under the intense scrutiny Garnett had. Every day, every arena, the writers and columnists camped in front of his locker, wondering how the kid was getting along. He heard and answered the same questions about his age again and again, until he could take it no more and announced he would accept no more such queries. "I'm looking forward to when I'm twenty," he said.

At least he was making no disturbing news, as many critics had expected him to. By the accounts of most close observers, Garnett had made few of the off-court mistakes that Joe Smith had. He was keeping his life relatively simple and sane.

Other than the obligatory luxury cars (Lexus and Range Rover), Garnett was playing it cool, lying low, following Eric Fleisher's financial advice. He told one close friend late in the season that he had earned and saved a good portion of $8 million from salary and endorsements.

His attentiveness eventually paid on-court dividends as well. Though the Wolves were a bickering, losing mess with a new head coach—McHale's college teammate and roommate Flip Saunders—Garnett's confidence was growing by leaps and bounds. He scored 16 points and grabbed 17 rebounds against the Bulls. He played with energy and emotion lacking on this team since its birth. It was obvious he—not Laettner—was its future, if it was going to have one. And after a frustrated Laettner had a trademark verbal eruption, McHale knew it was time to move.

"We've got some big britches on this team, people who know everything," Laettner complained after another loss. "There is not a winner on this team besides me."

Keeping in mind the T-Wolves had won 25 percent of their games with this kooky Dukie, McHale sent Laettner to Atlanta and officially placed the Franchise Player mantle on the shoulders of Garnett, who proved he was ready for it. At least as ready as Laettner had been.

While the Pistons dozed off that night at the Target Center, Minnesota played with heart, going on a 17-0 second-quarter tear, then holding on for a thrilling 94-93 victory. As a raucous Target Center crowd of 14,154 went home happy, Collins went nuts.

"We don't deserve to win this game," he fumed at his team. "You're not just playing out the last thirty games and trying to get a lottery pick. We're trying to make the playoffs."

Collins knew he had to do something. But what? In one of his more inspired and less confrontational moves, he borrowed from the Pat Riley school of jock psychology and decided to show a movie. A simple seven-minute tape of one Piston after another getting outrebounded, outrun, outscrambled, and outhustled to the ball.

"Just watch this," Collins told his bewildered wanna-bes, "and tell me how important it is for you to win."

Here was their answer. For only the second time since 1974, the Pistons went to Portland and won, pulling off a 93-81 victory built on steely eyes and a breakthrough defensive effort by Mills, of all people. In the game's final three minutes, Mills bumped and fronted and ultimately blanketed Arvidas Sabonis, the huge

Blazer center, as Detroit ran off 13 straight points to win going away.

"There are sixty days left and we are scrambling for a playoff spot," Hill said. "It's time to dig in and fight for it."

This was a different team now—poised, professional, intense. Playing without its captain—Dumars had suffered a deep thigh bruise in the Portland game—Detroit reeled off four victories in five tries, the only loss to Seattle, a game in which the Pistons led by 12. Hill had set the tone, as Money Players are supposed to, averaging 23.2 points, 10 rebounds, and 7.5 assists. But he wasn't alone. Houston was playing his best ball of the season. Thorpe. Mills. Hunter. Theo Ratliff. Don Reid. CBA pickup Michael Curry. Against Phoenix, Curry tallied a career-high 17 points, including an electrifying three-pointer to seal a 5-point win. In L.A., to wrap the best road trip in years, drop-dead shooting from Mills at crunch time highlighted a 107–103 defeat of the Clippers.

"I don't know if this trip could have been any better," Collins said.

Unfortunately, by halftime at the Omni, that kind of road warrior mentality had dissipated. The same somnambulant Pistons who had showed in Minnesota were snoozing right before Collins' disbelieving eyes. The result: a grand total of 34 first-half points.

It was here, in the locker room between halves, the captain decided it was time to speak. All season long, Dumars—no heroic speech-giver, by nature—had countered Collins' outbursts with occasional sermons of his own. Most importantly, he had stressed the importance of playing with a "sense of urgency" when the situation demanded. Forget about your pain, your problems, your family, your friends, he'd said. Don't wait around for the other team to fold, or the final five minutes. Go right for the heart from the start. Play every minute, all forty-eight, as if it's your last.

Often, he saw only dull eyes staring back at him. His teammates, their minds on late-night room service or delights even more tasty, would nod in agreement, but he didn't think they'd really heard or understood what he meant.

But he knew this Atlanta game was critical. It was time to send an urgent message to the Hawks, to the Cavaliers, to the whole damn league. He decided to try once more.

"Guys, don't just walk out there and get run over," he pleaded.

322

"Don't just come in here and lay down. You're representing yourself, your family, me, and this organization. Don't just walk out there and cash it in. Have some pride."

They tried. Even with Hill out from a third-quarter hip injury, they closed to 85–81 with 2:30 left. On the final 2 of a career-high 38 points, Houston got Detroit within 3 with 53 seconds to go. But Hawks guard Steve Smith came up big when it counted. Final score: 92–84, Atlanta.

Afterward, wedged into a hot, cramped corridor outside a junior high–sized locker room, a drained Collins wanted very much to keep his cool. He knew this was neither the time nor the place to blow off steam, so he held himself in check, acknowledging the obvious to the assembled press. "We were a tired team tonight," he said. "We just had no energy."

As one hangdog player after another headed off toward a postgame shower, Collins took a long pull of diet Coke and pored over the postgame stats. He knew this game had been lost in the first half. Tough schedule or not, there was no excuse for not showing up ready to go.

"Allan was great," he said. "But after Grant got hurt, we just couldn't create anything. Atlanta outplayed us the whole game, they really outplayed us." A quick shake of the head, then one more concession. "Five guys in double figures," he added, "and we've got one guy with thirty-eight."

Inside the locker room, the kid who'd loaded and fired that 38 special in front of a horde of family and friends spoke quietly, which was his way. Collins sat on a folding chair in the middle of the room, red-faced and alone, shaking his head. In one swift kick, his team (now 38-30) had dropped into seventh place in the conference playoff race.

"Tonight was the night we needed other guys to show up," he hissed, stabbing his finger at the stat sheet. "You tell me Mark West can't post up Christian Laettner. Fuck me." Stab. "You tell me Otis Thorpe can't post up Andrew Lang. Fuck me. Fuck me."

In retrospect, Collins' rage was fueled not so much by his players, but rather his growing frustration with the league and the game, changing right before his eyes. To Collins, players such as Anthony Bowie and Cedric Ceballos were symbols of the New NBA. That very day, in fact, the papers had carried a story on how Ceballos was apparently upset over losing playing time to Magic

Johnson and had been located at a resort in Lake Havasu City, Arizona, all while his team was fighting for playoff positioning, a position not helped by an 11-point loss to Seattle.

Collins got on an obscenity-laced roll and didn't want to stop: "Here's a guy who led Phoenix in scoring last year and they fucking gave him away to their archrivals in their own division," he began. "In their own division! They fucking gave him away! Gave him away! To the Lakers! Here, here's this cancer! This fucking cancer! You take him, let him fuck up your team!"

Late at night, unable to sleep after games, Collins would watch the Me First disease Ceballos and Bowie carried being spread around the league. There it was, on *SportsCenter*. Players attacking referees. Referees playing musical chairs with team mascots during time-outs, riding around the court on motorcycles.

"What the fuck is this league about anymore?" asked the coach in a voice that held no answers. "Is it substance or style?"

And just when he needed it, a player who was slowly but surely evolving into more than superficial ambled toward the locker-room door and another bus ride to another airport. A dapper black cap covered his head.

"Keep the faith, Coach," said Terry Mills. "We'll get there."

A small smile crossed Collins' face. On this night he would take a victory, any victory, where he could find it.

"Terry never said that before," Collins whispered. "Never."

It was something to take from the Omni to the next stop on the road to the playoffs.

Three weeks later, the Pistons clinched their first playoff spot in four years, and it wasn't easy. Or happy. On the second Sunday in April, they faced a Boston Celtics team long since eliminated from the playoffs but in a scrappy mood nonetheless. This time, Detroit would need a special effort, and get it. From Houston (27 points, career-high 11 rebounds). From Hill (a league-best tenth triple double). From Thorpe (20 points). But most of all, from the captain, the man Collins had hoped would be his MVP without being his best player.

With his team trailing by 5 at the half, Dumars took over. He reached back to the days of old, to the spring of '89. In forty-three minutes, old Joe scored 23 points, 12 in the final six minutes of regulation, to drag his wilting teammates into overtime, where they beat the Celtics. The playoff dream had come true.

Even opposing coach M. L. Carr, a towel-waving pain in the posterior during the epic Larry Bird era, could not help but admire the Pistons' growth, and the old warrior who had carried them into the playoff battlefield. "The old Joe Dumars stepped it up at the end," he said. "Even though it was against us, I like to see things like that."

"This is a great feeling," Dumars said. "I didn't know if I would ever get back into the playoffs. This is great."

"Joe was just phenomenal tonight," said Collins. "We needed him and he gave us a vintage Joe Dumars performance down the stretch. I don't think we realize what these guys have done the last seven months. They have brought a winning team to the city of Detroit, and I am proud of each and every one of them."

Yet for the players, something was missing. By now, playoffs or no playoffs, the unwavering verbal abuse had taken its toll.

"Doug kinda yelled the celebration out of us," Houston said, a solitary comment that seemed to speak volumes. About Collins, in particular. About young basketball players, in general. About a league Collins wished he could coach in and one he and the rest of his obsessive ilk were forced to endure.

Houston may have been thinking more of himself, for he was either Collins's pet project or verbal punching bag, depending on one's point of view. As one Pistons teammate told Dave D'Alessandro of the *Newark Star-Ledger*: "[Houston] could score 25 points and Collins would still get in his face and scream at him over one mistake. And it was nasty: 'I don't care how you're shooting, you suck tonight.' There was, like, one of those every week."

A full load of in-your-face defense poured from both sides during the opening minutes of Detroit's do-or-die game against Orlando. Late in the first quarter, play loosened a bit after a second foul sent Hill to the bench with 3:12 remaining. In a preview of things to come, Collins barked in referee Ed Middleton's ear, to no avail, and before the quarter was out, the Magic had turned a 6-point advantage into 9, 27–18.

But the Pistons fought on, behind the relentless hustle of undersized center Reid, the rookie from Georgetown with size-20 heart. It was 48-all with 54.3 seconds to go before the half, then 49–48 until Hardaway dribbled down the seconds to intermission and, with two ticks left, flipped the ball to Nick Anderson, who drilled an off-balance 16-footer as the clock ran out.

A small but telltale sign of how a team as talented as Orlando could crush the spirit of a young comer by simply stepping on the gas.

But the second half was the most important lesson of all, for it taught the Pistons that anything—*anything!*—could happen in the heat of the NBA playoff night. The Pistons' final twenty-four minutes of the season would be best remembered for the shot clock that stopped working, the baskets—and coaches—who disappeared, the young superstar who was humbled while another came of age, and the slow-motion replays that revealed nothing and everything.

It was all touched off, quite naturally, when the shot clock at the Pistons' end went haywire early in the third quarter, precipitating a seventeen-minute delay. When it was fixed, Hardaway drove down the right side of the lane, seemed to pick up his dribble, then sliced to the bucket for a layup that nobody but referee Nolan Fine figured was any good. Collins certainly didn't think so. And when Hill was called for his fourth personal foul with 4:46 to go in the period, Collins went right after Middleton, who quickly snapped off a T.

Near the end of the quarter Orlando had a 10-point lead (80–70). Here, Houston got hot, hitting from all over, keeping the Pistons in the chase. But when Middleton waved off a Houston bucket, signaling offensive foul with 2.4 seconds to play, Collins just lost it, or wanted his team to think so anyway. Though he later denied the suggestion, it was clear Collins knew, down by 11, he had to do something, anything, to ignite a team and a crowd increasingly accepting of its fate. Collins again set off after Middleton.

He followed him onto the court this time, leaving no room for misinterpretation, wanting this little lacquered-haired robot to have no chance to walk away. Five seconds later, Collins was hit with his second T—and automatic ejection—for only the second time in his pro career. He left to a standing ovation, a tribute to not only this night, but eighty-four others along the way.

"Fuck!" Collins raged while walking toward the locker room,

getting his money's worth. "They call every fucking foul against us!"

With Collins gone, the Pistons suddenly seemed to sense what was at stake, the sacrifice made on their behalf. The fans felt it, too. Chants of "De-fense" rang out. Sure enough, tick by tick, a transformation took place. The building began to rock, with a Bad Boy exterior, circa 1988.

When Houston buried a three-pointer, the place went wild. There was 4:18 to go. It was 91–87 Orlando. Two minutes later, Dumars drained a trademark rainbow jumper, making it 92–90. Now, down the stretch, it was time for the playoff battle–scarred to step forward. Unfortunately for Detroit, it wasn't Dumars as much as it was Horace Grant, he of the 16 points, 15 rebounds (on this night), and three Chicago championship rings. In succession, Grant hit two free throws, canned a clutch fifteen-footer, and shut down Houston in a defensive switch. That led to a seemingly secure 96–90 edge with 47.2 seconds to play.

But Detroit would not die. First, Houston hit a pair of free throws. Next, ten seconds later, Hill made it 97–95 with his first serious move of the game, a three-point play off a powerful drive. The Magic answered by putting the ball in the hands of a bright, shiny Penny named Hardaway. What happened next was questionable—some fans might argue criminal—given Detroit's furious comeback. Whatever, as Hardaway dribbled down the game clock to just under twelve seconds, he lofted a long, desperate shot that sailed over—way over—the left corner of the basket. It fell, like manna from heaven, into the hands of Grant, who banged it in.

It didn't matter that replays later showed air ball all the way, and that the shot clock should have been expired, giving the ball back to Detroit, trailing by only 2. It was 99–95 now, and all Houston could do was roar back down the court, fire in his eyes, and ice a three-pointer for his 33rd point of the night. But when Anderson coolly dropped in two free throws, the game, and season, were history.

Afterward, in a dead-silent locker room, both Collins and owner Bill Davidson told the team how proud they were.

"Anyone have anything else to say?" asked Collins.

Only one player did.

"Just work your ass off this summer," said Allan Houston.

As Collins related this comment later, he had tears in his eyes, and they were not made-for-TV.

"I think it's sorta interesting where Allan started and where he finished," Collins said. "I think some [of the press] sometimes think that I fly by the seat of my pants, but there's always thought in everything I do. I saw in Allan Houston something special. In the fourth quarter tonight, I saw steely eyes in a young kid. He jumped up and made the shots, big shots. He didn't blink. That was tremendous growth."

Just as Houston had grown, it was hoped by Collins that Hill had grown through failure. Late in the season, the legs that had lifted this team—his team—were nowhere to be found. For example, in the second-to-last game of the regular season, an absolutely crucial game against Cleveland, down by 1 with nine seconds to play, Hill drove the baseline, got double-teamed, and lost the ball. That one play cost Detroit the chance to play Cleveland or Indiana in the first round, instead of Orlando.

"It was the first time Grant just failed," said P.R. Director Dobek. "It was so great just to see it. Just to be a part of it. To see Grant Hill like that. He was so down on himself. It makes you know you're going the right way because it was a lesson learned."

It was clear from the sound of Hill's voice after the Orlando game that he had learned yet another humbling lesson. Just 1 field goal and 2 assists at halftime. Just 3 of 7 field goals, 6 rebounds, 5 assists, 17 silent points overall.

"I learned in the playoffs you gotta bring it," he said. "You gotta come with the total package, be at your best, and I wasn't at my best. I'll remember this series during the off-season, as opposed to the entire season. I'm not going to remember a career high. I'm going to remember this last game."

Dumars would remember it as well, but for very different reasons. Finally, he had seen what he had longed to see, signs that this team was learning how deep a team had to dig. "I think tonight we learned what we needed to learn in this series," he said in the dead quiet of a normally off-limits training room. "Tonight, a couple of guys learned, you know what, you lay your guts out there for forty-eight minutes, you've given yourself a chance to win. Playoff basketball forces you to know what urgency means. You don't have a choice. Tonight, no one has to tell you what urgency means. You lose, you go home. Now, next year, when it's the middle of the season, it's February and it's cold and I say, 'You've got to have a sense of urgency,' they'll understand what I mean."

It was just past midnight. Dressed in jacket and jeans, Dumars hopped off the table and started a slow walk down the hall. Despite the hour, the game long gone, the hallway was packed with people—family, friends, and team officials who weren't quite ready to say good-bye. Against one wall, one corner of this franchise's future stood signing every piece of paper in sight. That was Hill. Not twenty feet away, up against another wall, the same scene played out for Houston. Soon, they walked out together, side by side, the rocks on which, Collins believed, a future championship could rest.

A half hour later, Collins himself headed down the hall. The postgame tears had been replaced by bright eyes and a beaming grin. In many ways, it had been a season of absolution, a chance for a passionate coach to cleanse himself personally and professionally, to break away only to come back full circle. Back to the game, and the people he loved the most. A best friend from Philadelphia; his wife, Kathy, who was moving back into his life. As he prepared to walk out the door that night, Collins was a man at peace. His wife and his sense of team, his belief in the process, were back.

"The guy I'm most proud of is Allan Houston," he whispered, stopping one last time to make one final postgame introduction. Then he headed off into the night to celebrate a season. A good, honest season. He looked back once, to someone he'd befriended during those draining eighty-five games. He couldn't let them go. Not yet.

"I got one tonight," he said. "I got one."

He was talking about Allan Houston, and what he meant was that he'd gotten another star he could count on, build with. He had himself another Money Player, or so he thought.

Soon it would be time for Houston to get paid. And in the New NBA that Collins didn't always understand, or accept, wads of cash were much, much thicker than the loyalty a coach wanted too much to think he deserved. Than blood that was shared.

19

The One and Only

THE 1996 NBA FINALS FELT MORE LIKE A FORMALITY THAN A FRACAS. It had the atmosphere of a coronation, a reminder that the King, Elvis in baggy shorts, indeed was not dead.

Oh, Michael Jordan's Bulls became distracted for a few days, flattering themselves with historical declarations while using the powerful bargaining agent known as the international media to begin lucrative contract negotiations with combatively frugal owner Jerry Reinsdorf. Dennis Rodman climbed all over the boards, got under the SuperSonics' skin and inside their heads. Jordan didn't always shoot like a god but made the plays when he had to. The Bulls zippered the mouths of Seattle's brash Gary Payton and Shawn Kemp by winning the first three games, including an embarrassing game-three blowout at the Key Arena in the heart of the Great Northwest.

No NBA team had ever come from 0-3 to win the title, so winning game three more or less assured the Bulls their fourth title in six years. Even after winning their last two at home, leaving Jordan disgusted, seething in Seattle at his less obsessive team-mates, the Sonics were simply not capable of going back to Chicago and stealing games six and seven. They saved face by not being swept. They would have to be happy with that, with losing in six and watching as Jordan emerged from a celebration with the ball, sprinted off to the locker room, and threw himself on the floor, facedown. There, with NBC cameras on him, he sobbed and heaved.

This was no staged Nike moment, as it had been when Andre Agassi won Wimbledon in 1992 and was motioned by his handlers to lie facedown in the hallowed grass. Only the most cynical of critics would suspect that Jordan, who cried with James Jordan beside him after winning his first NBA title, was not admitting to millions of viewers that, unlike the hole often spoken of in the vernacular of the game, the one in his heart couldn't be filled.

He'd won his fourth championship on Father's Day.

"This is for Daddy," said the world's foremost sports hero.

It was highest drama the Finals produced, though Seattle's resistance to being executed at home, combined with Jordan's and Dennis Rodman's mere presence, helped make the six-game series the second-highest-rated Finals in history. Only the Jordan–Charles Barkley (Phoenix) 1993 showdown had attracted more viewers. It was more meaty evidence how Jordan drove the NBA.

In fact, the entire playoffs were strewn with lopsided series, Seattle's seven-game war with Utah in the Western Conference final being the most notable exception. Before Jerry West could say poof, Magic Johnson disappeared from view, the feuding Lakers losing to defending champion Houston in four. Johnson had predicted that the Western Conference winner would emerge from that series. It was wishful thinking on the Lakers' part and unrealistic in the case of the banged-up Rockets, who were swept in the next round by Seattle.

While Hakeem Olajuwon's reign as the NBA's best player was coming to an official and skidding halt, Johnson announced another retirement. Jordan, hearing the news from reporters on his way to the locker room for the fifth and final game of the Bulls' second-round series against the Knicks, said he wasn't surprised. Nor did he seem sad. This was, after all, the nineties.

Going into the Finals, the Bulls had lost one playoff game, in overtime, to Patrick Ewing's Knicks, whose aging infrastructure effectively rivaled New York City's. Then the most-anticipated playoff showdown, Bulls versus Magic, fizzled as if someone had stuck a pin into a giant inflatable Shaq. The Bulls blew Orlando out in game one at the United Center, with the Magic losing Horace Grant—the MVP of the previous spring's series—to an injured shoulder. And in game two came the pivotal and most telling game of not only the playoffs but the season and, in many ways, the competing generations.

On the off day between games one and two, Jordan received his fourth MVP award at a press conference in a Sheraton Hotel conference room near the Bulls' suburban practice facility. He'd received 109 of the 113 first-place votes, but that wasn't what was on the minds of the reporters in attendance. That morning, in the revered *Chicago Tribune* column of Bob Verdi, Jordan had fired his first free-agency salvo, setting a bottom-line figure at $18 million—deliberately low, most critics thought. He declared himself prepared to play someplace else for less if Reinsdorf didn't meet his price. It was a matter of principle, Jordan said. He had never demanded his contract be renegotiated, even as players who didn't belong on the same floor passed him by on the salary chart.

Naturally, at the press conference, not long after Jordan made his obligatory MVP acceptance speech, the contract issue came right to the fore. Jordan's reaction was a tap dance that included some of his best moves of the playoffs. He said he didn't know he was being quoted while he was talking to Verdi. Or he may have known he was being quoted but that he was quoted out of context. Or that he said it but he didn't mean it the way it came out. Or that he didn't mean for it to come out now. Everything but the truth: he was using his MVP moment to send Reinsdorf a clear signal. He'd be in to see him real soon, and the $18 million might be a good number with which to start the bidding.

The next night before game two, the subject of mega-money dominated the locker-room chatter. O'Neal, taking a few moments from dialing friends around the country on his cell phone, was asked for his reaction to speculation that Alonzo Mourning had already been promised $16 million a year in Miami.

"Alonzo's getting sixteen million dollars?" he said. He rolled his eyes, then went out and, in the first half, rolled over Luc Longley, Rodman, and anyone else the Bulls threw at him. In what Leonard Armato might describe as the result of a new-age form of motivation, O'Neal scored 26 points and grabbed 11 rebounds in the first twenty-four minutes as the Magic built a lead that would swell to 58–40 at the 9:10 mark of the third quarter. If one was looking for symbolism behind these stats, the 26 points and 11 rebounds added together and divided by two amounted to 18.5. Was this Shaq's way of saying that he, the NBA's version of Disney, was worth more than Jordan's Universal?

If it was, then Jordan's response was a virtual corporate takeover. He led a ferocious Bulls charge that rattled Orlando's perimeter players, shut Shaq down, and turned the Magic into mush. O'Neal got 10 harmless points in the second half, Jordan 25. O'Neal was no factor on defense. Jordan spearheaded the Bulls' press that took the ball out of the hands of Penny Hardaway, who surrendered it to Brian Shaw much too willingly, in a way Magic and Isiah would never have. Jordan would score the clutch baskets, finish the game with 15 free throws made in 16 attempts, a percentage O'Neal could not have achieved if he, as the rappin' genie Kazaam, had granted himself 100 wishes. Jordan then snuffed out Orlando's last hope by blocking Dennis Scott's three-point shot from the left corner.

From that moment on, there was absolutely no doubt who was the NBA's real Money Player. Nor was there any fight left in Orlando, and, as it would turn out, no future for the Shaq-and-Penny show. Jordan had sent a clear message that, as long as he cared enough to be in game shape, the Eastern Conference was his territory. Down in Orlando, the Magic mailed in games three and four and were eliminated from the playoffs for the third straight year in a sweep.

Orlando's unraveling should have surprised only those who believed that talent was all it took, as many of the young players did. The Anthony Bowie incident during the regular season against Detroit had demonstrated a chronic unprofessionalism and disregard for the wishes of the coach. As if that wasn't enough, O'Neal had seized the opportunity to embarrass Brian Hill again late in the season, and on national television to boot.

The Magic was pulling into New York to play the Knicks on April 3, when O'Neal's grandmother passed away, across the river in Newark. He left the team, quite naturally, missing that game and another the next night against Boston. With the Magic scheduled that Sunday for a NBC game against the Bulls, there was no word on whether O'Neal would return for the game with New York.

Before the game, Hill had said that he would not use O'Neal

unless he arrived prior to game time or called to say that he was on his way. There was no call, not so much as a sign of Shaq until the game began. With NBC's cameras rolling, O'Neal marched into the arena, through its bowels, into the locker room. Superman had arrived. Superman played. The Magic lost. And poor Brian Hill took another hit as an embattled coach who'd lost control of his team.

On the opposing bench, Phil Jackson could only shake his head and thank his lucky stars for Michael Jordan, for the opportunity to preach to an increasingly rare NBA congregation that believed in the team way as much as him.

The most startling news during the playoffs had nothing to do with the Bulls or the Sonics, or any of the other competing teams. It came out of the same Continental Airlines Arena where the Final Four had been played and involved the same coaches, Rick Pitino and John Calipari, who'd met in the tournament's most anticipated game.

During the Chicago-Orlando series, New Jersey's desperate Nets made Pitino a Pat Riley–type offer—minority ownership and a five-year package that guaranteed him more than $5 million a year plus complete control of the basketball operation. Pitino, wooed by his friends minority Nets owners Joe and Henry Taub at the Taubs' delicatessen in the suburb of Lyndhurst, New Jersey, tormented himself and everyone around him trying to decide whether to make the leap from Lexington.

The Kentucky people couldn't really blame him for going. He'd stayed seven years, restored the program, won the NCAA title. The issue for Pitino was the cloud over the Nets and their seven fractious and typically tremulous owners. This franchise had already had one coach (Larry Brown) walk out on the eve of the playoffs, another (Rollie Massimino) not show up for his own press conference to announce his hiring, and still another (the late Jim Valvano) who was signed by one owner after which another told reporters he'd never heard of him.

Finally and appropriately, on a golf tour of Ireland with UK alumni, Pitino announced to the alumni in dramatic fashion, his specialty, that he was staying. With the alumni's cheers still ringing in his ears, Pitino promptly called his pals the Taubs and suggested they grab Calipari out of the college ranks before someone else did. Thus did Pitino for a second time successfully lobby for his protégé. Calipari graduated from UMass to A Mess for the tidy sum of $15 million spread over five years. He, too, demanded and received front-office power.

Meanwhile, the man Calipari was replacing, Butch Beard, was leaning over a balcony at the Chicago predraft camp, convincing himself not to jump. Beard, a onetime championship point guard for Golden State, had waited sixteen years from the time of his retirement in 1978 for the chance to be a head NBA coach. For him, it was two years and out with an organization in utter chaos. Would he get another shot at a head-coaching job? The odds were not in his favor. The jobs did not come as easily for former black journeymen as they did for the Mike Dunleavys, the Pat Rileys, the Rick Adelmans. George Karl, coaching across town against Phil Jackson in the Finals, was working on his third NBA chance.

Five black coaches (out of twenty-nine teams) finished the 1995–96 season, not a terribly progressive percentage in a league that's been at least 70 percent black in players for years. Six blacks had jobs that gave them front-office power. "For years in this league, guys have been hiring their friends," said Doc Rivers. "The guys who do the hiring are white. Is that racism? Maybe not. But it's still a problem."

When Isiah Thomas hired a former teammate, Darrell Walker, to coach Toronto in the summer of '96, critics wondered if Thomas had lost his mind, handing the reins to a recently retired and much-traveled guard. But that was exactly how many of the more successful white ex-players had landed their positions. That was how Flip Saunders made the unlikely leap from the CBA to the NBA—far more than a natural candidate, he was Kevin McHale's friend.

Historically, black NBA coaches had been former star players, such as Bill Russell, Willis Reed, Wes Unseld, and Lenny Wilkens. And with the obvious exception of Wilkens, usually they were set up to fail with lousy teams. Only in recent years had the journeyman black players—men such as Beard and Boston's M. L. Carr—begun to make strides. For 1996–97, in addition to Walker's being hired by Toronto, Dallas grabbed Jim Cleamons off Chicago's talented coaching staff and Philadelphia replaced John Lucas with Johnny Davis. Camps opened with six black head coaches. Progress, but not much.

Most NBA teams typically attempted to pacify their black communities by hiring a black assistant coach, described by Buck Williams as "guys hired to communicate with black players." Ironically, this particular practice of tokenism had precipitated a reverse-discrimination suit in Orlando that had played out publicly, bitterly, for four long years.

It involved forty-six-year-old George Scholz, a onetime comer at Florida Southern, where he took his team to two Division II Final Fours. Scholz was hired by the Magic in 1990 as second assistant and advance scout by then-coach Matt Guokas. "Scholz Hired as Magic Assistant Coach" read the team's press release that day.

Scholz was perceived to be doing well and was at one point given a 40 percent pay raise. But forces beyond his control were working against him. In the early stages of the team's existence, a group called the Community Advisory Board (CAB) was created as a liaison between the Magic and the black community. In 1991, the year the DeVoss family, better known for their multibillion-dollar Amway Company, purchased the Magic, Scholz was in his second season. That December, according to the minutes of a CAB meeting, four CAB officials discussed a number of topics, "including the lack of minority representation on the Magic staff."

According to court records, in early 1992, Richard DeVoss asked Guokas to compile a list of black coaches on other NBA staffs. DeVoss was startled to discover that Orlando was one of three teams that had all-white staffs. Guokas, Scholz claimed, soon after told him that the team would soon hire a black second assistant for the 1992–93 season. Scholz, the son of an Illinois circuit court judge, said he told Guokas that "it was illegal to replace anyone because of their race."

Scholz was fired on April 20, 1992, the Magic claiming that Scholz was never an assistant coach, just a scout, and that the team was shaking up its scouting department. In other words, he was not being replaced as coach, he was fired in a staff reorganization. The long, contentious case—which would cost Scholz his family's savings and much of its sanity—was on.

Finally, in January 1996, Scholz got his day in court. Over several days his lawyers presented a strong argument including media guides and press releases identifying Scholz as an assistant coach. But then, in a stunning move, Judge Linda Gloeckner took the case away from the jury and exonerated the Magic, ruling that "while race may have been one of the many factors in Mr. Scholz's discharge, he had simply failed to submit sufficient evidence." One shocked juror said he had already decided to award Scholz $4 million in damages, and a bewildered Scholz was forced to scrape together the money for an appeal.

The Scholz case, covered extensively by *Court TV*, was still by no means a no national headline-grabber, but it was a fascinating example of how standard hiring practices in professional sports— the insular buddy system—had for once failed one of its own. George Scholz, who after two years of unemployment landed back at Jacksonville University, was gone from the seductive world of the NBA, unlikely to return. In late 1996, Scholz was ousted also from Jacksonville for, the school said, devoting too much time to his pending court battle.

Butch Beard, meanwhile, would have to start all over again, as an assistant to Jim Cleamons in Dallas. The two had been point-guard peers, onetime teammates. Cleamons threw his old friend a rope before he went under. At least Beard was back in the league, in the game. Out on the fringe, there were men who had never had a chance to work the big NBA stage and would have given their last drop of blood, if that's what it took.

On the night Seattle finally showed up in the Finals, learned what it took to run with the Bulls, perhaps the best young coach never to make the NBA in any capacity sat in a suburban Detroit living room. Game four had ended hours before, the clock on the mantel read 3:10 A.M., but neither the coach nor his friend, grieving the death of his mother, wanted to sleep.

Having just watched George Karl get a win against Phil Jackson, Gary Mazza was in something of his own grieving state. He was mourning the death of his career.

Who was Gary Mazza? Not even an Internet search could've dredged up his sad story, but Phil Jackson knew his name. So did Karl, and Riley, and much of the coaching fraternity that had come through the same summer league in Los Angeles, the most common training ground for NBA coaches in the 1980s, and the highways and byways of the CBA. Mazza had also coached in Jackson's "coach roach league." Coached his ass off in 1983 for the Detroit Spirits, all the way to the CBA Finals against Karl's Montana Golden Nuggets.

Mazza had been all of thirty, a combustible, ambitious climber. Tied 3-3, with game seven on his home floor, Karl was decked out in black tie to celebrate what he obviously believed would be a victory. Mazza made a monkey of the man in the suit, winning the title on the road.

Riley could tell you about Mazza as well. How right before game five of the 1988 NBA Finals against the Pistons, the series tied at 2-2 and the Lakers showing acute signs of vulnerability, Mazza had showed up at the team's hotel and handed Riley assistant Bill Bertka a three-page report, distilled from fifty pages of notes. Earlier, Bertka could barely contain himself when Mazza, at the team's request, provided a no-holds-barred scouting report on the Lakers themselves.

This time, Bertka took one long look and ran the report right into a team meeting, Mazza's advice aimed right at Riley. "I told him it was a TV series, to stop griping and bitching about the calls," Mazza said. "You have to establish what you need for the end of the game. Don't ask for any call but the last one."

Riley, still developing the jockspeak psychology that would become his calling card in New York, took heed. The last call in game six was the one that saved the Lakers—the phantom Bill Laimbeer foul on Kareem Abdul-Jabbar. Mazza got a well-deserved thanks from Riley. That was it.

Mazza only wanted a foot in the door, someone to take him on as an assistant. But he didn't have a rabbi. He didn't have the political, late-night, cocktail-lounge social skills. And he certainly didn't have any luck.

Back in 1981, in the midst of a long, news-depleted summer caused in part by a baseball strike, *Sports Illustrated* dispatched a writer to Los Angeles to work a feature on this twenty-eight-year old coaching phenom who was being hailed as a young Bobby Knight. The comparison made sense, based on the obsessive preparation, the compulsive need to work round the clock, to turn the screws on both ends of the floor. To control a game that, for years, was known for player spontaneity. It was the coming wave, from Knight to Hubie Brown to Riley to Pitino. NBA coaches, true sideline figures since Red Auerbach had puffed his last victory cigar, were becoming stars again in their own right.

Not Mazza, though. That summer he had taken a ragtag team of free agents and won 15 straight games in the free-agent and pro-level portion of the league. Fifteen straight against the likes of Riley, Chaney, and Del Harris. When the season was over he had been honored as Coach of the Year in the Summer League. But the story of that summer got canned, which was also the story of his life. Just as the magazine was going to press, the baseball strike ended and the editors weren't interested anymore in the man longtime L.A. summer-league director and NBA regular Larry Creger called "the best coach ever" to pass through his league.

Now, with a résumé by Rand McNally, after all the nights he'd slept in his car, after all the unpaid bills, the losses in love, the battles with frustrated players and penny-pinching, small-town owners, and the pleas from his parents to quit and get married, what was he supposed to do? He was forty-four, balding, with a teddy-bear body, a perpetual five-o'clock shadow tamed by soft blue eyes.

"How do you recover when you commit your life to something and it doesn't work out?" he said.

For most of the last six years, he has worked as a waiter at several fancy Detroit-area restaurants. They called him Coach in one place. In another, he offered counsel to Rodman and Grant Hill, who listened as they ordered salad and steak. He was living at home now, waiting tables, waiting for something good to happen, unable to stop himself from adding to the crates jammed with file folders titled "Basketball Philosophy," "Practice Preparation," "Style of Play (Being the Best)," "The Break."

If only he'd gotten one. Just one.

"Fucking A I want to be in the NBA," Mazza said. "A top assistant job. All the best coaches I came up with—Jackson, Riley, Del Harris—they're in the league. Karl knows. He knows I'm out here, somewhere. I've been with the best coaches in the game. They should know what I gave to the game."

Mazza took one last look at the clock. The time read 4 A.M. There were tears in his eyes when he spoke. "Everybody tells me to quit dreaming. Give up. Why? Why? I'm not crying. I'm not prejudiced. I've paid my dues. I've tried not to copy anyone. All I've done is love the game. I had my own system of plays. I've convinced players that I'm selling something that's me—all me. I gave a lot to the guys I came up with, but they never gave me a real job. They never gave me respect. I was lucky to come up with them, but whether they view you as a threat, I don't know. But I'll tell you what: I know I'm one of the best coaches. I know I used to be able to coach."

Karl, meanwhile, was somewhere over the rainbow, off in the Land of Oz. That's all he knew. And Jackson, too. Their days of driving CBA vans were long gone. Their focus was not on yesterday but tomorrow.

How much more they had coming. Both knew all about what John Calipari would be making in New Jersey the following season. Every NBA coach at the Chicago predraft camp couldn't stop talking about it. That night in his living room, Mazza heard the NBC announcers discuss how, the day before, Jackson had threatened to sit out a season unless Reinsdorf offered him market worth, which meant Calipari money. Karl, annoyed that Seattle owner Barry Ackerley was refusing to grant him a more lucrative contract extension, said he might follow Jackson into self-imposed exile.

This had to sound like insanity to Gary Mazza, but the plain truth was that it was just another by-product of how things work out, or don't. Once the gravy train left the station, it didn't much matter how you got on, or why you didn't.

It worked this way on various levels, even for famous and successful players who missed the big money and now had to sit back and watch as the likes of Derrick Coleman could play indifferently and live luxuriously off bank interest. To a certain extent, it was even this way for a legend such as Julius Erving, who had carried the sport through its most turbulent era and could now only shake his head at the once unimaginable fame that his foremost successor, Michael Jordan, had achieved.

"I'm not offended by it," Erving said one day during the Finals. "I always had the philosophy that if someone recognized me, it didn't make my day. So someone who doesn't recognize me doesn't break it."

That same day, between games one and two, traces of what were Erving's true feelings seemed to pour out, ironically in what was intended as another NBA feel-good production. Erving, David Stern, and Russ Granik were the principals at a press conference to promote the NBA's fiftieth anniversary (or at least the birth of the B.A.A.) and what would be a 1996–97 season-long celebration.

After Stern made the point of how today's players needed to

better understand the role of yesterday's heroes, Erving began to lobby the commissioner on behalf of his ABA brethren. He asked why ABA stats were not included in the makeup of the NBA record book.

With jerseys of the three teams he'd played for—the ABA Virginia Squires, the ABA Nets, and the NBA 76ers—hanging behind him, Erving went on to list his own long record of achievement, the MVPs he'd won, the All-Star teams he'd made, the records he'd set. It all seemed in good humor until he droned on too long, and the reporters in the audience looked at one another, instinctively recognizing that Erving was not at peace with this issue at all.

Had he been born a decade later, Erving would have been a Dream Teamer, too, and perhaps not found a country on earth where he could walk unmolested down a street. But he had run out of time a few years too soon, and Jordan was the man for whom the earth stood still.

This would be the exact message driven home the following night, after the Bulls had won game two. After finishing his press conference, Jordan left the press area and began making the walk through the winding tunnels of the United Center, followed by a small entourage of security and friends. Suddenly, about twenty yards from the Bulls' locker room, he bumped right into another celebrity group, this one centered by the actor Denzel Washington.

Jordan and Washington, from a suburb just north of New York City, had much in common, in the way each had transcended black typecasting in white America. Both were leading men of the entertainment industry whose skin color was almost, not quite, an irrelevancy.

Icon to icon, Jordan and Washington smiled, embraced each other warmly, and proceeded to spend the next few minutes, arms still on each other's shoulders, chatting softly so that they couldn't be heard. The crowd of about thirty just stood transfixed, as if it were a spectator event or a riveting film. Behind Jordan, David Falk stood holding the arm of Walter McCarty, the senior forward from NCAA champ Kentucky and now another Falk client. McCarty was as awestruck as any ten-year-old would have been.

And here, by sheer coincidence, came Julius Erving, having finished his NBC business, striding down the hall. Tall, handsome, distinguished, and gray, Erving himself was a striking, unmistakable figure in most places. But not here. Not now.

The legendary Dr. J turned no heads. He stood on the perimeter and watched, with everyone else, as Denzel Washington, who might be summoned one day to play the lead in the Michael Jordan story, continued his power chat with basketball's one and only.

20

Full Circle

On draft night, 1996, the scene shifted from Toronto's SkyDome to the New Jersey Meadowlands' Continental Arena, but it was the same irresistible show. Only the names and faces had changed. Once again, it was impossible to ignore the reality of poor black families striking it rich under the paternal big top of David Stern. The system at work all over again.

The Marbury men, from Don senior on down, had spent part of the day buying designer suits at Barneys. Young Stephon was decked out in a $1,500 Donna Karan model. And as he was getting dressed on the sealed-off nineteenth floor of the Meadowlands Sheraton Hotel, down the hall waiters were delivering a fourth bottle of Rémy Martin to the room of Mr. Allen Iverson, soon to become the successor to Joe Smith. No. 1 in his class. Stack's House in Philadelphia was about to receive another leading man.

Kobe Bryant, who would wind up in Hollywood, a Los Angeles Laker, made himself right at home in Star World, showing up at the Sheraton in a white stretch limo. The seventeen-year-old emerged from the backseat with five fine women in tow. The next day, he strode confidently onto the New York stage of the *Rosie O'Donnell Show*, plopped himself down next to the movie-star-

343

turned-chat-pack-maven, and handled himself with just the right touch of talk-show aplomb.

Thirty-six underclassmen had left school for the NBA by now, and though the NCAA was suddenly engaged in furious exploration of athletic stipends, its pie-in-the-sky piousness seemed more archaic than ever. For all of John Thompson's high-minded admonishments on *The Washington Post*'s Outlook opinion page—"I want everyone to recognize the harm we are doing ourselves as a society by diminishing the importance of education and magnifying the importance of immediate gratification," he wrote—the words of a teenager had a much more realistic ring:

"You can always go back to school," Stephon Marbury said at the Meadowlands Sheraton. "You can't always make four million dollars a year."

Who could argue with Marbury's decision to check out of Georgia Tech? It was all working out for him like a charm. He would be drafted No. 4 by the Milwaukee Bucks and immediately shipped right over to Minnesota in exchange for UConn's Ray Allen and a first-round draft pick. Eric Fleisher had worked the telephones, trying to make this deal happen, trying to keep the team of Kevin Garnett, Billy Taylor, himself, and Marbury intact. The agent, demonstrating increased influence in the Falkanized NBA, made it happen. Marc's kid brother—representing the Stockton and Malone of the hungry Wolves—was suddenly the most important nonplayer in the Minnesota camp, another chink in David Stern's armor.

Others would not be as fortunate as Marbury. Since 1990, nearly half of the underclassmen who have come out early have never played a single day in the NBA. And what of Thompson's stark warning of the message that it sent to young children who were trying to choose between bouncing a ball and reading a book? What about the words of the learned and caring Richard Lapchick, director of the prestigious Center for the Study of Sport in Society?

"If you were a young person growing up in this society, where hope has been eclipsed by despair, then making this money, making this fame, suddenly has to be an appealing thing to do," Lapchick said. "Unless you understand how tiny, tiny, tiny the odds of you making it are."

Stern liked to call it "the American dream," brought to life every three hundred seconds, the cameras getting a tight shot of another wild family celebration in the green room. Years ago, back when Stern was a kid, a popular television show, in black and white, was called *Queen for a Day*. Women would relate their sad-sack tales to America's enchanted audiences, and one would be selected to tearfully receive household wares. A television set. A washing machine.

The first round of the NBA draft, rookie cap notwithstanding, was worth much more than that.

By draft night, 1996, Stern's collective bargaining agreement was just about home free, though there would be one last bottleneck and lockout that lasted only as long as it took the parties to break for lunch. The union—with Billy Hunter, a former U.S. attorney for California's Northern District, just coming aboard as chief executive—still had no real direction or stomach for a fight. Jeffrey Kessler had extracted a few concessions from the league, but the rebellious fury of the previous summer was long gone. So was David Falk as the driving and leveraged dissident benefactor. He was on to other interests now, namely the free-agent sweepstakes, one that became every bit the mind-blowing spending orgy it was cracked up to be.

In a whirlwind of activity that would make a secondary story out of everything from the baseball season to the pre-Olympic drive, hundreds of millions were thrown around like Monopoly money, Jordan leading off with a one-year, $30-million thank-you note from Jerry Reinsdorf. With Jordan setting the ceiling, Falk moved quickly to get Alonzo Mourning ($105 million for seven years) and Juwan Howard ($100.8 million for seven) signed, both with Miami.

But Stern—exacting revenge on Micky Arison and Pat Riley for embarrassing him the previous summer while taking a poke at his nemesis, Falk—eventually voided the Howard deal. He ruled it in violation of his beloved cap, which would be circumvented no more. Despite reports that Riley had indeed played fast and loose with the rules, he countered by screaming of a league conspiracy. No one wanted to hear this from a man widely perceived as much too arrogant, in need of this swift and punitive rebuke.

"He's an asshole, and a lot of people around here think so," one high-ranking NBA official said. "Nobody's shocked the way it went down." Nor was it surprising that the beneficiary of the quashed deal was Washington owner Abe Pollin, the senior NBA owner and a longtime Stern ally. Pollin, not coincidentally, had a new downtown arena under construction and desperately needed a strong team to facilitate luxury-box sales.

The Bullets were thrilled to have a second chance at Howard. Even with Miami dragging the league into arbitration, the Bullets bestowed $105 million over seven years on the former Fab Fiver. Miami ultimately dropped its arbitration battle. If it had lost, Stern, empowered like the leader of the free world, could have imposed a $5-million fine and yearlong suspension on Arison or Riley.

Buck Williams, it turned out, was ecstatic that Portland didn't pick up his option. Though the Blazers traded Rod Strickland to Washington, the Blazers drafted the other high schooler, 6-11 Jermaine O'Neal, signed Kenny Anderson, and traded for Isaiah Rider, who continued to lead the league in police-blotter appearances. As far as Williams was concerned, it was good riddance to the Blazers and good luck to P. J. Carlesimo.

Rejecting less money to go elsewhere, Williams allied himself back in metropolitan New York with Patrick Ewing, of all people, his adversary in the previous summer's labor fight. Ewing himself was a fading star, but his Knicks had refilled their draining talent pool and again had the big town dreaming of epic battles with Jordan's Bulls. Madison Square Garden president Dave Checketts dealt for Larry Johnson and his $84-million contract, one he once ridiculed as a wantonly irresponsible act by Charlotte. That was then. Now, the Knicks and their corporate owners were raising ticket prices again. They had to keep the fannies in the seats.

In one swoop, Checketts and his Knicks chief executive, Ernie Grunfeld, bagged a backcourt, signing New Jersey's point guard Chris Childs for six years, $24 million, then the Pistons' Allan Houston for $56 million over seven years. Besides the cold cash, the Knicks flew Houston to New York on a corporate jet. En route, the "movie" featured appeals to Houston to please sign by Spike Lee, Robin Leach, and Peter Falk. Houston was ready to bite the Apple.

Doug Collins and the Pistons were crushed. Just like that, the foundation of a team-in-progress was irrevocably fractured, with the man who had stood in the locker room after the last playoff game to demand summer dedication gone in a New York minute. And the behind-the-scenes rumblings of what caused Houston to leave were a fresh and distressing reminder of how fragile every NBA program was, how a team's groundwork was a minefield of eggshells. A petty feud between players, their families, their wives, their girlfriends, and even their agents could eventually bring everyone down.

Some in the Detroit organization—Grant Hill for one—chose to believe that Houston's departure was simply about his wanting more endorsement opportunities. Others thought Houston didn't like the idea of spending his career in Hill's shadow. And then there were suspicions that something else factored into the decision.

This last theory went that taking Houston to New York was agent Bill Strickland's way of settling a two-year-old score with the Hills, Janet and Calvin. When Hill came out of Duke, Strickland made a presentation for IMG. According to a top Pistons official, Strickland showed up wearing no socks and with a marketing associate who didn't seem to know much about Grant—an unforgivable mistake when dealing with a sophisticated family such as the Hills.

It turned out that Janet Hill sat on the same college board as Mark McCormack, the head of IMG, and after the Hills rejected IMG, the Pistons official said that she candidly explained why to McCormack. "McCormack read Strickland the riot act, and he held that against the Hills," the official said. Strickland, for his part, denied that Houston's move had anything to do with the Hills.

Suddenly in a bind, the Pistons scrambled to obtain reinforcements from Atlanta, Grant Long and Stacey Augmon. But the official told the bottom-line truth: "Look at the quotes from the beginning of the year. 'The cornerstones of our franchise are going to be Allan and Grant.' We've got a lot of egg on our face."

Even if the Hill-Strickland theory had credence, the Pistons failed somehow to communicate their undying devotion to Houston. Their first offer was $30 million. Meanwhile, they were banging on Falk's door for Dikembe Mutombo or Juwan Howard, bidding as much as $90 million on Howard before realizing that Mourning had his ear—temporarily, as it turned out—down in Miami. When VP of Player Personnel Rick Sund finally turned back to Houston, it was too late.

"Let's face it, the Knicks overpaid," said the official. "But that's what he got."

Checketts, to his credit, wouldn't disagree. One night, after his whirlwind signing spree in the midst of attempting to do damage control following a Garden boxing riot, Checketts went home to an empty house in New Canaan, Connecticut. He threw a burger on the grill, opened a beer, and turned on a Dream Team exhibition from the West. His wife and kids were away, and he was exasperated, exhausted. The call about the melee following the Riddick Bowe–Andrew Golota bout had come from his hysterical secretary the previous night after eleven. Where was he? Bowing in the presence of David Falk at the agent's office in Washington, D.C.

"This is not sports," said Checketts, sighing. "This is just the way it is."

This seemed to be the story everywhere, with the talent war raging in full force. Falk got $70 million from Atlanta for Mutombo, an offensively inept center. He even got $50 million from Portland for spindly Kenny Anderson, whose own team, Charlotte, didn't bid for his tarnished point-guard services. And as good a shooter as Houston was, what had he really done to be worth $8 million a year?

The Pistons official claimed the league had lost control of itself. "David Stern has got to be shitting his pants right now," he said. "I predict he'll get out soon because twenty-nine owners are going to be screaming at him when they start losing money. How can anybody afford these salaries?"

Others echoed the alarm, but someone had to pay. Unlike baseball, there was still a cap, albeit a "soft" cap, to contend with. Already the dividing of the league into rich and relatively poor that was predicted by the agents—and scorned so convincingly by Stern in his office months before—was beginning to emerge. Scores of players were being renounced by teams as they scurried to make cap room for a big-time free agent. Atlanta had only a half dozen players under contract after it signed Mutombo. Miami renounced half its roster for Howard, then was left to scramble just to field a team. More players than ever were going to be making the minimum or what amounted in the NBA to chump change during the 1996–97 season.

There was bound to be resentment and other forms of fallout, as players who didn't live up to their gargantuan paychecks became symbols of failure, targets of fans shelling out big bucks. This had been the case in baseball, where many fans had grown sick of hearing about money and couldn't identify with players jumping from team to team.

The word association that Stern had played months before didn't work as well now for the NBA either. NBA stars were beginning to look like mercenaries, too. In less than a year, two expansion teams that had struck it rich in the draft were now wondering where they'd gone wrong. Alonzo Mourning and Larry Johnson were gone from Charlotte. And, in the final summer endgame, Shaquille O'Neal jumped Orlando and Michael Jordan territory for a $121-million payoff with the Lakers in L.A.

Farewell, central-Florida waffle houses. Hello, southern-California beachfront property.

That announcement came the morning after the Dream Team pulled into Atlanta for what would be a desultory—though incident-free—gold medal–winning Olympic performance. It was no coincidence that O'Neal waited to announce his departure until immediately after the Dreamers pulled out of a short training stay in Orlando, where newspaper polls overwhelmingly claimed he wasn't worth the money.

It was certainly worth it to the league to have him in L.A. And while the country mourned the shocking explosion that brought down TWA Flight 800 over Long Island the night before, Leonard Armato beamed as O'Neal flashed his toothy smile and insisted his leaving the Magic had nothing to do with Hollywood and financial considerations.

"I'm tired of hearing about money, money, money, money, money," he said. "I just want to play the game, drink Pepsi, wear Reebok."

And there it was, in one hilarious disclaimer, the realization of the American dream by the Dream Team center. Have your cake. Eat your cake. Insist you're on a fat-free diet.

The next day, a member of the NBA PR staff said that Stern had called in from a vacation in Alaska and sounded "very, very happy." Why not? The Lakers and Knicks were revitalized in the two biggest television markets, and the most famous team in the world was sitting pretty in the middle of the country.

Who could really blame O'Neal for getting out of flat, humid, landlocked, and family-infested Orlando? Hollywood had lifestyle rhythms more in tune with the NBA's. In Hollywood, weakness and immorality could be celebrated, treated as little more than fodder for profit. In Hollywood, on-screen with Bugs and Daffy, Michael Jordan could poke fun at his anemic hitting and even his vices. In *Space Jam*, the central plot involved a wager on which Jordan upped the ante and literally bet his freedom. Talk about art mimicking life!

In many ways, this was all nothing more than players practicing the very guidelines set by Stern himself: Shill and sell. Deal and deny. Always keep the smile on your face, and never stop to pick at the warts. Never admit they exist.

The NBA's ability to put just the right spin on any story was second to none in the sports and entertainment industry. Its ability to pay attention to detail, when it benefited the league, was remarkable. The army of fresh-faced PR assistants leading the rookies through the '96 draft haze, making their interview stops with train-schedule precision, was a testimony to the meticulous planning that went into each and every NBA event. Floor lights softened the look of the team banners for television. Tape on the back of the folding chairs designated seats for "Camby," for "Abdur-Rahim." David Stern's chair simply said "Commish."

When another first round was over, Stern stepped down from behind the podium, handing the second round, as usual, over to Rod Thorn. Stern was in a fine mood, chipper even, chuckling over how the league had, for once, been caught with its guard down. An Estonian forward named Martin Muursepp had been drafted late in the first round, and a placard with his name printed for the giant board could not be found.

The name eventually went up, scrawled in marker.

"These guys are coming from everywhere," Stern said, noting the six foreign-born players drafted in the first round alone.

The league was a burgeoning force with an enormous appetite, a beast that was feeding off the basketball revolution. Every week there seemed to be a new market to annex, a new path to take, a new venture to exploit. "You have a dish?" Stern asked excitedly one day in his office. He waxed passionately about the thousand games available for the 1996–97 season via Direct TV. About Internet endeavors. About new means of targeting fans. New television deals. New enterprises, such as the Women's National Basketball Association, on the way for summer 1997, already booked on three networks—NBC, ESPN, and Lifetime. Another McDonald's Championships a few months later. Another World Championships to trot out Dream Team IV in the summer of '98.

Money, money, money, money, money. No wonder Stern was too busy to have lunch with his aging mentor George Gallantz. No wonder his league had developed a defining case of selective hearing and vision, a myopia driven by its need to drive forward.

No wonder the NBA never went hard after the drug scandals in Phoenix or moved to prevent the Reggie Lewis tragedy in Boston. No wonder the most obvious informants and authorities in the so-called investigation of Michael Jordan's gambling were never contacted, much less interviewed. No wonder the odious and far-reaching Isiah Thomas saga was left virtually untouched. It would have brought incalculable dishonor to the NBA, an earthquake to the house of cards, and would have derailed the league from its higher calling to "grow the business."

In the two years since standing under the bleachers in Toronto and vowing to take back the game, Stern had bullied the union, been granted more money and power from the owners, had consolidated his power base, all without the loss of one regular-season game, without mudslinging, without denigrating his so-called adversaries, if not his enemies.

But like Joe Smith at Ridley's Restaurant and Lounge, like Anthony Mason taking on ten of New York City's finest one 1996 summer night in Times Square, too many of Stern's players continued to get dragged out of bars, into police stations, into situations that spoke ominously of a system that was dangerously close to the edge. More and more, there were owners who had no special bond with Stern, owners who had spent mega-millions to join the exclusive NBA club and didn't feel especially beholden to the veteran owners whose franchise values had soared.

As the '96–97 season moved closer, the rumblings began anew, behind the scenes and center stage. The league's Board of Governors struck an ominous chord when it approved a plan to provide financial assistance to low-revenue teams. At least three clubs were said to have lost money in 1995–96, while several others barely broke even. The assistance was to come out of a $50-million fund Stern said the league had been saving for a rainy day.

"It's just begun drizzling," the commissioner admitted.

The season's forecast was sunny, with Jordan and the Bulls primed for another run and the Knicks and Lakers revitalized on opposite coasts. But there was nonetheless much apprehension at Olympic Tower, about what would happen when Jordan quit for good. The majority of Stern's teams began the new season playing to non-sellouts and in some cases disturbingly sparse crowds. Fans were now taking a close look at some of the "stars" who'd struck it rich and in many cases found the whole process difficult to fathom.

Even Allan Houston made skeptical Knicks fans in New York do a few double takes with timid and sloppy early-season play, while out in Auburn Hills, Doug Collins' scrappy Pistons roared to a 30-11 record, earning their coach the right to coach the Eastern Conference All-Stars—ahead of Pat Riley. For however long it lasted, in Collins' mind it was all sweet justice, attributable to two faltering NBA concepts: loyalty and team. This, many believed, reflected more and more in the product; on the NBA grapevine, the feeling was growing that it was bland. Desultory, even, as the ESPN highlight generation flaunted a rattle-the-rim or shoot-the-three brand of ball that was woefully short of intermediate skill. The players were less diverse, making them easier to defend. A simple trip to the free-throw line had for too many become an adventure. Talent-diluted teams were struggling to reach 80 points in many an unsightly game. There was a justifiable fear that the NBA's bridge to the twenty-first century might be far more unsteady than the one Bill Clinton was promising voters just as the new season was commencing with the Knicks playing at Toronto—a rematch of the 1946 inaugural of the BAA, which would three years later take the NBA name.

Not long after that nostalgic occasion north of the border, John Bitove left his position as the Raptors' president and controlling partner. That left his handpicked basketball organization chief and 9 percent owner, Isiah Thomas, to fend off speculation that he was the next to go, despite the fact that Thomas, to the surprise of no one, had in less than two seasons constructed a spunky team more competitive than some of the drearier veteran outfits that were stinking up arenas all across the NBA map.

There was no way professional basketball could return to those days when it was merely an event to stage on dark hockey nights.

But the product's substantial slippage was obvious in the one playoff season Jordan had missed. For all the money they were making, there wasn't one young star—except, perhaps, Hill—who was ready to carry the league the way Johnson, Bird, and Jordan had. No matter how the league artificially inflated them, as when an undeserving O'Neal was included as a member of the league's Top 50 all-time players, announced just in time for the NBA's fiftieth campaign.

Critics panned O'Neal's inclusion, but, as one NBA official said, "Leave him off the team and good luck trying to get him to do any promotions." The official shrugged. It was just life in the NBA in the late twentieth century. The Big Shill.

Speaking of which, Stephon Marbury was the featured star of an ad campaign for a new company, And 1, but already his parents were wondering if Eric Fleisher would have done better for their son by signing him with a more established brand. And, as one Marbury family member asked of Fleisher, "What kind of agent sues his brother?" It sounded like the beginning of a story that Len Elmore might know the ending to. When Elmore was hired by ESPN to do college basketball commentary, he was asked by *USA Today* why he'd left the agent business. His reply was comically cosmic. With no apologies to the makers of *Star Trek*, he said he'd grown tired of "fighting the cling-ons."

And, as it turned out, "the federation" as well. As autumn began, Elmore was contacted by a head-hunting firm about a possible vice presidency with the Basketball Hall of Fame in Springfield, Massachusetts. After interviewing and being told he was a finalist, he said he had received a call the following week from the headhunter. The NBA office, he was told, had used its influence to nix his candidacy.

Meanwhile, with the malicious-wounding charge safely behind him, Joe Smith found himself on the cover of the "Official NBA Register," symbolically chasing a man whose level in the NBA was his approximate destination. Shawn Kemp was pictured as he prepared to throw down one of his patented power dunks, not to be confused with the power play he was pulling on Seattle's front office. Kemp roared from the mouth of his agent that he was unhappy with the long-term contract that now left him the sixth-highest-paid Sonics player. He skipped the first three weeks of the team's training camp, though the collective bargaining rules prevented the Sonics from giving him more money even if they were so inclined. Back in Orlando, at the Rookie Transition Program, Allen Iverson, heir to Joe Smith as first pick in the draft, was bailing out a couple of days early, asking for no one's permission. And one of the most celebrated Money Players, Jason Kidd, was tossed out of Dallas, traded to Phoenix in December 1996.

Rodman carried his Bad Boy act to the limit, kicking a courtside television cameraman in the groin. He paid for it with the second-longest suspension in league history and a reported $200,000 out-of-court settlement.

And finally, more than three years after Reggie Lewis' death, the NBA even began to tacitly admit that its once-celebrated drug program was something less than exemplary. Powerless to do anything after two players, Portland's Isaiah Rider, and Atlanta's Mookie Blaylock, were reportedly caught red-handed with marijuana, the league began quiet talks with the union in an effort to toughen the existing policies.

The comparisons had been made many times between NBA players and rock stars, and the best players were the lead singers. And with all the head-spinning, commercial benefits that accompanied such status came the vulnerability to temptation, to the predators of the nightlife. Only a wish-it-away, made-for-TV mentality could actually accept the NBA's typical refrains, its so-called investigations of itself, its inevitable proclamations of no harm, no foul.

Those who didn't—people such as James Keppel and Ron Suskind and all the rest—were written off as troublemaking intruders. Practitioners of a witch-hunt. So would others who unlocked an NBA closet and dragged out skeletons. The league counted on its enormous popularity and appeal to carry it through every storm. It staked its credibility on rebounds and revenue. Stern had the players. Dick Ebersol had the cameras. As long as the games went on and the ratings went up, there could be nothing wrong. Explore new worlds, go where no sports league has gone before. The New NBA was its own USS *Enterprise,* Stern a real-life Jean-Luc Picard. He was a powerful man with a vision, with a poker face and the capacity to outbluff opponents without tipping his hand. And like the great point men of the game that he had so successfully sold, Stern had mastered the art of looking in one direction, dealing in the other.

Michael Jordan represented the NBA's highest peak, but what the league had accomplished overall in less than fifteen years was magic. Pure magic, and all David Stern and his minions had to do was to keep out the destructive influences, hold together the divergent forces and warring factions. Stern's job was to keep his house from blowing apart, from going up in a cloud of smoke.

Authors' Note

ALTHOUGH THE TOILS AND TRIBULATIONS OF THIS PROJECT DATE back to the summer of 1990, it picked up reportorial steam about three years ago. More than four hundred people with various associations with the NBA, past and present, were interviewed, many of them several times. Whenever possible, these interviews were taped; a wide variety were supplemented with material gathered from public record, the courts, along with national and local newspapers and magazines. Conversations, when reconstructed, were based on interviews or documents dealing directly with one of the principals.

The most explosive subject matter of this book—the Isiah Thomas scandal—began as a television investigation by one of the authors of this work and a former ABC colleague, the talented Richard Greenberg, now one of Steve Kroft's producers at *60 Minutes*. Another ABC News producer, Dan Green, deserves credit for digging into the NBA's antidrug program as part of a report that eventually aired on *World News Tonight with Peter Jennings*. Along those same lines, every serious discussion of antidrug programs in sports—as we believe ours to be—begins with the seminal reporting of Ron Suskind, the Pulitzer

Prize–winning reporter who broke the Reggie Lewis story for the *Wall Street Journal.*

On the subject of the rise, fall, and rebirth of the Detroit Pistons, we owe a huge debt of gratitude to Corky Meinicke of the *Detroit Free Press,* who covered the team with distinction for years, and Chris McCoskey of the *Detroit News.* We also owe far more than a passing nod to Dan Desmond of the *Oakland Press,* and *Free Press* columnist Charlie Vincent and his compatriot Joe Falls, over at the *News.*

Our Kevin Garnett saga would have been nowhere near as lively or complete without the writings of Steve Aschburner of the *Minneapolis Star Tribune,* Ray Richardson of the *St. Paul Pioneer Press,* and Jill Lieber, the extraordinary feature writer and reporter now gracing the pages of *USA Today.*

So much occurs during a single NBA season, and it would have been impossible to cover it all without true professionals such as Brian McIntyre, Jan Hubbard, and Terry Lyons of the NBA PR staff; former NBA staffer Ellen Brandon; Julie Marvel of the Golden State Warriors; and Josh Rosenfeld, formerly of the New York Knicks.

The renowned journalism of David Halberstam, who wrote the pro basketball bible; along with *Sports Illustrated*'s Phil Taylor, Jack McCallum, and Tim Crothers; Ric Bucher of the *San Jose Mercury News;* Bill Brubaker of *The Washington Post;* and Sam Smith of the *Chicago Tribune* provided incalculable assistance. That, plus friendship and support from some of the country's smartest newspaper people—Aileen Voisin of the *Atlanta Constitution;* Ira Berkow, Mike Wise, and Cliff Brown of the *New York Times;* Barry Stanton of the Gannett Suburban Newspapers; Filip Bondy, Ian O'Connor, and David Kaplan of the *New York Daily News*—made a daunting endeavor that much easier. So did David Black's wisdom and guidance

Special thanks to Jim Ornstein for his yeoman's work on David Stern, the early years, and to Michael Jaffe, Don Yaeger, and Desmond Wallace of *Sports Illustrated* for their superb efforts.

On a more personal note, to Matt Dobek and his professional staff in the Detroit Pistons PR office (Bill Wickett, Sue Emerick, and Brian Bierley) for all their hospitality, and for keeping us honest; to Jackie Marucci, for her fast fingers, and especially to ABC News researcher Sean Carr, for righting the wrongs.

To our agent Basil Kane, publisher Jack Romanos, whose wisdom and belief brought this project to life, and editors Peter Wolverton and Tristram Coburn, who tightened and focused our tale.

To our bosses at ABC News (President Roone Arledge and Senior Vice President Paul Friedman and *World News Tonight* Executive Producer Kathy Christensen), the *New York Times* (Executive Sports Editor Neil Amdur, along with Rich Rosenbush, Bill Brink, Jay Schreiber, and Kathleen McElroy), and *Sports Illustrated* (Managing Editor Bill Colson and Executive Editor Peter Carry) for their understanding, patience, and support.

And most importantly to those who believed in us, who trusted us to speak the truth and watched our backs. Especially one very special person who did all that and so much more, who risked a great deal to keep us on the right side of the street.

Finally, we'd like to dedicate this book to the following:

From A.K.: To Virginia Keteyian and Jack Tobin, mother and mentor. Despite passing last year, your voices remain. I listen. I love. And I never forget.

From H.A.: To the magical Beth, Alex, and Charlie, and Michelle M., a true fan.

From Martin F. Dardis: The way one conducts one's life, especially in one's association with others, is guided and motivated by people one learns from along the way: Harold Gilliland, who was my friend when I was friendless as a young boy; he died before I could repay him. First Lt. Dixon L. Pyles, who taught me civics, justice, and the fact that Thomas Jefferson was right. Chief Leroy Wike and Richard E. Gerstein, who were always there in my thoughts as I negotiated my long journey through the criminal justice system, with two powerful words provided by them— *compassion* and *justice*. After applying those criteria, the rest was easy.

To Gil Rogin who (1) hired me at *Sports Illustrated;* (2) was editor of the biggest *SI* story I ever worked on; (3) always returned phone calls no matter how high up the ladder he was; and (4) was always there when I needed him.

For the past sixteen years at *Sports Illustrated*, the words were *ethics* and *integrity*, as practiced by my two editors, Sandy Padwe and Steve Robinson. The same principles applied to my coworkers on numerous investigations, for whom I have great admiration and respect: Jill Lieber, Sonja Steptoe, Michael Jaffe, and my coauthor Armen Keteyian.

To best-selling author and *Miami Herald* columnist Carl Hiassen—as the guy on early TV once said, "You're the greatest." And last but not least in the print world, my friend and champion of social justice, Gene Miller of the *Herald*. Gene, I love you. Closer to home, my best friend, William Scanlon, an attorney who puts the lie to all lawyer jokes.

And finally, to Barbara Joan, whose love, understanding, and support made it all possible. And to all my children, who accomplished what I hoped they would. I am very proud.

P.S. The other dinosaur is gone. I miss you, Jack Tobin.